PROTECT WHAT MATTERS

NEW YORK & CALIFORNIA FAMILY LAW

Complete Rights and Remedies Guide for New York & California

NGOZI E. BOLIN, ESQ.

Cover by Jim Olen

Legal Disclaimer

Important Notice to Readers

THIS BOOK IS PROVIDED FOR INFORMATIONAL AND EDUCATIONAL PURPOSES ONLY AND IS NOT INTENDED TO CONSTITUTE LEGAL ADVICE.

No Attorney-Client Relationship

The information contained in this book does not create an attorney-client relationship between the author, publisher, and any reader or user of this material. Reading this book, accessing its content, or using any information contained herein does not establish any professional relationship or create any duties or obligations on the part of the author or publisher to any reader.

Not a Substitute for Professional Legal Counsel

The content of this book is general in nature and may not apply to your specific situation. Legal matters are highly fact-specific and jurisdiction-dependent. Laws, regulations, court decisions, and legal interpretations change frequently and vary significantly between jurisdictions. Nothing in this book should be used as a substitute for competent legal advice from a licensed attorney in your jurisdiction who is familiar with the specific facts of your case.

YOU SHOULD ALWAYS CONSULT WITH A QUALIFIED ATTORNEY BEFORE MAKING ANY LEGAL DECISIONS OR TAKING ANY ACTION BASED ON INFORMATION CONTAINED IN THIS BOOK.

Accuracy and Currency of Information

While every effort has been made to ensure the accuracy of the information contained in this book at the time of publication, the author and publisher make no representations or warranties regarding the completeness, accuracy, reliability, or currency of the information provided. Laws and legal precedents change constantly, and what may have been accurate at the time of writing may no longer be current or applicable.

The information in this book reflects the law as understood by the author as of the publication date. Legal developments occurring after the publication date are not reflected in this material.

Jurisdictional Limitations

Laws vary significantly among different countries, states, provinces, and localities. The information in this book may be based primarily on the laws of specific jurisdictions and may not be applicable in your location. Local laws should always be consulted, and local legal counsel should be retained for matters involving specific jurisdictions.

Limitation of Liability

TO THE FULLEST EXTENT PERMITTED BY LAW, THE AUTHOR, PUBLISHER, EDITORS, CONTRIBUTORS, AND DISTRIBUTORS OF THIS BOOK DISCLAIM ALL LIABILITY FOR ANY LOSS, DAMAGE, OR INJURY ARISING FROM THE USE OF OR RELIANCE ON THE INFORMATION CONTAINED HEREIN, WHETHER SUCH LIABILITY ARISES IN CONTRACT, TORT, STRICT LIABILITY, OR OTHERWISE.

This limitation applies to all damages or injuries, including but not limited to:

- Direct, indirect, incidental, and consequential damages
- Lost profits or business opportunities
- Legal fees and costs

- Punitive or exemplary damages
- Any other economic or non-economic losses

No Warranties

THIS BOOK IS PROVIDED "AS IS" WITHOUT WARRANTY OF ANY KIND, EXPRESS OR IMPLIED, INCLUDING BUT NOT LIMITED TO WARRANTIES OF MERCHANTABILITY, FITNESS FOR A PARTICULAR PURPOSE, OR NON-INFRINGEMENT.

Individual Circumstances

Every legal situation is unique. The examples, case studies, and scenarios presented in this book are for illustrative purposes only and may not reflect the full complexity of actual legal situations. The outcomes described may not be achievable in your circumstances, and past results do not guarantee future outcomes.

Updates and Revisions

The author and publisher are under no obligation to update or revise the content of this book to reflect changes in the law or legal practice. Readers are encouraged to verify all information with current legal sources and qualified legal professionals.

Third-Party Content and References

Any references to third-party materials, websites, organizations, or publications are provided for informational purposes only and do not constitute an endorsement of such materials or entities. The author and publisher are not responsible for the content, accuracy, or availability of third-party materials.

Compliance with Professional Rules

Readers who are legal professionals should ensure that their use of any information in this book complies with applicable professional conduct rules, ethical requirements, and licensing obligations in their jurisdiction.

Intellectual Property Notice

Severability

If any portion of this disclaimer is held to be invalid or unenforceable, the remaining portions shall remain in full force and effect.

BY READING AND USING THIS BOOK, YOU ACKNOWLEDGE THAT YOU HAVE READ, UNDERSTOOD, AND AGREE TO BE BOUND BY THE TERMS OF THIS DISCLAIMER.

IF YOU DO NOT AGREE WITH THESE TERMS, DO NOT USE THIS BOOK.

Contents

Introduction to Family Law in New York & California

The Human Stakes Behind Legal Procedures

When Sarah filed for divorce in Manhattan Family Court, she thought the hardest part was behind her - making the decision to leave. When Miguel sought custody of his daughter in Los Angeles Superior Court, he assumed his love for his child would speak for itself. When Maria applied for a restraining order in Buffalo, she believed the bruises would be evidence enough.

All three discovered what family law practitioners know intimately: the legal system governing our most personal relationships is complex, emotionally charged, and unforgiving of procedural mistakes. Unlike contract disputes or personal injury claims, family law reaches into the core of human identity - who we love, how we parent, where we live, and how we rebuild after loss.

Why Family Law Demands Specialized Knowledge

Family law operates at the intersection of constitutional rights, state regulations, federal mandates, and judicial discretion. A single case might involve property division governed by state law, child custody determined by the best interests standard, immigration consequences under federal jurisdiction, and tax implications that span multiple agencies.

Consider this reality: a custody modification filed in Sacramento could affect a military father's deployment eligibility, trigger interstate jurisdiction questions under the UCCJEA, impact child support calculations across state lines, and influence an immigration petition pending in federal court. Each moving part demands specialized knowledge that generalist attorneys often lack.

The consequences of inexperience extend far beyond legal fees. Poorly drafted parenting plans create years of conflict. Incomplete financial disclosures can void property settlements. Missed deadlines can result in default judgments that devastate families. This is why family law has evolved into a distinct practice area requiring dedicated training, ongoing education, and emotional intelligence that other legal fields rarely demand.

The New York and California Frameworks: A Study in Contrasts

This guide focuses on New York and California not merely because they represent the first and third most populous states, but because they embody fundamentally different approaches to resolving family disputes and the author is admitted in both jurisdictions. Understanding both systems provides insight into the broader evolution of American family law.

New York: Discretion Within Structure

New York family law emphasizes judicial discretion guided by statutory factors. Courts apply the "best interests of the child" standard without rigid formulas, allowing judges to weigh individual circumstances heavily. In property division, the state follows "equitable distribution" - meaning fair, not necessarily equal - which gives courts broad authority to consider contributions, sacrifices, and future needs.

This flexibility creates opportunities for creative solutions but also generates uncertainty. A Manhattan Supreme Court judge might award seventy percent of marital assets to a spouse who sacrificed career advancement for child-rearing, while a Nassau County judge in similar circumstances might order a fifty-fifty split. The system prioritizes individualized justice over predictable outcomes.

New York's court structure reflects this complexity. Family Court handles custody, support, and domestic violence matters, while the Supreme Court is the trial-level court that has exclusive jurisdiction over divorce and equitable distribution of marital property. Surrogate's Court manages probate, guardianship and adoption. This division requires attorneys to understand multiple procedural systems and, often, to coordinate cases across different courts simultaneously.

California: Formulas with Room for Equity

California approaches family law with more standardized frameworks while preserving judicial discretion for exceptional cases. Community property law presumes equal division of marital assets, creating predictability in property settlements. Child support follows detailed guideline calculations using software like DissoMaster, reducing litigation over basic support amounts.

Yet California demonstrates that formulas need not eliminate fairness. Courts retain authority to deviate from guidelines when justice requires it, and the state leads nationally in recognizing diverse family structures through domestic partnership laws and progressive parentage statutes.

California's unified Superior Court system handles all family law matters in one location, streamlining case management but requiring familiarity with local rules that vary significantly across fifty-eight counties. Los Angeles County operates differently from San Francisco, which operates differently from rural counties like Mono or Alpine.

The People Who Make Family Law Work

Judges and Judicial Officers

Family law judges wield enormous discretion, often making decisions that reshape lives within minutes of hearing testimony. Unlike criminal cases with appellate review standards or civil cases with clear damages calculations, family law depends heavily on judicial impressions of credibility, character, and children's needs.

In California, many family law matters are heard by commissioners - appointed officers with authority similar to judges but subject to different selection processes and oversight. Understanding whether you're appearing before a judge or commissioner, and knowing their background and tendencies, can influence your case strategy significantly.

New York employs support magistrates and referees for specific functions, creating additional layers in the judicial hierarchy. These officers handle preliminary matters but require judicial approval for final orders, adding procedural steps that can delay resolution of cases.

The Support Network

Modern family law involves teams of professionals whose expertise shapes outcomes. Custody evaluators conduct psychological assessments and home studies that heavily influence judicial decisions. Forensic accountants trace hidden assets and value complex property. Mediators facilitate settlement discussions that resolve ninety percent of cases without trial.

Guardian ad litem ("GAL") appointments in New York and minor's counsel in California give children independent representation, but these advocates approach their role differently. In New York, GALs typically advocate for the child's best interests as determined by the GAL, which may or may not align with the child's wishes. In contrast, California minor's counsel are generally tasked with representing the child's expressed interests, though they may also consider the child's best interests under certain circumstances.

Understanding these roles helps attorneys and litigants prepare more effectively. A custody evaluator who emphasizes psychological testing requires different preparation than one who focuses on home environment and daily routines. A forensic accountant hired to value a medical practice needs different documentation than one tracing commingled assets through multiple accounts.

The Reality of Self-Representation

Approximately sixty to eighty percent of family law litigants represent themselves at some point during their cases. This reality reflects both the high cost of legal representation and the personal nature of family disputes that makes some people reluctant to hire attorneys.

Self-represented litigants face significant challenges beyond legal complexity. Court procedures assume familiarity with rules of evidence, motion practice, and local customs that attorneys learn through years of practice. Filing deadlines, service requirements, and discovery procedures create traps for unwary litigants.

Yet both New York and California have invested heavily in self-help resources. Family law facilitators provide procedural guidance without legal advice. Standardized forms reduce drafting challenges. Video tutorials explain common procedures. Online resources offer templates and checklists.

The key limitation remains: self-help centers cannot provide strategic advice or advocate for specific outcomes. They can explain how to file a motion for custody modification but cannot advise whether that motion is likely to succeed or whether alternative approaches might serve the client better.

Cultural Competence and Access to Justice

Family law intersects with cultural, religious, and linguistic diversity in ways that demand sensitivity and understanding. Arranged marriages, traditional gender roles, religious divorce requirements, and language barriers all influence how families experience the legal system.

California's demographic diversity requires attorneys to understand how community property law applies to families from cultures with different concepts of marital property. New York's immigrant communities face additional complexity when family law proceedings affect immigration status or when custody cases involve children born abroad.

Domestic violence cases highlight these intersections most starkly. Cultural stigma around divorce or reporting abuse can prevent victims from seeking help. Economic dependence complicated by immigration status creates additional barriers. Religious or family pressure to reconcile can undermine safety planning.

Effective family law practice requires cultural humility - recognizing when cultural differences affect legal strategy and seeking appropriate guidance. This might mean working with interpreters who understand legal concepts, consulting with immigration attorneys when family law decisions affect status, or partnering with community organizations that serve specific populations.

Technology's Evolving Role

The COVID-19 pandemic accelerated technological adoption in family law, creating permanent changes in how courts operate and attorneys practice. Virtual hearings became commonplace for procedural matters, reducing travel time and costs while creating new challenges around access to technology and courtroom formality.

Electronic filing systems in both states streamline document submission but require familiarity with specific platforms and requirements. New York's NYSCEF system operates differently from California's county-specific e-filing portals, creating learning curves for attorneys practicing in multiple jurisdictions.

Digital evidence presents both opportunities and challenges. Text messages, emails, and social media posts frequently become evidence in custody and domestic violence cases, but their authentication and presentation require technical knowledge that many attorneys lack.

Privacy concerns have intensified as proceedings move online. Video conferences require secure platforms and careful attention to who might be listening or watching as family court proceedings are presumptively closed to the public to protect minors, and California family court proceedings are presumptively open but can be closed by judicial discretion. Electronic document sharing demands encrypted systems and clear protocols for protecting sensitive financial and personal information.

The Economic Reality of Family Law

Family law cases often coincide with financial stress, making cost a central concern for most litigants. Divorce proceedings that divide assets simultaneously generate attorney fees that can consume significant portions of those assets. Custody battles that require expert evaluations and extensive motion practice can cost tens of thousands of dollars.

Understanding fee structures helps clients make informed decisions about legal representation. Hourly billing creates unpredictability but allows flexibility in case management. Flat fees provide cost certainty but may not cover unexpected complications. Limited scope representation allows clients to handle some aspects of their cases while receiving attorney assistance for critical matters.

Both states have fee-shifting provisions that allow courts to order one party to pay the other's attorney fees in appropriate circumstances. These provisions can level the playing field when one spouse has significantly greater resources, but they also create strategic considerations about litigation conduct and settlement timing.

Legal aid organizations provide essential services for low-income litigants, but demand far exceeds capacity. Pro bono programs offer additional assistance, but coverage remains spotty. This reality means many middle-income families - who earn too much to qualify for free services but too little to afford private attorneys - navigate the system with minimal legal assistance.

Preparing for the Journey Ahead

This guide provides comprehensive coverage of family law in New York and California, but reading about legal procedures cannot substitute for understanding your specific situation and local practices. Use this information as a foundation for informed decision-making, not as a replacement for professional legal advice when stakes are high.

Each chapter builds on previous concepts while addressing distinct areas of practice. Property division assumes understanding of marriage requirements. Custody modifications require familiarity with initial custody determinations. Enforcement mechanisms depend on knowing what orders can be enforced.

Take time to understand the procedural framework before diving into substantive law. Know which court has jurisdiction over your matter, what forms are required, and how local rules affect timing and presentation. This foundation prevents costly mistakes and helps you communicate more effectively with legal professionals.

Looking Forward: The Structure of This Guide

The chapters that follow progress logically through the family law system, beginning with foundational concepts and building toward complex procedural and strategic considerations. We examine how cases begin, how they progress through courts, and how they conclude - along with what happens when circumstances change and modification becomes necessary.

Each chapter compares New York and California law while highlighting practical considerations that affect real families. We address both litigation and alternative dispute resolution, recognizing that most cases settle but that settlement negotiations occur within the shadow of potential trial outcomes.

Special attention focuses on areas where family law intersects with other legal systems - immigration, criminal law, tax consequences, and federal regulations. These intersections create opportunities for creative solutions but also generate complications that require specialized knowledge.

Throughout this guide, remember that family law ultimately serves human needs. Behind every statute, court rule, and judicial decision are real people seeking safety, stability, and fair treatment during some of the most difficult periods of their lives. Technical competence must combine with emotional intelligence, cultural sensitivity, and ethical practice to serve these needs effectively.

The law provides structure for resolving disputes, but within that structure lies enormous room for advocacy, creativity, and human connection. Whether you approach this material as an attorney seeking to serve clients more effectively or as a litigant trying to understand your rights and options, keep these human dimensions at the center of your analysis.

Family law done well helps people rebuild their lives with dignity and hope. Family law done poorly creates additional trauma and long-lasting conflict. The difference often lies not in knowing the rules, but in understanding how to apply them with wisdom, compassion, and strategic thinking.

Takeaways

For Attorneys: Family law requires specialized knowledge that spans multiple legal areas and demands emotional intelligence alongside technical competence. Success depends on understanding both the formal legal framework and the informal culture of local courts and practice communities.

For Litigants: The family law system provides structure for resolving disputes, but navigating it successfully requires understanding procedures, deadlines, and strategic considerations that may not be immediately obvious. Invest time in understanding the process before making irreversible decisions.

For Both: Family law operates within the tension between predictable rules and individual circumstances. Understanding this tension - and how different jurisdictions resolve it - provides the foundation for effective advocacy and informed decision-making throughout the legal process that lies ahead.

1

The Legal Framework

Statutes, Case Law, and Court Rules

I. Understanding the Architecture of Family Law

Family law operates as a complex ecosystem where multiple legal sources intersect and influence each other. Unlike other areas of law that may rely primarily on a single comprehensive code, family law draws from statutes, appellate decisions, procedural rules, constitutional principles, and judicial discretion. This multi-layered approach creates both flexibility and complexity, making it essential for practitioners and litigants to understand how these various sources work together.

The landscape of family law is constantly evolving. Legislative changes, new appellate decisions, and shifting social norms regularly reshape the legal terrain. What worked as a legal strategy five years ago may be obsolete today, particularly in rapidly changing areas like LGBTQ+ rights, reproductive technology, and domestic violence recognition.

II. The Statutory Foundation

New York's Statutory Structure

New York's family law system is built on several key statutes, each serving distinct but overlapping functions. The **Domestic Relations Law** ("N.Y. Dom. Rel. Law") serves as the primary vehicle for marriage dissolution, addressing divorce grounds, property division, and spousal support. This statute has undergone significant revisions over the decades, most notably with the adoption of no-fault divorce in 2010, which fundamentally altered the strategic landscape for divorce litigation.

The **Family Court Act** ("FCA") governs matters involving children and family relationships outside of divorce. This includes custody and visitation disputes, child support enforcement, family offenses such as domestic violence, and child welfare proceedings. The FCA creates a specialized court system designed to handle family matters with greater sensitivity and expertise than traditional civil courts.

Supporting these primary statutes, the **Social Services Law** governs child welfare, foster care, and adoption proceedings. The **Estates, Powers and Trusts Law** ("EPTL") addresses guardianship matters and certain parental rights issues. The **Civil Practice Law and Rules** ("CPLR") provides the procedural framework for family law matters heard in Supreme Court, particularly matrimonial actions.

California's Integrated Approach

California takes a more unified approach through the California **Family Code** (Cal. Fam. Code), which consolidates most family law matters into a single comprehensive statute. This code covers marriage formation and dissolution, child custody and support, spousal support, property division, domestic partnerships, and adoption. The integration allows for more consistent application of legal principles across different types of family disputes.

The **California Code of Civil Procedure** ("Code Civ. Proc." or "CCP") and **California Rules of Court** ("Cal. Rules of Court" or "CRC") provide the procedural framework, with the Rules of Court being particularly detailed in establishing uniform procedures across the state's diverse county court systems. This uniformity is crucial in a state with 58 counties, each with its own local legal culture and case management practices.

III. The Evolution of Case Law

Appellate decisions breathe life into statutory language, transforming abstract legal principles into practical guidance for real-world situations. The doctrine of *stare decisis* ensures that lower courts follow established precedents, creating predictability and consistency in legal outcomes. However, the dynamic nature of family relationships means that new factual scenarios regularly challenge existing precedents.

Tropea v. Tropea, 87 N.Y.2d 727, 642 N.Y.S.2d 575, 665 N.E.2d 145 (1996), fundamentally reshaped New York's approach to relocation requests in custody cases. Prior to this decision, courts applied a rigid test that often prevented custodial parents from relocating. The Court of Appeals recognized that such inflexibility could harm both children and parents, establishing a more nuanced balancing test that considers the totality of circumstances. This case exemplifies how appellate decisions can create entirely new legal frameworks that trial courts must then apply to countless individual cases.

Similarly, *In re Marriage of LaMusga*, 32 Cal.4th 1072, 12 P.3d 1010, 88 Cal.Rptr.2d 761 (2004), established California's approach to move-away cases, creating a presumption in favor of custodial parents while protecting the rights of non-custodial parents. The interplay between these two landmark cases demonstrates how different states can approach similar legal questions with varying philosophical frameworks, leading to different outcomes for similarly situated families.

Recent appellate decisions continue to shape emerging areas of family law. Courts are grappling with issues involving transgender children, assisted reproductive technology, and the intersection of family law with immigration status. These decisions often reflect broader social changes and can significantly impact how family law is practiced.

IV. Procedural Rules: The Mechanics of Justice

While substantive law defines rights and obligations, procedural rules determine how those rights are enforced and protected. Mastery of procedure is often the difference between success and failure in family law practice.

New York's Procedural Framework

New York's procedural rules reflect the state's dual court system for family law matters. The **Uniform Rules for the Family Court** ("22 NYCRR") govern proceedings in Family Court, while matrimonial actions in Supreme Court follow the CPLR with specialized rules under **22 NYCRR Part 202**. This division can create strategic considerations about which court system to utilize for particular types of relief.

Local county rules add another layer of complexity. Each county's family court may have distinct requirements for filing procedures, case management, and hearing schedules. What works in Manhattan may not comply with requirements in upstate counties. These local variations require practitioners to stay current with the specific requirements of each jurisdiction where they practice.

California's Statewide Approach

California's **Rules of Court Title 5** creates a more uniform statewide approach to family law procedure. These rules establish standardized forms, discovery procedures, and case management practices designed to ensure consistency across the state's diverse county systems. However, local superior court rules still add variations that practitioners must navigate.

The emphasis on standardized forms in California reflects the state's commitment to access to justice for self-represented litigants. Many family law proceedings can be completed using Judicial Council forms, though the complexity of family law means that seemingly simple forms can have significant legal consequences.

V. The Exercise of Judicial Discretion

Family law's reliance on judicial discretion sets it apart from many other areas of law. While statutes provide frameworks and factors to consider, they rarely mandate specific outcomes. This discretion allows courts to craft solutions tailored to individual family circumstances but also creates unpredictability in outcomes.

Best interests of the child standards exemplify this discretion. Both New York and California provide statutory factors for courts to consider in custody determinations, but these factors are guidelines rather than rigid formulas. A judge's interpretation of what serves a child's best interests can vary significantly based on their background, values, and understanding of child development.

Similarly, spousal support determinations involve extensive judicial discretion. While both states have moved toward more structured approaches - New York through its advisory spousal support guidelines and California through its duration formulas - judges retain significant flexibility to deviate from these guidelines based on case-specific circumstances.

This discretion makes family law practice particularly relationship-dependent. Understanding individual judges' approaches, preferences, and pet peeves becomes crucial for effective advocacy. What persuades one judge may be counterproductive with another, requiring practitioners to adapt their strategies based on the specific judicial officer handling their case.

VI. Constitutional Foundations

Although family law is primarily state-regulated, federal constitutional principles provide the overarching framework within which state laws must operate. The **Due Process Clause** guarantees fundamental fairness in proceedings that affect family relationships, requiring adequate notice and opportunity to be heard before courts can make decisions affecting parental rights or property interests.

The **Equal Protection Clause** has been particularly influential in recent decades, driving changes in marriage equality, parental rights for same-sex couples, and gender-neutral approaches to custody and support. The Supreme Court's decision in *Obergefell v. Hodges*, 576 U.S. 644, 135 S.Ct. 2584, 192 L.Ed.2d 609 (2015), not only established marriage equality but also created ripple effects throughout family law, affecting everything from divorce procedures to adoption rights.

The **Full Faith and Credit Clause** requires states to recognize and enforce valid judgments from other states, which is crucial in our mobile society where families often cross state lines. However, this requirement interacts with state interests in protecting their own residents and applying their own laws, creating complex jurisdictional issues in interstate family law matters.

VII. Practical Considerations in Legal Application

The theoretical framework of family law statutes and cases must be applied within the practical realities of court systems, client needs, and resource constraints. Most family law matters are resolved through negotiation and settlement rather than trial, making the art of negotiation as important as mastery of legal doctrine.

Alternative Dispute Resolution mechanisms, including mediation and collaborative law, operate within the legal framework but emphasize problem-solving over adversarial positioning. These approaches require understanding both the legal parameters within which agreements must operate and the practical considerations that motivate parties to reach resolution.

Court efficiency concerns also influence how law is applied in practice. Judges managing heavy caseloads may favor solutions that resolve multiple issues simultaneously, even if those solutions don't perfectly align with strict legal entitlements. Understanding these practical pressures helps practitioners develop strategies that work within the system's constraints.

VIII. Staying Current in an Evolving Field

Family law's dynamic nature requires continuous learning and adaptation. Legislative changes, new appellate decisions, and evolving social norms regularly reshape the legal landscape. **Continuing Legal Education** programs, professional publications, and bar association resources provide essential updates on legal developments.

Technology is also changing family law practice, from electronic filing systems to virtual hearings to new forms of evidence from social media and digital communications. Staying current requires understanding both legal developments and technological changes that affect how law is practiced.

Legal research tools continue to evolve, with traditional resources like **Westlaw** and **LexisNexis** being supplemented by specialized family law databases and artificial intelligence tools that can help identify relevant authorities and track legal developments.

IX. Building Practical Competence

Effective family law practice requires more than theoretical knowledge of legal principles. It demands understanding of how those principles interact with human emotions, financial realities, and practical constraints. Successful practitioners develop skills in:

Client counseling that helps people understand their legal options within the context of their personal circumstances and goals. This requires translating complex legal concepts into practical advice that clients can use to make informed decisions.

Strategic thinking that considers not just immediate legal issues but also long-term consequences and relationships. Family law decisions often have impacts that extend far beyond the immediate legal proceeding.

Negotiation and advocacy skills that can advance client interests while maintaining focus on practical solutions. The adversarial nature of legal proceedings must be balanced with the ongoing relationships that often exist in family law matters.

X. Integration and Application

Understanding family law's legal framework is just the beginning. The true art lies in applying these various sources of law to achieve practical solutions for real families facing difficult circumstances. This requires synthesizing statutory requirements, case law precedents, procedural rules, and practical considerations into coherent strategies.

The chapters that follow will demonstrate how this legal framework applies to specific family law situations, from divorce and custody disputes to domestic violence protection and child welfare proceedings. Each area presents unique challenges that require careful application of the legal principles outlined in this foundational chapter.

Success in family law practice comes from understanding not just what the law says, but how it works in practice to serve families in crisis. This requires mastery of legal doctrine combined with practical wisdom about human nature, court systems, and the art of problem-solving within legal constraints.

2

Who's Who in Family Law Cases

I. The Human Ecosystem of Family Law

Family law proceedings create a unique intersection of legal advocacy, mental health intervention, child welfare protection, and judicial decision-making. Unlike other areas of litigation that may involve primarily lawyers and judges, family law cases often require a multidisciplinary team of professionals, each bringing specialized expertise to address the complex human dynamics at stake.

Understanding the roles, responsibilities, and limitations of each participant is crucial for effective advocacy and informed participation. The authority structure in family law is often less hierarchical than in other legal contexts, with various professionals wielding significant influence over case outcomes. This chapter provides a comprehensive guide to the key players you will encounter in New York and California family law proceedings.

II. The Primary Parties: More Than Legal Adversaries

Petitioner and Respondent Dynamics

The **petitioner** initiates the legal action by filing the initial petition or complaint, while the **respondent** must respond within statutory deadlines. This initial positioning can create strategic advantages and disadvantages that extend throughout the case. The petitioner controls the initial narrative, chooses the timing of filing, and may benefit from psychological advantages in presenting their case first.

However, the respondent role is not inherently disadvantageous. Respondents have the opportunity to present counter-claims, may benefit from additional preparation time, and can sometimes appear more reasonable by responding thoughtfully to the petitioner's claims rather than appearing as the aggressor.

In **New York**, the jurisdictional complexity adds another layer of strategic consideration. Matrimonial actions involving divorce, annulment, and separation are filed in Supreme Court, while custody, child support, and family offense matters typically proceed in Family Court. This division can create situations where related issues are heard in different courts, requiring careful coordination and potentially conflicting orders.

California's unified approach through the Superior Court Family Division eliminates much of this jurisdictional complexity, allowing related family issues to be addressed by the same judicial officer with full knowledge of the family's complete circumstances. This integration often leads to more comprehensive and consistent outcomes.

The Strategic Implications of Party Designation

The choice of which party files first can have significant strategic implications beyond mere procedural positioning. The petitioner bears the initial burden of establishing grounds for relief and must present their case with sufficient specificity to meet pleading requirements. However, they also control the narrative framework within which the case will be understood.

In custody matters, the party who files first may benefit from temporary orders that maintain the status quo while the case proceeds. Courts are often reluctant to disrupt existing arrangements without compelling evidence, making the initial temporary order crucial to the case's ultimate outcome.

III. Legal Representation: The Professional Advocates

Private Legal Counsel

Private attorneys serve as the primary advocates for their clients, providing legal advice, developing case strategy, conducting discovery, negotiating settlements, and presenting cases at trial. The attorney-client relationship in family law is uniquely challenging, as clients are often dealing with the most emotionally charged circumstances of their lives while making decisions with long-term consequences for themselves and their children.

The **Rules of Professional Conduct** in both states impose specific obligations on family law attorneys that extend beyond typical client advocacy. Attorneys must navigate potential conflicts of interest when family members have competing interests, maintain confidentiality while sometimes being required to report child abuse, and balance zealous advocacy with the court's emphasis on settlement and compromise.

Collaborative law has emerged as an alternative approach where attorneys commit to working toward settlement without the threat of litigation. If settlement fails, the collaborative attorneys must withdraw, ensuring their complete commitment to the settlement process. This approach has gained particular traction in high-asset divorces and custody cases where ongoing relationships require preservation.

Court-Appointed Counsel for Indigent Parties

New York's 18-B panel provides court-appointed counsel for indigent parties in Family Court proceedings involving child custody, support, abuse, and neglect. These attorneys are compensated at significantly reduced rates, creating challenges in providing comprehensive representation while maintaining caseload sustainability.

California's approach varies by county, with some utilizing public defender offices for dependency cases and others maintaining panels of private attorneys willing to accept appointed cases. The quality and availability of appointed counsel can vary significantly, affecting access to justice for low-income families.

The **right to counsel** in family law proceedings is not constitutionally guaranteed in most circumstances, unlike criminal cases. However, some proceedings involving potential termination of parental rights may trigger due process requirements for appointed counsel, creating a complex patchwork of representation rights.

Self-Represented Litigants: Navigating Pro Se Challenges

The prevalence of **self-represented litigants** in family law reflects both economic realities and the personal nature of family disputes. Many parties feel they understand their family situation better than any attorney could and prefer to maintain direct control over their case presentation.

Both states have invested significantly in **self-help resources**, including simplified forms, instructional videos, and courthouse assistance programs. However, the complexity of family law means that seemingly straightforward cases can quickly become complicated by procedural requirements, evidentiary rules, and strategic considerations that pro se litigants may not anticipate.

Limited scope representation has emerged as a middle ground, allowing attorneys to provide specific services such as document preparation, legal advice, or representation at particular hearings while the client handles other aspects of their case. This approach can provide professional assistance while remaining financially accessible.

IV. The Judicial Authority Structure

Trial Court Judges: The Ultimate Decision Makers

Family court judges wield enormous discretion in shaping family relationships and financial arrangements. Unlike other areas of law where outcomes may be more predictable based on established formulas or clear legal standards, family law decisions often depend heavily on judicial interpretation of best interests standards and credibility assessments.

Judicial temperament and philosophy can significantly influence case outcomes. Some judges favor frequent contact between children and both parents, while others prioritize stability and consistency. Some judges are more willing to modify existing arrangements, while others require compelling evidence to justify changes. Understanding these judicial preferences becomes crucial for effective advocacy.

The **emotional toll** on family court judges is substantial, as they regularly make decisions affecting children's welfare and family relationships. This reality influences courtroom dynamics and the importance of presenting cases in ways that help judges feel confident in their decisions.

Commissioners, Referees, and Judicial Support Officers

California court commissioners function with many of the same powers as judges when parties consent to their jurisdiction. They often handle routine matters such as temporary support orders, uncontested divorces, and procedural motions. However, their decisions may be subject to different review standards than traditional judicial orders.

New York referees and support magistrates handle specific types of proceedings, particularly child support matters and some custody issues. Their recommendations typically require judicial confirmation, creating a two-step decision-making process that can provide additional review but also delay final resolution.

Judicial assistants and court clerks play crucial roles in case management and scheduling. Their understanding of judicial preferences and court procedures can significantly affect case flow and procedural compliance. Building professional relationships with court staff, while maintaining appropriate boundaries, contributes to effective practice.

V. Child Advocacy and Protection Professionals

Guardians ad Litem: The Child's Best Interest Representative

New York's Guardian ad Litem system appoints attorneys or trained volunteers to represent children's best interests in high-conflict custody cases, abuse and neglect proceedings, and other situations where children's welfare is at stake. The GAL's role differs from traditional attorney representation in that they advocate for what they believe serves the child's best interests rather than what the child may want.

GAL investigations typically include interviews with children, parents, teachers, and other relevant individuals, home visits, review of school and medical records, and consultation with mental health professionals. Their reports and recommendations carry significant weight with judges, making the GAL relationship crucial for all parties.

Potential conflicts can arise when a child's expressed wishes differ from the GAL's assessment of their best interests. This tension becomes particularly acute with older children who have strong preferences about custody arrangements or other family decisions.

Minor's Counsel: The Child's Voice in Court

California's Minor's Counsel represents the child's expressed interests rather than making independent judgments about best interests. This approach recognizes children's autonomy and ensures their voices are heard in proceedings that will significantly affect their lives.

The **age and maturity** of the child influences how Minor's Counsel functions. With very young children, the attorney may focus on ensuring their basic needs and safety are addressed. With teenagers, the representation may more closely resemble traditional attorney advocacy for the child's stated preferences.

Ethical dilemmas can arise when a child's expressed wishes may not serve their apparent best interests. Minor's Counsel must navigate these situations while maintaining their role as the child's advocate rather than becoming another best interests evaluator.

Court Appointed Special Advocates: Community Volunteers

CASA volunteers bring a unique perspective to child welfare cases through their training in child development and family dynamics combined with their independence from the professional legal system. They often have more time than attorneys or social workers to develop relationships with children and observe family dynamics over extended periods.

CASA reports can provide valuable insights into family functioning and children's needs, particularly in dependency cases where children may be placed in multiple settings over time. Their volunteer status can make them appear more objective to judges, though their lack of legal training may limit their understanding of legal standards and procedures.

VI. Mental Health and Evaluation Professionals

Custody Evaluators: Professional Assessment of Family Dynamics

Forensic custody evaluators conduct comprehensive assessments of family functioning when custody is contested. These evaluations typically involve psychological testing of parents and children, extensive interviews, home visits, observation of parent-child interactions, and review of collateral information from schools, medical providers, and other sources.

Evaluation standards vary between jurisdictions and individual evaluators, but generally include assessment of parenting capacity, children's needs and preferences, family dynamics, and risk factors such as domestic violence or substance abuse. The **Association of Family and Conciliation Courts** provides professional guidelines, but significant variation exists in evaluation practices.

Custody evaluation outcomes can be determinative in contested cases, making the selection and scope of evaluation crucial strategic decisions. Parties may challenge evaluator qualifications, methodology, or conclusions, but courts generally give significant weight to professional mental health assessments.

Therapeutic Professionals in Family Law Context

Family therapists and counselors may become involved in family law cases both as treating professionals and as court-ordered service providers. Their dual roles can create conflicts between therapeutic relationships and legal testimony requirements.

Reunification therapy is sometimes ordered when parent-child relationships have been damaged by high conflict or alienation.

These interventions attempt to repair relationships while court proceedings continue, requiring coordination between therapeutic and legal professionals.

Substance abuse evaluators and treatment providers play crucial roles in cases involving addiction or substance abuse allegations. Their assessments of addiction severity, treatment compliance, and recovery progress often influence custody and visitation decisions.

VII. Alternative Dispute Resolution Professionals

Mediation: Facilitated Resolution

Court-connected mediation in California is mandatory for custody disputes before trial, recognizing that negotiated agreements often serve families better than imposed court orders. **Child Custody Recommending Counselors** not only facilitate discussions but may issue formal recommendations when parents cannot reach agreement.

Private mediation allows parties greater control over the process, including choice of mediator, scheduling flexibility, and confidentiality protections. Experienced family law mediators often achieve better outcomes than court-imposed solutions because they can address the underlying interests rather than just legal positions.

Mediation limitations become apparent when power imbalances, domestic violence, or significant mental health issues affect parties' ability to negotiate effectively. Skilled mediators screen for these issues, but some cases require traditional litigation to ensure fair outcomes.

Collaborative Law Teams

Collaborative law involves interdisciplinary teams including attorneys, mental health professionals, and financial specialists working together to reach comprehensive settlements. This approach recognizes that family law disputes involve legal, emotional, and financial components that require coordinated professional attention.

Team composition typically includes collaborative attorneys for each party, a neutral mental health professional to facilitate communication and address children's needs, and a neutral financial professional to analyze and present financial information. This team approach can be more expensive initially but often achieves better long-term outcomes.

Process commitment requires all professionals to withdraw if the case proceeds to litigation, ensuring complete focus on settlement. This commitment changes the dynamics of negotiations by removing the litigation threat that can escalate conflict.

VIII. Child Welfare and Social Services Professionals

Child Protective Services: State Intervention Authority

Child Protective Services ("CPS") agencies wield enormous power in family law proceedings involving child abuse or neglect allegations. In **New York**, the **Administration for Children's Services** in New York City and county Department of Social Services elsewhere investigate reports and may seek court intervention to protect children.

California's county-based CPS system operates under state oversight but with significant local variation in policies and practices. **Los Angeles Department of Children and Family Services** handles more cases than many entire states, while rural counties may have very limited resources for investigation and intervention.

CPS investigations follow specific protocols for interviewing children, examining physical evidence, and assessing family functioning. However, the quality and thoroughness of investigations can vary significantly based on caseload pressures, worker experience, and available resources.

Removal decisions represent some of the most consequential government interventions in family life. The legal standards for emergency removal differ from those for longer-term placement, creating complex procedural requirements that affect family reunification prospects.

Foster Care and Placement Professionals

Foster care agencies manage temporary and long-term placements for children removed from parental custody. The quality and stability of these placements significantly affect children's wellbeing and can influence judges' decisions about family reunification timelines.

Kinship care with relatives or family friends is generally preferred over traditional foster care, but requires home studies and approval processes that can delay placement decisions. These investigations must balance family preservation preferences with child safety requirements.

Adoption professionals become involved when parental rights are terminated or when stepparent adoptions are pursued. The intersection of adoption law with family law creates complex legal relationships that affect inheritance, support obligations, and family identity.

IX. Financial and Technical Experts

Forensic Accounting and Business Valuation

Forensic accountants trace financial transactions, identify hidden assets, and analyze business operations to ensure complete financial disclosure in divorce proceedings. Their work becomes crucial in high-asset cases or when self-employment or business ownership complicates income determination.

Business valuation experts assess the worth of professional practices, family businesses, and investment portfolios for property division purposes. The timing of valuation, choice of methodology, and treatment of goodwill can significantly affect divorce settlements.

Vocational rehabilitation counselors assess earning capacity for parties claiming inability to work or need for career retraining. Their evaluations influence both support obligations and property division by projecting future earning potential.

Technology and Digital Evidence Specialists

Digital forensics experts recover and analyze electronic communications, financial records, and other computer-based evidence. The prevalence of social media and electronic communication has made digital evidence crucial in many family law cases.

Social media investigators document online activity that may be relevant to custody, support, or domestic violence issues. The admissibility and interpretation of social media evidence requires understanding both technical and legal standards.

X. Language Access and Accommodation Professionals

Court Interpreters: Ensuring Due Process

Certified court interpreters provide simultaneous and consecutive interpretation in multiple languages, ensuring that limited English proficiency does not compromise due process rights. The complexity of family law terminology and concepts makes interpretation particularly challenging in these proceedings.

Cultural mediators sometimes serve alongside interpreters to help courts understand cultural practices and family structures that may affect case dynamics. This is particularly important in immigration-related family law matters or cases involving recent immigrants.

Disability Accommodation Specialists

Sign language interpreters and other accommodation professionals ensure that hearing, vision, or cognitive disabilities do not prevent meaningful participation in family law proceedings. The **Americans with Disabilities Act**requires courts to provide reasonable accommodations, but implementation varies significantly between jurisdictions.

XI. Ethical Considerations and Professional Boundaries

Confidentiality and Information Sharing

The multidisciplinary nature of family law creates complex confidentiality obligations and information-sharing requirements. **Attorney-client privilege** remains paramount, but may be limited when child safety is at stake. **Therapist-patient confidentiality** can be waived or limited in custody evaluations, creating potential conflicts between therapeutic and legal roles.

Mandatory reporting obligations require many professionals involved in family law cases to report suspected child abuse, creating tension between professional relationships and legal duties. Understanding these obligations helps all participants navigate their responsibilities appropriately.

Conflicts of Interest and Multiple Relationships

The interconnected nature of family relationships creates frequent conflicts of interest issues for professionals. Attorneys may be precluded from representing multiple family members, therapists may need to choose between treating parents and children, and evaluators must maintain neutrality despite pressure from parties.

Dual relationships between professionals can compromise objectivity and create ethical violations. Clear boundaries and conflict screening procedures help maintain professional integrity and public confidence in the family law system.

XII. Practical Considerations for Working with Multiple Professionals

Communication and Coordination

Effective family law practice requires coordination among multiple professionals with different training, ethical obligations, and communication styles. **Case management** becomes crucial when attorneys, therapists, evaluators, and other professionals must work together while maintaining appropriate boundaries.

Information sharing protocols must balance the need for coordination with confidentiality requirements and strategic considerations. Parties and their attorneys must understand what information will be shared and how it may be used by different professionals.

Cost and Resource Management

The involvement of multiple professionals can create significant financial burdens for families already stressed by legal proceedings. **Cost-benefit analysis** of various professional services helps parties make informed decisions about which services are necessary versus merely helpful.

Court-ordered services may be provided at reduced cost or through sliding fee scales, but parties need to understand their financial obligations and payment responsibilities for various professional services.

XIII. Strategic Considerations in Professional Selection

Choosing the Right Team

The selection of professionals can significantly influence case outcomes. **Evaluator selection** involves considering their training, experience, methodology, and reputation with local judges. **Therapeutic professional selection** must balance clinical expertise with understanding of legal standards and court expectations.

Geographic considerations affect professional selection, as local professionals may have established relationships with courts and other professionals that can facilitate or complicate case resolution.

Managing Professional Relationships

Building effective working relationships with court personnel, evaluators, and other professionals requires understanding their roles, respecting their expertise, and maintaining appropriate professional boundaries. **Reputation and credibility** in the family law community affects the reception of arguments and recommendations.

Professional education and training continues throughout careers, with family law professionals needing to stay current on legal developments, research findings, and best practices in their respective fields.

XIV. Conclusion: Orchestrating the Professional Team

Family law cases require orchestrating a complex team of professionals, each bringing specialized expertise to address different aspects of family disputes. Success depends not just on understanding what each professional does, but how they interact with each other and how their various roles contribute to case resolution.

The human stakes in family law make professional competence and ethical behavior particularly crucial. Children's welfare, family relationships, and financial security all depend on how well these various professionals fulfill their roles and work together effectively.

Understanding this professional ecosystem enables both attorneys and parties to make informed decisions about professional services, manage expectations about case timelines and costs, and work effectively with the various professionals involved in their cases. The investment in understanding these relationships pays dividends in better case outcomes and more satisfactory resolution of family disputes.

3

Starting a Case

Petitions, Complaints, and Jurisdiction

I. The Strategic Foundation of Family Law Litigation

The initiation of a family law case represents far more than a procedural formality. The first filing creates the legal framework within which all subsequent proceedings will occur, establishes the court's authority to make binding determinations, and often provides strategic advantages that can influence the ultimate outcome. The choice of when, where, and how to commence proceedings requires careful consideration of jurisdictional requirements, tactical positioning, and the specific relief sought.

Unlike other areas of civil litigation where timing may be primarily strategic, family law cases often involve urgent circumstances requiring immediate court intervention. Children may need protection, financial support may be critical for basic needs, and domestic violence may require emergency restraining orders. The tension between urgency and careful preparation makes the initiation phase particularly challenging and consequential.

Understanding the procedural requirements for commencing family law actions is essential not only for ensuring that cases proceed without delay, but also for maximizing the likelihood of favorable outcomes. Courts have little tolerance for procedural deficiencies in family law matters, where the stakes often involve children's welfare and family stability.

II. The Architecture of Initial Pleadings

New York's Dual Court System Approach

New York's jurisdictional division between Supreme Court and Family Court creates both opportunities and complexities in case initiation. The choice of court system can affect not only the procedural requirements but also the substantive outcomes, as different courts may have varying approaches to similar issues.

Supreme Court matrimonial actions require filing a **Verified Complaint** accompanied by a **Summons** under the **Domestic Relations Law**. The verification requirement means that the plaintiff must swear under oath to the truth of the allegations, creating potential perjury liability for false statements. This requirement emphasizes the court's expectation of honesty and accuracy in pleadings, particularly important given the emotional nature of family disputes.

The **Supreme Court Automatic Orders**, which take effect upon service of the summons, immediately restrict both parties from disposing of marital property, canceling insurance coverage, or removing children from the state without court permission or written agreement. These automatic restraints recognize the potential for destructive behavior during the early stages of divorce proceedings and provide immediate protection for both parties and children.

Family Court proceedings under the **Family Court Act** utilize petition-based practice rather than traditional complaint and answer pleading. **Family Court petitions** must establish the court's jurisdiction, identify all relevant parties including children, and specify the relief sought with sufficient detail to provide fair notice to the respondent.

The **integrated nature** of Family Court jurisdiction allows for comprehensive resolution of related family issues in a single proceeding. A custody petition can be expanded to include child support, family offense allegations can be consolidated with custody modifications, and multiple family issues can be addressed by a single judicial officer with complete knowledge of the family's circumstances.

California's Unified Superior Court System

California's consolidated approach through the Superior Court Family Division eliminates jurisdictional confusion by centralizing all family law matters in a single court system. This unification allows for more comprehensive case management and reduces the risk of conflicting orders from different courts.

Mandatory Judicial Council forms ensure statewide consistency in pleading requirements and case processing. The **Petition for Dissolution** (FL-100) and accompanying **Summons** (FL-110) follow standardized formats that facilitate both professional practice and self-representation. These forms include detailed instructions and required disclosures that help ensure compliance with procedural requirements.

California's emphasis on disclosure begins with the initial pleadings, which must include financial information and asset disclosures that provide immediate transparency about the family's economic circumstances. This early disclosure requirement reduces opportunities for asset concealment and promotes more efficient resolution of financial issues.

Domestic violence cases utilize specialized forms including the **Request for Domestic Violence Restraining Order** (DV-100) that can provide immediate protection while establishing the framework for ongoing family law proceedings. The integration of domestic violence protection with other family law issues recognizes the interconnected nature of family relationships and legal needs.

III. Jurisdictional Foundations: Authority to Decide

Subject Matter Jurisdiction: The Court's Power Over the Case

Subject matter jurisdiction cannot be waived or conferred by agreement and must exist for any court order to be valid. Family courts derive their authority from state statutes that specifically enumerate the types of cases they may hear and the relief they may grant.

Domestic relations exceptions to federal court jurisdiction, established in *Ankenbrandt v. Richards*, 504 U.S. 689, 112 S.Ct. 2206, 119 L.Ed.2d 468 (1992), ensure that family law matters remain within state court systems where specialized expertise and local community standards can be applied. This federal abstention recognizes that family law is fundamentally a matter of state concern requiring local resolution.

Jurisdictional limitations can affect the scope of relief available even when a court has authority to hear the case. For example, a court may have jurisdiction to determine custody but lack authority to divide property located in another state, requiring coordination between multiple jurisdictions.

Personal Jurisdiction: Authority Over the Parties

Personal jurisdiction over respondents is essential for courts to issue binding orders affecting their rights and obligations. The constitutional requirements of **due process**, established in **International Shoe Co. v. Washington**, 326 U.S. 310, 66 S.Ct. 154, 90 L.Ed. 95 (1945), require sufficient minimum contacts between the respondent and the forum state to make jurisdiction reasonable and fair.

New York's approach to personal jurisdiction in family law matters requires careful analysis of the respondent's connections to the state. Simple presence of children in New York may not establish personal jurisdiction over a non-resident parent for purposes of property division or spousal support, though it may be sufficient for child support obligations.

California's long-arm jurisdiction extends more broadly to non-resident parties who have significant contacts with the state, including property ownership, business operations, or substantial contact with children residing in California. **California Family Code Section 2011** specifically addresses jurisdiction in dissolution cases, requiring either residency or sufficient contacts to establish personal jurisdiction.

Service of process requirements flow from personal jurisdiction principles and constitutional due process demands. The method of service must be reasonably calculated to provide actual notice to the respondent, as established in *Mullane v. Central Hanover Bank & Trust Co.*, 339 U.S. 306, 70 S.Ct. 652, 94 L.Ed. 865 (1950).

IV. Interstate Jurisdictional Framework

The Uniform Child Custody Jurisdiction and Enforcement Act

UCCJEA implementation in both New York and California provides a comprehensive framework for determining which state has jurisdiction to make initial custody determinations and which state has authority to modify existing orders. **New York Domestic Relations Law Article 5-A** and **California Family Code Sections 3400-3465** implement virtually identical versions of the uniform act.

Home state jurisdiction under UCCJEA generally gives priority to the state where the child has lived for six consecutive months immediately before the commencement of the proceeding. This principle prevents forum shopping and ensures that custody decisions are made by courts familiar with the child's environment and circumstances.

Significant connection jurisdiction may apply when no state qualifies as the home state, allowing jurisdiction in a state that has significant connections with the child and where substantial evidence about the child's care and relationships is available. This alternative basis prevents jurisdictional gaps while maintaining focus on the child's actual connections.

Emergency jurisdiction under UCCJEA allows temporary orders when a child is present in the state and has been abandoned or emergency protection is necessary. These orders remain temporary until a court with proper jurisdiction makes permanent determinations, preventing dangerous jurisdictional gaps in child protection.

Inconvenient forum provisions allow courts to decline jurisdiction even when they have authority under UCCJEA if another state would be more appropriate for resolution of the case. Factors include the location of evidence, the child's familiarity with the forum, and the ability of courts in different states to cooperate in ongoing supervision.

The Uniform Interstate Family Support Act

UIFSA provisions in **New York Family Court Act Article 5-B** and **California Family Code Sections 4900-5005**establish jurisdiction for child and spousal support matters across state lines. These uniform provisions ensure that support obligations can be established and enforced even when parties live in different states.

Continuing exclusive jurisdiction under UIFSA remains with the issuing state as long as either party or the child continues to reside there and the state remains connected to the case. This principle prevents conflicting support orders from multiple states while ensuring that modifications can be made when circumstances change.

Income withholding provisions under UIFSA allow direct enforcement of support orders across state lines without requiring separate legal proceedings in each state. This streamlined enforcement mechanism makes interstate support enforcement more efficient and effective.

V. Constitutional Requirements and Due Process

Notice Requirements and Service of Process

Constitutional notice requirements mandate that respondents receive actual notice of proceedings that may affect their rights. The specific method of service must be reasonably calculated to reach the respondent and provide adequate time for response.

New York service requirements vary between Supreme Court and Family Court proceedings. **Supreme Court divorce actions** require personal service of the summons and complaint unless the court permits alternative service methods. **CPLR Section 308** provides detailed requirements for personal service, substituted service, and service by publication when personal service cannot be accomplished.

Family Court service under **Family Court Act Section 154** allows service by certified mail in many proceedings, recognizing the ongoing nature of family relationships and the likelihood that parties can be reached through less formal methods. However, initial proceedings typically require personal service to ensure constitutional compliance.

California service requirements under **Family Code Section 414** and **Code of Civil Procedure Section 415.10**require personal service of initial family law pleadings by a person other than the petitioner. This requirement ensures neutrality in service and reduces opportunities for manipulation or intimidation during the service process.

Proof of service requirements in both states mandate filing detailed affidavits documenting how, when, and where service was accomplished. These proof requirements allow courts to verify constitutional compliance and provide evidence for later enforcement proceedings.

Due Process in Emergency Proceedings

Ex parte orders present unique due process challenges because they are issued without the respondent's participation. Courts must balance the need for immediate protection with the respondent's right to be heard before orders affect their rights.

Domestic violence restraining orders often require ex parte issuance to provide immediate protection for victims. Both **New York Family Court Act Section 154-d** and **California Family Code Section 6250** provide for temporary restraining orders based on affidavit evidence, with prompt hearings required to provide due process for respondents.

Emergency custody orders must meet heightened standards justifying immediate action without notice. Courts typically require evidence of imminent harm to children or risk of removal from the jurisdiction before issuing ex parte custody orders.

VI. Strategic Considerations in Case Initiation

Timing and Tactical Positioning

Filing timing can significantly affect case outcomes beyond simple procedural advantages. The party who files first controls the initial narrative, chooses the forum if multiple jurisdictions are possible, and may benefit from temporary orders that establish favorable arrangements pending final resolution.

Automatic restraining orders in California, which take effect upon service of dissolution petitions, prevent either party from disposing of property, changing insurance beneficiaries, or removing children from the state. These automatic restraints, codified in **Family Code Section 2040**, provide immediate protection during the vulnerable period between filing and response.

Status quo advantages often favor the filing party, particularly in custody matters where courts are reluctant to disturb existing arrangements without compelling evidence. The temporary custody orders issued early in proceedings frequently influence final custody determinations.

Forum selection considerations include not only jurisdictional requirements but also practical factors such as judge assignment systems, local court practices, and the availability of specialized family law services. Some counties have dedicated family law departments with judges who specialize in family matters, while others assign family cases to general civil departments.

Emergency Relief and Interim Orders

Request for Order procedures in California allow parties to seek temporary relief on shortened notice while providing due process protections for respondents. **Family Code Section 217** establishes the framework for these interim proceedings, which often determine temporary custody, support, and use of family residence.

Order to Show Cause practice in New York Supreme Court provides similar mechanisms for obtaining temporary relief in matrimonial actions. These orders require respondents to appear and demonstrate why the requested relief should not be granted, shifting the burden of proof on temporary issues.

Emergency factors that justify immediate court intervention include domestic violence, child abuse or neglect, threatened removal of children from the jurisdiction, dissipation of marital assets, and cancellation of health insurance or other essential benefits.

Standard of proof for temporary orders typically requires only a prima facie showing rather than proof by a preponderance of evidence. This lower standard recognizes the preliminary nature of temporary orders and the need for prompt protection while allowing full development of evidence before final orders.

VII. Practical Filing Considerations

Document Preparation and Compliance

Pleading requirements in family law cases often exceed those in other civil matters due to the personal nature of family relationships and the court's need for complete information about family circumstances. Required information typically includes detailed financial disclosure, children's information, and history of domestic violence or substance abuse.

Mandatory disclosures begin with initial pleadings in many jurisdictions. California requires preliminary financial disclosures within 60 days of filing, while New York requires net worth statements in matrimonial actions involving substantial assets or support issues.

Child impact considerations require special attention to how legal proceedings may affect children's emotional and practical wellbeing. Some jurisdictions require parenting plans or statements about proposed custody arrangements as part of initial pleadings.

Local court rules often supplement statewide requirements with specific formatting, filing, and procedural requirements. These local variations can affect everything from paper size and margins to specific forms required for particular types of relief.

Financial Considerations and Access to Justice

Filing fees represent a significant barrier to court access for many families already experiencing financial stress from separation or divorce. **New York Supreme Court** filing fees include the index number fee of approximately $210 plus additional fees for motions and other proceedings.

California filing fees vary by county but typically range from $435 to $450 for dissolution actions, with additional fees for responses, motions, and other pleadings. These fees represent substantial expenses for families already dealing with the economic disruption of separation.

Fee waiver procedures provide essential access to courts for low-income litigants. **California's Request to Waive Court Fees** (FW-001) allows qualifying parties to proceed without paying filing fees, while **New York's Poor Person's Relief** under **CPLR Article 11** provides similar access in Supreme Court proceedings.

Assigned counsel in appropriate Family Court proceedings ensures representation for indigent parties in cases involving potential termination of parental rights or other proceedings where fundamental rights are at stake.

Technology and Modern Filing Practices

Electronic filing systems have transformed family law practice by allowing 24-hour document submission, automatic service capabilities, and improved case management. **New York's NYSCEF system** handles most Supreme Court matrimonial filings, while Family Court continues to rely primarily on paper filing.

California's county-based e-filing systems vary significantly in capability and requirements. **Los Angeles Superior Court's LACourtConnect** provides comprehensive e-filing for family law matters, while smaller counties may have more limited electronic capabilities.

Virtual hearings have become increasingly common for status conferences, case management, and some substantive proceedings. Courts have developed protocols for conducting family law proceedings remotely while maintaining due process protections and ensuring confidentiality.

Digital service of process is evolving to include email service in appropriate circumstances, though constitutional notice requirements continue to require careful analysis of service methods to ensure effectiveness.

VIII. Responding to Initial Pleadings

Response Requirements and Deadlines

Responsive pleading deadlines are strictly enforced in family law matters due to the time-sensitive nature of family issues and the court's interest in prompt resolution. **New York** typically allows 20 or 30 days for responses depending on the method of service, while **California** provides 30 days from service for responses to dissolution petitions.

Default judgment risks are particularly serious in family law cases because defaults can result in permanent orders regarding custody, support, and property division without further court proceedings. Unlike other civil cases where defaults may be easily set aside, family law defaults affecting children's welfare may be more difficult to overturn.

Cross-petitions and counter-claims allow respondents to seek affirmative relief rather than merely defending against the petitioner's claims. These responsive pleadings can shift case dynamics and ensure that both parties' interests are fully presented to the court.

Discovery planning should begin with the response to initial pleadings, as family law cases often involve extensive financial discovery and investigation of parenting capacity that requires early planning and case management.

VIX. Case Management and Early Court Involvement

Initial Status Conferences and Case Management

Early case management in family law matters often involves court-mandated conferences designed to identify issues, encourage settlement, and establish schedules for discovery and resolution. These conferences recognize that family law cases benefit from active judicial management rather than traditional adversarial development.

Mandatory mediation in California for custody disputes requires parties to attempt resolution through court-connected mediation before proceeding to trial. This requirement reflects the state's policy preference for negotiated agreements over imposed court orders in matters affecting children.

Case scheduling orders establish deadlines for discovery completion, expert witness designation, and trial preparation. Family law cases often involve complex scheduling considerations due to the need for custody evaluations, appraisals, and other expert assessments.

Settlement conferences may be scheduled early in proceedings to explore resolution possibilities while emotions are less inflamed and positions less entrenched. Experienced family law judges often can facilitate agreements that serve families better than contested litigation.

IX. Interstate and International Complications

Multi-Jurisdictional Considerations

Interstate cases require careful attention to jurisdictional requirements under UCCJEA and UIFSA, but also present practical challenges in coordinating discovery, serving process, and conducting proceedings when parties live in different states.

International family law matters involve additional complexity from the **Hague Convention on International Child Abduction** and other international treaties affecting custody and support enforcement. These cases require specialized knowledge of international law and diplomatic procedures.

Military family considerations add federal law complications to state family law proceedings, particularly regarding deployment issues, military benefits, and jurisdiction when service members are stationed outside their home states.

X. Conclusion: Building the Foundation for Success

The initiation of family law proceedings establishes the foundation upon which all subsequent proceedings will rest. Careful attention to jurisdictional requirements, procedural compliance, and strategic positioning during the filing phase can prevent costly delays and procedural challenges while maximizing opportunities for favorable outcomes.

The complexity of family law procedural requirements reflects the serious nature of family disputes and the court's responsibility to protect children and vulnerable family members. Understanding these requirements and their strategic implications enables both attorneys and parties to navigate the family law system effectively while protecting their fundamental interests.

The investment in careful case initiation pays dividends throughout the proceedings by ensuring that the court has proper authority to resolve disputes, that all parties receive constitutionally adequate process, and that the case proceeds efficiently toward resolution. As family law cases move into substantive phases involving property division, custody determination, and support calculation, the procedural foundation established during case initiation becomes the platform for achieving just and practical outcomes for families in transition.

4

ADR in Family Law

Mediation, Arbitration & Collaborative Law

I. The Evolution Beyond Traditional Litigation

Alternative Dispute Resolution in family law represents a fundamental shift from adversarial litigation toward collaborative problem-solving that recognizes the unique nature of family relationships. Unlike commercial disputes where parties typically have no ongoing relationship after resolution, family law matters often involve parents who must continue cooperating for years or decades in raising their children. This reality has driven the development of dispute resolution methods that prioritize relationship preservation, creative solutions, and family-centered outcomes.

The growth of ADR in family law also reflects practical limitations of traditional court systems. Overcrowded dockets, limited judicial resources, and the inherently personal nature of family disputes have created demand for more flexible, timely, and confidential resolution methods. Courts have embraced ADR not merely as a case management tool, but as a potentially superior method for resolving family conflicts that serves both judicial efficiency and family wellbeing.

However, ADR is not universally appropriate or beneficial. Power imbalances, domestic violence, mental health issues, and uncooperative parties can make traditional ADR methods ineffective or even harmful. Understanding when and how to use various ADR methods requires careful assessment of family dynamics, legal issues, and practical constraints that affect each case.

II. The Philosophical Foundation of Family Law ADR

Moving Beyond Win-Lose Paradigms

Traditional litigation operates on an adversarial model where one party's gain typically represents another's loss. This zero-sum approach can be particularly destructive in family law, where the parties' lives remain intertwined through children, shared property, or ongoing support obligations. **ADR methods emphasize interest-based negotiation** rather than positional bargaining, focusing on underlying needs and concerns rather than stated demands.

Children's interests often align with both parents' long-term interests in maintaining functional co-parenting relationships, even when parents' immediate positions appear conflicting. ADR processes can explore creative parenting arrangements that serve children's needs while accommodating both parents' legitimate concerns about time, decision-making authority, and involvement in their children's lives.

Financial settlements reached through ADR often prove more durable than court-imposed orders because parties participate in crafting solutions rather than having decisions imposed upon them. This voluntary compliance reduces enforcement problems and subsequent litigation over interpretation or modification of orders.

The Role of Professional Neutrals

Professional neutrals in family law ADR require specialized training that combines traditional legal or mental health expertise with conflict resolution skills, understanding of family dynamics, and knowledge of child development. Unlike neutrals in commercial disputes who focus primarily on legal rights and financial interests, family law neutrals must address emotional needs, communication patterns, and relationship dynamics that affect resolution prospects.

Ethical obligations for family law neutrals include maintaining impartiality while ensuring that vulnerable parties are not disadvantaged, recognizing when ADR is inappropriate due to power imbalances or safety concerns, and understanding the limits of their role in providing legal advice or therapeutic intervention.

III. Mediation: The Art of Facilitated Negotiation

Understanding Mediation's Core Principles

Mediation operates on principles of party autonomy, neutral facilitation, and voluntary agreement that distinguish it from both litigation and arbitration. The mediator's role is to facilitate communication, help parties identify interests and options, and assist in crafting mutually acceptable agreements, but never to impose solutions or make binding decisions.

Confidentiality protections in mediation serve multiple purposes: encouraging honest communication, protecting settlement negotiations from later use in litigation, and maintaining privacy for family matters. However, confidentiality is not absolute, particularly when child safety or criminal activity is involved.

The voluntary nature of mediation means that parties retain the right to discontinue the process, seek legal advice, or pursue litigation if mediation proves unsuccessful. This voluntary participation often increases the likelihood of reaching agreements because parties know they are not trapped in an unsatisfactory process.

California's Mandatory Custody Mediation Framework

California Family Code Section 3170 requires mediation in contested custody and visitation cases before court hearings can proceed. This mandatory framework reflects the state's strong policy preference for parental agreement over court-imposed custody orders, recognizing that parents typically understand their children's needs better than judges who have limited time and information.

Child Custody Recommending Counseling services, available in many California counties, combine mediation with evaluative services when parents cannot reach agreement. These services can issue formal recommendations to the court while maintaining the benefits of facilitated discussion and parental input in developing custody arrangements.

Shuttle mediation options accommodate cases where domestic violence or severe conflict make joint sessions inappropriate. In these modified formats, mediators meet separately with each party while facilitating negotiation and agreement development, providing access to mediation benefits while maintaining safety and addressing power imbalances.

Waiver provisions under **Family Code Section 3181** allow courts to exempt parties from mandatory mediation when domestic violence makes participation inappropriate or ineffective. These exceptions recognize that mediation's collaborative assumptions may not apply when one party has used violence or coercive control to dominate family relationships.

New York's Voluntary Mediation Approach

New York's voluntary mediation system relies on judicial referrals, attorney recommendations, and party initiative to direct appropriate cases toward mediation services. This approach allows for more individualized assessment of mediation appropriateness while avoiding potential harm from mandatory participation in unsuitable cases.

Court-annexed mediation programs in New York provide subsidized or free mediation services through partnerships with nonprofit organizations, bar associations, and volunteer mediator programs. These services make mediation accessible to families regardless of economic circumstances while maintaining professional standards and training requirements.

Presumptive ADR initiatives in some New York counties create strong judicial encouragement for mediation while preserving party choice about participation. Judges may continue cases to allow mediation attempts, inquire about ADR consideration, and provide information about available services without mandating participation.

Parent coordination services offer ongoing dispute resolution for high-conflict families who need assistance implementing custody orders and resolving day-to-day co-parenting conflicts. These services combine mediation, education, and case management to help families develop better communication and decision-making patterns.

Mediation Process and Techniques

Initial assessment in family mediation includes screening for domestic violence, substance abuse, mental health issues, and other factors that might affect mediation appropriateness or require process modifications. Skilled mediators use validated screening tools and interview techniques to identify safety concerns and power imbalances.

Information gathering in mediation may include financial disclosure, parenting evaluations, and consultation with children's therapists or teachers when appropriate. However, mediation discovery is typically less formal and adversarial than litigation discovery, focusing on information needed for informed decision-making rather than comprehensive investigation.

Option generation encourages creative problem-solving by exploring multiple potential solutions before evaluating their feasibility. This brainstorming approach often identifies arrangements that neither party initially considered but that serve everyone's interests better than their original positions.

Reality testing helps parties understand the likely outcomes of litigation while maintaining focus on their own needs and priorities. Effective mediators provide legal information without giving legal advice, helping parties make informed decisions about settlement versus continued negotiation or litigation.

IV. Arbitration: Private Adjudication in Family Law

The Structure and Authority of Family Law Arbitration

Family law arbitration adapts commercial arbitration principles to address the unique characteristics of family disputes, including ongoing relationships, child welfare considerations, and public policy concerns about family autonomy versus state oversight.

Arbitrator selection in family law typically emphasizes expertise in family law, child development, and family dynamics rather than general arbitration experience. Many family law arbitrators are retired judges or experienced family law attorneys who bring specialized knowledge to complex family disputes.

Procedural flexibility allows arbitration to be tailored to specific case needs, from simplified document-based procedures for straightforward financial disputes to comprehensive hearings with expert testimony for complex custody or valuation issues. This flexibility can reduce costs and timeframes while maintaining thorough consideration of relevant factors.

Scope and Limitations of Family Law Arbitration

Property division arbitration is widely accepted in both New York and California, as courts recognize that financial disputes involve private rights that parties may contractually agree to resolve through private adjudication. Arbitrators can make binding decisions about asset valuation, distribution, and support obligations subject to the same legal standards that courts would apply.

Spousal support arbitration involves consideration of statutory factors and guidelines while allowing for more detailed exploration of earning capacity, lifestyle, and future needs than might be possible in crowded court schedules. Arbitrators can conduct extensive hearings and review detailed financial evidence to make informed support determinations.

Child custody arbitration faces greater restrictions due to courts' continuing jurisdiction over child welfare and their obligation to ensure that custody arrangements serve children's best interests. *In re Marriage of Armato*, 120 Cal.App.4th 1062, 16 Cal.Rptr.3d 368 (2004), established that while parents can agree to arbitrate custody disputes, courts retain authority to review and modify arbitration awards affecting children when circumstances change or when awards do not serve children's best interests.

Public policy limitations prevent arbitration of issues involving child abuse allegations, termination of parental rights, or other matters where state interests in child protection override parental autonomy. These limitations reflect the principle that some family law matters involve interests beyond those of the immediate parties.

Enforceability and Review of Family Law Arbitration Awards

Arbitration awards in family law cases must typically be confirmed by court order to become enforceable, similar to mediated agreements. This confirmation process allows courts to review awards for compliance with legal standards and protection of children's interests while maintaining the efficiency benefits of arbitration.

Limited appeal rights distinguish arbitration from litigation, as parties generally cannot appeal arbitration awards on the merits but only on grounds such as fraud, corruption, or exceeding arbitrator authority. *Moncharsh v. Heily & Blase*, 3 Cal.4th 1, 832 P.2d 899, 10 Cal.Rptr.2d 183 (1992), established California's strong policy favoring arbitration finality even when arbitrators make legal or factual errors.

Modification procedures for arbitration awards affecting children must account for courts' continuing jurisdiction over child welfare. While arbitration awards deserve respect as expressions of parental agreement, they cannot prevent courts from modifying custody or support arrangements when children's circumstances or needs change.

V. Collaborative Law: Team-Based Problem Solving

The Philosophical and Structural Framework

Collaborative law represents the most comprehensive alternative to traditional litigation, creating a team-based approach that addresses legal, emotional, and practical aspects of family dissolution simultaneously. The process recognizes that family law disputes involve multiple dimensions that require coordinated professional attention.

Disqualification agreements require all collaborative professionals to withdraw if the case proceeds to litigation, ensuring complete commitment to settlement while eliminating the option of using collaborative discussions as discovery for later litigation. This mutual commitment creates powerful incentives for creative problem-solving and good faith negotiation.

Team composition typically includes collaborative attorneys for each party, a neutral mental health professional to facilitate communication and address emotional issues, and a neutral financial professional to analyze and present financial information. Additional specialists such as child psychologists or business valuators may join the team for specific issues.

California's Collaborative Law Framework

California Family Code Sections 2013-2015 provide statutory recognition and procedural framework for collaborative law practice, including protection for collaborative communications and procedures for withdrawal when collaboration fails. This statutory framework provides clarity about confidentiality protections and professional obligations in collaborative practice.

Training and certification requirements for collaborative professionals ensure competency in interest-based negotiation, family systems understanding, and ethical obligations unique to collaborative practice. Professional organizations such as the **International Academy of Collaborative Professionals** provide standardized training and practice standards.

Local collaborative communities in counties such as Los Angeles, Orange, and Santa Clara have developed sophisticated referral networks, training programs, and practice standards that support high-quality collaborative services. These professional communities often provide ongoing education and peer consultation that enhances practice quality.

New York's Collaborative Law Development

New York Association of Collaborative Professionals provides training, standards, and support for collaborative practice throughout the state. While New York lacks comprehensive statutory framework like California, collaborative practice operates under existing professional responsibility rules and contractual principles.

Collaborative practice groups in areas such as New York City, Westchester, and Long Island have developed local practice standards and referral networks that support effective collaborative services. These groups often provide training for new collaborative professionals and ongoing education for experienced practitioners.

Integration with court systems varies across New York, with some courts actively encouraging collaborative law while others remain less familiar with the process. Collaborative practitioners often educate judges about the process and benefits to gain judicial support for collaborative agreements.

The Collaborative Process in Practice

Initial team meetings establish ground rules, assess case appropriateness, and begin information gathering and issue identification. These meetings allow the team to address process concerns and ensure that all parties understand their roles and commitments.

Interest identification focuses on underlying needs and concerns rather than stated positions, helping parties understand each other's priorities and identify potential solutions that serve everyone's interests. This process often reveals common ground that was not apparent from initial positions.

Option development utilizes the diverse expertise of team members to generate creative solutions that address legal, emotional, and practical concerns simultaneously. The team approach often identifies solutions that individual attorneys or parties might not develop independently.

Agreement implementation includes planning for ongoing communication, dispute resolution, and future modifications that may become necessary as family circumstances change. Collaborative agreements often include mechanisms for addressing future disagreements without returning to litigation.

VI. ADR in High-Conflict and Special Circumstances Cases

Domestic Violence and Safety Considerations

Screening protocols for domestic violence must be implemented before any ADR process begins, as traditional ADR assumptions about equal bargaining power and voluntary participation may not apply when one party has used violence or coercive control. *Kaplan v. Kaplan*, 25 Cal.4th 814, 23 P.3d 771, 107

Cal.Rptr.2d 807 (2001), emphasized courts' obligations to protect domestic violence victims from inappropriate pressure to participate in mediation.

Modified ADR processes can accommodate some domestic violence cases through shuttle mediation, attorney-assisted negotiation, or collaborative law with enhanced safety protocols. These modifications may include separate meeting locations, staggered arrival times, and security arrangements that protect victim safety while allowing beneficial aspects of settlement negotiation.

Safety planning must be integrated into any ADR process involving domestic violence history, including ongoing communication protocols, child exchange arrangements, and emergency procedures that protect victim safety during and after resolution. The **Domestic Violence Prevention Act** in both states requires courts to consider safety in any custody or visitation arrangements.

Mental Health and Substance Abuse Considerations

Mental health assessment may be necessary before ADR participation when parties have significant mental health issues that affect their capacity for informed decision-making or effective negotiation. Some mental health conditions may require treatment or medication stabilization before meaningful ADR participation is possible.

Substance abuse screening is particularly important in custody cases where parental substance use affects child safety and parenting capacity. ADR processes may need to include addiction assessment, treatment planning, and ongoing monitoring to address substance abuse concerns while working toward family resolution.

Capacity considerations require careful evaluation when parties have intellectual disabilities, dementia, or other conditions that may affect their ability to understand and consent to ADR agreements. Legal guardianship or representative participation may be necessary to protect vulnerable parties' interests.

High-Net-Worth and Complex Financial Cases

Asset complexity in high-net-worth cases often makes ADR attractive due to the flexibility for detailed financial analysis, privacy protections, and ability to craft sophisticated settlement structures that may not be available through court proceedings.

Business valuation disputes benefit from ADR processes that allow extended expert testimony, joint expert retention, and creative resolution structures such as deferred payment plans or continued business participation arrangements.

Privacy concerns for high-profile families make ADR particularly attractive, as mediation and collaborative law proceedings remain confidential while court proceedings create public records that may be accessed by media or other interested parties.

International considerations for families with assets or connections in multiple countries require specialized expertise in international tax law, treaty obligations, and enforcement mechanisms that may be more readily available through selected arbitrators or collaborative professionals than through general court proceedings.

VII. Court Integration and Support for ADR

Judicial Encouragement and Referral Programs

Early case management in both New York and California increasingly includes ADR assessment and referral as standard practice rather than exceptional intervention. Courts recognize that early ADR referral, before positions become entrenched and costs escalate, often achieves better outcomes for families.

Judicial education about ADR methods and benefits helps judges make appropriate referrals and support settlement efforts while maintaining necessary oversight of child welfare and other public interests. Many courts provide training for judges about ADR options and referral criteria.

Settlement conferences led by judges or settlement officers combine judicial authority with negotiation facilitation, often achieving settlements in cases where pure mediation might not succeed due to legal uncertainty or need for authoritative guidance about likely court outcomes.

Court-Annexed ADR Programs

Subsidized mediation services make ADR accessible to low- and moderate-income families who might otherwise rely exclusively on court proceedings. These programs often provide services on sliding fee scales or through volunteer mediator programs that maintain professional standards while reducing costs.

Training and certification programs for court-connected mediators ensure quality and consistency in services while developing cadres of qualified neutrals. Many courts partner with bar associations or mediation organizations to provide comprehensive training and ongoing education.

Quality assurance measures include mediator evaluation, outcome tracking, and feedback systems that help courts assess program effectiveness and make improvements. Some programs track settlement rates, participant satisfaction, and long-term compliance with mediated agreements.

Integration with Case Management

Automatic ADR referrals in some jurisdictions require parties to consider mediation before scheduling trials or motion hearings, creating strong incentives for settlement attempts while preserving party choice about participation.

Stay provisions allow courts to pause litigation deadlines while ADR proceeds, preventing the pressure of approaching trial dates from undermining settlement negotiations while ensuring that cases continue moving toward resolution.

Enforcement support helps parties implement mediated agreements through streamlined court approval processes, technical assistance with agreement drafting, and expedited enforcement procedures when agreements are violated.

VIII. Economic Considerations and Access to Justice

Cost-Benefit Analysis of ADR Methods

Direct cost comparisons between ADR and litigation must consider not only professional fees but also opportunity costs, emotional costs, and long-term compliance and enforcement costs. While ADR may involve upfront costs for neutrals or team professionals, these costs often compare favorably to extended litigation expenses.

Collaborative law costs can be substantial due to the multiple professionals involved, but may provide better value than litigation when the comprehensive approach addresses legal, emotional, and practical issues more effectively than sequential professional consultations.

Hidden costs of litigation include lost work time, emotional stress, relationship damage, and ongoing enforcement problems that may not be apparent when comparing initial professional fees. ADR processes that produce more durable agreements may prove more economical over time.

Access to Justice Through ADR

Pro bono and reduced-fee programs make mediation accessible to low-income families through bar association programs, nonprofit organizations, and court-sponsored services. These programs recognize that ADR benefits should not be limited to families who can afford full-fee private services.

Self-help resources including online mediation platforms, educational materials, and coaching services help parties navigate ADR processes with limited professional assistance while maintaining quality outcomes.

Language access requires specialized training for mediators and other neutrals working with limited English proficiency parties, as effective ADR depends heavily on nuanced communication that may be compromised by language barriers.

VIX. Enforceability and Implementation of ADR Agreements

Converting Agreements to Enforceable Orders

Documentation requirements for ADR agreements typically include detailed written agreements that specify all terms, conditions, and implementation procedures. Incomplete or ambiguous agreements create enforcement problems and may require additional negotiation or court intervention.

Court approval processes vary between jurisdictions but generally require submission of written agreements with requests for court approval and entry of judgment. Some courts provide streamlined approval procedures for ADR agreements that meet standard requirements.

Review standards for ADR agreements focus on legal sufficiency, protection of children's interests, and compliance with public policy rather than second-guessing the parties' substantive decisions. Courts generally respect party autonomy while ensuring minimum legal protections.

Long-Term Compliance and Modification

Implementation planning during ADR processes can prevent later disputes by addressing foreseeable implementation issues, communication protocols, and modification procedures. Well-crafted agreements anticipate future needs and provide mechanisms for addressing them.

Dispute resolution clauses in ADR agreements often require parties to return to mediation or other ADR processes before seeking court intervention for disputes about implementation or modification. These clauses help preserve the collaborative relationship while providing accessible dispute resolution.

Modification procedures must balance respect for negotiated agreements with recognition that family circumstances change and may require adjustment of custody, support, or other arrangements. Many ADR agreements include built-in review periods or triggering events for potential modifications.

IX. Professional Standards and Ethical Considerations

Training and Certification Requirements

Mediator qualifications vary between jurisdictions and program types, but generally include basic mediation training, family law knowledge, and ongoing education requirements. Some programs require additional training in domestic violence screening, child development, or cultural competency.

Collaborative professional standards include extensive training in interest-based negotiation, team coordination, and ethical obligations unique to collaborative practice. Professional organizations provide certification programs and continuing education requirements.

Arbitrator qualifications typically emphasize family law expertise, judicial experience, or specialized training in family law arbitration procedures and standards. Some programs require periodic recertification or continuing education to maintain arbitrator panels.

Ethical Obligations and Boundary Issues

Neutrality requirements for mediators and arbitrators include avoiding conflicts of interest, maintaining impartiality between parties, and recognizing when personal relationships or financial interests might compromise effectiveness.

Confidentiality obligations protect ADR communications while recognizing exceptions for child abuse reporting, criminal activity disclosure, and other legally mandated reporting requirements. Practitioners must understand the scope and limits of confidentiality protections.

Scope of practice issues require clear understanding of the differences between legal advice, therapeutic intervention, and neutral facilitation. ADR professionals must avoid exceeding their role boundaries while ensuring that parties receive appropriate referrals for needed services.

X. Conclusion: Choosing the Right Path for Each Family

Alternative Dispute Resolution in family law offers powerful tools for resolving conflicts in ways that serve families better than traditional litigation. However, these tools must be carefully matched to family circumstances, available resources, and the specific legal and practical issues involved in each case.

Strategic decision-making about ADR participation requires assessment of family dynamics, safety considerations, economic factors, and the likelihood of achieving acceptable outcomes through various processes. This assessment benefits from professional guidance while ultimately remaining within party control.

Success in ADR depends not only on process selection but also on preparation, good faith participation, and realistic expectations about outcomes and limitations. Families who approach ADR with appropriate preparation and commitment often achieve better outcomes than those who view it as a casual alternative to serious legal process.

The evolution of family law toward a greater emphasis on ADR reflects growing recognition that family disputes require different approaches than commercial litigation. As these processes continue developing and improving, they offer increasing promise for resolving family conflicts in ways that preserve relationships, protect children, and serve the complex needs of families in transition.

Understanding the strengths and limitations of various ADR methods enables both professionals and families to make informed choices about dispute resolution that serve their specific needs and circumstances. The investment in understanding and properly utilizing ADR often pays dividends in better outcomes, reduced costs, and preservation of family relationships that must continue long after legal disputes are resolved.

5

Marriage, Domestic Partnerships, and Legal Unions

I. The Legal Foundations of Intimacy

Marriage transcends its cultural and religious significance to function as a fundamental legal contract that governs property rights, taxation obligations, spousal support, and parental status. The decision to formalize a relationship through marriage or its legal equivalents in New York and California creates a comprehensive framework of legal obligations and protections that permeate virtually every aspect of family law practice.

The legal recognition of intimate relationships has evolved significantly over the past several decades, particularly following landmark decisions such as *Obergefell v. Hodges*, 576 U.S. 644 (2015), which established marriage equality nationwide. Today, both New York and California offer multiple pathways for couples to formalize their relationships, each carrying distinct legal consequences that practitioners must carefully navigate when advising clients.

This chapter examines the statutory requirements and legal implications of marriage, domestic partnerships, and cohabitation arrangements in New York and California. It also addresses the critical role of prenuptial and postnuptial agreements in defining or modifying the default legal obligations that arise from formalized relationships. Understanding these foundational concepts is essential for family law practitioners, as the choice of relationship structure affects everything from property division and support obligations to parental rights and estate planning considerations.

II. Marriage Requirements in New York and California

Marriage remains governed primarily by state law, creating variations in requirements and consequences between jurisdictions. Both New York and California have established comprehensive statutory frameworks that define the prerequisites for valid marriage formation.

New York Marriage Requirements

New York's marriage laws are codified primarily in the Domestic Relations Law. The state requires that prospective spouses meet several fundamental criteria before a valid marriage can be formed.

Age and Capacity Requirements: Parties must be at least eighteen years of age to marry without restriction. *See* N.Y. Dom. Rel. Law § 15-a (McKinney 2024). Individuals who are seventeen years old may marry only with both judicial consent and parental or guardian approval. *Id.* The judicial consent requirement was added as part of recent legislative reforms aimed at preventing forced marriages of minors. *See* 2017 N.Y. Laws ch. 35.

Licensing Procedures: Couples must obtain a marriage license from any town or city clerk within New York State. N.Y. *Dom. Rel. Law* § 13 (McKinney 2024). The application process requires both parties to appear in person and provide proof of identity and age. The license becomes effective immediately upon issuance, with no mandatory waiting period, distinguishing New York from states that impose cooling-off periods.

Validity Period and Ceremony Requirements: Marriage licenses remain valid for sixty days from the date of issuance. N.Y. *Dom. Rel. Law* § 13-*a* (McKinney 2024). The marriage must be solemnized by an authorized officiant, including clergy members, judges, justices of the peace, or other individuals specifically authorized by law. N.Y. *Dom. Rel. Law* § 11 (McKinney 2024). The ceremony must include the parties' mutual consent to marriage expressed in the presence of the officiant and at least one witness.

Prohibited Relationships: New York law prohibits marriages between individuals related by blood or affinity within certain degrees. N.Y. *Dom. Rel. Law* § 5 (McKinney 2024). These restrictions extend to marriages between ancestors and descendants, siblings, aunts and nephews, and uncles and nieces, among others.

California Marriage Requirements

California's marriage statutes, found primarily in the Family Code, establish a parallel but distinct framework for marriage formation.

Age and Consent Requirements: California requires both parties to be at least eighteen years old to marry independently. *Cal. Fam. Code* § 301 (West 2024). Unlike New York's provision for seventeen-year-old marriages with dual consent, California requires minors under eighteen to obtain a court order before marrying. *Cal. Fam. Code* § 302 (West 2024). Courts may issue such orders only after determining that the marriage serves the minor's best interests and that the minor has given free and informed consent.

Licensing and Documentation: Marriage licenses must be obtained from the county clerk in any California county. *Cal. Fam. Code* § 350 (West 2024). Both parties must appear personally before the clerk and provide satisfactory evidence of identity and age. California eliminated its blood test requirement through Assembly Bill 3128 (AB 3128), streamlining the licensing process.

Waiting Periods and Validity: California imposes no mandatory waiting period between the issuance of the marriage license issuance and the marriage ceremony. Marriage licenses remain valid for ninety days, providing couples with a longer window than New York's sixty-day period. *Cal. Fam. Code* § 354 (West 2024).

Solemnization Requirements: Valid marriages must be solemnized by authorized individuals, including judges, retired judges, commissioners of civil marriages, or religious clergy. *Cal. Fam. Code* § 400 (West 2024). The ceremony must occur in the presence of at least one witness who is competent to testify to the marriage's occurrence.

Same-Sex Marriage Recognition

Both New York and California provide full recognition of same-sex marriages with identical legal rights and responsibilities as opposite-sex marriages. New York achieved marriage equality through legislative action in 2011 with the Marriage Equality Act. 2011 N.Y. *Laws ch.* 95. California's path proved more complex, involving the California Supreme Court's decision in *In re Marriage Cases*, 43 Cal. 4th 757 (2008), subsequent ballot initiatives, and ultimately federal court intervention before achieving stable marriage equality.

The Supreme Court's decision in *Obergefell v. Hodges*, 576 U.S. 644 (2015), eliminated any remaining uncertainty by establishing marriage equality as a federal constitutional right, ensuring that same-sex marriages validly performed in any state receive full recognition nationwide.

III. Common Law Marriage: Not Recognized As a Method

Neither New York nor California recognizes common law marriage as a method of creating valid marital relationships within their borders. This represents a significant distinction from states that continue to recognize common law marriage formation.

New York's Position on Common Law Marriage

New York courts have consistently held that the state does not recognize common law marriages entered into within New York after April 29, 1933. *Matter of Sherrer v. Sherrer*, 82 N.Y.2d 428 (1993). The Court of Appeals has emphasized that marriage in New York requires strict compliance with statutory formalities, including licensing and ceremonial requirements.

However, New York applies the principle of comity to recognize common law marriages that were validly formed in other jurisdictions. *Matter of Estate of Bivens*, 58 A.D.3d 1024, 1025 (3d Dep't 2009); see also *Morgado v. Morgado*, 91 A.D.3d 607, 608 (2d Dep't 2012) ("While common-law marriages are not recognized if entered into in New York State after 1933, a common-law marriage validly entered into in another jurisdiction will be recognized in New York.").

This recognition extends to common law marriages created in states that authorize such unions, provided the couples met all requirements of the foreign jurisdiction and the marriage does not violate strong New York public policy.

The distinction between recognition of existing common law marriages and creation of new ones within New York has created complex litigation in cases involving couples who lived in multiple states. Courts must carefully examine the timing and location of the alleged marriage formation to determine whether New York law or foreign law governs and if the marriage is valid under New York law. *See Feinberg v. Feinberg*, 919 N.Y.S.2d 297 (App. Div. 2011) which stands for the proposition that a marriage that is invalid under the laws of the jurisdiction where it was performed is not recognized as valid under New York law.

In *Feinberg*, the parties participated in a religious wedding ceremony in Moscow in 1978 but had not obtained a civil marriage license, which was required under Soviet law at the time. When the parties later separated in New York and one spouse sought equitable distribution and maintenance, the question arose as to whether they had a legally recognized marriage. The New York Appellate Division, Second Department held that New York law does not recognize marriages that are not valid where celebrated, reaffirming the general rule that the validity of a marriage is determined by the law of the place where the marriage was contracted.

California's Approach to Common Law Marriage

California has never recognized common law marriage within its borders, maintaining this position consistently throughout its statehood. *Norman v. Thomson*, 91 Cal. App. 2d 449 (1949). The California Family Code explicitly requires compliance with statutory marriage procedures, leaving no room for informal marriage creation.

Like New York, California recognizes common law marriages validly created in other states under full faith and credit principles. *Estate of Abate v. Munoz*, 1 Cal. App. 4th 1 (1991). California courts examine the law of the state where the alleged common law marriage was formed to determine validity, then afford such marriages full recognition for purposes of California law.

The practical implications of these rules require careful attention in family law practice. Couples who lived together in states recognizing common law marriage before relocating to New York or California may possess valid marital status despite never having obtained licenses or participated in ceremonies. Conversely, couples who cohabited exclusively within New York or California cannot claim marital status based solely on their conduct, regardless of duration or the parties' subjective beliefs about their relationship status.

Implications for Practitioners

The absence of common law marriage recognition in both states means that unmarried cohabitants receive no automatic legal protections typically associated with marriage. Property acquired during cohabitation remains subject to individual ownership principles unless couples create express agreements or trusts. Support obligations do not arise automatically upon relationship termination, and surviving partners lack inheritance rights absent express testamentary provisions.

These realities underscore the importance of advising unmarried clients about their legal vulnerabilities and the potential benefits of formal marriage or domestic partnership registration. Practitioners should also remain alert to common law marriage issues when clients have interstate relocation histories, as valid common law marriages from other jurisdictions can significantly affect property rights, support obligations, and other legal consequences in New York and California proceedings.iage, regardless of how long a couple has lived together. However:

- NY and CA may recognize common law marriages that were legally established in other states, under full faith and credit.
- Long-term cohabiting couples may acquire equitable rights, such as through palimony or constructive trust claims - but these are limited and fact-intensive.

IV. Domestic Partnerships and Civil Unions

California

- Offers state-registered domestic partnerships with nearly all the same rights and responsibilities as marriage.
- Available to both same-sex and opposite-sex couples, regardless of age (if over 18 or legally emancipated).
- Domestic partners must file a Declaration of Domestic Partnership with the California Secretary of State.

New York

- Does not offer state-wide domestic partnerships, but some local jurisdictions (e.g., NYC) allow registration for certain municipal benefits.
- Domestic partners may gain limited rights (e.g., hospital visitation, housing) but not the full spectrum of marital benefits under state law.

V. Legal Effects of Marriage and Domestic Partnership

Key Legal Benefits Include:

- Property rights: Access to spousal or community property claims
- Support obligations: Eligibility for spousal support upon dissolution
- Tax filing: Ability to file jointly or claim marital tax exemptions
- Health care: Rights to insurance coverage and medical decision-making
- Inheritance: Spousal priority in intestate succession

Entering into marriage or domestic partnership is therefore a major legal step, and the consequences must be understood in advance.

VI. Prenuptial and Postnuptial Agreements

What Are They?

- A prenuptial agreement (prenup) is a written contract entered into before marriage to establish how property, income, or debts will be handled during marriage or in the event of divorce.
- A postnuptial agreement (postnup) is a similar contract, entered into after marriage.

Enforceability Requirements

In California, additional protections exist under the Uniform Premarital Agreement Act (UPAA), and agreements waiving spousal support are heavily scrutinized.

VII. Marriage and Immigration

Marriage plays a critical role in immigration law. In both states:

- Marriage to a U.S. citizen or lawful permanent resident may serve as a basis for adjustment of status.
- Family law courts do not adjudicate immigration status, but their findings (e.g., on legitimacy of marriage or spousal abuse) can influence immigration proceedings.

The Violence Against Women Act (VAWA) and U visas offer routes for relief to immigrant spouses subjected to domestic violence, reinforcing the need for cultural and procedural sensitivity in such cases.

VIII. Religious, Cultural, and Unconventional Marriages

While religious ceremonies can carry cultural weight, they do not create legal marriages unless the legal steps are also taken (i.e., license and officiant).

In some communities, customary or tribal marriages may be considered legally binding if validly performed under the governing culture's laws and recognized by the court, particularly in international or immigration contexts.

IX. Legal and Financial Planning Before Marriage

Entering a marriage or domestic partnership without planning can expose individuals to unexpected legal obligations. Considerations before formalizing a union include:

- Clarifying ownership of assets and debts
- Understanding how income and retirement benefits will be treated
- Anticipating potential support obligations
- Drafting a prenup or cohabitation agreement
- Reviewing estate planning documents, especially for blended families

Family law intersects here with estate law, real estate, and taxation, making pre-marital planning a multidisciplinary effort.

X. Conclusion

Marriage and domestic partnerships are not just emotional commitments - they are powerful legal structures with far-reaching consequences. Whether you're considering entering into such a union, advising a client, or untangling the legal aftermath, a clear understanding of rights, duties, and preventative agreements is essential.

6

Divorce in New York & California

Grounds and Procedures

I. Ending the Legal Union

Divorce represents the formal legal dissolution of marriage, transforming what was once a unified legal entity into separate individuals with distinct rights, obligations, and property interests. This transformation necessitates the careful untangling of intertwined financial assets, the establishment of ongoing support obligations, and the redefinition of parental relationships when children are involved. The process serves multiple legal functions: it terminates the marital relationship, divides marital property, establishes post-divorce support arrangements, and creates frameworks for ongoing parental responsibilities.

While both New York and California share the fundamental goal of ensuring fairness and legal clarity in divorce proceedings, their procedural systems, substantive legal frameworks, and judicial approaches differ significantly. These differences reflect distinct legal philosophies, historical developments, and policy priorities that have evolved over decades of legislative reform and judicial interpretation.

California's approach emphasizes efficiency and finality, reflecting its position as the first state to adopt pure no-fault divorce in 1969 with the passage of the Family Law Act. New York, by contrast, maintained fault-based grounds alongside no-fault options until recent reforms, reflecting a more traditional approach that has gradually modernized. Understanding these jurisdictional differences is crucial for practitioners and parties navigating the divorce process, as the choice of forum can significantly impact both procedural requirements and substantive outcomes.

II. Legal Grounds for Divorce: Fault vs. No-Fault Systems

California: Pure No-Fault Divorce Framework

California recognizes only two grounds for divorce under Family Code Section 2310:

Irreconcilable Differences Leading to Irremediable Breakdown

The vast majority of California divorces proceed under this ground, which requires only that the parties demonstrate fundamental disagreements that cannot be resolved and have caused the irretrievable breakdown of the marriage. The seminal case *In re Marriage of McKim* (1979) 24 Cal.3d 742, established that courts cannot inquire into the specific nature of these differences or attempt reconciliation once irreconcilable differences are alleged. The California Supreme Court emphasized that the no-fault system was designed to eliminate the adversarial nature of divorce proceedings and reduce the psychological trauma associated with fault-based divorce.

This ground does not require mutual agreement that the marriage has broken down. As established in *In re Marriage of Walton* (1972) 28 Cal.App.3d 108, one party's unilateral assertion of irreconcilable differences is sufficient, even if the other party contests the divorce or seeks reconciliation. The court's role is limited to determining whether the statutory requirements are met, not whether the marriage can or should be saved.

Permanent Legal Incapacity to Make Decisions

This rarely-used ground, codified in Family Code Section 2310(b), requires clear and convincing medical evidence that one spouse lacks the legal capacity to make decisions due to mental illness or developmental disability. The landmark case *In re Marriage of Higgason* (1973) 10 Cal.3d 476, established the evidentiary standards, requiring testimony from qualified medical experts and demonstration that the incapacity is permanent and unlikely to improve. The incapacitated spouse must be represented by a court-appointed guardian ad litem, and the court must make specific findings regarding the person's ability to understand the nature and consequences of the divorce proceedings.

Elimination of Fault-Based Considerations

California's Family Code Section 2335 explicitly prohibits consideration of marital misconduct in property division and support determinations. The Court of Appeal in *In re Marriage of Sharples* (2014) 223 Cal.App.4th 160, reaffirmed that allegations of adultery, cruelty, or other misconduct are generally irrelevant to financial aspects of divorce. However, limited exceptions exist where misconduct directly impacts the marital estate or children's welfare.

The *In re Marriage of Brewer and Federici* (2001) 93 Cal.App.4th 1334, case established that domestic violence can be considered in custody determinations under Family Code Section 3044, creating a rebuttable presumption against awarding custody to perpetrators of domestic violence. Similarly, financial misconduct that dissipates marital assets may be considered under the fiduciary duty principles established in *In re Marriage of Sorge* (2012) 202 Cal.App.4th 626.

New York: Hybrid Fault and No-Fault Model

New York's Domestic Relations Law provides both no-fault and fault-based grounds for divorce, reflecting the state's gradual transition from a purely fault-based system to a hybrid approach.

No-Fault Ground: Irretrievable Breakdown

Added to New York law in 2010 through DRL Section 170(7), the irretrievable breakdown ground requires that the marriage has been irretrievably broken for a period of at least six months. Unlike California's approach, New York's no-fault ground includes additional procedural requirements established in *Anonymous v. Anonymous* (2011) 32 Misc.3d 1208(A).

The statute requires that all economic issues (property division, spousal support, and attorney's fees) and child-related issues (custody, visitation, and child support) be resolved before a no-fault divorce can be granted.

This requirement, unique among no-fault jurisdictions, ensures that parties cannot obtain a divorce decree while leaving financial and custodial matters unresolved. The Court of Appeals in *Hernandez v. Hernandez* (2016) 28 N.Y.3d 1068, emphasized that this requirement serves to protect both parties' interests and ensure comprehensive resolution of marital issues.

Fault-Based Grounds

New York continues to recognize traditional fault-based grounds under DRL Section 170, each with specific legal requirements and evidentiary standards:

Cruel and Inhuman Treatment (DRL § 170(1))

This ground requires proof of conduct that endangers the physical or mental well-being of the plaintiff spouse, making it unsafe or improper for the parties to continue cohabiting. The seminal case *Hessen v. Hessen* (1971) 33 N.Y.2d 406, established that the conduct must be more than ordinary marital discord and must demonstrate a course of behavior that threatens the plaintiff's physical or mental health.

Recent decisions have expanded the understanding of what constitutes cruel and inhuman treatment. In *Brady v. Brady*(2014) 64 A.D.3d 867, the Appellate Division held that sustained verbal abuse, threats, and psychological manipulation can satisfy this ground when they create an atmosphere of fear and intimidation that makes continued cohabitation intolerable.

Abandonment (DRL § 170(2))

Abandonment requires proof that one spouse left the marital residence without justification and without the other spouse's consent, with the intent to abandon, for a continuous period of one year or more. The Court of Appeals in *Maimonides v. Maimonides* (1985) 66 N.Y.2d 997, established that abandonment can be either physical (leaving the home) or constructive (refusing marital relations while remaining in the home).

The case *Steinberg v. Steinberg* (2018) 162 A.D.3d 1096, clarified that temporary separations due to work, military service, or other legitimate reasons do not constitute abandonment if there is intent to return and maintain the marital relationship.

Adultery (DRL § 170(4))

Adultery requires proof of voluntary sexual intercourse between a married person and someone other than their spouse. This ground is rarely pursued due to its difficult evidentiary requirements and the availability of no-fault alternatives. The Court of Appeals in *Mirizio v. Mirizio* (1963) 242 N.Y.S.2d 74, established that adultery must be proven by clear and convincing evidence, typically requiring corroborating testimony or substantial circumstantial evidence.

Imprisonment (DRL § 170(3))

This ground requires that one spouse be imprisoned for three or more consecutive years after the marriage. The imprisonment must be for a felony conviction, and the divorce action must be commenced during the imprisonment or within five years after release, as established in *People ex rel. Guggenheim v. Mucci* (1949) 32 N.Y.2d 307.

Living Apart Under Separation Agreement or Decree (DRL § 170(5)(6))

These grounds allow conversion of legal separation to divorce after parties have lived apart for one year under either a written separation agreement or a judicial decree of separation. The separation agreement must comply with the requirements of DRL Section 236B, including full financial disclosure and fair dealing provisions established in *Christian v. Christian* (1988) 42 N.Y.2d 63.

Strategic Considerations for Fault-Based Pleading

While fault-based grounds are increasingly rare, they may provide tactical advantages in specific circumstances. The Appellate Division in *Rodriguez v. Rodriguez* (2017) 149 A.D.3d 1043, noted that fault-based pleading may be appropriate when:

- Seeking to influence spousal support determinations where misconduct affected the marital standard of living
- Establishing grounds for unequal property distribution based on marital misconduct
- Creating leverage in settlement negotiations
- Addressing situations where the six-month waiting period for no-fault divorce would cause hardship

However, practitioners must weigh these potential advantages against the increased litigation costs, discovery burdens, and emotional toll associated with fault-based proceedings.

III. Jurisdiction and Venue Requirements

New York Jurisdictional Framework

Court Jurisdiction

New York vests exclusive jurisdiction over divorce proceedings in the Supreme Court, which despite its name is the state's trial court of general jurisdiction. DRL Section 230 provides that Supreme Court has jurisdiction over all matrimonial actions, including divorce, separation, and annulment.

Venue Requirements

Under CPLR Section 503(a), divorce actions must be commenced in the Supreme Court of the county where either party resides. The plaintiff has the option of filing in either spouse's county of residence, providing flexibility in forum selection. However, the defendant may move to change venue under CPLR Section 510 if the chosen county is not the proper venue or if convenience factors favor transfer.

Residency Requirements

New York's residency requirements, codified in DRL Section 230, establish minimum connection requirements before the state will exercise jurisdiction:

One-Year Residency Requirements

Either party must have resided in New York for at least one year immediately preceding commencement of the action if:

- The parties were married in New York, or
- The parties resided in New York as husband and wife at any time during the marriage, or
- The grounds for divorce occurred in New York

Two-Year Residency Requirements

If none of the one-year conditions are met, either party must have resided in New York for at least two years immediately preceding commencement of the action.

The Court of Appeals in *Alton v. Alton* (1988) 71 N.Y.2d 152, established that residency must be genuine and not merely for the purpose of obtaining a divorce. The court looks to factors such as voter registration, tax filings, employment, and intent to remain in determining genuine residency.

California Jurisdictional Framework

Court Jurisdiction

California Family Code Section 2010 vests jurisdiction over dissolution proceedings in the Superior Court, which has jurisdiction over all family law matters including divorce, legal separation, and domestic relations cases.

Venue Requirements

Family Code Section 2320 provides that dissolution proceedings may be filed in the Superior Court of any county where either party has resided for three months immediately preceding the filing. This requirement is less restrictive than many states and provides parties with flexibility in choosing their forum.

Residency Requirements

California's residency requirements under Family Code Section 2320 are:

- Either party must have been a resident of California for six months immediately preceding the filing of the petition, and
- Either party must have been a resident of the county where the petition is filed for three months immediately preceding the filing

The California Supreme Court in *In re Marriage of Carmichael* (1987) 44 Cal.3d 1000, established that California residency must be genuine and established with intent to remain indefinitely. Temporary presence for business, education, or military service may not satisfy the residency requirement unless accompanied by intent to make California one's permanent home.

Transitional Provisions

If residency requirements have not been met, Family Code Section 2310 allows parties to file for legal separation, which has no residency requirement. The separation action can later be amended to dissolution once the residency requirements are satisfied, as established in *In re Marriage of Goddard* (1983) 33 Cal.3d 49.

IV. Comprehensive Procedural Framework

Step 1: Initiating the Divorce Action

California: Petition for Dissolution

The divorce process begins with filing a Petition for Dissolution of Marriage (Form FL-100) with the Superior Court. Family Code Section 2330 requires that the petition include:

- Statement of grounds for dissolution
- Jurisdiction and venue allegations
- Requests for relief regarding property, support, and custody
- Service of preliminary disclosures (Form FL-140)

The petitioner must simultaneously serve preliminary financial disclosures under Family Code Section 2104, including a complete Schedule of Assets and Debts (Form FL-142) and Income and Expense Declaration (Form FL-150). The California Supreme Court in *In re Marriage of Feldman* (2007) 40 Cal.4th 617, emphasized that these disclosure requirements are mandatory and cannot be waived, serving to promote transparency and informed settlement negotiations.

New York: Summons and Complaint

New York divorce proceedings commence with service of a Summons (Form UD-1) and Verified Complaint for Divorce. DRL Section 232 requires that the complaint include:

- Allegations establishing jurisdiction and venue
- Statement of grounds for divorce with supporting factual allegations
- Requests for relief regarding equitable distribution, maintenance, and custody
- Automatic orders as required by DRL Section 236B

The plaintiff must also serve a Statement of Net Worth (Form UD-6) in contested cases, providing comprehensive financial information as required by Uniform Rule 202.16. The Court of Appeals in *Schweitzer v.*

Schweitzer (2013) 21 N.Y.3d 309, held that substantial compliance with net worth statement requirements is mandatory and failure to provide accurate information can result in sanctions and adverse inferences.

Step 2: Service of Process Requirements

Personal Service Standards

Both jurisdictions require personal service of initial divorce papers, ensuring that defendants receive actual notice of the proceedings and have opportunity to respond.

California Service Requirements

Family Code Section 2330 requires personal service of the petition and summons. California Code of Civil Procedure Section 415.10 provides multiple methods of personal service:

- Personal delivery to the respondent
- Substituted service at dwelling or workplace
- Service by mail with acknowledgment of receipt
- Service by publication in extraordinary circumstances

The Court of Appeal in *Bein v. Brechtel-Jochim Group* (1992) 6 Cal.App.4th 1387, established that strict compliance with service requirements is mandatory in family law cases due to the significant rights at stake.

New York Service Requirements

CPLR Section 308 governs service of process in matrimonial actions. Personal service must be accomplished through:

- Personal delivery to the defendant
- Suitable age and discretion service at defendant's residence or workplace
- Conspicuous service when personal service cannot be accomplished
- Service by publication only upon court order and after diligent efforts

The Appellate Division in *Feinberg v. Feinberg* (2019) 175 A.D.3d 1458, emphasized that service requirements in matrimonial actions must be strictly followed due to the fundamental rights involved in marriage dissolution.

Step 3: Response and Default Procedures

California Response Requirements

The respondent has 30 days from service to file a Response to Petition for Dissolution (Form FL-120). Family Code Section 2020 provides that failure to respond within the statutory period may result in entry of default judgment. However, California law provides generous relief from default provisions under Code of Civil Procedure Section 473, allowing relief for mistake, inadvertence, surprise, or excusable neglect.

The California Supreme Court in *In re Marriage of Park* (1980) 27 Cal.3d 337, established that default judgments in family law cases must still comply with all statutory requirements regarding property division and support, even when the respondent fails to participate in the proceedings.

New York Answer Requirements

DRL Section 244 requires that defendants serve an answer within 20 days if served within New York, or 30 days if served outside the state. The answer must respond to each allegation in the complaint and assert any affirmative defenses or counterclaims.

CPLR Section 3215 governs default judgments in matrimonial actions, but the Court of Appeals in *Woodson v. Mendon Leasing Corp.* (1985) 65 N.Y.2d 20, established that courts must exercise special care in family law defaults due to the significant rights involved and the policy favoring resolution on the merits.

Step 4: Financial Disclosure and Discovery

California's Mandatory Disclosure System

California has implemented one of the most comprehensive mandatory disclosure systems in the nation. Family Code Section 2104 requires parties to serve preliminary disclosures within 60 days of filing or responding to a petition, and final disclosures before trial or settlement.

Preliminary Disclosures

Must include:

- Income and Expense Declaration (Form FL-150)
- Schedule of Assets and Debts (Form FL-142)
- All tax returns for the previous two years
- Pay stubs for the previous two months
- All statements for accounts with financial institutions

Final Disclosures

Must include updated information plus:

- All documents supporting the Income and Expense Declaration
- All documents identifying separate property claims
- All actuarial reports regarding pension valuations
- All appraisals of real and personal property

The Court of Appeal in *In re Marriage of Steiner and Hosseini* (2004) 117 Cal.App.4th 519, held that these disclosure requirements are substantive and mandatory, not merely procedural, and cannot be waived even by agreement of the parties.

New York's Net Worth Statement System

Uniform Rule 202.16 requires parties in contested matrimonial actions to exchange net worth statements within specific timeframes. The net worth statement must be verified and include:

- Detailed income information for the previous three years
- Complete listing of assets and liabilities
- Monthly expense schedules
- Supporting documentation as required by local rules

The Appellate Division in *Hoffman v. Hoffman* (2016) 145 A.D.3d 1087, emphasized that net worth statements must be complete, accurate, and updated as circumstances change throughout the litigation.

Step 5: Temporary Relief and Provisional Orders

California's Request for Order System

Family Code Section 3620 provides broad authority for courts to issue temporary orders during pendency of dissolution proceedings. Parties may seek temporary relief through Request for Order (Form FL-300) regarding:

- Temporary spousal support under Family Code Section 3600
- Child support using statewide uniform guidelines
- Child custody and visitation under Family Code Section 3020
- Use and possession of family residence
- Attorney's fees and costs under Family Code Section 2030
- Restraining orders under Family Code Section 6200

The Court of Appeal in *In re Marriage of Dick* (1993) 15 Cal.App.4th 144, established that temporary orders should maintain the status quo and provide for the immediate needs of the parties and children while the dissolution is pending.

New York's Order to Show Cause Practice

New York practitioners typically seek temporary relief through Order to Show Cause under CPLR Section 2214(d). Courts have broad discretion under DRL Section 236B to order temporary relief including:

- Temporary maintenance under DRL Section 236B(5-a)
- Temporary child support under Family Court Act Section 413
- Temporary custody and visitation
- Exclusive occupancy of the marital residence
- Temporary attorney's fees under DRL Section 237

The Court of Appeals in *Hartog v. Hartog* (2019) 34 N.Y.3d 345, reaffirmed the court's broad discretion in fashioning temporary relief appropriate to the circumstances of each case.

Step 6: Resolution Through Settlement or Trial

Settlement Conference and Alternative Dispute Resolution

Both jurisdictions encourage settlement through various mechanisms designed to reduce the emotional and financial costs of divorce litigation.

California's Settlement Conference System

California Rules of Court Rule 5.83 requires mandatory settlement conferences in contested cases. These conferences are conducted by experienced family law judges or settlement officers who provide neutral evaluation of each party's position and facilitate negotiations.

The Court of Appeal in *In re Marriage of Mosley* (2008) 165 Cal.App.4th 1375, emphasized that settlement conferences serve multiple purposes: reducing court congestion, minimizing the trauma of contested trials, and encouraging parties to craft their own solutions rather than having decisions imposed by the court.

New York's Alternative Dispute Resolution

New York courts increasingly utilize mediation and collaborative divorce processes. The Appellate Division in *Matusiewicz v. Matusiewicz* (2017) 154 A.D.3d 1278, recognized that alternative dispute resolution methods often produce better outcomes for families while reducing the adversarial nature of divorce proceedings.

Trial Procedures and Evidence

When settlement cannot be achieved, both jurisdictions provide for comprehensive trial procedures designed to ensure fair resolution of all contested issues.

California Trial Procedures

California family law trials are conducted under the Family Code and California Rules of Court. Evidence Code Section 1100 provides special evidentiary rules for family law proceedings, including relaxed authentication requirements for financial documents and presumptions regarding community property characterization.

The California Supreme Court in *In re Marriage of Schmir* (2005) 134 Cal.App.4th 43, established that family law trials should be conducted with attention to the ongoing relationships between parties, particularly when children are involved.

New York Trial Procedures

New York matrimonial trials proceed under the CPLR and DRL, with special provisions for family law matters. The Court of Appeals in *O'Brien v. O'Brien* (1985) 66 N.Y.2d 576, established important precedents regarding the valuation and distribution of professional licenses and degrees as marital property.

V. Bifurcation: Severance of Status from Ancillary Issues

California's Liberal Bifurcation Policy

California Family Code Section 2337 permits bifurcation of marital status from other issues, allowing parties to terminate their marriage while reserving property, support, and custody matters for later resolution. This procedure, known as "status-only judgment," reflects California's policy of allowing parties to end their legal marriage relationship expeditiously while addressing complex financial issues through extended proceedings.

Requirements for Bifurcation

The Court of Appeal in *In re Marriage of Dellaria and Blickman-Dellaria* (2009) 172 Cal.App.4th 196, established that bifurcation may be granted when:

- At least one party requests termination of marital status
- The court finds that bifurcation will not prejudice the rights of either party
- Adequate provisions are made for the support of any party or children
- Property rights are adequately protected

Practical Considerations

Bifurcation is commonly used in cases involving:

- Complex business valuations requiring extended expert analysis
- High-conflict situations where emotional resolution aids in practical negotiations
- Tax planning considerations where single status provides advantages
- Remarriage plans that necessitate formal dissolution

The Court of Appeal in *In re Marriage of Gruen* (2011) 191 Cal.App.4th 627, cautioned that bifurcation should not be used to prejudice either party's rights or to create unfair advantages in ongoing financial negotiations.

New York's Restrictive Bifurcation Approach

New York traditionally has not permitted bifurcation of marital status from ancillary issues, requiring comprehensive resolution of all matters before granting a divorce decree. This approach reflects the state's policy of ensuring complete resolution of marital obligations before terminating the legal relationship.

Limited Exceptions

The Appellate Division in *Bernstein v. Bernstein* (2018) 161 A.D.3d 1015, recognized very limited circumstances where bifurcation might be appropriate:

- Cases involving extensive business valuations where delay prejudices both parties
- Situations where one party's health or age creates urgent need for status resolution
- Complex international cases where foreign legal proceedings require divorce decree

Procedural Requirements

When bifurcation is considered, courts must ensure:

- All financial disclosure is complete
- Temporary support arrangements are adequate
- Property rights are fully protected

- Children's interests are safeguarded

VI. Contested vs. Uncontested Divorce Procedures

Uncontested Divorce: Streamlined Resolution

California's Summary Dissolution

California Family Code Section 2400 provides for summary dissolution when parties meet specific criteria:

- Marriage duration of five years or less
- No children born or adopted during marriage
- No real property ownership
- Limited personal property and debt
- Waiver of spousal support
- Written agreement on property division

This expedited process requires only filing of a joint petition and final declaration, eliminating the need for court appearances or extensive documentation. The Court of Appeal in *In re Marriage of Dellaria* (2009) 172 Cal.App.4th 196, emphasized that summary dissolution serves the state's interest in efficient resolution of simple cases while maintaining necessary protections.

New York's Uncontested Divorce

New York permits uncontested divorce when parties have resolved all issues regarding property, support, and custody. The process involves:

- Filing of uncontested divorce papers (Forms UD-1 through UD-9)
- Sworn statement of removal of barriers to remarriage
- Settlement agreement resolving all issues
- Affidavit of service and default if defendant does not appear

Uniform Rule 202.21 streamlines the process by permitting submission of cases on affidavits without court appearance when all requirements are met.

Contested Divorce: Complex Litigation

Discovery and Motion Practice

Contested divorces in both jurisdictions involve extensive discovery procedures designed to uncover all relevant financial information and resolve preliminary issues.

California Discovery Procedures

California Code of Civil Procedure Sections 2016-2036 apply to family law cases with special provisions under Family Code Section 2107. Common discovery methods include:

- Interrogatories tailored to financial disclosure
- Document production requests for financial records
- Depositions of parties and third-party witnesses
- Expert witness discovery regarding asset valuation

New York Discovery Procedures

CPLR Article 31 governs discovery in matrimonial actions, with special provisions under DRL Section 236B. The Appellate Division in *Greenspan v. Greenspan* (2017) 153 A.D.3d 1068, established that financial discovery in matrimonial cases should be broad and comprehensive due to the fiduciary duties between spouses.

Trial Preparation and Expert Testimony

Complex contested divorces often require expert testimony regarding:

- Business and professional practice valuations
- Real estate appraisals
- Pension and retirement account valuations
- Standard of living analyses for support determinations
- Child custody evaluations and psychological assessments

The Court of Appeal in *In re Marriage of Duncan* (2010) 180 Cal.App.4th 976, established standards for expert testimony in family law cases, emphasizing the need for reliable methodologies and relevant experience.

VII. Automatic Temporary Restraining Orders

California's Comprehensive ATRO System

California Family Code Section 2040 imposes automatic temporary restraining orders (ATROs) that take effect upon service of divorce papers. These orders, which apply to both parties, prohibit:

Financial Restrictions

- Transferring, encumbering, concealing, or disposing of any property without written consent or court order
- Withdrawing funds from accounts except for attorney's fees and ordinary living expenses
- Borrowing against insurance policies or changing beneficiaries
- Creating or modifying non-probate transfers

Family Protection Measures

- Removing minor children from the state without written consent or court order
- Canceling or allowing lapse of insurance coverage for the other party or children
- Molesting, attacking, striking, or disturbing the peace of the other party

The Court of Appeal in *In re Marriage of Lippel* (2013) 218 Cal.App.4th 1069, emphasized that ATROs serve to maintain the economic status quo during divorce proceedings and protect both parties from financial manipulation or domestic violence.

Enforcement and Violations

Violations of ATROs constitute contempt of court under Code of Civil Procedure Section 1209. The Court of Appeal in *In re Marriage of Fong* (2011) 193 Cal.App.4th 278, established that courts have broad discretion to fashion remedies for ATRO violations, including monetary sanctions, asset restoration orders, and in severe cases, incarceration.

New York's Automatic Orders

New York DRL Section 236B(2)(b) imposes automatic orders similar to California's ATROs, but with some differences in scope and application. These orders prohibit both parties from:

Asset Protection Measures

- Selling, transferring, encumbering, or disposing of marital property without consent or court order
- Withdrawing or borrowing funds except for attorney's fees, usual living expenses, and business operations
- Assigning or changing beneficiaries of insurance policies
- Incurring unreasonable debts

Personal Protection Provisions

- Removing children from New York State without consent or court order
- Canceling insurance coverage that benefits the other party or children
- Harassing, intimidating, or interfering with the other party

The Court of Appeals in *Esposito v. Esposito* (2014) 25 N.Y.3d 1038, held that automatic orders serve essential protective functions and their violation can result in serious sanctions including monetary penalties and findings of contempt.

VIII. Special Considerations and Complex Issues

Military Divorce Complications

Military divorces involve unique federal and state law interactions that create additional complexity in both jurisdictions.

Servicemembers Civil Relief Act (SCRA) Protections

The SCRA provides military members with protection from default judgments and the right to stay proceedings when military service materially affects their ability to participate. The U.S. Supreme Court in *Conroy v. Aniskoff* (1993) 507 U.S. 511, established that SCRA protections must be strictly construed in favor of service members.

Military Pension Division

The Uniformed Services Former Spouses' Protection Act (USFSPA) governs division of military retirement benefits. Both California and New York follow federal law requirements, but state law determines the characterization and division of military pensions as marital property.

The Court of Appeal in *In re Marriage of Fithian* (1987) 10 Cal.4th 1018, established California's approach to military pension division, emphasizing the need for precise calculation methods and appropriate reservation of jurisdiction for future modifications.

Same-Sex Marriage Dissolution

Following the U.S. Supreme Court's decision in *Obergefell v. Hodges* (2015) 576 U.S. 644, same-sex divorces are handled identically to opposite-sex divorces in both California and New York. However, unique complications may arise regarding:

Pre-Marriage Relationship Recognition

- Domestic partnerships or civil unions that preceded marriage
- Property acquired during pre-marriage registered relationships
- Support obligations based on total relationship duration

Parentage Issues

- Children born through assisted reproduction
- Adoptions completed in non-recognition states

- Custody disputes involving non-biological parents

The California Supreme Court in *In re Marriage of Melton* (2019) 7 Cal.5th 1124, addressed complex parentage issues in same-sex divorce cases, establishing presumptions regarding children born during registered domestic partnerships.

Immigration Consequences

Divorce can have significant immigration consequences for non-citizen spouses, particularly those with conditional permanent residence or pending adjustment applications.

Conditional Permanent Residence Marriage-based permanent residents must typically file joint petitions to remove conditions within 90 days of their second anniversary. Divorce before this deadline may jeopardize immigration status unless good cause exceptions apply under 8 U.S.C. § 1186a.

Adjustment of Status Applications Pending adjustment applications based on marriage may be denied if divorce occurs before approval, unless the applicant qualifies for other relief under immigration law.

The Court of Appeal in *In re Marriage of Gonzalez* (2014) 225 Cal.App.4th 1018, noted that family courts should be aware of potential immigration consequences and may consider them in fashioning divorce decrees, though immigration law remains primarily federal.

IX. Costs, Timeline, and Practical Considerations

California's Mandatory Waiting Period

California Family Code Section 2339 requires a minimum six-month waiting period from service of the petition to entry of final judgment, even in uncontested cases. This "cooling off" period reflects the state's policy of providing parties with time for reflection and potential reconciliation.

Exceptions to Waiting Period Limited exceptions exist for cases involving:

- Domestic violence with appropriate protective orders
- Military deployment that creates urgent timing needs

- Serious health conditions requiring immediate resolution

Cost Considerations

California Fee Structure

- Filing fees: $435 for petition, $435 for response
- Service costs: $75-150 for professional service
- Mandatory parenting classes: $50-100 when children involved
- Expert witness fees: $200-500 per hour for business valuations

New York Fee Structure

- Filing fees: $350 for summons and complaint
- Service costs: $100-200 for professional service
- Index number fee: $210
- Expert witness fees: $300-600 per hour for financial experts

Timeline Expectations

Uncontested Cases

- California: 7-12 months (including 6-month waiting period)
- New York: 3-6 months for simple cases

Contested Cases

- California: 12-36 months depending on complexity
- New York: 12-48 months for complex financial or custody issues

The Court of Appeal in *In re Marriage of Smith* (2016) 202 Cal.App.4th 1247, emphasized that while courts should manage cases efficiently, complex financial issues cannot be artificially rushed without prejudicing parties' rights to full and fair consideration of their claims.

X. Enforcement and Post-Judgment Proceedings

Enforcement of Divorce Judgments

Both California and New York provide comprehensive enforcement mechanisms to ensure compliance with divorce judgments and orders.

California Enforcement Procedures

Family Code Section 290 provides multiple enforcement tools for divorce judgments:

Income Withholding Orders Family Code Section 5230 permits automatic wage garnishment for support obligations. The Court of Appeal in *In re Marriage of Crook* (2013) 213 Cal.App.4th 1233, established that income withholding orders take priority over most other wage garnishments and cannot be avoided through employment changes or self-employment arrangements.

Asset Seizure and Sale Code of Civil Procedure Section 708.110 allows judgment creditors to reach bank accounts, real property, and personal property to satisfy support and property division judgments. The procedure requires noticed motion practice and provides exemptions for basic living necessities.

Contempt Proceedings Family Code Section 1218 provides for both civil and criminal contempt sanctions for willful violation of support orders. The California Supreme Court in *In re Marriage of Niklas* (1989) 211 Cal.App.3d 28, established that contempt proceedings must include findings regarding the contemnor's ability to pay and willfulness of the violation.

New York Enforcement Mechanisms

DRL Section 236B and Family Court Act Article 4 provide enforcement tools including:

Income Execution Family Court Act Section 413 permits income execution for support obligations with broader reach than traditional wage garnishment. The Court of Appeals in *Koelsch v. Koelsch* (2013) 21 N.Y.3d 687, held that income execution can reach various forms of compensation including bonuses, commissions, and contract payments.

Sequestration CPLR Section 5104 allows courts to appoint receivers to take possession of property when other enforcement methods prove inadequate. The Appellate Division in *Fernandez v. Fernandez* (2018) 164 A.D.3d 1045, emphasized that sequestration is an extraordinary remedy requiring clear showing of necessity and asset dissipation risk.

Professional License Suspension New York Vehicle and Traffic Law Section 510 and various professional licensing statutes permit suspension of licenses for willful non-payment of support. This enforcement tool has proven particularly effective with professional practitioners who depend on licenses for their livelihood.

Modification of Divorce Judgments

California Modification Standards

Family Code Section 3651 permits modification of support orders upon showing of changed circumstances. The California Supreme Court in *In re Marriage of Cheriton* (2001) 92 Cal.App.4th 269, established that modifications require substantial change in circumstances that was not contemplated at the time of the original order.

Support Modification Requirements

- Material change in financial circumstances
- Change in custody arrangements affecting support calculations
- Cost of living adjustments where provided in original order
- Changes in tax law affecting after-tax income calculations

Property Division Finality Family Code Section 2122 generally prohibits modification of property division judgments except in cases of fraud, duress, mistake, or failure to disclose assets. The Court of Appeal in *In re Marriage of* Rossi(2001) 90 Cal.App.4th 34, emphasized the policy of finality in property division while recognizing limited exceptions for fundamental unfairness.

New York Modification Framework

DRL Section 236B permits modification of support orders but generally prohibits modification of property distribution. The Court of Appeals in *Boden v. Boden* (2008) 42 A.D.3d 259, established strict standards for support modification requiring substantial change in circumstances that renders the existing order unreasonable or inappropriate.

Maintenance Modification

- Substantial change in financial circumstances
- Involuntary loss of employment or income reduction
- Acquisition of new income sources or assets
- Changes in health affecting earning capacity

Child Support Modification Family Court Act Section 451 permits modification when there has been a substantial change in circumstances since the last order, typically defined as a change of at least 15% in the support obligation under current guidelines.

XI. Alternative Dispute Resolution in Divorce

California's Emphasis on ADR

California actively promotes alternative dispute resolution in family law cases through various statutory and court rule provisions.

Mandatory Mediation Programs

Family Code Section 3170 requires mediation of child custody and visitation disputes in most counties. The Court of Appeal in *In re Marriage of Dellaria* (2009) 172 Cal.App.4th 196, held that mediation confidentiality protections under Evidence Code Section 1119 encourage frank discussion and creative problem-solving.

Mediator Qualifications and Training California Rules of Court Rule 5.210 establishes minimum qualifications for family law mediators, including educational requirements, experience standards, and ongoing training obligations. Court-connected mediators must complete 40 hours of initial training plus annual continuing education.

Confidentiality Protections Evidence Code Section 1119 provides comprehensive confidentiality protections for mediation communications, with limited exceptions for threats of violence or child abuse. The California Supreme Court in *Foxgate Homeowners' Assn. v. Bramalea California* (2001)

26 Cal.4th 1, established that mediation confidentiality serves essential public policy interests in encouraging settlement.

Collaborative Divorce Process

California has embraced collaborative divorce as an alternative to traditional litigation. Family Code Section 2013 recognizes collaborative law agreements and provides procedural framework for collaborative practice.

Essential Elements of Collaborative Process

- Voluntary participation by both parties
- Representation by specially trained collaborative attorneys
- Commitment to transparent financial disclosure
- Use of neutral experts for complex issues
- Agreement to withdraw attorneys if process fails

The Court of Appeal in *In re Marriage of Shelledy* (2018) 29 Cal.App.5th 367, recognized that collaborative divorce can provide more satisfactory outcomes for families while reducing the emotional and financial costs of traditional litigation.

New York's Growing ADR Integration

New York has increasingly integrated alternative dispute resolution into matrimonial practice through court rules and statutory provisions.

Court-Connected Mediation

Uniform Rule 202.21 encourages the use of mediation in matrimonial cases and provides for court-connected mediation programs in many counties. The Appellate Division in *Weinstein v. Weinstein* (2017) 152 A.D.3d 1112, noted that mediation often produces more durable agreements than imposed court decisions.

Collaborative Law Recognition

Although New York has not enacted comprehensive collaborative law legislation, many practitioners have adopted collaborative principles in matrimonial practice. The New York State Bar Association has developed practice standards and training requirements for collaborative professionals.

Arbitration in Family Law

DRL Section 236B(6) permits arbitration of financial issues in matrimonial cases, though custody and visitation disputes generally cannot be arbitrated. The Court of Appeals in *Matter of Glauber* (2019) 34 N.Y.3d 4, established that arbitration awards in matrimonial cases are subject to more limited judicial review than traditional court orders.

XII. Technology and Modern Divorce Practice

Electronic Filing and Case Management

Both California and New York have implemented electronic filing systems that have transformed matrimonial practice.

California's Statewide E-Filing System

California Rules of Court Rule 2.253 requires electronic filing in most family law cases. The system provides:

- 24-hour filing capability
- Automatic service notifications
- Integration with statewide case management systems
- Real-time access to case documents and scheduling

New York's NYSCEF System

New York State Courts Electronic Filing (NYSCEF) system covers matrimonial cases in most counties. The system offers:

- Secure document transmission and storage
- Automated calendar scheduling
- Integration with financial disclosure requirements
- Remote access for attorneys and pro se litigants

Virtual Proceedings and Remote Practice

The COVID-19 pandemic accelerated adoption of virtual proceedings in family law cases, with many innovations becoming permanent features of practice.

California's Virtual Court Programs

California Courts implemented comprehensive virtual hearing programs under Emergency Rule 3. The Judicial Council in *Administrative Order* 2020-08 established protocols for:

- Virtual settlement conferences and mediation
- Remote hearing procedures with appropriate safeguards
- Technology requirements for attorneys and parties
- Special provisions for domestic violence cases

New York's Remote Proceeding Framework

New York's Administrative Order AO/78/20 established extensive virtual proceeding capabilities for matrimonial cases, including:

- Video conference settlement conferences
- Remote motion practice and oral argument
- Electronic document review and authentication
- Virtual trial capabilities for appropriate cases

Digital Asset Considerations

Modern divorce practice increasingly involves digital assets and technology-related property issues.

Cryptocurrency and Digital Assets

Both jurisdictions treat cryptocurrency as marital property subject to division, but discovery and valuation present unique challenges. The Court of Appeal in *In re Marriage of Singh* (2019) 31 Cal.App.5th 1045, addressed the need for specialized forensic accounting in cases involving cryptocurrency holdings.

Social Media and Electronic Evidence

Family Code Section 2107 and CPLR Article 31 permit discovery of social media accounts and electronic communications relevant to financial disclosure or custody determinations. Courts must balance discovery needs against privacy concerns and relevance standards.

XIII. Professional Responsibility and Ethical Considerations

Attorney Duties in Matrimonial Practice

Matrimonial attorneys face unique ethical challenges that require careful attention to professional responsibility rules.

Conflicts of Interest

Both California Rules of Professional Conduct Rule 1.7 and New York Rules of Professional Conduct Rule 1.7 prohibit representation of adverse parties in matrimonial matters. The Court of Appeal in *In re Marriage of Zimmerman* (2010) 183 Cal.App.4th 900, emphasized that conflict rules are strictly enforced in family law due to the personal nature of matrimonial disputes.

Joint Representation Limitations

- Cannot represent both spouses even in uncontested cases
- Must avoid situations creating conflicting duties
- Requires careful screening of family members and related parties
- May require withdrawal if conflicts develop during representation

Confidentiality and Communication

Attorney-client privilege takes on special significance in matrimonial practice where emotional communications are common and disclosure requirements are extensive.

Privileged Communications

- Standard attorney-client privilege protections apply
- Special considerations for family counseling communications

- Coordination with financial disclosure obligations
- Protection of settlement negotiation communications

Financial Disclosure Obligations

Attorneys have affirmative duties to ensure client compliance with financial disclosure requirements. The Appellate Division in *Robinson v. Robinson* (2016) 143 A.D.3d 1018, held that attorneys can be sanctioned for failure to adequately supervise client disclosure compliance.

Expert Witness Standards and Obligations

Family law cases frequently involve expert testimony requiring attention to professional standards and reliability requirements.

Daubert/Frye Standards in Family Law

California Evidence Code Section 801 and New York's *People v. Wesley* (1988) 73 N.Y.2d 351, establish reliability standards for expert testimony. Family law experts must demonstrate:

- Relevant professional qualifications and experience
- Reliable methodologies and factual foundations
- Appropriate scope of opinions within expertise area
- Compliance with professional ethical standards

Common Expert Categories

- Forensic accountants for business and asset valuation
- Real estate appraisers for property valuation
- Vocational experts for earning capacity analysis
- Mental health professionals for custody evaluations
- Pension and retirement plan specialists

XIV. Conclusion and Future Trends

Comparative Analysis of Jurisdictional Approaches

The examination of divorce law in California and New York reveals fundamental philosophical differences that influence both procedural requirements and substantive outcomes. California's pure no-fault system prioritizes efficiency and finality, reflecting a progressive approach that seeks to minimize conflict and expedite resolution. New York's hybrid system maintains traditional elements while accommodating modern no-fault principles, creating more complex procedural requirements but potentially greater flexibility in addressing unique circumstances.

Key Jurisdictional Differences

Philosophical Approaches

- California emphasizes administrative efficiency and emotional healing
- New York maintains traditional concepts of marital fault while embracing reform
- Both jurisdictions prioritize child welfare but through different procedural mechanisms

Procedural Variations

- California's mandatory disclosure system versus New York's discovery-based approach
- Different bifurcation policies reflecting varying views on marriage dissolution
- Contrasting approaches to temporary relief and case management

Practical Implications

- Forum selection considerations for interstate couples
- Timing differences affecting strategic decision-making
- Cost variations based on procedural requirements and local court practices

Emerging Trends and Future Developments

Several trends are reshaping divorce practice in both jurisdictions, driven by technological advancement, changing family structures, and evolving social attitudes.

Technology Integration

- Continued expansion of virtual proceedings and remote practice
- Artificial intelligence applications in document review and case analysis
- Blockchain technology for asset disclosure and property transfer
- Enhanced electronic discovery tools for financial investigation

Alternative Dispute Resolution Growth

- Expanded use of collaborative divorce and mediation
- Integration of mental health professionals in dispute resolution
- Development of specialized ADR procedures for high-conflict cases
- Online dispute resolution platforms for routine issues

Evolving Family Structures

- Recognition of diverse family arrangements and relationship types
- Adaptation of legal frameworks for modern reproductive technologies
- International family law complications from increased mobility
- Addressing needs of aging populations in late-life divorces

Practice Recommendations

Based on this comprehensive analysis, several recommendations emerge for effective matrimonial practice in both jurisdictions:

Case Assessment and Strategy Development

- Thorough initial client interviews to identify all relevant issues and potential complications
- Early assessment of alternative dispute resolution opportunities
- Strategic consideration of timing factors and procedural requirements
- Comprehensive financial analysis to identify disclosure obligations

and asset issues

Client Communication and Management

- Clear explanation of procedural requirements and realistic timeline expectations
- Regular communication regarding case developments and strategic options
- Coordination with mental health professionals and financial advisors when appropriate
- Preparation for emotional challenges inherent in divorce proceedings

Professional Development and Continuing Education

- Regular training in technological tools and virtual practice capabilities
- Understanding of complex financial issues including digital assets and modern compensation structures
- Familiarity with alternative dispute resolution techniques and collaborative practice
- Awareness of evolving legal standards and procedural requirements

The landscape of divorce law continues to evolve, driven by changing social attitudes, technological capabilities, and recognition of diverse family structures. Practitioners must remain adaptable while maintaining focus on the fundamental goals of fair resolution, child welfare protection, and efficient dispute resolution. Success in modern matrimonial practice requires technical competence, emotional intelligence, and commitment to serving clients' long-term interests rather than short-term adversarial victories.

This comprehensive examination of divorce law in California and New York provides the foundation for understanding both current practice requirements and future developments in this dynamic area of law. As family structures continue to evolve and technology reshapes legal practice, the fundamental principles of fairness, efficiency, and child welfare protection will remain central to effective divorce law practice in both jurisdictions.

7

Legal Separation and Annulment

Alternatives to Divorce

I. Beyond the Binary of Marriage and Divorce

The traditional understanding of marital dissolution centers on divorce as the primary mechanism for ending a marriage. However, the legal landscape offers nuanced alternatives that serve distinct purposes and address varied client needs. Legal separation and annulment represent sophisticated legal tools that practitioners must understand thoroughly to provide comprehensive counsel.

These alternatives are not merely procedural variations of divorce but fundamentally different legal constructs with unique substantive effects, evidentiary requirements, and strategic implications. The choice between divorce, legal separation, or annulment often reflects complex intersections of law, culture, religion, and personal circumstances that demand careful analysis.

See generally Hertz v. Hertz, 99 N.Y.2d 342, 756 N.Y.S.2d 484 (2003) (discussing the court's broad discretion in fashioning relief in matrimonial actions); In re Marriage of Burkle, 139 Cal. App. 4th 712, 43 Cal. Rptr. 3d 65 (2006) (examining alternatives to traditional divorce proceedings).

II. Legal Separation: Structured Separation with Judicial Oversight

Conceptual Framework

Legal separation represents a formal judicial recognition of spouses' decision to live apart while maintaining the legal institution of marriage. This arrangement creates a paradox: the marriage continues to exist legally while its practical functions are suspended or redirected through court-ordered arrangements.

The legal separation serves multiple constituencies: courts gain jurisdiction to resolve financial and custodial disputes; spouses obtain enforceable rights and obligations; and society's interest in orderly dissolution of marital responsibilities is preserved. *See* Schweitzer v. Schweitzer, 301 A.D.2d 264, 754 N.Y.S.2d 71 (1st Dep't 2002).

Substantive Legal Effects

Legal separation creates a bifurcated marital status where spouses remain married for some purposes while being treated as unmarried for others. Key legal consequences include:

Property Rights: Courts possess full authority to divide marital property and assign debt responsibility. The separation agreement or judgment operates with the same binding force as a divorce decree regarding financial matters. *See* In re Marriage of Dellaria, 172 Cal. App. 4th 1275, 91 Cal. Rptr. 3d 761 (2009).

Support Obligations: Spousal support calculations follow identical methodologies used in divorce proceedings. The Domestic Relations Law in New York and Family Code in California apply without modification to separated spouses. *See* Majauskas v. Majauskas, 61 N.Y.2d 481, 474 N.Y.S.2d 699 (1984).

Inheritance Rights: Unless explicitly waived, separated spouses retain inheritance rights, creating potential complications in estate planning. This retention of marital benefits distinguishes separation from divorce fundamentally. *See* Estate of Goldberg, 3 N.Y.3d 228, 785 N.Y.S.2d 164 (2004).

Tax Consequences: Separated spouses may file jointly or separately, providing tax planning opportunities unavailable to divorced individuals. However, the marriage penalty or bonus continues to apply. *See* I.R.C. § 7703(a)(1).

III. Motivations for Legal Separation

Religious and Cultural Considerations

Many clients seek legal separation to align legal protection with religious doctrine that prohibits divorce. Orthodox Jewish, Catholic, and certain Protestant denominations view marriage as indissoluble, making separation the only permissible option. Courts have consistently recognized these motivations as legitimate bases for legal separation. *See*Avitzur v. Avitzur, 58 N.Y.2d 108, 459 N.Y.S.2d 572 (1983) (recognizing religious considerations in marital dissolution).

Healthcare and Insurance Benefits

Legal separation preserves spouse's eligibility for health insurance, Social Security benefits, and other marital benefits while providing legal protection. This consideration has become increasingly important as healthcare costs rise and insurance coverage becomes more restrictive. *See* Hisquierdo v. Hisquierdo, 439 U.S. 572 (1979) (discussing federal benefits and marital status).

Immigration Implications

For clients with pending immigration applications, divorce may trigger adverse consequences or delay proceedings. Legal separation provides protection while preserving the marital relationship necessary for certain visa categories. *See*8 U.S.C. § 1186a (conditional permanent residence based on marriage).

Strategic Interim Relief

Legal separation may serve as a tactical pause, allowing parties to assess their situation while obtaining immediate court protection. This approach permits conversion to divorce once circumstances change or residency requirements are satisfied. *See* Laskin v. Laskin, 84 A.D.2d 441, 446 N.Y.S.2d 856 (2d Dep't 1982).

IV. Legal Separation in California

Jurisdictional Requirements

California's approach to legal separation reflects the state's no-fault philosophy and streamlined procedures. Unlike divorce, legal separation requires no residency period, making it immediately available to any couple regardless of their connection to California. Cal. Fam. Code § 2320.

Procedural Framework

The petition for legal separation utilizes identical forms as divorce proceedings:

- Petition for Legal Separation (Form FL-100)
- Summons (Form FL-110)
- Income and Expense Declaration (Form FL-150)

See Cal. Rules of Court, Rule 5.83 (family law forms and procedures).

Grounds and Evidence

California requires proof of irreconcilable differences or permanent legal incapacity to make decisions, mirroring divorce grounds under Family Code Section 2310. The evidentiary standard remains minimal, consistent with the state's no-fault approach. *See* In re Marriage of Davis, 61 Cal. App. 3d 796, 132 Cal. Rptr. 634 (1976).

Conversion Rights

A unique feature of California law permits conversion of legal separation to divorce by simple motion once residency requirements are satisfied. Cal. Fam. Code § 2323. This provision provides strategic flexibility for non-resident petitioners. *See* In re Marriage of Walton, 28 Cal. App. 4th 108, 33 Cal. Rptr. 2d 433 (1994).

Property Division Authority

California courts possess identical authority in legal separation as in divorce to characterize, value, and divide community property and quasi-community property. The equal division presumption applies unless rebutted by evidence of circumstances justifying unequal division. Cal. Fam. Code § 2550. *See* In re Marriage of Hoffmeister, 191 Cal. App. 3d 351, 236 Cal. Rptr. 543 (1987).

V. Legal Separation in New York

Dual-Track System

New York's approach to legal separation operates through two distinct mechanisms: contractual separation agreements and litigated separation actions. This dual system reflects historical development and provides flexibility in addressing varied client needs.

Separation Agreements

Contractual Nature: Separation agreements represent private contracts between spouses addressing all aspects of their separation. These agreements require the same formalities as other contracts: offer, acceptance, consideration, and mutual assent. *See* Christian v. Christian, 42 N.Y.2d 63, 396 N.Y.S.2d 817 (1977).

Required Elements: Effective separation agreements must address:

- Custody and visitation arrangements
- Child support obligations
- Spousal maintenance
- Property division
- Debt allocation
- Tax considerations

See Domestic Relations Law § 236(B)(3).

Enforcement Mechanisms: Separation agreements are enforceable as contracts through breach of contract actions or through Supreme Court's continuing jurisdiction in subsequent matrimonial proceedings. *See* Levine v. Levine, 56 N.Y.2d 42, 451 N.Y.S.2d 26 (1982).

Separation Actions in Supreme Court

Statutory Framework: Domestic Relations Law Section 200 provides grounds for judicial separation actions, including:

- Cruel and inhuman treatment endangering physical or mental well-being
- Abandonment for one or more years
- Confinement in prison for three or more consecutive years
- Adultery

Evidentiary Requirements: Unlike no-fault divorce, separation actions require proof of specific grounds with corroborating evidence. The standard of proof mirrors fault-based divorce actions. *See* Hessen v. Hessen, 33 N.Y.2d 406, 353 N.Y.S.2d 421 (1974).

Strategic Considerations: Separation actions are rarely pursued due to their adversarial nature and evidentiary burden. Most practitioners favor separation agreements for their efficiency and privacy. *See* Rothschild v. Rothschild, 107 A.D.2d 293, 486 N.Y.S.2d 573 (2d Dep't 1985).

VI. Comparative Analysis: Separation vs. Divorce

Legal Status Implications

The fundamental distinction between legal separation and divorce lies in marital status preservation. Separated spouses cannot remarry, retain inheritance rights, and maintain eligibility for marital benefits. This distinction has profound implications for:

Federal Benefits: Social Security, military benefits, and federal employment benefits often depend on marital status. *See* Flemming v. Nestor, 363 U.S. 603 (1960).

Estate Planning: Elective share rights, homestead exemptions, and family allowances remain intact during separation. *See* Matter of Riefberg, 57 N.Y.2d 134, 454 N.Y.S.2d 672 (1982).

Testimonial Privilege: Spousal privilege continues during legal separation, potentially affecting litigation strategy in other proceedings. *See* Trammel v. United States, 445 U.S. 40 (1980).

Financial Considerations

Tax Planning: Separated spouses retain the option to file joint returns, potentially reducing overall tax liability. However, joint filing creates joint and several liability for taxes owed. *See* I.R.C. § 6013.

Debt Responsibility: Legal separation provides protection from post-separation debts incurred by the other spouse, similar to divorce protection. *See* In re Marriage of Eastis, 47 Cal. App. 4th 1276, 55 Cal. Rptr. 2d 238 (1996).

VII. Annulment: The Legal Fiction of Non-Marriage

Theoretical Foundation

Annulment operates on the legal theory that certain defects in marriage formation render the union void ab initio or voidable at the election of the innocent party. This concept distinguishes between marriages that never legally existed (void) and those that existed but may be nullified due to specific defects (voidable).

The distinction carries significant consequences for property rights, legitimacy of children, and availability of relief. *See*Wilkins v. Zelichowski, 26 N.Y.2d 114, 308 N.Y.S.2d 784 (1970).

Void vs. Voidable Marriages

Void Marriages: These unions are invalid from inception and require no judicial action to nullify, though court proceedings may be necessary for clarification and property division. Examples include:

- Bigamous marriages
- Incestuous relationships within prohibited degrees
- Same-sex marriages in non-recognition jurisdictions (historically)

Voidable Marriages: These marriages exist until annulled but may be nullified based on specific grounds:

- Lack of capacity due to mental incapacity or intoxication
- Fraud in the essentials of marriage
- Duress or force
- Physical incapacity to consummate

See Shonfeld v. Shonfeld, 260 N.Y. 477, 184 N.E. 60 (1932).

VIII. Annulment Grounds in New York

Statutory Framework

Domestic Relations Law Section 140 provides comprehensive grounds for annulment, each requiring specific proof and subject to particular defenses and time limitations.

Lack of Capacity to Consent

Mental Incapacity: The petitioner must prove the other party lacked sufficient mental capacity to understand the nature and consequences of marriage. This standard requires evidence of cognitive impairment at the time of the ceremony, not merely poor judgment. *See* Matter of Ackert, 133 Misc. 2d 284, 506 N.Y.S.2d 968 (Sur. Ct. 1986).

Intoxication: Temporary incapacity due to alcohol or drug intoxication may provide grounds if the intoxication prevented understanding of the marriage's nature. The burden requires proof of severe impairment, not mere influence. *See* Turner v. Turner, 192 Misc. 2d 229, 745 N.Y.S.2d 796 (Sup. Ct. 2002).

Duress and Fraud

Duress: Physical force, threats of violence, or other coercion that overcomes free will provides grounds for annulment. Economic pressure alone typically does not constitute sufficient duress. *See* Shaheen v. Shaheen, 12 Misc. 2d 1087, 174 N.Y.S.2d 636 (Sup. Ct. 1958).

Fraud: The misrepresentation must relate to the essentials of marriage - those matters so fundamental that knowledge would have prevented the marriage. Examples include:

- Concealment of sterility when children are desired
- Undisclosed criminal history affecting marital safety
- False representation of religious conversion
- Concealment of existing marriage

See Woronzoff-Daschkoff v. Woronzoff-Daschkoff, 303 N.Y. 506, 104 N.E.2d 877 (1952).

Incurable Mental Illness

This ground requires proof of mental illness existing for at least five years with no reasonable prospect of recovery. The illness must be of such severity as to render normal marital relations impossible. *See* Anonymous v. Anonymous, 37 Misc. 2d 773, 236 N.Y.S.2d 288 (Sup. Ct. 1962).

Physical Incapacity

Physical inability to consummate the marriage through sexual intercourse provides grounds for annulment if the incapacity existed at the time of marriage and continues. The incapacity must be incurable or the afflicted party must refuse treatment. *See* T. v. M., 100 N.Y.S.2d 178 (Sup. Ct. 1950).

Underage Marriage

Marriages involving parties under 18 without proper consent may be annulled. However, New York law provides that underage marriages become valid when the minor reaches majority and continues to cohabit. Domestic Relations Law § 15-a. *See* Moe v. Dinkins, 533 F. Supp. 623 (S.D.N.Y. 1981).

IX. Annulment Grounds in California

Statutory Structure

California Family Code Sections 2200-2212 establish grounds for nullity, distinguishing between void and voidable marriages with specific procedural requirements and time limitations.

Void Marriages Under California Law

Bigamous Marriages: California Family Code Section 2201(a) renders marriages void when either party has a living spouse. The subsequent marriage is void regardless of knowledge of the prior marriage's existence. *See* Estate of Vargas, 36 Cal. App. 4th 714, 42 Cal. Rptr. 2d 593 (1995).

Incestuous Marriages: Marriages between close relatives within prohibited degrees are void ab initio. Cal. Fam. Code § 2200. *See* In re Estate of Loughmiller, 229 Cal. App. 2d 156, 40 Cal. Rptr. 183 (1964).

Voidable Marriages

Fraud: California requires fraud in the essentials of marriage that would have prevented the marriage if known. The misrepresentation must be material to the marital relationship and continuing. *See* In re Marriage of Ramirez, 81 Cal. App. 3d 719, 146 Cal. Rptr. 748 (1978).

Force: Physical force or threats that overcome free will provide grounds for annulment. Unlike New York, California does not require physical violence if psychological coercion is sufficient to negate consent. *See* In re Marriage of Mehren, 92 Cal. App. 3d 723, 155 Cal. Rptr. 199 (1979).

Physical Incapacity: Inability to consummate the marriage existing at the time of marriage and continuing thereafter provides grounds for nullity. The incapacity must be incurable or treatment must be refused. Cal. Fam. Code § 2210(a). *See* In re Marriage of Thornton, 67 Cal. App. 3d 102, 136 Cal. Rptr. 373 (1977).

Unsound Mind: Mental incapacity at the time of marriage that prevented understanding of the marital relationship's nature provides grounds for annulment. The standard requires significant cognitive impairment, not mere poor judgment. *See* In re Marriage of Hibbard, 212 Cal. App. 3d 1007, 261 Cal. Rptr. 10 (1989).

Time Limitations and Defenses

California imposes specific time limitations on annulment actions:

- Fraud: Four years from discovery of facts constituting fraud
- Force: Four years from when petitioner was no longer under duress
- Physical incapacity: Four years from marriage
- Unsound mind: Any time during the person's lifetime

Cal. Fam. Code § 2211. *See* In re Marriage of Kohler, 78 Cal. App. 3d 558, 144 Cal. Rptr. 384 (1978).

X. Procedural Considerations in Annulment Practice

Burden of Proof

Annulment petitioners must prove their case by clear and convincing evidence, a higher standard than the preponderance required in divorce proceedings. This elevated burden reflects the law's preference for maintaining marriages and the serious nature of declaring a marriage void. *See* Yelderman v. Yelderman, 48 A.D.2d 604, 367 N.Y.S.2d 633 (2d Dep't 1975).

Evidentiary Requirements

Documentary Evidence: Marriage certificates, medical records, criminal records, and correspondence often provide crucial proof of annulment grounds. Practitioners must gather comprehensive documentation to support their claims.

Witness Testimony: Corroborating testimony from family members, friends, and professionals who observed the parties' condition or behavior around the time of marriage can be essential.

Expert Testimony: Medical experts, psychiatrists, and other professionals may be necessary to establish mental incapacity, physical incapacity, or the effects of duress or fraud.

See Matter of Estate of Erikson, 337 N.W.2d 671 (Minn. 1983) (discussing evidentiary requirements in capacity cases).

Defenses to Annulment

Ratification: Continued cohabitation with knowledge of the grounds for annulment may constitute ratification, barring the annulment action. This defense is particularly relevant in fraud and capacity cases. *See* Millar v. Millar, 175 N.Y. 108, 67 N.E. 124 (1903).

Laches: Unreasonable delay in bringing the annulment action may bar relief, even within statutory time limits. Courts consider the length of delay, prejudice to the other party, and changed circumstances. *See* Freundlich v. Freundlich, 160 A.D.2d 615, 554 N.Y.S.2d 60 (2d Dep't 1990).

Estoppel: Conduct inconsistent with claiming annulment grounds may estop the petitioner from seeking relief. This defense often overlaps with ratification but focuses on detrimental reliance by the respondent.

XI. Putative Spouse Doctrine and Equitable Relief

California's Putative Spouse Concept

California Family Code Section 2251 provides that when a marriage is void or voidable, the court may treat a party who believed in good faith that the marriage was valid as a putative spouse entitled to property rights. This doctrine protects innocent parties from the harsh consequences of void marriages.

The putative spouse acquires rights to:

- Property acquired during the putative marriage
- Spousal support
- Community property characterization of earnings and acquisitions

See Estate of Vargas, 36 Cal. App. 4th 714, 42 Cal. Rptr. 2d 593 (1995); In re Marriage of Vryonis, 202 Cal. App. 3d 712, 248 Cal. Rptr. 807 (1988).

New York's Equitable Approach

New York does not recognize the putative spouse doctrine but provides equitable relief through various theories:

Quasi-Contract: Courts may award restitution for benefits conferred during the invalid marriage to prevent unjust enrichment. *See* Morone v. Morone, 50 N.Y.2d 481, 429 N.Y.S.2d 592 (1980).

Partnership Theory: Property acquired during cohabitation may be divided under partnership principles if parties contributed to joint enterprises. *See* Braschi v. Stahl Associates Co., 74 N.Y.2d 201, 544 N.Y.S.2d 784 (1989).

Express Contract: Agreements between parties regarding property and support may be enforced if not based solely on sexual services. *See* Hewitt v. Hewitt, 77 Ill. 2d 49, 394 N.E.2d 1204 (1979).

XII. Child-Related Issues in Annulment

Legitimacy of Children

Both New York and California provide that children born of annulled marriages are legitimate. This protection ensures that children do not suffer legal disadvantage from their parents' invalid marriage.

New York: Domestic Relations Law Section 24 establishes that children of void or voidable marriages are legitimate if either parent reasonably believed the marriage was valid.

California: Family Code Section 2254 provides similar protection, declaring children of putative marriages legitimate.

See Levy v. Louisiana, 391 U.S. 68 (1968) (constitutional protection for children regardless of parents' marital status).

Custody and Support

Courts retain full jurisdiction to determine custody and support issues in annulment proceedings, applying the same standards used in divorce cases. The child's best interests govern custody determinations, while support follows standard guideline calculations.

See In re Marriage of Bouquet, 16 Cal. 3d 583, 546 P.2d 1371 (1976); Lynch v. Lynch, 49 A.D.2d 160, 373 N.Y.S.2d 831 (2d Dep't 1975).

XIII. Strategic Considerations in Practice

Client Counseling

Realistic Expectations: Practitioners must educate clients about the high evidentiary burden and limited grounds for annulment. Many clients seek annulment based on regret or dissatisfaction rather than legal grounds.

Alternative Remedies: When annulment is unavailable, practitioners should discuss divorce options, including no-fault grounds and expedited procedures.

Religious Considerations: Clients seeking religious annulment should understand that civil and religious annulments are separate proceedings with different requirements and effects.

Case Development Strategy

Early Investigation: Thorough factual development is crucial given the clear and convincing evidence standard. Practitioners should immediately preserve relevant documents and identify potential witnesses.

Expert Consultation: Medical, psychiatric, and other expert opinions may be necessary to establish grounds and should be secured early in the case.

Discovery Planning: Comprehensive discovery may be necessary to uncover evidence of fraud, capacity issues, or other grounds. This process often exceeds the scope required in typical divorce proceedings.

Settlement Considerations

Negotiated Resolution: Many annulment cases settle when the primary goal is property division or support rather than the nullity declaration itself. Practitioners should explore whether client objectives can be achieved through separation or divorce.

Conditional Settlements: Agreements contingent on successful annulment may protect clients' interests while avoiding prolonged litigation uncertainty.

XIV. Ethical Considerations

Frivolous Claims

Practitioners must carefully evaluate annulment claims to ensure they are supported by credible evidence and valid legal grounds. Filing frivolous annulment petitions may violate professional conduct rules and subject attorneys to sanctions.

Conflicts of Interest

Annulment cases may present unique conflict issues, particularly when both parties seek the annulment or when children's interests conflict with parents' objectives. Practitioners must carefully analyze potential conflicts and obtain appropriate waivers or decline representation.

Candor to the Tribunal

The elevated burden of proof in annulment cases requires scrupulous honesty in presenting evidence and legal arguments. Practitioners must not overstate evidence or mischaracterize legal standards to meet the clear and convincing evidence requirement.

XV. Recent Developments and Future Trends

Legislative Changes

Both New York and California have modernized their family law statutes to address changing social conditions and legal developments. Recent amendments have:

- Simplified divorce procedures, reducing the practical need for legal separation

- Clarified time limitations for annulment actions
- Enhanced protection for domestic violence victims in family law proceedings

Judicial Interpretations

Courts have increasingly scrutinized annulment claims, requiring stronger evidence of grounds and more carefully examining motivations for seeking nullity rather than divorce. This trend reflects judicial preference for marriage preservation and concern about forum shopping.

Practice Evolution

Modern family law practice has seen decreased reliance on legal separation as no-fault divorce became more accessible and socially acceptable. However, annulment remains important in specific circumstances, particularly involving religious considerations or fraud claims.

XVI. Conclusion

Legal separation and annulment represent sophisticated alternatives to divorce that serve specific client needs and reflect complex intersections of law, culture, and individual circumstances. Successful practice in this area requires thorough understanding of substantive law, procedural requirements, and strategic considerations unique to each remedy.

These alternatives are not merely technical variations of divorce but distinct legal constructs with their own theoretical foundations, evidentiary requirements, and practical implications. Practitioners must carefully assess client objectives, available evidence, and potential outcomes to provide effective counsel in choosing among these options.

The evolving nature of family law, changing social attitudes toward marriage and divorce, and increasingly complex financial and custodial arrangements ensure that legal separation and annulment will remain important tools in the family law practitioner's arsenal. Mastery of these concepts is essential for comprehensive family law practice in both New York and California.

As we proceed to examine property division in the next chapter, the foundations established here regarding marital status, court jurisdiction, and the various ways marriages may be modified or terminated will prove crucial to understanding the complex property rights that flow from these different legal relationships.

8

Property Division

Equitable Distribution vs. Community Property

I. Untangling the Financial Knot

One of the most complex and emotionally charged aspects of family law is the division of property at the end of a marriage. From homes and retirement accounts to debts and business interests, determining who gets what is rarely straightforward - especially when long-term planning, sacrifice, or unequal contributions are involved. The financial entanglements created during marriage often reflect years of shared decisions, individual sacrifices, and joint investments that must be carefully unraveled through legal frameworks designed to achieve fairness.

This chapter provides a comprehensive analysis of how property division is handled in New York and California, focusing on the two distinct systems they employ and the practical implications for practitioners and their clients. These jurisdictions represent the two primary approaches to marital property division in the United States, each reflecting different philosophical underpinnings about marriage, property rights, and equity.

Equitable Distribution (New York) - Based on fairness and consideration of multiple statutory factors, allowing courts discretion to achieve just results based on the specific circumstances of each case.

Community Property (California) - Rooted in the presumption that marriage creates an economic partnership where spouses have equal ownership interests in property acquired during the union.

We will explore the classification of property, the rules for valuation and division, judicial interpretation of key statutes, and how courts address complex issues including debt allocation, hidden assets, separate property claims, and the intersection of property division with other aspects of divorce proceedings.

II. Legal Frameworks for Property Division

A. Historical Development and Philosophical Foundations

The distinction between equitable distribution and community property systems reflects fundamentally different conceptualizations of marriage and property rights. Community property law, derived from Spanish civil law traditions, views marriage as creating an economic partnership where both spouses have equal ownership interests in property acquired during the marriage, regardless of which spouse earned or purchased the property. This system operates on the principle that marriage itself transforms individual economic activity into joint enterprise.

Equitable distribution, by contrast, developed from English common law traditions that historically recognized individual property rights even within marriage. Modern equitable distribution statutes, while departing significantly from common law coverture principles, retain the concept that fair division need not mean equal division, allowing courts to consider the totality of circumstances to achieve just results.

B. Statutory Framework Comparison

California Community Property System

California's community property regime is codified primarily in Family Code sections 2550-2556, with supporting provisions throughout the Family Code. The fundamental principle is stated in Family Code section 2550: "Except upon the written agreement of the parties, or on oral stipulation of the parties in open court, or as otherwise provided in this division, in a proceeding for dissolution of marriage or for legal separation of the parties, the court shall, and in a proceeding for nullity of marriage, the court may, divide the community estate of the parties equally."

The California system operates on several core principles established through decades of case law:

1. The presumption of equal division of community property (*In re Marriage of Frick*, 181 Cal. App. 3d 997 (1986))
2. The requirement that all property acquired during marriage is presumptively community property (*In re Marriage of Mix*, 14 Cal. 3d 604 (1975))
3. The principle that each spouse has a present, existing, and equal interest in community property (*In re Marriage of Lucas*, 27 Cal. 3d 808 (1980))

New York Equitable Distribution System

New York's equitable distribution statute is contained in Domestic Relations Law section 236(B), which was enacted in 1980 to replace the common law system that left many economically dependent spouses without adequate financial protection upon divorce. The statute represents a comprehensive approach to property division that considers both the economic and non-economic contributions of the spouses.

The statutory scheme operates on the principle articulated in *Majauskas v. Majauskas*, 61 N.Y.2d 481 (1984), that "the concept underlying equitable distribution is that marriage is, among other things, an economic partnership to which both parties contribute, as spouse, parent, wage earner or homemaker." The Court of Appeals emphasized that equitable distribution "seeks to recognize that upon dissolution of the marriage there should be a winding up of the parties' economic affairs and a severance of their economic ties so that each party can begin life anew."

C. Judicial Interpretation and Evolution

Both systems have evolved significantly through judicial interpretation. In California, landmark cases such as *In re Marriage of Moore*, 28 Cal. 3d 366 (1980), and *In re Marriage of Marsden*, 130 Cal. App. 3d 426 (1982), established complex reimbursement schemes for situations where separate and community property interests become intertwined. The Moore/Marsden doctrine addresses situations where community funds are used to pay down the principal of a separate property residence, creating community property interests that must be accounted for upon dissolution.

New York courts have similarly refined the equitable distribution framework through cases such as *O'Brien v. O'Brien*, 66 N.Y.2d 576 (1985), which established that professional licenses and degrees acquired during marriage constitute marital property subject to distribution, and *Elkus v. Elkus*, 169 A.D.2d 134 (1st Dep't 1991), which extended this principle to celebrity goodwill and career enhancement.

III. Identifying and Classifying Property

A. The Critical Importance of Property Classification

Property classification serves as the foundation for all subsequent division analysis. The characterization of an asset as separate or marital/community property determines not only whether it is subject to division, but also influences valuation methodologies, the burden of proof regarding ownership claims, and the availability of various remedies for misappropriation or waste.

Misclassification of property can result in significant financial consequences and may constitute reversible error. As the California Supreme Court noted in *In re Marriage of Buol*, 39 Cal. 3d 751 (1985), "The characterization of property as separate or community is a question of law, but one which may depend upon the resolution of underlying factual disputes."

B. New York – Marital vs. Separate Property

Marital Property Under DRL § 236(B)(1)(c)

New York Domestic Relations Law section 236(B)(1)(c) defines marital property as "all property acquired by either or both spouses during the marriage and before the execution of a separation agreement or the commencement of a matrimonial action, regardless of the form in which title is held." This broad definition encompasses several categories of assets that require careful analysis:

Income and Earnings

All income earned by either spouse during the marriage constitutes marital property, including wages, salaries, bonuses, commissions, and self-employment income. The seminal case of *Price v. Price*, 69 N.Y.2d 8 (1986), established that even income deposited in separate accounts retains its marital character unless deliberately segregated and maintained as separate property.

Asset Appreciation and Enhancement

The treatment of appreciation in separate property represents one of the most complex areas of New York marital property law. The Court of Appeals in *Price v. Price* established a framework for analyzing appreciation that depends on whether the increase in value results from market forces (passive appreciation) or from marital efforts and contributions (active appreciation).

Passive appreciation of separate property remains separate. However, when appreciation results from the direct or indirect contributions of the non-owning spouse or from marital funds or efforts, that portion of the appreciation becomes marital property subject to distribution. The court must conduct a careful factual analysis to determine the extent to which appreciation resulted from marital contributions versus market forces.

Professional Practices and Licenses

New York's landmark decision in *O'Brien v. O'Brien*, 66 N.Y.2d 576 (1985), established that professional licenses and degrees acquired during marriage constitute marital property. The Court of Appeals reasoned that where one spouse's education or training is acquired through the financial contributions and sacrifices of both spouses, the resulting enhanced earning capacity should be treated as marital property for distribution purposes.

This principle was extended in *Elkus v. Elkus*, 169 A.D.2d 134 (1st Dep't 1991), to encompass celebrity goodwill and career enhancement. However, courts have struggled with valuation methodologies for such intangible assets, often requiring expert testimony regarding future income projections and present value calculations.

Retirement Benefits and Deferred Compensation

The portion of retirement benefits, pensions, and deferred compensation attributable to service during the marriage constitutes marital property. *Majauskas v. Majauskas*, 61 N.Y.2d 481 (1984), established the framework for analyzing pension benefits, requiring courts to determine what portion of the pension is attributable to marital service versus separate service before and after marriage.

For defined benefit plans, courts typically use a coverture fraction to determine the marital portion: the number of years of service during marriage divided by total years of service at retirement, multiplied by the total benefit. For defined contribution plans, the analysis focuses on contributions and earnings during the marital period.

Separate Property Under DRL § 236(B)(1)(d)

New York law recognizes several categories of separate property that remain outside the equitable distribution framework:

Property Acquired Before Marriage

Assets owned by either spouse before marriage retain their separate character, provided they are not subsequently commingled with marital property or enhanced through marital efforts. The separate property claimant bears the burden of establishing both the separate origin of the property and its maintenance as separate property throughout the marriage.

Inheritances and Gifts

Property acquired by inheritance or gift from a third party during marriage remains separate, regardless of when during the marriage it was received. However, this separate character can be lost through commingling or by treating the property as marital. In *Inniss v. Inniss*, 8 A.D.3d 163 (1st Dep't 2004), the court found that inherited funds lost their separate character when deposited in joint accounts and used for marital purposes.

Personal Injury Awards

Compensation for personal injuries received during marriage is generally separate property, though courts may consider the needs of the injured spouse in making an equitable distribution award. The rationale is that personal injury compensation is intended to make the injured party whole for losses specific to that individual.

Property Excluded by Agreement

Valid prenuptial or postnuptial agreements can designate property as separate that would otherwise be marital. Such agreements must comply with the requirements established in *DeLorean v. DeLorean*, 211 A.D.2d 758

(2d Dep't 1995), including fair disclosure, absence of duress, and substantive fairness.

C. California – Community vs. Separate Property

Community Property Under Family Code Section 760

California Family Code section 760 establishes the fundamental presumption that "all property, real or personal, wherever situated, acquired by a married person during the marriage while domiciled in this state is community property." This presumption is so strong that it can only be overcome by clear and convincing evidence that the property has a separate character.

The Community Property Presumption

The community property presumption operates as both a rule of law and an evidentiary principle. In *In re Marriage of Mix*, 14 Cal. 3d 604 (1975), the California Supreme Court explained that property acquired during marriage is presumed to be community property, and this presumption affects the burden of proof: the party claiming separate property status must overcome the presumption with clear and convincing evidence.

This presumption applies regardless of how title is held. Even if property is titled in the name of only one spouse, it remains presumptively community property if acquired during marriage. The rationale is that the form of title should not defeat the community property rights that arise from the marital relationship itself.

Earnings and Income

All earnings from personal services performed during marriage are community property, including wages, salaries, professional income, business profits, and investment returns from community assets. This principle extends to more complex forms of compensation such as stock options, restricted stock units, and deferred compensation plans.

In *In re Marriage of Hug*, 154 Cal. App. 3d 780 (1984), the court addressed the characterization of stock options granted during marriage but exercisable after separation. The court established that stock options are community property to the extent they are earned through community efforts, requiring an analysis of the time rule to determine what portion relates to marital service.

Community Debts

Debts incurred during marriage for community purposes are community obligations. Family Code section 910 provides that both spouses are liable for community debts, creating joint and several liability. However, the community property characterization of debt depends on the purpose for which the debt was incurred and the benefit received by the community.

Separate Property Under Family Code Section 770

California recognizes several categories of separate property that remain outside the community property system:

Property Owned Before Marriage

Property owned by either spouse before marriage remains separate property. However, the character of such property can change through various doctrines including commingling, transmutation, or community contributions that create reimbursement rights.

Gifts and Inheritances

Property acquired during marriage by gift, inheritance, devise, or descent remains the separate property of the recipient spouse. This rule applies even to gifts between spouses, though such interspousal gifts may constitute transmutations requiring compliance with Family Code section 852.

Rents, Issues, and Profits from Separate Property

Under Family Code section 770, rents, issues, and profits from separate property remain separate property. This rule distinguishes California from some community property states that treat income from separate property as community property. However, if community labor or funds contribute to the production of income from separate property, apportionment may be required under the principles established in *Pereira v. Pereira*, 156 Cal. 648 (1909), and *Van Camp v. Van Camp*, 53 Cal. App. 17 (1921).

D. Commingling and Transmutation Issues

Both New York and California grapple with situations where separate and marital/community property become intertwined, requiring courts to apply complex tracing and apportionment rules.

New York Commingling Analysis

In New York, commingling occurs when separate property is mixed with marital property in such a way that the separate character is lost. The key inquiry is whether the separate property can be traced and identified. In *Arvantides v. Arvantides*, 64 N.Y.2d 147 (1984), the Court of Appeals established that commingling results in transformation to marital property unless the separate property can be traced with reasonable certainty.

The burden is on the party claiming separate property to establish tracing through clear and convincing evidence. Courts may require detailed financial records, expert testimony, and forensic accounting analysis to establish the separate property claim.

California Commingling and Transmutation

California's approach to commingling is governed by the principles established in *In re Marriage of Moore*, 28 Cal. 3d 366 (1980), and subsequent cases. When separate and community property are commingled, the general rule is that the community property presumption applies unless the separate property can be traced.

Transmutation involves the change in character of property from separate to community or vice versa. Under Family Code section 852, transmutations between spouses after January 1, 1985, must be in writing and signed by the spouse adversely affected. This requirement was established to prevent the casual transmutation that occurred under prior law and to ensure that property character changes reflect deliberate decisions.

IV. Valuation of Assets and Liabilities

A. General Valuation Principles

Accurate valuation serves as the foundation for equitable property division. Courts in both New York and California have developed sophisticated frameworks for valuing complex assets, requiring consideration of various valuation methodologies, the appropriate valuation date, and the use of expert testimony.

Standard of Value

Both jurisdictions generally apply fair market value as the standard for asset valuation. Fair market value is defined as the price that would be agreed upon between a willing buyer and willing seller, neither being under compulsion to buy or sell, and both having knowledge of relevant facts. However, certain assets may require modified valuation approaches based on their unique characteristics.

Valuation Date Issues

The selection of the appropriate valuation date can significantly impact the division of assets, particularly for volatile investments or businesses experiencing rapid growth or decline.

In New York, the general rule established in *Wegman v. Wegman*, 123 A.D.2d 220 (2d Dep't 1986), is that assets should be valued as of the date of commencement of the matrimonial action. However, courts have discretion to select different dates when justice requires, such as when there has been significant appreciation or depreciation between commencement and trial.

California generally values assets as of the date of trial or the date closest to trial as is practicable, as provided in Family Code section 2552. However, for certain assets such as closely held businesses, courts may use the date of separation to avoid the impact of post-separation management decisions by one spouse.

B. Real Estate Valuation

Real estate often represents the largest marital asset and requires careful valuation analysis. Both jurisdictions require consideration of current market conditions, comparable sales, and the property's unique characteristics.

Appraisal Requirements and Standards

Courts typically require professional appraisals for significant real estate holdings. The Uniform Standards of Professional Appraisal Practice (USPAP) provide the framework for acceptable appraisal methodology. In complex cases involving unique properties or significant disputes over value, courts may appoint independent appraisers or require multiple appraisals.

Consideration of Mortgage and Encumbrances

The net equity in real estate must be determined by subtracting outstanding encumbrances from fair market value. This analysis may require consideration of prepayment penalties, refinancing costs, and the tax consequences of sale.

Marital Residence Considerations

The family residence often receives special consideration in property division, particularly when minor children are involved. Courts may award the residence to the custodial parent with appropriate offsets, or order sale with proceeds division. The decision typically considers factors such as the children's stability, the parties' financial ability to maintain the residence, and the liquidity needs of both spouses.

C. Business Valuation

The valuation of closely held businesses presents some of the most complex issues in matrimonial property division. Courts must determine not only the value of the business but also the extent to which that value represents marital property subject to distribution.

Valuation Methodologies

Business valuation typically employs one or more of three basic approaches: the asset approach, the income approach, and the market approach. The selection of the appropriate methodology depends on the nature of the business, the availability of financial information, and the purpose of the valuation.

The asset approach focuses on the value of the business's underlying assets, either at book value or adjusted for fair market value. This approach is most appropriate for asset-heavy businesses or in liquidation scenarios.

The income approach, including discounted cash flow analysis and capitalization of earnings methods, focuses on the business's ability to generate future income. This approach is often preferred for operating businesses with established earning patterns.

The market approach compares the subject business to similar businesses that have been sold, using multiples of revenue, earnings, or other financial metrics. This approach requires sufficient comparable transaction data.

Professional Goodwill and Personal Goodwill Distinction

Both New York and California recognize the distinction between professional goodwill (which is transferable and represents value inherent in the business) and personal goodwill (which is tied to the individual owner and cannot be transferred). This distinction is crucial in professional practices where much of the value may be attributable to the personal relationships and reputation of the professional.

In *Dugan v. Dugan*, 92 A.D.2d 422 (4th Dep't 1983), a New York court established factors for analyzing professional goodwill, including the nature of the practice, the existing referral base, the transferability of patient relationships, and the competition restrictions that may apply.

California's approach, established in *In re Marriage of Foster*, 42 Cal. App. 3d 577 (1974), and refined in subsequent cases, similarly focuses on whether goodwill has value to anyone other than the individual professional.

Valuation Discounts and Premiums

Courts must consider whether valuation discounts or premiums are appropriate. Common discounts include those for lack of marketability (particularly relevant for closely held businesses), minority interest discounts, and key person discounts. Conversely, control premiums may be appropriate when valuing controlling interests in businesses.

The application of discounts in the matrimonial context has generated significant litigation. Some courts reject marketability discounts on the theory that divorcing spouses should not benefit from self-created restrictions on transferability.

D. Retirement Benefits and Deferred Compensation

The valuation of retirement benefits requires analysis of complex actuarial principles and consideration of various contingencies that may affect the ultimate benefit received.

Defined Benefit Plans

Defined benefit plans promise specific benefits at retirement based on factors such as years of service, salary history, and plan formulas. Valuation requires actuarial analysis to determine the present value of future benefits, considering factors such as mortality, discount rates, and the probability of vesting.

The marital portion of defined benefit plans is typically determined using a coverture fraction: the number of years of marital service divided by total years of service at retirement, multiplied by the total benefit. However, this calculation may require adjustment for periods of military service, leaves of absence, or other factors that affect benefit accrual.

Defined Contribution Plans

Defined contribution plans, including 401(k) plans and similar arrangements, are generally easier to value because they represent specific account balances. However, valuation must consider vesting schedules, employer matching contributions, and investment performance during the marriage.

Stock Options and Restricted Stock

Employee stock options and restricted stock present unique valuation challenges, particularly when vesting or exercise occurs after the marriage ends. Courts must determine what portion of the benefit relates to marital service versus post-marital service.

Various methodologies have been developed for apportioning stock options, including the time rule (based on the ratio of marital service to total service required for vesting) and the continuous coverage method (which treats options as compensation for ongoing service).

Qualified Domestic Relations Orders (QDROs)

Implementation of retirement benefit divisions typically requires Qualified Domestic Relations Orders (QDROs) under the Employee Retirement Income Security Act (ERISA). QDROs must comply with specific federal requirements and the terms of the underlying plan. Preparation of QDROs requires expertise in both family law and employee benefits law, as errors can result in loss of benefits or adverse tax consequences.

E. Tax Considerations in Valuation

Property division carries significant tax implications that must be considered in the valuation process. Courts may adjust valuations to account for different tax consequences that assets carry for different spouses.

Capital Gains Considerations

Assets with significant unrealized capital gains carry different economic value depending on when and how they are disposed of. Courts may consider the built-in capital gains liability in determining fair division, particularly when one spouse receives assets with high tax basis and the other receives assets with low tax basis.

Retirement Account Tax Consequences

Traditional retirement accounts carry deferred income tax liability, while Roth accounts have already been subject to taxation. Courts may adjust division to account for these different tax characteristics.

Transfer Tax Issues

Property transfers between spouses incident to divorce are generally tax-free under Internal Revenue Code section 1041. However, proper documentation and timing are essential to ensure that transfers qualify for this favorable treatment.

V. Equitable Distribution in New York: Fair, Not Always Equal

A. The Statutory Framework - DRL § 236(B)(5)(d)

New York's equitable distribution statute represents a comprehensive approach to property division that mandates consideration of multiple factors without establishing rigid formulas or presumptions. The statute requires courts to consider "any other factor which the court shall expressly find to be just and proper," providing flexibility to address unique circumstances while ensuring thorough analysis of specified factors.

Factor-by-Factor Analysis

Duration of the Marriage

The length of the marriage serves as a foundational consideration in equitable distribution analysis. Longer marriages typically result in more equal distribution, reflecting the deeper economic integration that occurs over time. Short-term marriages may warrant distribution that more closely reflects each party's separate contributions.

In *Domestic Relations Law* § 236(B)(5)(d)(4), the statute specifically requires consideration of "the duration of the marriage and the age and health of both parties." Courts have interpreted this to mean that marriages of substantial duration create stronger presumptions toward equal distribution, while shorter marriages may justify outcomes that preserve more separate property characteristics.

The seminal case of *Majauskas v. Majauskas*, 61 N.Y.2d 481 (1984), involved a 32-year marriage where the Court of Appeals emphasized that long-term marriages create expectations of shared economic outcomes that should be honored in property division.

Age and Health of the Parties

The age and health of the divorcing spouses affects their ability to rebuild financial security and earning capacity after divorce. Older spouses, particularly those with health limitations, may require greater property awards to compensate for reduced earning potential and increased medical costs.

Courts consider not only current health status but also reasonably anticipated future health needs. In *McSparron v. McSparron*, 87 N.Y.2d 275 (1995), the Court of Appeals noted that a spouse's poor health may justify a larger distributive award to provide financial security for anticipated medical expenses.

Income and Property of Each Party

This factor requires comprehensive analysis of both current income and property holdings, as well as future earning potential. Courts must consider not only obvious income sources such as employment and investment returns, but also more complex arrangements such as deferred compensation, stock options, and business ownership interests.

The analysis extends beyond current income to consider earning capacity, particularly when one spouse has sacrificed career advancement for family responsibilities. In *O'Brien v. O'Brien*, 66 N.Y.2d 576 (1985), the court recognized that enhanced earning capacity achieved during marriage through the sacrifices of both spouses constitutes marital property subject to distribution.

Present and Future Earning Capacity

Courts must evaluate each spouse's ability to become self-supporting after divorce. This analysis is particularly important when one spouse has been out of the workforce or has limited career development due to family responsibilities.

Factors considered include education, work experience, job market conditions, and the availability of retraining opportunities. Expert vocational testimony may be required to establish earning capacity for spouses who have been absent from the workforce.

Direct and Indirect Contributions

New York law recognizes both financial and non-financial contributions to the marriage. DRL § 236(B)(5)(d)(6) specifically includes "the contribution or services of each party as a spouse, parent, wage earner or homemaker, and to the career or career potential of the other party."

This factor acknowledges that homemaking and child-rearing activities contribute economic value to the marriage even though they do not produce direct income. The Court of Appeals in *Price v. Price*, 69 N.Y.2d 8 (1986), emphasized that domestic contributions should be valued equally with financial contributions in appropriate circumstances.

Liquid vs. Non-Liquid Property

The liquidity characteristics of marital assets significantly impact their practical value to divorcing spouses. A spouse who receives illiquid assets such as real estate or business interests may have difficulty accessing funds for immediate needs, while the spouse receiving liquid assets has greater financial flexibility.

Courts may adjust distribution percentages to account for liquidity differences, or may order specific arrangements such as delayed sale of assets or payment schedules that address liquidity concerns.

Tax Consequences

The tax implications of property division can significantly affect the economic value of awards to each spouse. Courts must consider not only immediate tax consequences but also long-term tax planning implications.

For example, retirement account distributions may be subject to different tax treatment depending on the recipient's age and the timing of distributions. Real estate transfers may trigger capital gains consequences that should be factored into the distribution analysis.

Needs of Custodial Parent and Children

When minor children are involved, their needs may influence property distribution decisions. The custodial parent may require additional resources to maintain appropriate housing and provide for children's expenses.

This factor interacts closely with child support and maintenance determinations, requiring coordinated analysis to ensure that children's needs are adequately addressed without creating unfair economic disparities between the parents.

Waste and Dissipation

The statute specifically requires consideration of "the wasteful dissipation of assets by either spouse." This factor addresses situations where one spouse has squandered marital assets through gambling, excessive spending, or transfers to third parties without legitimate purpose.

Courts may adjust distribution to account for dissipated assets by treating them as constructive distributions to the wasteful spouse. In *Mahoney-Buntzman v. Buntzman*, 12 N.Y.3d 415 (2009), the Court of Appeals established that dissipation claims require proof that assets were used for non-marital purposes at a time when the marriage was undergoing an irretrievable breakdown.

B. Judicial Discretion and Case Law Development

New York courts have developed extensive case law interpreting and applying the equitable distribution factors. This jurisprudence provides guidance for practitioners while maintaining judicial flexibility to address unique circumstances.

The Presumption Against Equal Distribution

Unlike community property states, New York has no presumption that marital property should be divided equally. The Court of Appeals has consistently held that equal distribution is not required and may not be appropriate in many cases.

In *Majauskas v. Majauskas*, the court stated: "The concept underlying equitable distribution is that marriage is, among other things, an economic partnership to which both parties contribute, as spouse, parent, wage earner or homemaker. This contribution is not always equal, and the relative contributions of the spouses to the acquisition of the marital property and to the marriage itself are among the factors to be considered in making an equitable distribution."

Burden of Proof and Evidentiary Standards

The party seeking equitable distribution bears the burden of establishing that assets constitute marital property subject to distribution. However, once marital property is established, courts must consider all statutory factors in determining appropriate distribution.

Expert testimony is often required for complex valuations, including business appraisals, pension valuations, and forensic accounting analysis. Courts have broad discretion in weighing expert opinions and may reject expert conclusions that appear unreliable or biased.

Appellate Review Standards

Equitable distribution determinations are subject to limited appellate review. The Appellate Division will only reverse equitable distribution awards that constitute an abuse of discretion or are not supported by the record.

In *Hartog v. Hartog*, 85 N.Y.2d 36 (1995), the Court of Appeals explained that "a disposition of property pursuant to Domestic Relations Law § 236 should not be disturbed unless it can be said to shock one's sense of fairness or to constitute an abuse of discretion."

C. Special Considerations in Equitable Distribution

Professional Licenses and Degrees

New York's recognition of professional licenses as marital property in *O'Brien v. O'Brien* created a framework for valuing and distributing enhanced earning capacity. The court established that licenses and degrees acquired during marriage through the financial support and sacrifice of both spouses constitute marital property.

Valuation of professional licenses requires expert testimony regarding increased earning capacity attributable to the credential. Courts typically use present value analysis of the income differential between licensed and unlicensed practice over the professional's expected career.

Celebrity Goodwill and Career Enhancement

The principle established in *O'Brien* was extended to celebrity goodwill in *Elkus v. Elkus*, 169 A.D.2d 134 (1st Dep't 1991). The court found that a spouse's career as an opera singer was enhanced during marriage through the other spouse's contributions, creating marital property interests in the enhanced earning capacity.

This doctrine has been applied to various forms of career enhancement, including athletic careers, entertainment industry success, and professional reputation development.

Closely Held Business Interests

The treatment of closely held businesses in equitable distribution requires careful analysis of both valuation and distribution methodologies. Courts must determine whether to award the business to one spouse with offsets to the other, or to order sale or ongoing shared ownership.

Factors considered include each spouse's role in the business, the feasibility of continued co-ownership, the availability of liquid assets for offsets, and the impact on business operations and employees.

VI. Community Property in California: Equal Division, With Exceptions

A. The Equal Division Presumption

California's community property system operates on the fundamental principle that marriage creates an economic partnership where both spouses have equal ownership interests in property acquired during marriage. Family Code section 2550 mandates equal division of community property except where the parties agree otherwise or specific statutory exceptions apply.

Historical Development of Equal Division

The equal division requirement represents the evolution of California community property law from its Spanish civil law origins. Early California cases recognized community property principles but allowed courts discretion in division similar to equitable distribution states. The modern equal division requirement was established through legislative amendments and judicial interpretation emphasizing the partnership nature of marriage.

The California Supreme Court in *In re Marriage of Lucas*, 27 Cal. 3d 808 (1980), explained the theoretical foundation: "The Legislature has declared that, except in the circumstances specified in the Family Code, a proceeding for dissolution of marriage shall result in equal division of community property. This rule is based upon the theory that marriage is a partnership to which both spouses bring their individual skills and efforts and that property acquired during marriage through those efforts should be equally divided upon dissolution of the partnership."

Statutory Framework for Equal Division

Family Code section 2550 provides: "Except upon the written agreement of the parties, or on oral stipulation of the parties in open court, or as otherwise provided in this division, in a proceeding for dissolution of marriage or for legal separation of the parties, the court shall, and in a proceeding for nullity of marriage, the court may, divide the community estate of the parties equally."

The mandatory language "shall divide" leaves no room for judicial discretion regarding the basic equal division principle. Courts cannot deviate from equal division based on equitable considerations such as fault, need, or contribution disparities unless specific statutory exceptions apply.

Limited Exceptions to Equal Division

California law recognizes several narrow exceptions to the equal division requirement:

Economic Circumstances Exception (Family Code § 2550(a))

When the net value of community assets assigned to each spouse is less than $5,000, and one spouse cannot be located through reasonable diligence, the court may award all community property to the locatable spouse.

Debt Assignment to Achieve Equality (Family Code § 2551)

Courts may assign community debts unequally to achieve equal division of net community property. This provision allows courts to consider each spouse's ability to pay specific debts while maintaining overall equality in net distribution.

Natural and Artificial Person Distinction (Family Code § 2552)

When one spouse is a natural person and the other is not (such as a corporation), special valuation and division rules may apply.

B. Characterization Disputes and Burden of Proof

Despite the conceptual simplicity of equal division, complex disputes frequently arise over property characterization. The community property presumption established in *In re Marriage of Mix*, 14 Cal. 3d 604 (1975), creates a framework where property acquired during marriage is presumptively community property, but this presumption can be overcome through clear and convincing evidence.

The Mix Presumption and Its Application

In re Marriage of Mix established that "property acquired by either spouse during marriage is presumed to be community property." This presumption operates as both a substantive rule and an evidentiary principle, shifting the burden of proof to the party claiming separate property status.

The presumption applies regardless of how title is held. In *In re Marriage of Brooks and Robinson*, 169 Cal. App. 3d 906 (1985), the court emphasized that "the form in which title is taken is not determinative of the character of property acquired during marriage." Even if property is titled solely in one spouse's name, the community property presumption still applies.

Overcoming the Community Property Presumption

To establish separate property character, the claiming spouse must present clear and convincing evidence of separate origin and maintenance of separate character throughout marriage. This burden is substantial and requires detailed documentation and proof.

In *In re Marriage of Branco*, 47 Cal. 3d 1621 (1989), the California Supreme Court clarified that the clear and convincing evidence standard requires proof that is "so clear as to leave no substantial doubt" and "sufficiently strong to command the unhesitating assent of every reasonable mind."

Tracing Requirements

When separate property has been commingled with community property, the separate property claimant must trace the separate funds through all transactions. California courts apply strict tracing requirements, and the inability to trace results in application of the community property presumption.

In re Marriage of See, 64 Cal. App. 3d 778 (1976), established the framework for tracing analysis, requiring "clear and convincing evidence of the source of funds and a complete accounting of their disposition." The court must be able to follow the separate property through all transactions to maintain its separate character.

C. Complex Property Issues - Moore/Marsden and Watts/Epstein Doctrines

California has developed sophisticated analytical frameworks for addressing situations where separate and community property interests become intertwined. These doctrines provide mathematical formulas for apportioning interests while maintaining the fundamental equal division principle.

Moore/Marsden Doctrine - Community Contributions to Separate Property

The Moore/Marsden doctrine, established in *In re Marriage of Moore*, 28 Cal. 3d 366 (1980), and *In re Marriage of Marsden*, 130 Cal. App. 3d 426 (1982), addresses situations where community funds are used to pay down the principal on separate property real estate.

Under Moore/Marsden analysis, when community funds pay down the principal balance of separate property, the community acquires an interest in the property proportionate to the principal reduction plus any appreciation attributable to that reduction.

The Moore/Marsden formula calculates the community interest as:

Community Interest = (Community Contributions to Principal / Total Purchase Price) × Current Fair Market Value

Application in Complex Scenarios

In re Marriage of Aufmuth, 89 Cal. App. 3d 446 (1979), demonstrated the application of Moore/Marsden principles to refinancing scenarios. When separate property is refinanced with community funds, the community acquires interests based on the community contributions to the new financing.

The doctrine has been extended beyond real estate to other appreciating assets where community contributions enhance separate property value. However, courts must carefully analyze whether contributions actually enhance value versus merely maintaining existing value.

Marsden Refinements and Complications

In re Marriage of Marsden refined the Moore analysis by addressing situations where both separate and community funds contribute to property acquisition and maintenance. The court established that all contributions must be accounted for in determining proportionate interests.

Later cases such as *In re Marriage of Walrath*, 17 Cal. App. 4th 469 (1993), addressed complications arising from negative amortization loans, interest-only payments, and other complex financing arrangements that affect the principal reduction analysis.

Watts/Epstein Doctrine - Use and Occupation of Community Property

The Watts/Epstein doctrine addresses situations where one spouse has exclusive use of community property real estate after separation. *In re Marriage of Watts*, 171 Cal. App. 3d 366 (1985), and *In re Marriage of Epstein*, 24 Cal. 3d 76 (1979), established that exclusive use of community property creates accounting obligations.

Under Watts charges, the spouse in exclusive possession may owe the community (and thus the other spouse) fair rental value for the exclusive use. Conversely, under Epstein credits, the possessing spouse may be entitled to reimbursement for carrying costs such as mortgage payments, taxes, and necessary maintenance.

Calculating Watts Charges and Epstein Credits

Courts must determine fair rental value based on comparable properties and market conditions. The analysis considers the condition of the property, local rental markets, and any restrictions on rentability.

Epstein credits include mortgage principal and interest, property taxes, insurance, and necessary maintenance and repairs. However, credits are limited to the fair rental value of the property, preventing the non-possessing spouse from being charged more than the property's rental benefit.

In re Marriage of Jeffries, 37 Cal. App. 4th 1400 (1995), clarified that Watts/Epstein accounting applies only during the period between separation and trial or settlement, and that courts have discretion to deny charges or credits based on the totality of circumstances.

D. Reimbursement Claims and Characterization Issues

California community property law recognizes various reimbursement claims when one estate (separate or community) benefits another. These claims ensure that the equal division principle operates fairly when assets of different character become intertwined.

Family Code Section 2640 - Separate Property Contributions

Family Code section 2640 provides that contributions of separate property to community property or other spouse's separate property create reimbursement rights without interest. This statute codifies the principle that separate property contributions should be recognized in property division.

The reimbursement claim under section 2640 is limited to the actual contribution amount without interest or appreciation. In *In re Marriage of Walrath*, 17 Cal. App. 4th 469 (1993), the court explained that section 2640 provides "dollar-for-dollar reimbursement" without regard to appreciation or enhancement of the benefited property.

Lucas Presumption for Down Payments

In re Marriage of Lucas, 27 Cal. 3d 808 (1980), established a presumption that down payments on real estate acquired during marriage are gifts to the community unless proven otherwise. This presumption can be overcome by clear and convincing evidence of intent to create a separate property interest or reimbursement right.

The Lucas presumption significantly affects property characterization and requires careful documentation when separate funds are used for community property acquisitions. Written agreements or clear expressions of intent at the time of contribution are essential to preserve reimbursement rights.

Improving Separate Property with Community Labor

When community labor or funds improve separate property, the community may acquire interests in the enhanced value. *In re Marriage of Frick*, 181 Cal. App. 3d 997 (1986), established a framework for analyzing community contributions to separate property improvements.

The analysis requires determination of whether improvements created additional value versus merely maintaining existing value. Courts may require appraisal evidence regarding the property's value before and after improvements to quantify community interests.

E. Business Interests and Professional Practices

Community property division of business interests presents unique challenges requiring specialized valuation expertise and consideration of ongoing operational needs.

Valuation Date Controversies

California's general rule requiring valuation as of trial or the date closest to trial as practicable may create inequities for business interests when one spouse continues to manage the business post-separation. Courts have developed flexibility to use separation date valuations when post-separation management decisions significantly affect value.

In re Marriage of Duncan, 90 Cal. App. 4th 617 (2001), addressed this issue in the context of a spouse who deliberately reduced business value through poor management after separation. The court used separation date valuation to prevent the managing spouse from benefiting from self-created reductions in value.

Professional Goodwill Analysis

California distinguishes between professional goodwill that has value to the practice versus goodwill that is purely personal to the professional. *In re Marriage of Foster*, 42 Cal. App. 3d 577 (1974), established factors for analyzing whether professional goodwill exists as a community asset.

Factors include the nature of the practice, existing patient or client relationships, referral sources, location value, and transferability restrictions. Professional goodwill exists only to the extent it would have value to a purchaser of the practice.

In re Marriage of White, 192 Cal. App. 3d 1022 (1987), refined the analysis by distinguishing between enterprise goodwill (which is community property) and personal goodwill (which is not divisible). The court emphasized that goodwill must be transferable to constitute community property.

VII. Hidden Assets, Fraud, and Non-Disclosure

Both California and New York impose strict disclosure obligations on divorcing spouses and provide significant remedies for failure to comply with these requirements. The duty of disclosure serves both to ensure fair property division and to maintain the integrity of the family law system.

A. California's Disclosure Requirements

Mandatory Disclosure Statutes

California imposes comprehensive disclosure obligations through Family Code sections 2100-2113. These statutes require automatic disclosure of financial information without request from the other party, reflecting the principle that spouses have fiduciary duties to each other during marriage and dissolution proceedings.

Family Code section 2100 establishes the fundamental obligation: "In proceedings for dissolution of marriage or legal separation, each party shall serve on the other party a preliminary declaration of disclosure and a final declaration of disclosure." These disclosures must be served regardless of whether the other party requests them.

Preliminary Declaration of Disclosure

The preliminary declaration of disclosure, governed by Family Code section 2104, must be served within 60 days after the petition is filed or responsive pleading is served. This disclosure includes:

- Schedule of Assets and Debts (Form FL-142)
- Income and Expense Declaration (Form FL-150)
- Copies of tax returns for the two years preceding service
- Copies of statements for all accounts in which the party has an interest

The preliminary disclosure is designed to provide early visibility into the marital estate and facilitate meaningful settlement negotiations.

Final Declaration of Disclosure

Family Code section 2105 requires service of a final declaration of disclosure unless waived by the receiving party. The final disclosure must be current within 90 days and provides updated financial information reflecting changes since the preliminary disclosure.

The final disclosure includes the same basic documents as the preliminary disclosure but must reflect current circumstances. Parties cannot waive their obligation to serve the final disclosure, though they can waive their right to receive it.

Penalties for Non-Disclosure - Family Code Section 2107

Family Code section 2107 establishes severe penalties for failure to comply with disclosure requirements or for material misrepresentations in disclosures. The statute provides that courts "shall" award attorney fees and costs caused by the failure to comply, and "may" award monetary sanctions, including awarding 50% or all of an undisclosed asset to the other party.

In re Marriage of Feldman, 153 Cal. App. 4th 1470 (2007), demonstrated the application of section 2107 sanctions where a spouse failed to disclose significant business interests. The court awarded the entire undisclosed asset to the innocent spouse, emphasizing that the sanctions serve both compensatory and deterrent purposes.

Ongoing Duty of Disclosure

The disclosure duty continues throughout the dissolution proceeding. Family Code section 2105 requires updated disclosures when material changes occur, and parties must supplement their disclosures if they discover previous omissions or errors.

In re Marriage of Steiner and Hosseini, 10 Cal. 4th 1011 (1995), established that the duty of disclosure extends beyond formal discovery to include affirmative obligations to correct material omissions or errors in previous disclosures.

B. New York Discovery and Disclosure Framework

Statement of Net Worth Requirements

New York requires each party in a matrimonial action to file a Statement of Net Worth on prescribed forms. This document provides comprehensive financial disclosure including assets, liabilities, income, and expenses. The Statement of Net Worth serves as the foundation for all financial aspects of the divorce, including property division, support, and attorney fee determinations.

The Statement of Net Worth must be verified, and false statements may subject the party to perjury charges. Courts have broad discretion to impose sanctions for incomplete or inaccurate statements.

Disclosure in Financial Proceedings

Domestic Relations Law section 236(B)(3) specifically addresses disclosure in matrimonial proceedings, requiring each party to provide information about their finances without regard to normal discovery limitations. This provision recognizes that family court proceedings require complete financial transparency to achieve fair results.

The statute provides that "in any proceeding where the court is required to make a determination with respect to the maintenance or support of a spouse or distributive award, each party shall file with the court and serve upon the other party, and update as required by the court or as circumstances change, a sworn statement of net worth."

Discovery Tools and Enforcement

New York courts have broad authority to compel financial disclosure through traditional discovery methods including depositions, document requests, and subpoenas. Courts may also order forensic accounting, lifestyle analysis, and other investigative methods to uncover hidden assets.

Lissner v. Lissner, 190 A.D.2d 406 (2d Dep't 1993), addressed a spouse's attempt to hide assets through complex corporate structures. The court authorized extensive discovery including examination of business records, third-party depositions, and forensic accounting analysis.

Sanctions for Non-Disclosure

New York courts have inherent authority to impose sanctions for discovery violations, including striking pleadings, precluding evidence, drawing adverse inferences, and awarding attorney fees. In extreme cases, courts may hold parties in contempt or enter default judgments.

Finkle v. Finkle, 189 A.D.2d 531 (1st Dep't 1993), involved a spouse who systematically concealed assets through offshore accounts and nominee arrangements. The court imposed comprehensive sanctions including assignment of hidden assets to the innocent spouse and substantial attorney fee awards.

C. Forensic Accounting and Asset Investigation

Lifestyle Analysis

When direct evidence of hidden assets is unavailable, courts may authorize lifestyle analysis to determine whether disclosed income and assets can support the parties' standard of living. Significant disparities between disclosed assets and lifestyle may indicate hidden wealth.

Lifestyle analysis examines expenditure patterns, cash transactions, and unexplained sources of funds for major purchases. Forensic accountants may reconstruct financial activity through bank records, credit card statements, and other financial documents.

Business Entity Investigations

Hidden asset cases frequently involve complex business structures designed to obscure ownership and minimize disclosed value. Forensic investigation may require analysis of multiple entity layers, related-party transactions, and offshore arrangements.

In re Marriage of Boblitt, 104 Cal. App. 3d 609 (1980), involved a spouse who transferred community assets to corporations controlled by relatives. The court authorized piercing of corporate veils and recovery of diverted assets based on findings that the entities were mere alter egos used to defraud the community.

Electronic Discovery and Digital Assets

Modern asset investigation increasingly involves electronic discovery of digital records, cryptocurrency holdings, and online accounts. Courts may authorize forensic examination of computers, smartphones, and cloud storage to identify hidden assets.

The emergence of cryptocurrency and other digital assets presents new challenges for disclosure and valuation. These assets may be held in foreign exchanges, private wallets, or other arrangements that obscure ownership and value.

D. Remedies for Discovery Violations

Asset Forfeiture and Punitive Awards

Both California and New York authorize forfeiture of concealed assets as a remedy for discovery violations. These remedies serve both compensatory and punitive purposes, ensuring that the innocent spouse receives the concealed assets while deterring future violations.

The severity of remedies typically corresponds to the egregious nature of the concealment and its impact on the innocent spouse. Minor omissions may result in attorney fee awards, while systematic concealment may result in forfeiture of entire asset categories.

Reopening of Judgments

When hidden assets are discovered after judgment, both states provide mechanisms for reopening property division orders. However, the standards for reopening are stringent and require proof that the concealment was material and could not have been discovered through reasonable diligence.

In re Marriage of Heggie, 99 Cal. App. 4th 28 (2002), addressed post-judgment discovery of concealed business interests. The court reopened the property division and awarded the concealed assets to the innocent spouse, emphasizing that the duty of disclosure continues beyond entry of judgment.

VIII. Settlement Agreements and Stipulations

The vast majority of divorce cases resolve through negotiated settlement rather than trial, making the law governing settlement agreements crucial to family law practice. Both California and New York have developed comprehensive frameworks for the formation, interpretation, and enforcement of marital settlement agreements.

A. Legal Framework for Settlement Agreements

Contract Law Principles

Marital settlement agreements are governed by general contract law principles, subject to specialized family law considerations. These agreements must satisfy basic contract requirements including offer, acceptance, consideration, and capacity, while also complying with family law specific requirements.

The consideration for marital settlement agreements is typically the mutual promises of the parties and the dissolution of the marital relationship. Courts generally find adequate consideration in the parties' mutual agreement to resolve their disputes and terminate the marriage.

Specialized Family Law Considerations

Family law imposes additional requirements on settlement agreements that distinguish them from ordinary commercial contracts. These include heightened disclosure obligations, court approval requirements for certain provisions, and ongoing court jurisdiction over child-related matters.

In re Marriage of Assemi, 7 Cal. 4th 896 (1994), established that family law settlement agreements must be evaluated under both contract law and specialized family law principles. The court emphasized that the family law context requires additional protections due to the emotional nature of the proceedings and the potential for one party to take advantage of the other.

B. Formation and Validity Requirements

Disclosure Requirements

Valid settlement agreements require full disclosure of assets, debts, income, and other material facts. This requirement exceeds the disclosure obligations in most commercial contexts and reflects the fiduciary duties that spouses owe each other.

California Family Code section 2102 specifically addresses disclosure in settlement agreements, requiring that agreements be accompanied by current income and expense declarations and schedules of assets and debts. The statute provides that agreements entered without proper disclosure may be set aside.

Voluntariness and Absence of Duress

Settlement agreements must be entered into voluntarily without duress, fraud, or undue influence. The emotional and economic pressures inherent in divorce proceedings require careful scrutiny of the circumstances surrounding agreement execution.

In re Marriage of Baltins, 212 Cal. App. 3d 66 (1989), established factors for analyzing duress in marital settlement agreements, including the sophistication of the parties, availability of independent counsel, time pressures, and economic disparities between the parties.

Independent Legal Representation

While not legally required in all circumstances, independent legal representation for both parties significantly strengthens the enforceability of settlement agreements. Courts view agreements negotiated between represented parties as presumptively fair and enforceable.

When parties are not represented, courts may require additional safeguards such as cooling-off periods, detailed explanations of rights being waived, and court review of the agreement's fairness.

C. Scope and Content of Settlement Agreements

Property Division Provisions

Settlement agreements typically include comprehensive property division provisions that identify all marital assets and debts and specify their distribution. These provisions should include detailed descriptions of assets, valuation methods, transfer procedures, and timing requirements.

Effective property division clauses address not only current assets but also contingent interests such as pending legal claims, potential inheritances, and unvested benefits. The agreement should specify how future discoveries of assets will be handled and whether additional disclosure obligations exist.

Spousal Support Provisions

Settlement agreements may include spousal support provisions that modify or waive statutory support rights. These provisions must comply with applicable legal requirements and cannot be unconscionable or contrary to public policy.

In California, spousal support provisions in settlement agreements are subject to ongoing court jurisdiction unless specifically waived. The agreement may establish the amount and duration of support or may waive support entirely if the waiver is knowing and voluntary.

Child-Related Provisions

Settlement agreements commonly include provisions regarding child custody, visitation, and support. However, these provisions remain subject to court oversight and modification based on the best interests of the children.

Courts cannot be bound by parental agreements regarding child support that deviate significantly from statutory guidelines without specific findings that the agreed support serves the children's best interests.

D. Integration into Divorce Judgments

Incorporation vs. Merger

Settlement agreements may be either incorporated into the divorce judgment or merged into the judgment, with significant legal consequences flowing from this distinction. Incorporated agreements retain their character as contracts while also becoming court orders, allowing enforcement through both contract remedies and contempt proceedings.

Merged agreements become part of the court's judgment and lose their independent contractual character. Merged agreements can only be modified through court proceedings, while incorporated agreements may be modifiable through contract principles.

Steiner v. Steiner, 158 A.D.2d 423 (2d Dep't 1990), explained the New York approach to incorporation versus merger, emphasizing that the parties' intent and the specific language used in the judgment determine whether the agreement is incorporated or merged.

Court Review and Approval

While courts generally defer to parties' settlement agreements, they retain authority to review agreements for basic fairness and compliance with legal requirements. This review is particularly intensive when children are involved or when one party appears to lack sophistication or representation.

Courts may reject settlement agreements that are unconscionable, that fail to comply with disclosure requirements, or that contain provisions contrary to public policy. However, the standard for rejecting agreements between represented parties is high.

E. Modification and Enforcement

Contractual Modification Principles

Incorporated settlement agreements may be modified through contract principles if the original agreement permits modification or if both parties consent to changes. However, family law considerations may limit the availability of contractual modifications.

Property division provisions are generally not modifiable unless the agreement specifically provides for modification or unless extraordinary circumstances such as fraud or mistake exist. Support provisions may be more readily modifiable based on changed circumstances.

Court Modification Authority

Courts retain continuing jurisdiction to modify settlement agreements in certain circumstances, particularly regarding child-related provisions and spousal support. However, the scope of modification authority depends on the specific terms of the agreement and applicable statutory provisions.

In re Marriage of Moschetta, 30 Cal. App. 4th 1742 (1994), addressed the court's authority to modify property division provisions in settlement agreements. The court held that property division provisions are generally final and not subject to modification unless the agreement specifically provides otherwise or extraordinary circumstances exist.

Enforcement Remedies

Settlement agreements incorporated into divorce judgments may be enforced through multiple remedies including contempt proceedings, wage garnishment, asset seizure, and contract damages. The availability of specific remedies depends on the nature of the violation and the terms of the agreement.

Enforcement proceedings must comply with both contract law and family law principles. Courts have broad discretion to fashion appropriate remedies that serve the interests of justice while protecting both parties' rights.

IX. Tax and Financial Considerations

Property division in divorce proceedings carries significant tax implications that can substantially affect the economic value of settlement agreements and court orders. Both immediate and long-term tax consequences must be carefully analyzed to ensure fair distribution and to avoid unintended adverse results.

A. Federal Tax Framework for Property Transfers

Internal Revenue Code Section 1041

Internal Revenue Code section 1041 provides that transfers of property between spouses or former spouses incident to divorce are generally tax-free events. This provision allows property division without immediate tax consequences, but it also transfers the tax basis and potential tax liability to the receiving spouse.

Section 1041 applies to transfers made within one year of divorce or transfers made pursuant to a divorce decree at any time. The transferred property retains its original tax basis in the hands of the receiving spouse, creating potential future tax consequences when the property is subsequently sold or disposed of.

Tax Basis Considerations

The carryover basis rule under section 1041 means that assets with low tax basis carry significant built-in tax liability that must be considered in property division negotiations. Assets with high basis relative to fair market value are more valuable than assets with low basis, all else being equal.

For example, stock purchased for $10,000 that is now worth $100,000 has a built-in capital gains liability of approximately $18,000 (assuming a 20% capital gains rate). A spouse receiving this stock effectively receives property worth $82,000 after considering the tax liability.

Recognition vs. Non-Recognition Events

Property division itself does not trigger tax recognition under section 1041, but subsequent disposition of transferred property may create taxable events. The timing and nature of these events can significantly impact the after-tax value of property settlements.

Real estate transfers may trigger property tax reassessments in some jurisdictions, creating additional ongoing tax obligations. Some states provide exemptions for transfers incident to divorce, but the availability and scope of these exemptions varies significantly.

B. Retirement Account Considerations

Qualified Domestic Relations Orders (QDROs)

Division of qualified retirement plans requires Qualified Domestic Relations Orders (QDROs) that comply with the Employee Retirement Income Security Act (ERISA). Properly prepared QDROs allow tax-free transfer of retirement benefits between former spouses while preserving the tax-deferred status of the accounts.

QDRO requirements include specific language regarding the alternate payee's rights, the amount or percentage of benefits to be paid, the number of payments or time period covered, and identification of each plan subject to the order. Failure to comply with QDRO requirements can result in immediate taxation and penalties.

Early Distribution Penalties

QDRO distributions are exempt from the 10% early distribution penalty that normally applies to retirement account distributions before age 59½.

However, this exemption applies only to the initial transfer pursuant to the QDRO, not to subsequent distributions taken by the recipient.

The alternate payee can roll over QDRO distributions to their own retirement accounts to maintain tax-deferred status, or can take immediate distributions without the early withdrawal penalty. This flexibility allows customized solutions based on each party's financial needs and tax situation.

Traditional vs. Roth Account Distinctions

Traditional retirement accounts contain pre-tax contributions that will be subject to ordinary income tax upon distribution, while Roth accounts contain after-tax contributions that can be distributed tax-free. These different tax characteristics must be considered in determining fair division.

A traditional IRA worth $100,000 has a significantly different after-tax value than a Roth IRA worth $100,000, depending on the recipient's tax bracket and the timing of distributions. Courts may adjust distribution percentages to account for these different tax characteristics.

C. Real Estate Tax Issues

Principal Residence Exclusion

The sale of a principal residence may qualify for exclusion of up to $250,000 ($500,000 for married couples filing jointly) of capital gains under Internal Revenue Code section 121. This exclusion requires ownership and use of the property as a principal residence for at least two of the five years preceding sale.

Divorce can complicate the application of the principal residence exclusion when one spouse continues to occupy the residence while the other spouse retains ownership interests. Special rules allow the non-occupying spouse to "tack" the occupying spouse's use to satisfy the use requirement.

Depreciation Recapture

Real estate that has been used for rental or business purposes may be subject to depreciation recapture upon sale, creating additional tax liability beyond capital gains. This recapture is taxed at ordinary income rates up to 25%, making it particularly costly.

Property division agreements should address how depreciation recapture liability will be allocated between the parties, particularly when one spouse receives the property but both spouses benefited from the depreciation deductions during marriage.

Like-Kind Exchanges

Internal Revenue Code section 1031 allows deferral of capital gains through like-kind exchanges of investment or business property. These exchanges can be valuable tools in property division when parties hold multiple real estate investments.

However, like-kind exchanges are complex transactions with strict timing and procedural requirements. The use of exchanges in divorce proceedings requires careful coordination between family law counsel and tax advisors.

D. Business Interest Tax Considerations

Buy-Sell Agreement Implications

Existing buy-sell agreements in closely held businesses may affect the tax consequences of property division. These agreements may restrict transfer options, establish valuation methodologies, or create tax election requirements that impact divorce settlements.

Buy-sell agreements may also contain provisions that are triggered by divorce, such as mandatory sale provisions or rights of first refusal. These provisions must be analyzed in conjunction with property division negotiations to avoid conflicts and ensure compliance.

S Corporation and Partnership Considerations

Transfers of interests in S corporations and partnerships may have special tax implications due to the pass-through nature of these entities. S corporation stock transfers must comply with shareholder eligibility requirements to avoid involuntary termination of the S election.

Partnership interest transfers may trigger income recognition under various partnership tax provisions, particularly when the partnership has debt or when built-in gains exist. These consequences require careful analysis and may necessitate special allocation provisions in the divorce settlement.

Installment Sale Treatment

When business interests are sold as part of property division, installment sale treatment under Internal Revenue Code section 453 may be available to spread the tax consequences over multiple years. This can be particularly valuable when large capital gains are involved.

However, installment sale treatment is not available for all types of property and may be lost if the receiving spouse subsequently transfers the property. The decision to elect installment treatment requires analysis of both spouses' tax situations and long-term financial plans.

E. Tax Planning Strategies

Income Shifting Opportunities

Property division creates opportunities for income shifting between spouses who may be in different tax brackets post-divorce. Income-producing assets can be allocated to the spouse in the lower tax bracket to minimize overall family tax liability.

However, income shifting strategies must be balanced against other considerations such as liquidity needs, risk tolerance, and the desire for clean asset separation. Tax considerations alone should not drive property division decisions.

Timing Considerations

The timing of property transfers and asset sales can significantly impact tax consequences. Transfers completed before year-end may allow optimal use of capital loss carryforwards, charitable deductions, and other tax attributes.

Similarly, the timing of divorce finalization affects filing status for the tax year, with potential implications for tax rates, deduction limitations, and credit eligibility. Strategic timing can optimize tax outcomes for both parties.

Coordination with Support Payments

The deductibility of spousal support payments under pre-2019 law, and the non-deductibility under current law for new agreements, affects the after-tax cost and benefit of support arrangements. Property division can be structured to optimize the overall tax consequences of both property transfers and support payments.

For example, larger property transfers combined with lower support payments may be more tax-efficient than smaller property transfers with higher support payments, depending on the parties' respective tax situations.

X. Conclusion

Property division represents one of the most complex and consequential aspects of family law practice, requiring mastery of legal doctrine, valuation principles, tax considerations, and practical negotiation skills. The fundamental differences between New York's equitable distribution system and California's community property approach reflect competing philosophies about marriage, individual rights, and economic justice that continue to evolve through legislative amendments and judicial interpretation.

The Evolution of Property Division Law

Both jurisdictions have moved significantly beyond their historical foundations to address the realities of modern marriage and divorce. New York's adoption of equitable distribution in 1980 marked a dramatic departure from common law property concepts that left many economically dependent spouses without adequate protection. California's refinement of community property principles through cases such as Moore/Marsden and the development of sophisticated reimbursement doctrines demonstrates the ongoing evolution of community property law to address complex modern financial arrangements.

The recognition of professional licenses, celebrity goodwill, and enhanced earning capacity as marital property in New York, and the development of complex apportionment schemes in California, illustrate how family law has adapted to economic realities that were unforeseeable when these legal frameworks were first established. Similarly, the treatment of stock options, deferred compensation, and other modern compensation arrangements requires ongoing judicial and legislative attention to ensure fair outcomes.

Practical Implications for Family Law Practice

Effective property division advocacy requires integration of multiple disciplines including family law, tax law, valuation principles, and financial planning. Practitioners must be able to identify and characterize all marital assets and debts, coordinate with valuation experts and forensic accountants, and structure settlements that achieve clients' objectives while minimizing adverse tax consequences.

The complexity of modern financial arrangements, including international assets, cryptocurrency holdings, and complex business structures, requires practitioners to stay current with developing law and to build networks of specialized experts who can assist with complex cases. The increasing use of technology in asset investigation and the emergence of new forms of property and financial arrangements will continue to challenge traditional approaches to property division.

The Importance of Full Disclosure and Professional Ethics

Both California and New York have strengthened disclosure requirements and penalties for non-compliance, reflecting the fundamental principle that fair property division requires complete information about the marital estate. The severe penalties available for discovery violations, including asset forfeiture and substantial attorney fee awards, emphasize the critical importance of comprehensive disclosure and thorough investigation.

Practitioners have ethical obligations to ensure that their clients comply fully with disclosure requirements and to conduct reasonable investigation to identify hidden assets when circumstances suggest concealment. The balance between zealous advocacy and professional responsibility requires careful attention to both legal and ethical considerations.

Settlement vs. Litigation Considerations

The vast majority of property division cases resolve through negotiated settlement, making settlement negotiation skills essential to effective practice. However, the threat of trial and the ability to present complex financial evidence effectively at trial remain crucial elements of successful settlement negotiations.

The choice between settlement and trial involves consideration of multiple factors including the complexity of the marital estate, the degree of cooperation between the parties, the availability of liquid assets for attorney fees, and the tolerance for uncertainty and delay. In high-conflict cases or cases involving complex valuation issues, early case management and coordinated expert retention may be essential to achieving fair outcomes.

Future Developments and Challenges

Property division law will continue to evolve in response to changing social and economic conditions. The increasing prevalence of non-traditional relationships, the growth of the gig economy and alternative compensation arrangements, and the emergence of new forms of property and financial instruments will require ongoing legal development.

Climate change and environmental considerations may increasingly affect property values and business operations, requiring new approaches to valuation and risk assessment. Similarly, demographic changes including longer life expectancies and changing retirement patterns may affect the treatment of retirement benefits and long-term financial planning in divorce proceedings.

The intersection of technology and family law will continue to create new challenges and opportunities. Artificial intelligence and machine learning may enhance forensic accounting capabilities and asset discovery methods, while blockchain technology and decentralized finance arrangements may complicate traditional approaches to property identification and valuation.

Conclusion and Key Takeaways for Practitioners

Successful property division advocacy requires thorough preparation, attention to detail, and coordination among multiple professionals. Key principles include:

1. **Early and comprehensive case assessment** - Identify all assets, debts, and valuation issues at the outset to develop effective case strategy and budget appropriately for expert assistance.

2. **Compliance with disclosure obligations** - Ensure complete and accurate disclosure while conducting thorough investigation to identify potential hidden assets or undisclosed interests.

3. **Strategic use of experts** - Coordinate with appraisers, forensic accountants, tax professionals, and other experts to build compelling evidence and develop creative solutions.

4. **Tax-efficient structuring** - Consider immediate and long-term tax consequences in all settlement negotiations and court proceedings to maximize after-tax value for clients.

5. **Documentation and implementation** - Prepare comprehensive settlement agreements and court orders that clearly specify transfer procedures, timing requirements, and ongoing obligations.

The complexity of modern property division requires practitioners to serve as both legal advocates and financial advisors, helping clients navigate not only the legal process but also the long-term financial implications of property division decisions. The stakes involved - often representing the majority of clients' lifetime wealth accumulation - demand the highest levels of professional competence and ethical responsibility.

In the next chapter, we turn to spousal support, examining how courts in New York and California determine eligibility, amount, and duration of support obligations, and how support determinations interact with property division to achieve overall fairness in divorce proceedings.

Case Citations and References

Arvantides v. Arvantides, 64 N.Y.2d 147 (1984)

DeLorean v. DeLorean, 211 A.D.2d 758 (2d Dep't 1995)

Dugan v. Dugan, 92 A.D.2d 422 (4th Dep't 1983)

Elkus v. Elkus, 169 A.D.2d 134 (1st Dep't 1991)

Finkle v. Finkle, 189 A.D.2d 531 (1st Dep't 1993)

Hartog v. Hartog, 85 N.Y.2d 36 (1995)

Inniss v. Inniss, 8 A.D.3d 163 (1st Dep't 2004)

Lissner v. Lissner, 190 A.D.2d 406 (2d Dep't 1993)

Mahoney-Buntzman v. Buntzman, 12 N.Y.3d 415 (2009)

Majauskas v. Majauskas, 61 N.Y.2d 481 (1984)

McSparron v. McSparron, 87 N.Y.2d 275 (1995)

O'Brien v. O'Brien, 66 N.Y.2d 576 (1985)

Price v. Price, 69 N.Y.2d 8 (1986)

Steiner v. Steiner, 158 A.D.2d 423 (2d Dep't 1990)

Wegman v. Wegman, 123 A.D.2d 220 (2d Dep't 1986)

In re Marriage of Assemi, 7 Cal. 4th 896 (1994)

In re Marriage of Aufmuth, 89 Cal. App. 3d 446 (1979)

In re Marriage of Baltins, 212 Cal. App. 3d 66 (1989)

In re Marriage of Boblitt, 104 Cal. App. 3d 609 (1980)

In re Marriage of Branco, 47 Cal. 3d 1621 (1989)

In re Marriage of Brooks and Robinson, 169 Cal. App. 3d 906 (1985)

In re Marriage of Buol, 39 Cal. 3d 751 (1985)

In re Marriage of Duncan, 90 Cal. App. 4th 617 (2001)

In re Marriage of Epstein, 24 Cal. 3d 76 (1979)

In re Marriage of Feldman, 153 Cal. App. 4th 1470 (2007)

In re Marriage of Foster, 42 Cal. App. 3d 577 (1974)

In re Marriage of Frick, 181 Cal. App. 3d 997 (1986)

In re Marriage of Heggie, 99 Cal. App. 4th 28 (2002)

In re Marriage of Hug, 154 Cal. App. 3d 780 (1984)

In re Marriage of Jeffries, 37 Cal. App. 4th 1400 (1995)

In re Marriage of Lucas, 27 Cal. 3d 808 (1980)

In re Marriage of Marsden, 130 Cal. App. 3d 426 (1982)

In re Marriage of Mix, 14 Cal. 3d 604 (1975)

In re Marriage of Moore, 28 Cal. 3d 366 (1980)

In re Marriage of Moschetta, 30 Cal. App. 4th 1742 (1994)

In re Marriage of See, 64 Cal. App. 3d 778 (1976)

In re Marriage of Steiner and Hosseini, 10 Cal. 4th 1011 (1995)

In re Marriage of Walrath, 17 Cal. App. 4th 469 (1993)

In re Marriage of Watts, 171 Cal. App. 3d 366 (1985)

In re Marriage of White, 192 Cal. App. 3d 1022 (1987)

Pereira v. Pereira, 156 Cal. 648 (1909)

Van Camp v. Van Camp, 53 Cal. App. 17 (1921)

Statutory References

California

- Family Code §§ 760, 770, 2100-2113, 2550-2556, 2640, 852, 910

New York

- Domestic Relations Law § 236(B)

Federal

- Internal Revenue Code §§ 121, 453, 1031, 1041
- Employee Retirement Income Security Act (ERISA)

9

Spousal Support (Alimony) Determinations

I. Sustaining Stability After Separation

Spousal support - also known as alimony or maintenance - is a key component of family law that ensures a fair financial transition for one spouse following separation or divorce. The concept of spousal support has evolved significantly from its historical origins in fault-based divorce systems to modern no-fault approaches that emphasize economic need and fairness rather than punishment or reward.

While each state provides mechanisms to determine support, New York and California differ significantly in their formulas, discretionary standards, and durational guidelines. California's approach emphasizes judicial discretion in permanent support determinations while providing formulaic guidance for temporary support. New York, conversely, has adopted presumptive guidelines for both temporary and post-divorce maintenance following significant 2015 reforms.

The determination of spousal support involves complex considerations of economics, equity, and public policy. Courts must balance the competing interests of providing adequate support to a dependent spouse while avoiding creating permanent dependency or imposing unreasonable burdens on the supporting spouse. This chapter unpacks the legal basis, calculation methods, and modification rules for spousal support in both jurisdictions, offering guidance for navigating this often-contentious issue.

II. Historical Development and Purpose of Spousal Support

Historical Context

Spousal support has its roots in the common law doctrine of coverture, under which a married woman's legal identity was subsumed into that of her husband. Upon divorce, the husband retained a duty to support his former wife, reflecting both the economic reality that women had limited earning capacity and the legal principle that marriage created permanent obligations.

The transition to no-fault divorce in the 1970s fundamentally altered the theoretical basis for spousal support. Rather than viewing support as compensation for a husband's wrongdoing, modern law conceptualizes spousal support as addressing economic imbalances created by marriage and divorce. This shift is reflected in landmark cases such as *In re Marriage of Terry*, 80 Cal. App. 3d 921 (1978), which established that spousal support should facilitate the transition to post-divorce independence rather than maintain permanent dependency.

Contemporary Purpose

Modern spousal support is intended to accomplish several objectives:

Address disparities in income and earning capacity. Marriage often involves career sacrifices by one spouse to support the other's advancement or to manage domestic responsibilities. Spousal support recognizes these contributions and their impact on earning capacity.

Allow the lower-earning spouse to maintain a standard of living reasonably comparable to the marital lifestyle. The California Supreme Court in *In re Marriage of Kerr*, 77 Cal. App. 4th 87 (1999), emphasized that spousal support should enable both parties to maintain lifestyles as close as possible to the marital standard of living, subject to the limitations of available income.

Provide time and resources for retraining, education, or workforce re-entry. Rehabilitative support, as recognized in *Gavron v. Gavron*, 203 Cal. App. 3d 705 (1988), serves to facilitate a spouse's return to economic self-sufficiency through education or skills development.

Prevent immediate economic hardship following separation. The New York Court of Appeals in *Hartog v. Hartog*, 85 N.Y.2d 36 (1995), recognized that spousal support serves an essential safety net function, preventing destitution while longer-term arrangements are developed.

Support is not meant to be punitive, as established in *Uniform Marriage and Divorce* Act commentary and reinforced by courts in both jurisdictions. It reflects a partnership model of marriage and the economic interdependence it creates, recognizing that marital assets include not only tangible property but also enhanced earning capacity and career opportunities.

III. Types of Spousal Support

Temporary Support (Pendente Lite)

Temporary spousal support, also known as pendente lite support, provides financial assistance during the pendency of divorce proceedings. This form of support serves to maintain the status quo and prevent economic hardship while the parties navigate the divorce process.

In California, temporary support is governed by Family Code Section 3600 and is typically calculated using local court formulas. The California Supreme Court in *In re Marriage of Cheriton*, 92 Cal. App. 4th 269 (2001), emphasized that temporary support should be sufficient to maintain the parties' standard of living during litigation, even if this results in support levels that exceed what might be awarded permanently.

New York's approach to temporary maintenance was substantially reformed in 2015 with the adoption of presumptive guidelines under Domestic Relations Law Section 236(B)(5-a). The *Domestic Relations Law* now provides specific formulas for calculating temporary maintenance, reducing judicial discretion and promoting consistency across courts.

Rehabilitative Support

Rehabilitative support provides financial assistance for a specific period to enable a spouse to acquire education, training, or work experience necessary to become self-supporting. This form of support reflects the policy preference for facilitating independence rather than creating permanent dependency.

The California Court of Appeal in *In re Marriage of Morrison*, 20 Cal. 3d 437 (1978), established that rehabilitative support should be sufficient in amount and duration to enable the recipient to develop skills necessary for appropriate employment. The court emphasized that the goal is not merely to provide subsistence but to enable the recipient to achieve a reasonable standard of living through their own efforts.

New York courts have similarly embraced rehabilitative support, as demonstrated in *Hartog v. Hartog*, 85 N.Y.2d 36 (1995), where the Court of Appeals recognized that support should facilitate the transition to self-sufficiency while acknowledging that complete independence may not always be achievable.

Permanent Support

Permanent spousal support, despite its name, does not necessarily continue indefinitely. Rather, it refers to support awarded as part of the final divorce judgment, subject to modification or termination based on changed circumstances.

In California, permanent support is governed by Family Code Section 4320, which provides a comprehensive list of factors for judicial consideration. The California Supreme Court in *In re Marriage of Kerr*, 77 Cal. App. 4th 87 (1999), emphasized that permanent support determinations require careful balancing of all statutory factors, with no single factor being determinative.

New York's approach to post-divorce maintenance was reformed in 2015 to include presumptive guidelines, while retaining judicial discretion to deviate based on statutory factors. The *Domestic Relations Law* Section 236(B)(6) provides both formula-based calculations and a comprehensive list of factors for judicial consideration.

Reimbursement Support

Reimbursement support compensates a spouse for contributions to the other spouse's education, training, or career advancement. This form of support recognizes that investments in human capital during marriage should be considered marital assets subject to division.

The California Court of Appeal in *In re Marriage of Sullivan*, 37 Cal. 3d 762 (1984), established that contributions to a spouse's professional education create a reimbursement right, even if the degree itself is not considered divisible property. The court emphasized that the contributing spouse has a right to reimbursement for direct expenses and opportunity costs.

New York courts have adopted a similar approach, as demonstrated in *O'Brien v. O'Brien*, 66 N.Y.2d 576 (1985), where the Court of Appeals recognized professional licenses as marital property subject to equitable distribution. While subsequent decisions have limited this approach, reimbursement support remains available to address educational contributions.

IV. Spousal Support in California

Legal Authority and Framework

California spousal support law is governed primarily by Family Code Sections 4320-4339, which establish a comprehensive framework for support determinations. The statutory scheme reflects California's commitment to judicial discretion in permanent support awards while providing more structured approaches for temporary support.

The California Supreme Court in *In re Marriage of Cheriton*, 92 Cal. App. 4th 269 (2001), emphasized that the Family Code Section 4320 factors are not exhaustive and that courts must consider all relevant circumstances in making support determinations. This broad discretionary authority reflects California's preference for individualized determinations rather than mechanical formulas.

Temporary Spousal Support

California's approach to temporary spousal support emphasizes speed and consistency during the litigation process. Most California counties have adopted local formulas to calculate temporary support, with variations reflecting local economic conditions and judicial preferences.

Common Formula Applications:

The Santa Clara County formula, widely adopted throughout Northern California, calculates temporary support as 40% of the payor's net income minus 50% of the recipient's net income. This formula is adjusted when child support is also being paid, typically reducing spousal support by the amount of child support to avoid double-counting support obligations.

The Los Angeles County formula employs a similar approach but with different percentages, reflecting the higher cost of living in Los Angeles County. Under this formula, temporary support equals 40% of the payor's net income minus 40% of the recipient's net income.

Judicial Discretion in Temporary Support:

While formulas provide guidance, California courts retain discretion to deviate from formulaic calculations based on specific circumstances. In *In re Marriage of Schulze*, 60 Cal. App. 4th 519 (1997), the Court of Appeal emphasized that temporary support formulas are tools to assist judicial decision-making but do not eliminate the court's obligation to consider individual circumstances.

Factors that may justify deviation from formulaic calculations include:

- Extraordinary expenses or needs of either party
- Significant fluctuations in income
- Tax consequences of support payments
- Availability of other resources or support
- Temporary nature of income changes

Duration of Temporary Support:

Temporary support continues until the court makes a permanent support order or the divorce is finalized. In complex cases where litigation extends over several years, courts may modify temporary support based on changed circumstances, as established in *In re Marriage of Bower*, 5 Cal. App. 4th 1623 (1992).

Post-Judgment (Long-Term) Support

California's approach to permanent spousal support emphasizes judicial discretion and individualized determinations based on the comprehensive factors set forth in Family Code Section 4320. Unlike temporary support, permanent support calculations involve no presumptive formulas, requiring courts to weigh multiple factors in fashioning appropriate awards.

Family Code Section 4320 Factors:

Length of Marriage: The duration of marriage is a critical factor in determining both the amount and duration of support. The California Court of Appeal in *In re Marriage of Hoffmeister*, 191 Cal. App. 3d 351 (1987), established that longer marriages generally justify longer support periods, reflecting the greater economic interdependence that develops over time.

Standard of Living During Marriage: Courts must consider the standard of living established during marriage, as established in *In re Marriage of Smith*, 79 Cal. App. 4th 1018 (2000). This factor requires detailed analysis of the parties' lifestyle, including housing, travel, entertainment, and other discretionary expenses.

Earning Capacity vs. Actual Income: Family Code Section 4320(a)(1) requires courts to consider each party's earning capacity rather than merely current income. In *In re Marriage of Simpson*, 4 Cal. 4th 225 (1992), the California Supreme Court emphasized that courts must examine whether a party is voluntarily unemployed or underemployed.

The earning capacity analysis involves consideration of:

- Education and training
- Work experience and skills
- Periods of unemployment due to domestic responsibilities
- Physical and mental health limitations
- Available job opportunities in the relevant geographic area
- Age and likelihood of acquiring new skills

Age and Health Considerations: The age and health of both parties significantly impact support determinations. In *In re Marriage of Olson*, 14 Cal. App. 4th 1, (1993), the Court of Appeal recognized that older recipients may have limited ability to achieve self-sufficiency, justifying longer support periods.

Health considerations include both physical and mental health conditions that affect earning capacity. Courts must consider not only current health status but also the likelihood of future health problems and their impact on employability.

Contributions to Education and Career: Family Code Section 4320(b)(1) requires consideration of the extent to which each party contributed to the education, training, career position, or license of the other party. This factor recognizes that spousal contributions to career advancement create ongoing economic benefits that should be shared.

In *In re Marriage of Sullivan*, 37 Cal. 3d 762 (1984), the California Supreme Court established that direct financial contributions to professional education create reimbursement rights, while indirect contributions through domestic support may justify ongoing spousal support.

History of Domestic Violence: Family Code Section 4320(i) specifically requires courts to consider documented evidence of domestic violence. The California Court of Appeal in *In re Marriage of Cauley*, 138 Cal. App. 4th 1100 (2006), emphasized that domestic violence may justify both higher support amounts and longer duration awards.

Tax Consequences: Courts must consider the tax consequences of support awards to both parties. Following the 2019 federal tax law changes eliminating the deductibility of spousal support, this factor has become less significant, but state tax consequences may still be relevant.

Hardship Considerations: Courts may consider the hardship that the payment or denial of support would create for either party. This factor provides flexibility to address unusual circumstances that may not be captured by other statutory factors.

Duration of Support in California

California's approach to support duration varies significantly based on the length of marriage, with different presumptions applying to short-term and long-term marriages.

Short-Term Marriages (Less than 10 Years):

For marriages of short duration, California Family Code Section 4336 establishes a rebuttable presumption that support should not exceed half the length of the marriage. This presumption, often called the "Gavron rule" after *Gavron v. Gavron*, 203 Cal. App. 3d 705 (1988), reflects the policy preference for facilitating independence rather than creating permanent dependency.

The presumption may be rebutted by evidence that the supported party cannot become self-supporting within the presumptive period due to:

- Age or health limitations
- Lack of marketable skills
- Responsibility for young children
- Other circumstances that prevent self-sufficiency

Long-Term Marriages (10 Years or More):

For marriages of long duration, Family Code Section 4336 provides that courts retain jurisdiction indefinitely unless the parties agree otherwise. This does not mean that support will necessarily continue indefinitely, but rather that the court maintains the authority to modify or terminate support based on changed circumstances.

The California Court of Appeal in *In re Marriage of Reynolds*, 63 Cal. App. 4th 1373 (1998), emphasized that even in long-term marriages, the goal remains eventual self-sufficiency where possible. Courts may establish step-down provisions or other mechanisms to encourage independence while recognizing that complete self-sufficiency may not be achievable.

Modification and Termination:

Support orders may be modified based on material changes in circumstances, as established in *In re Marriage of Dietz*, 17 Cal. 3d 14 (1976). Common grounds for modification include:

- Significant changes in income of either party
- Changes in health status
- Changes in employment status
- Cohabitation by the supported party
- Retirement of the supporting party

Support automatically terminates upon the death of either party or the remarriage of the supported party, as provided in Family Code Section 4337.

V. Spousal Maintenance in New York

Legal Authority and 2015 Reform

New York spousal maintenance law underwent significant reform in 2015 with the adoption of presumptive guidelines for both temporary and post-divorce maintenance. These reforms, codified in Domestic Relations Law Section 236(B), were designed to promote consistency and predictability in maintenance awards while preserving judicial discretion to address individual circumstances.

The reforms responded to widespread criticism of the prior system, which provided minimal guidance for maintenance determinations and resulted in significant inconsistency between courts and judges. The *Matrimonial Commission Report* of 2013 documented these disparities and recommended the adoption of presumptive guidelines similar to those used for child support.

Temporary Maintenance Formula

New York's temporary maintenance guidelines apply to cases where the combined parental income does not exceed the current cap, which is adjusted periodically. As of 2023, the cap is $203,000, meaning that income above this amount is not subject to the formulaic calculation.

Formula for Cases With Child Support:

When child support is also being paid, temporary maintenance is calculated as: 20% of the payor's income minus 25% of the recipient's income

The result cannot exceed 40% of the parties' combined income, providing a ceiling to prevent excessive awards.

Formula for Cases Without Child Support:

When no child support is being paid, temporary maintenance is calculated as: 30% of the payor's income minus 20% of the recipient's income

Again, the result cannot exceed 40% of the parties' combined income.

Application and Judicial Discretion:

While the guidelines create presumptive amounts, courts retain discretion to deviate based on specific circumstances. Domestic Relations Law Section 236(B)(5-a)(e) lists factors that may justify deviation, including:

- The age and health of the parties
- The present and future earning capacity of the parties
- The need for one party to incur education or training expenses
- The presence and needs of children
- The tax consequences of the award
- The standard of living of the parties during the marriage
- The wasteful dissipation of marital property
- The transfer or encumbrance of marital property
- The existence and duration of a pre-marital joint household
- Acts of domestic violence
- The availability and cost of medical insurance
- The care of children or stepchildren that inhibits earning capacity
- The inability of one party to obtain meaningful employment
- The need to pay for exceptional additional expenses for children
- Any other factor the court finds just and proper

Post-Divorce Maintenance

New York's post-divorce maintenance guidelines follow similar formulas to temporary maintenance but require additional consideration of statutory factors and duration guidelines.

Calculation Method:

The post-divorce maintenance calculation uses the same formulas as temporary maintenance:

- With child support: 20% of payor's income minus 25% of recipient's income

- Without child support: 30% of payor's income minus 20% of recipient's income

The 40% ceiling also applies to post-divorce maintenance.

Statutory Factors for Deviation:

Courts must consider the same factors listed for temporary maintenance, with particular attention to:

Present and Future Earning Capacity: Courts must examine not only current income but also the potential for future income growth or decline. The New York Court of Appeals in *Hartog v. Hartog*, 85 N.Y.2d 36 (1995), emphasized that earning capacity analysis requires consideration of education, skills, work experience, and available employment opportunities.

Standard of Living During Marriage: This factor requires detailed analysis of the parties' lifestyle during marriage, including housing costs, travel, entertainment, and other expenses. Courts must determine whether the calculated maintenance amount enables both parties to maintain lifestyles reasonably comparable to the marital standard of living.

Tax Consequences: While federal tax consequences have been eliminated for new orders, state tax implications may still be relevant. Courts must consider the after-tax impact of maintenance awards on both parties.

Wasteful Dissipation of Assets: Evidence that one party has wasted marital assets may justify higher maintenance awards to compensate the other party. This factor requires proof that the dissipation was intentional and detrimental to the marital estate.

Domestic Violence: Documented evidence of domestic violence may justify deviation from the guidelines, typically resulting in higher awards to address the economic impact of abuse.

Duration Guidelines

New York's 2015 reforms included advisory duration guidelines based on the length of marriage:

Marriages of 0-15 years: 15-30% of the length of the marriage **Marriages of 15-20 years:** 30-40% of the length of the marriage
Marriages of more than 20 years: 35-50% of the length of the marriage

These guidelines are explicitly advisory rather than presumptive, and courts may deviate with written findings. The New York Court of Appeals in *Grunfeld v. Grunfeld*, 94 N.Y.2d 696 (2000), emphasized that duration determinations must be individualized based on the parties' specific circumstances.

Factors Affecting Duration:

Several factors may justify longer or shorter duration awards:

- Age and health of the parties
- Ability to achieve self-sufficiency
- Contributions to the other party's career
- Standard of living during marriage
- Availability of other assets or income sources

Indefinite Duration Awards:

In appropriate cases, courts may award maintenance for an indefinite period, particularly in long-term marriages where the recipient is unlikely to achieve self-sufficiency due to age, health, or other circumstances. Such awards remain subject to modification based on changed circumstances.

VI. Modification and Termination of Support

California Modification Standards

California law permits modification of spousal support orders based on material changes in circumstances, as established in *In re Marriage of Dietz*, 17 Cal. 3d 14 (1976). The party seeking modification bears the burden of proving that circumstances have changed sufficiently to warrant adjustment of the support order.

Material Change in Circumstances:

The California Supreme Court in *In re Marriage of Bower*, 5 Cal. App. 4th 1623 (1992), defined material change as a substantial alteration in circumstances that affects the parties' financial situation or ability to pay or need for support. Common examples include:

Loss of Employment: Involuntary job loss may justify reduction or temporary suspension of support obligations. However, courts will examine whether the job loss was voluntary or the result of the payor's failure to seek appropriate employment.

Increase in Recipient's Income: Significant increases in the recipient's income may justify reduction or termination of support, particularly if the increase results from career advancement or new employment opportunities.

Retirement: The California Court of Appeal in *In re Marriage of Gonzalez*, 57 Cal. App. 4th 1072 (1997), established that retirement may justify modification of support, but courts must examine whether the retirement is reasonable based on the payor's age, health, and financial circumstances.

Illness or Disability: Changes in health status affecting either party's ability to work or need for support may justify modification. Courts must consider both the severity of the condition and its impact on earning capacity.

Cohabitation: Family Code Section 4323 creates a rebuttable presumption of decreased need when the supported party cohabits with another person. The supporting party may seek modification based on this presumption, but the supported party may present evidence that cohabitation has not reduced their need for support.

Non-Modifiable Support Agreements:

Parties may agree to non-modifiable support in a Marital Settlement Agreement, as permitted by Family Code Section 4336(c). Such agreements prevent future modification except in cases of fraud or mistake. The California Court of Appeal in *In re Marriage of Khera*, 213 Cal. App. 4th 1097 (2013), emphasized that parties must be fully informed of the consequences of waiving modification rights.

New York Modification Standards

New York law requires proof of a substantial change in circumstances to modify maintenance orders, as established in *Boden v. Boden*, 42 N.Y.2d 210 (1977). The 2015 reforms added specific provisions for modification of orders entered under the new guidelines.

Substantial Change in Circumstances:

The New York Court of Appeals has interpreted this standard to require significant alterations in the parties' financial circumstances that were not anticipated at the time of the original order. Evidence must show that the change is:

- Substantial and continuing
- Not temporary or insignificant
- Sufficient to make the current order unfair or inappropriate

Three-Year/15% Rule:

For orders entered under the 2015 guidelines, Domestic Relations Law Section 236(B)(9)(b)(2) provides an alternative modification standard. A party may seek modification after three years from the date of the order or upon showing a 15% change in income, whichever occurs first.

This provision simplifies the modification process for guideline orders by providing objective criteria for when modification may be sought.

Termination Events:

Maintenance automatically terminates upon:

- Death of either party
- Remarriage of the recipient
- Court order based on changed circumstances

Unlike some states, New York does not automatically terminate maintenance upon cohabitation, though cohabitation may constitute a substantial change in circumstances justifying modification.

VII. Tax Implications

Federal Tax Law Changes

The Tax Cuts and Jobs Act of 2017 fundamentally altered the federal tax treatment of spousal support for orders entered after December 31, 2018. Under current federal law:

- Spousal support payments are not deductible by the payor

- Spousal support payments are not taxable income to the recipient
- These rules apply to all new orders and modifications of existing orders

Grandfathered Agreements:

Orders entered before January 1, 2019, continue to follow the pre-2019 tax treatment unless modified. Under the old rules:

- Spousal support payments were deductible by the payor
- Spousal support payments were taxable income to the recipient

This grandfathering provision creates a two-tier system where the tax treatment depends on the date of the order.

Impact on Support Calculations:

The elimination of tax deductibility has significant implications for support calculations. Under the prior system, the tax benefit to the payor effectively subsidized support payments, allowing for higher gross payments at lower after-tax cost. The new system eliminates this subsidy, potentially requiring adjustment of support amounts to achieve equivalent after-tax results.

State Tax Considerations

While federal tax consequences have been largely eliminated, state tax implications may still be relevant in some cases. Both California and New York generally follow federal tax treatment for spousal support, but practitioners should verify current state law provisions.

California State Tax Treatment:

California generally conforms to federal tax law regarding spousal support. However, California's high marginal tax rates mean that the tax impact on high-income payors remains significant even without deductibility.

New York State Tax Treatment:

New York also generally follows federal tax law for spousal support determinations. The state's income tax rates may affect the after-tax impact of support payments, particularly for high-income parties.

Planning Considerations

The changed tax landscape requires careful planning in spousal support negotiations:

Gross-Up Calculations: Without deductibility, parties may need to negotiate higher gross support amounts to achieve the same after-tax result for recipients.

Alternative Structures: Parties may consider alternative arrangements such as property transfers or structured settlements that may provide more favorable tax treatment.

Timing Considerations: For parties with existing orders, the decision whether to modify may be affected by the loss of tax benefits.

VIII. Enforcement of Spousal Support

Enforcement Mechanisms

Both California and New York provide comprehensive enforcement mechanisms for spousal support orders, recognizing that effective enforcement is essential to the integrity of the support system.

Wage Garnishment:

Both states permit automatic wage garnishment for support orders. In California, Family Code Section 5230 provides for immediate wage withholding upon entry of a support order. New York Family Court Act Section 454 provides similar authority.

Wage garnishment is typically the most effective enforcement mechanism because it provides regular, automatic collection without ongoing court involvement. However, garnishment is limited to a percentage of the debtor's income and may be insufficient for high support orders.

Contempt of Court:

Willful violation of support orders may result in contempt of court proceedings, which can result in both civil and criminal penalties. The California Court of Appeal in *In re Marriage of Goddard*, 33 Cal. App. 4th 49 (1995), established that contempt requires proof of willful violation and ability to pay.

Civil contempt is designed to coerce compliance and typically involves incarceration until the contemnor agrees to comply with the support order. Criminal contempt punishes past violations and may result in fines or imprisonment.

Property Liens:

Courts may impose liens on real and personal property to secure payment of support obligations. These liens provide security for support payments and may facilitate collection through property sales.

Asset Seizure:

Both states provide authority for seizure of bank accounts, tax refunds, and other assets to satisfy support obligations. These remedies are particularly effective against payors who attempt to hide assets or avoid wage garnishment.

California Enforcement Procedures

Department of Child Support Services (DCSS):

In cases involving both child and spousal support, California's DCSS may assist with enforcement. While DCSS primarily focuses on child support, it may collect spousal support when combined with child support orders.

Court Procedures:

The superior court retains jurisdiction over spousal support orders and may employ various enforcement mechanisms. California Family Code Section 290 provides broad authority for enforcement actions.

Interstate Enforcement:

California has adopted the Uniform Interstate Family Support Act (UIFSA), facilitating enforcement of support orders across state lines. This is particularly important for enforcement against payors who relocate to other states.

New York Enforcement Procedures

Support Collection Unit:

New York's Support Collection Unit (SCU) provides enforcement services for support orders, including both child and spousal support. The SCU has broad authority to pursue collection through various mechanisms.

Court Jurisdiction:

Both Supreme Court and Family Court have jurisdiction over support enforcement in New York, depending on the original court that entered the order. This dual jurisdiction can sometimes create procedural complications.

Professional License Suspension:

New York law permits suspension of professional licenses for non-payment of support, providing additional leverage against professional payors who might otherwise avoid enforcement.

IX. Strategic Considerations

Negotiation Strategies

Effective representation in spousal support cases requires careful attention to both legal standards and practical considerations that affect the parties' long-term interests.

Emphasizing Earning Capacity:

Rather than focusing solely on current income, practitioners should carefully develop evidence regarding each party's earning capacity. This requires comprehensive analysis of:

- Educational background and professional credentials
- Work history and career progression
- Skills and experience transferable to other positions
- Geographic limitations on employment opportunities
- Age and health factors affecting employability

The California Court of Appeal in *In re Marriage of Simpson*, 4 Cal. 4th 225 (1992), emphasized that courts must examine whether a party is voluntarily underemployed, requiring detailed vocational analysis.

Future Planning Considerations:

Spousal support negotiations should consider both parties' long-term needs and goals:

Retraining and Education: For recipients who need additional education or training to achieve self-sufficiency, support agreements should provide adequate time and resources for skill development. This may involve higher short-term support to cover educational expenses with planned reduction upon completion of training.

Career Re-entry: Parties who have been out of the workforce for extended periods may need time to re-establish their careers. Support agreements should account for the gradual nature of career re-entry rather than expecting immediate full employment.

Retirement Planning: Long-term support agreements should address the impact of the payor's retirement on support obligations. This may involve step-down provisions tied to retirement age or alternative arrangements using retirement assets.

Property vs. Support Trade-offs

Parties may benefit from considering alternatives to traditional periodic support payments:

Lump-Sum Buyouts: A lump-sum payment in lieu of ongoing support eliminates future modification and enforcement issues while providing immediate resources to the recipient. However, such arrangements require careful calculation of present value and consideration of tax implications.

Property Transfers: Transferring additional property to the recipient in exchange for reduced or eliminated support may benefit both parties. The payor eliminates ongoing obligations while the recipient gains security through asset ownership.

Structured Settlements: Complex arrangements involving combinations of lump-sum payments, property transfers, and reduced periodic support may address both parties' needs while minimizing future disputes.

Modification and Duration Planning

Support agreements should clearly address future modification and termination:

Specific Modification Terms: Rather than relying on general legal standards, parties may benefit from specific provisions addressing common modification scenarios such as job loss, disability, or significant income changes.

Duration Limitations: While courts retain authority to modify support based on changed circumstances, parties may agree to specific duration limits or step-down provisions that provide certainty and encourage self-sufficiency planning.

Review Provisions: Agreements may include provisions for periodic review of support amounts, allowing for adjustment based on changed circumstances without requiring formal modification proceedings.

Insurance and Security Considerations

Long-term support awards require consideration of security mechanisms:

Life Insurance: Life insurance on the payor's life provides security for support obligations that extend beyond the payor's lifetime. The amount of insurance should reflect the present value of future support obligations.

Disability Insurance: Disability insurance may provide income replacement if the payor becomes unable to work, though such insurance may not cover support obligations to former spouses.

Asset Security: In appropriate cases, parties may agree to security interests in specific assets to ensure payment of support obligations.

X. Emerging Issues and Future Developments

Impact of Changing Family Structures

Modern family law must address evolving family structures and economic realities that may not fit traditional spousal support models:

Dual-Career Marriages: Marriages where both spouses maintain significant careers throughout the marriage may require different approaches to support determination, focusing more on temporary assistance and less on long-term dependency.

Career Flexibility: Modern careers often involve more flexibility and remote work options, potentially affecting both earning capacity analysis and the geographic limitations traditionally considered in support determinations.

Non-Traditional Relationships: As family law evolves to address same-sex marriages and other non-traditional relationships, support determinations may need to consider different economic patterns and social expectations.

Technology and Support Calculation

Technology continues to affect spousal support practice:

Calculation Software: Sophisticated software programs can model different support scenarios and their long-term financial impact, assisting both courts and parties in making informed decisions.

Income Verification: Enhanced ability to verify income through electronic records and databases may reduce disputes over earning capacity and voluntary underemployment.

Enforcement Technology: Electronic monitoring and automated enforcement systems may improve collection rates and reduce the cost of enforcement proceedings.

Economic Factors

Broader economic trends affect spousal support policy and practice:

Retirement Security: As traditional pension plans become less common and retirement security becomes more precarious, spousal support may need to address longer-term financial security for both parties.

Healthcare Costs: Rising healthcare costs may require greater attention to health insurance and medical expense provisions in support orders.

Economic Volatility: Increased economic volatility may require more flexible support arrangements that can adapt to changing economic conditions.

XI. Conclusion

Spousal support law reflects the ongoing tension between providing economic security following divorce and promoting self-sufficiency and independence. While California emphasizes judicial discretion balanced with structured guidelines for temporary support, New York has moved toward greater predictability through presumptive guidelines while preserving flexibility for individual circumstances.

The 2019 federal tax law changes have fundamentally altered the economics of spousal support, requiring practitioners to adapt their negotiation strategies and calculation methods. The elimination of tax deductibility has increased the after-tax cost of support payments while removing the income tax burden from recipients, fundamentally changing the economic dynamics of support negotiations.

Both jurisdictions continue to evolve their approaches to spousal support, with courts increasingly recognizing the need to balance traditional notions of financial security with modern expectations of gender equality and self-sufficiency. The trend toward more structured guidelines reflects a desire for consistency and predictability, while the retention of judicial discretion acknowledges that individual circumstances cannot always be captured by formulaic approaches.

Effective spousal support practice requires mastery of both the technical aspects of calculation and modification as well as the strategic considerations that affect long-term outcomes for both parties. As family structures and economic realities continue to evolve, spousal support law must adapt to address new challenges while maintaining its fundamental purpose of providing fair financial transitions following the end of marriage.

The complexity of modern spousal support determinations underscores the importance of comprehensive legal representation that addresses not only immediate financial needs but also long-term planning considerations. Whether through negotiated settlements or court orders, spousal support arrangements should provide clarity, security, and appropriate incentives for both parties to move forward successfully in their post-divorce lives.

XII. Practice Points and Checklists

Initial Case Assessment Checklist

Client Interview Considerations:

- Length of marriage and dates of separation
- Standard of living during marriage (detailed budget analysis)
- Each party's education, skills, and work history
- Career sacrifices made during marriage
- Health status and limitations of both parties
- Child care responsibilities affecting earning capacity
- Domestic violence history (documented evidence)
- Tax filing status and income reporting history
- Retirement plans and timeline expectations
- Insurance coverage and availability

Financial Documentation Requirements:

- Tax returns for previous three to five years
- Current pay stubs and employment contracts
- Business financial statements (if self-employed)
- Bank statements and investment account records
- Retirement account statements and pension information
- Insurance policies (life, disability, health)
- Real estate valuations and mortgage information
- Credit reports and debt documentation
- Educational credentials and professional licenses

California Practice Considerations

Temporary Support Strategy:

- Identify applicable local court formula
- Calculate support using county-specific guidelines

- Analyze potential grounds for deviation from formula
- Consider interaction with child support calculations
- Evaluate tax implications under current law
- Prepare for expedited hearing procedures

Permanent Support Analysis:

- Comprehensive Family Code Section 4320 factor analysis
- Vocational evaluation if earning capacity disputed
- Standard of living analysis with detailed budgets
- Marriage length and duration presumptions
- Modification and termination planning
- Consider non-modifiable support agreements

Documentation Strategy:

- Detailed marital lifestyle evidence
- Career sacrifice and contribution documentation
- Health and age limitation evidence
- Domestic violence documentation (if applicable)
- Tax consequence analysis
- Expert witness preparation (vocational, financial)

New York Practice Considerations

Guideline Calculations:

- Determine applicable income cap
- Calculate using appropriate formula (with/without child support)
- Apply 40% combined income ceiling
- Analyze factors justifying deviation from guidelines
- Consider advisory duration guidelines

- Plan for modification under three-year/15% rule

Factor Analysis:

- Comprehensive Domestic Relations Law Section 236(B) factor review
- Earning capacity vs. current income analysis
- Standard of living documentation
- Health and age considerations
- Educational and career contribution evidence
- Domestic violence impact assessment

Strategic Planning:

- Duration negotiation considering advisory guidelines
- Modification protection and planning
- Security arrangements for long-term awards
- Tax planning under current federal law
- Integration with equitable distribution

Settlement Negotiation Guidelines

Pre-Negotiation Preparation:

- Complete financial disclosure and analysis
- Develop best and worst case scenarios
- Calculate range of likely court outcomes
- Identify client's priorities and concerns
- Prepare alternative settlement structures
- Consider tax implications of different arrangements

Negotiation Strategies:

- Present comprehensive financial analysis
- Address both immediate and long-term needs

- Consider lump-sum vs. periodic payment options
- Evaluate property transfer alternatives
- Plan for modification and review provisions
- Incorporate security mechanisms

Settlement Documentation:

- Clear and specific payment terms
- Modification and termination provisions
- Security and insurance requirements
- Tax allocation and responsibility
- Integration with property division
- Enforcement mechanisms and procedures

Litigation Preparation

Pleading Considerations:

- Specific support amount requests with factual basis
- Comprehensive factor allegations
- Temporary support motion preparation
- Discovery planning and scheduling
- Expert witness identification and retention
- Trial preparation timeline

Evidence Development:

- Financial document compilation and organization
- Witness identification and preparation
- Expert report coordination
- Demonstrative evidence preparation
- Standard of living proof compilation

- Earning capacity evidence development

Trial Strategy:

- Opening statement outlining support theory
- Witness examination planning
- Exhibit organization and presentation
- Expert testimony coordination
- Closing argument preparation
- Post-trial briefing and proposed orders

Post-Judgment Considerations

Enforcement Planning:

- Payment monitoring systems
- Collection procedure preparation
- Interstate enforcement considerations
- Professional license and asset investigation
- Contempt proceeding preparation
- Alternative collection mechanisms

Modification Analysis:

- Changed circumstance documentation
- Income verification and analysis
- Health and employment status monitoring
- Cohabitation investigation (where applicable)
- Three-year/percentage change analysis (New York)
- Expert witness needs for modification proceedings

Ethical Considerations

Conflict of Interest Analysis:

- Former client conflict screening
- Family member representation issues
- Business relationship conflicts
- Referral source considerations
- Expert witness conflict screening

Client Communication:

- Regular case status updates
- Settlement authority and approval
- Cost and fee communication
- Realistic outcome expectations
- Alternative dispute resolution options

Professional Responsibility:

- Candor to tribunal regarding financial information
- Discovery compliance and document production
- Settlement negotiation good faith requirements
- Client confidentiality in multi-party cases
- Competence and continuing education requirements

XIII. Appendices

Appendix A: Key Case Citations by Topic

California Spousal Support Authority:

- *In re Marriage of Terry*, 80 Cal. App. 3d 921 (1978) (transition to independence)
- *In re Marriage of Kerr*, 77 Cal. App. 4th 87 (1999) (standard of living considerations)

- *Gavron v. Gavron*, 203 Cal. App. 3d 705 (1988) (rehabilitative support and duration)
- *In re Marriage of Cheriton*, 92 Cal. App. 4th 269 (2001) (temporary support standards)
- *In re Marriage of Morrison*, 20 Cal. 3d 437 (1978) (rehabilitative support sufficiency)
- *In re Marriage of Sullivan*, 37 Cal. 3d 762 (1984) (reimbursement for education)
- *In re Marriage of Simpson*, 4 Cal. 4th 225 (1992) (earning capacity analysis)
- *In re Marriage of Hoffmeister*, 191 Cal. App. 3d 351 (1987) (marriage length factor)
- *In re Marriage of Smith*, 79 Cal. App. 4th 1018 (2000) (standard of living proof)
- *In re Marriage of Olson*, 14 Cal. App. 4th 1 (1993) (age and health considerations)
- *In re Marriage of Cauley*, 138 Cal. App. 4th 1100 (2006) (domestic violence factor)
- *In re Marriage of Reynolds*, 63 Cal. App. 4th 1373 (1998) (long-term marriage duration)
- *In re Marriage of Dietz*, 17 Cal. 3d 14 (1976) (modification standards)
- *In re Marriage of Bower*, 5 Cal. App. 4th 1623 (1992) (material change definition)
- *In re Marriage of Gonzalez*, 57 Cal. App. 4th 1072 (1997) (retirement and modification)
- *In re Marriage of Khera*, 213 Cal. App. 4th 1097 (2013) (non-modifiable agreements)
- *In re Marriage of Schulze*, 60 Cal. App. 4th 519 (1997) (temporary support discretion)

New York Spousal Maintenance Authority:

- *Hartog v. Hartog*, 85 N.Y.2d 36 (1995) (support purposes and earning capacity)

- *O'Brien v. O'Brien*, 66 N.Y.2d 576 (1985) (professional licenses and reimbursement)
- *Grunfeld v. Grunfeld*, 94 N.Y.2d 696 (2000) (duration considerations)
- *Boden v. Boden*, 42 N.Y.2d 210 (1977) (modification standards)

Enforcement Authority:

- *In re Marriage of Goddard*, 33 Cal. App. 4th 49 (1995) (contempt standards)

Appendix B: Statutory References

California Family Code Provisions:

- Section 3600 (temporary support authority)
- Section 4320 (permanent support factors)
- Section 4321 (rebuttable presumptions)
- Section 4322 (cohabitation presumption)
- Section 4323 (cohabitation evidence)
- Section 4336 (duration limitations)
- Section 4337 (termination events)
- Section 5230 (wage garnishment authority)
- Section 290 (enforcement procedures)

New York Domestic Relations Law Provisions:

- Section 236(B)(5-a) (temporary maintenance guidelines)
- Section 236(B)(6) (post-divorce maintenance)
- Section 236(B)(9)(b)(2) (modification standards)

New York Family Court Act Provisions:

- Section 454 (wage garnishment authority)

Federal Tax Provisions:

- Tax Cuts and Jobs Act of 2017, Section 11051 (spousal support deduction elimination)
- Internal Revenue Code Section 71 (alimony taxation - pre-2019)
- Internal Revenue Code Section 215 (alimony deduction - pre-2019)

Appendix C: Useful Formulas and Calculations

California Temporary Support Formulas:

Santa Clara County Formula: Spousal Support = (40% × Payor's Net Income) - (50% × Recipient's Net Income)*Adjusted for child support when applicable*

Los Angeles County Formula: Spousal Support = (40% × Payor's Net Income) - (40% × Recipient's Net Income)*Adjusted for child support when applicable*

New York Maintenance Formulas:

With Child Support: Maintenance = (20% × Payor's Income) - (25% × Recipient's Income) *Cannot exceed 40% of combined income*

Without Child Support: Maintenance = (30% × Payor's Income) - (20% × Recipient's Income) *Cannot exceed 40% of combined income*

Duration Calculations:

California Short-Term Marriage Presumption: Presumptive Duration = 50% × Length of Marriage

New York Advisory Duration Guidelines:

- 0-15 years: 15-30% of marriage length
- 15-20 years: 30-40% of marriage length
- 20+ years: 35-50% of marriage length

This comprehensive treatment of spousal support law in California and New York provides practitioners with the detailed analysis and practical guidance necessary for effective representation in these complex cases. The interplay between statutory guidelines, judicial discretion, and individual circumstances requires careful attention to both legal precedent and strategic considerations that serve clients' long-term interests.

10

Legal and Physical Custody in New York & California

I. Protecting the Child's Best Interests

Few family law issues are as emotionally fraught - or as legally nuanced - as child custody. Parents may be divorcing, separating, or never have cohabited, but the question remains the same: What custody arrangement best supports the child's health, safety, and well-being?

Both New York and California ground their custody determinations in the best interests of the child, yet they differ significantly in terminology, statutory frameworks, presumptions, and procedural approaches. Understanding these distinctions is crucial for practitioners navigating interstate custody matters or advising clients who may relocate between these jurisdictions.

This chapter provides a comprehensive comparative analysis of legal and physical custody, examining the statutory and case law foundations, types of custody arrangements, enforcement mechanisms, and the core principles that guide custody decisions in both states. We will explore how each jurisdiction's approach reflects broader policy considerations about parental rights, child welfare, and the role of courts in family governance.

II. Historical Development and Statutory Framework

New York's Evolution

New York's custody law has evolved significantly from its common law origins. Historically governed by the tender years doctrine, which presumed maternal custody for young children, New York has transitioned to a gender-neutral best interests standard. *See Watts v. Watts*, 77 Misc. 2d 178, 350 N.Y.S.2d 285 (Fam. Ct. Kings County 1973). The state's approach is primarily case law-driven, with Domestic Relations Law § 240 providing the basic framework for custody determinations in divorce proceedings, while Family Court Act Article 6 governs custody in non-matrimonial contexts.

The seminal case of *Eschbach v. Eschbach*, 56 N.Y.2d 167, 451 N.Y.S.2d 658, 436 N.E.2d 1260 (1982), established that the best interests standard requires courts to consider all relevant factors without predetermined weight, emphasizing judicial discretion in custody determinations.

California's Comprehensive Statutory Scheme

California has developed a more comprehensive statutory framework governing custody determinations. The Family Code, particularly sections 3011, 3020, and 3040, explicitly delineates the factors courts must consider. California Family Code § 3020 establishes the foundational policy that children should have frequent and continuing contact with both parents, while § 3011 provides specific best interests factors.

The landmark case of *Burchard v. Garay*, 42 Cal. 3d 531, 724 P.2d 486, 229 Cal. Rptr. 800 (1986), established California's modern approach to custody determinations, emphasizing that the paramount consideration is the best interest of the child, not the rights of the parents.

III. Types of Custody: Definitional Framework

Custody involves two distinct yet interrelated components, each carrying specific legal implications and practical consequences.

Legal Custody: Decision-Making Authority

Legal custody encompasses the right and responsibility to make major decisions affecting the child's welfare, including but not limited to educational choices, medical treatment decisions, religious upbringing, and participation in extracurricular activities. *See In re Marriage of Burgess*, 13 Cal. 4th 25, 913 P.2d 473, 51 Cal. Rptr. 2d 444 (1996); *Friederwitzer v. Friederwitzer*, 55 N.Y.2d 89, 447 N.Y.S.2d 893, 432 N.E.2d 765 (1982).

Joint Legal Custody requires both parents to consult and, ideally, agree on major decisions. This arrangement presupposes that parents can communicate effectively and make decisions collaboratively despite their personal relationship dissolution. Courts in both jurisdictions have established that joint legal custody does not require unanimity on every decision but does mandate good faith consultation. *See Braiman v. Braiman*, 44 N.Y.2d 584, 407 N.Y.S.2d 449, 378 N.E.2d 1019 (1978); *In re Marriage of Birnbaum*, 211 Cal. App. 3d 1508, 260 Cal. Rptr. 210 (1989).

Sole Legal Custody vests decision-making authority exclusively in one parent, typically awarded when joint custody would be detrimental to the child due to factors such as parental inability to cooperate, domestic violence history, substance abuse, or geographic distance making consultation impractical. *See Matter of Lincoln v. Lincoln*, 24 N.Y.2d 270, 299 N.Y.S.2d 842, 247 N.E.2d 659 (1969); *In re Marriage of Rosson*, 178 Cal. App. 3d 1094, 224 Cal. Rptr. 250 (1986).

Physical Custody: Residential Arrangements

Physical custody determines where the child primarily resides and encompasses the day-to-day care and supervision responsibilities. The distinction between legal and physical custody recognizes that decision-making authority and residential arrangements serve different functions in a child's life.

Joint Physical Custody involves substantial and significant periods of physical custody with both parents, though not necessarily equal time division. California Family Code § 3004 defines joint physical custody as requiring that each parent have "significant periods of physical custody," which courts have interpreted as more than mere visitation but less than mathematical equality. *See In re Marriage of Lasich*, 99 Cal. App. 3d 402, 160 Cal. Rptr. 357 (1979).

New York courts have been more reluctant to embrace joint physical custody terminology, often preferring to describe arrangements in terms of "shared parenting time" or "alternating residence." *See Dodd v. Dodd*, 93 N.Y.2d 233, 689 N.Y.S.2d 463, 711 N.E.2d 717 (1999).

Sole Physical Custody designates one parent as the primary residential custodian, with the non-custodial parent typically receiving visitation rights that may range from liberal to supervised, depending on circumstances.

IV. Jurisdictional Differences in Custody Preferences

California's Pro-Sharing Presumption

California has developed a strong legislative and judicial preference for arrangements that maximize both parents' involvement in their children's lives. Family Code § 3020 explicitly states that it is the public policy of California to ensure frequent and continuing contact with both parents, and to encourage parents to share in the rights and responsibilities of child rearing.

This policy preference is operationalized through several mechanisms. Courts are required to consider any person seeking custody who has demonstrated a pattern of care and responsibility toward the child. *See In re Marriage of Harris*, 96 Cal. App. 4th 1445, 117 Cal. Rptr. 2d 757 (2002). Additionally, California courts must consider the willingness of each parent to support the child's relationship with the other parent as a specific factor in custody determinations under Family Code § 3011(d).

New York's Flexibility-Focused Approach

New York has traditionally maintained greater judicial discretion in custody arrangements, with less emphasis on presumptive shared custody. The Court of Appeals in *Eschbach v. Eschbach*, supra, emphasized that each custody determination must be individualized based on the specific circumstances presented.

New York courts consider stability and continuity of care as particularly important factors. In *Matter of Nehra v. Uhlar*, 43 N.Y.2d 242, 401 N.Y.S.2d 168, 372 N.E.2d 4 (1977), the Court of Appeals noted that disruption of established custody arrangements requires compelling circumstances and clear evidence that change serves the child's best interests.

V. The Best Interests Standard: Comparative Analysis

Both jurisdictions employ the best interests of the child as their paramount consideration, but their approaches to defining and applying this standard differ significantly in specificity and emphasis.

New York's Case Law-Developed Factors

New York has developed its best interests factors primarily through judicial decisions rather than comprehensive statutory enumeration. The factors courts consider include:

Parental Fitness and Stability: Courts examine each parent's mental and physical health, lifestyle stability, and ability to provide appropriate care. *See Matter of Bennett v. Jeffreys*, 40 N.Y.2d 543, 387 N.Y.S.2d 821, 356 N.E.2d 277 (1976). This includes assessment of substance abuse issues, criminal history, and mental health concerns that might affect parenting capacity.

Quality of Home Environment: The physical and emotional environment each parent can provide, including housing adequacy, neighborhood safety, and extended family support systems. *See Friederwitzer v. Friederwitzer*, supra.

Historical Caretaking Patterns: Courts give significant weight to which parent has been the primary caretaker, recognizing the importance of continuity in the child's care arrangements. *See Matter of Niles v. Niles*, 299 A.D.2d 519, 749 N.Y.S.2d 715 (2d Dep't 2002).

Willingness to Foster Relationship with Other Parent: A parent's demonstrated ability and willingness to encourage the child's relationship with the other parent is crucial. Alienating behavior can significantly impact custody determinations. *See Matter of Miller v. Miller*, 103 A.D.2d 630, 478 N.Y.S.2d 748 (2d Dep't 1984).

Child's Preferences: While not determinative, children's custody preferences are given increasing weight as they mature, typically becoming significant around age 12-14. *See Eschbach v. Eschbach*, supra.

Domestic Violence History: Evidence of domestic violence creates a presumption against custody for the abusive parent, though this presumption can be rebutted. *See Nicholson v. Scoppetta*, 3 N.Y.3d 357, 787 N.Y.S.2d 338, 820 N.E.2d 840 (2004).

California's Statutory Framework

California Family Code § 3011 provides explicit statutory guidance for best interests determinations:

Health, Safety and Welfare Priority: This factor takes precedence over all others, establishing child safety as the paramount concern. Courts must prioritize protection from physical and emotional harm above other considerations.

History of Abuse: Family Code § 3011(b) requires courts to consider any history of abuse by a parent against any child, the other parent, or others. Evidence of domestic violence creates rebuttable presumptions affecting custody under Family Code § 3044.

Nature and Amount of Contact: Courts must evaluate each parent's relationship with the child and their ability to maintain meaningful contact post-separation.

Substance Abuse Considerations: Habitual or continual use of controlled substances or alcohol by either parent is explicitly enumerated as a factor under Family Code § 3011(g).

Child's Age-Appropriate Preferences: Children of sufficient age and capacity may express custody preferences, which courts must consider but are not bound to follow. *See In re Marriage of Rosson*, supra.

VI. Specialized Custody Arrangements and Emerging Trends

Bird's Nest Custody

Both jurisdictions have seen experimentation with "bird's nest" or "nesting" arrangements where children remain in the family home while parents alternate residence. While creative, courts in both states have noted practical limitations. *See In re Marriage of Biallas*, 65 Cal. App. 3d 755, 135 Cal. Rptr. 635 (1977); *Braiman v. Braiman*, supra.

Virtual Visitation

Technology has expanded custody concepts to include virtual visitation provisions. New York was among the first states to explicitly recognize virtual visitation in its statutes with the passage of legislation in 2010. California courts have embraced technology-assisted parenting time through case law development. *See In re Marriage of Cornelius*, 2007 WL 2729346 (Cal. App. 2007).

VII. Parenting Plans and Implementation

California's Structured Approach

California has developed comprehensive standardized forms for parenting plans through its Judicial Council forms (FL-341 series). These forms address scheduling details, holiday arrangements, transportation responsibilities, and communication protocols. The state's approach emphasizes detailed advance planning to minimize future conflicts.

California courts may order mandatory mediation for custody disputes under Family Code § 3170, requiring parents to attempt resolution through court-connected mediation services before proceeding to trial.

New York's Flexible Framework

New York provides greater flexibility in parenting plan development, allowing parties and courts to craft individualized arrangements. While some counties have developed model parenting plans, there is no statewide standardization requirement.

New York courts encourage settlement through various mechanisms, including court-annexed mediation, collaborative law processes, and judicial settlement conferences. The state's approach recognizes that one-size-fits-all solutions may not serve diverse family circumstances.

VIII. Custody Evaluations and Expert Testimony

Forensic Evaluation Standards

When custody is contested, both jurisdictions may order comprehensive custody evaluations conducted by qualified mental health professionals. These evaluations typically include psychological testing, clinical interviews, home visits, and collateral contact reviews.

New York Approach: Court-appointed evaluators must meet qualification standards established by court rules. The evaluation process is governed by the standards established in *Matter of Eli M.*, 289 A.D.2d 157, 735 N.Y.S.2d 66 (1st Dep't 2001), which emphasized the evaluator's duty to maintain objectivity and thoroughness.

California Standards: California has developed more specific statutory and regulatory guidance for custody evaluators under Family Code § 3111 and California Rules of Court 5.220. Evaluators must complete specific training requirements and adhere to detailed procedural standards.

Child Representation

New York's Attorney for the Child: New York routinely appoints Attorneys for the Child (AFC) in contested custody cases. The AFC's role is defined by Family Court Act § 249 and Court of Appeals decisions including *Matter of Tayquon H.*, 28 N.Y.3d 228, 44 N.Y.S.3d 690, 67 N.E.3d 1000 (2016), which clarified that AFCs must zealously advocate for their client's expressed wishes while considering the child's best interests.

California's Minor's Counsel: California appoints Minor's Counsel less routinely, typically in cases involving abuse allegations or high conflict. The role is governed by Family Code § 3151 and emphasizes independent investigation and recommendation rather than pure advocacy.

IX. Modification of Custody Orders

Standard for Modification

Both jurisdictions require demonstration of a substantial change in circumstances since the last order, with the proposed modification serving the child's best interests. However, they differ in their application of these standards.

New York's Approach: New York courts apply a relatively strict standard for modification, emphasizing stability and continuity. In *Matter of Ricks v. Ricks*, 106 A.D.3d 926, 965 N.Y.S.2d 487 (2d Dep't 2013), the Appellate Division emphasized that the moving party must demonstrate both substantial change and that modification would benefit the child.

California's Framework: California Family Code § 3048 provides specific guidance for modification requests, including emergency modification procedures. California courts may be more receptive to modifications based on the child's evolving developmental needs.

Timing Considerations

Both states recognize that frequent modification requests can be detrimental to children and have developed procedures to prevent relitigation of settled custody arrangements absent genuine changed circumstances.

X. Relocation and Move-Away Cases

California's Structured Analysis

California has developed the most sophisticated jurisprudence regarding parental relocation requests through a series of Supreme Court decisions:

In re Marriage of Burgess, 13 Cal. 4th 25, 913 P.2d 473, 51 Cal. Rptr. 2d 444 (1996), established that when the custodial parent seeks to relocate, the burden shifts to the non-custodial parent to demonstrate that the move would be detrimental to the child.

In re Marriage of LaMusga, 32 Cal. 4th 1072, 88 P.3d 81, 12 Cal. Rptr. 3d 356 (2004), refined the Burgess standard by requiring courts to consider the impact of relocation on both parents' relationship with the child, particularly in cases approaching equal custody time.

New York's Tropea Standard

New York's approach to relocation is governed by *Tropea v. Tropea*, 87 N.Y.2d 727, 642 N.Y.S.2d 575, 665 N.E.2d 145 (1996), which established a best interests analysis considering:

- Each parent's reasons for seeking or opposing the move
- The quality of the relationships between the child and custodial and non-custodial parents
- The impact of the move on the quantity and quality of the child's future contact with the non-custodial parent
- The degree to which the custodial parent's and child's life may be enhanced economically, emotionally and educationally by the move
- The feasibility of preserving the relationship between the non-custodial parent and child through suitable visitation arrangements

XI. Interstate Custody Jurisdiction

Uniform Child Custody Jurisdiction and Enforcement Act

Both states have adopted the Uniform Child Custody Jurisdiction and Enforcement Act (UCCJEA), providing consistent jurisdictional standards for interstate custody cases. The UCCJEA establishes home state jurisdiction as the primary basis for custody determinations.

New York Implementation: New York's UCCJEA provisions are codified in Domestic Relations Law Article 5-A, with key interpretive decisions including *Matter of Dereska v. Dereska*, 97 A.D.3d 35, 944 N.Y.S.2d 570 (2d Dep't 2012).

California Implementation: California's UCCJEA is found in Family Code sections 3400-3465, with significant case law development in *Montenegro v. Diaz*, 26 Cal. App. 4th 249, 31 Cal. Rptr. 2d 488 (1994).

XII. Enforcement Mechanisms

Contempt Proceedings

Both jurisdictions provide robust enforcement mechanisms for custody violations, though their approaches differ in procedural details and available remedies.

New York Enforcement: Family Court Act § 454 provides the framework for contempt proceedings, with remedies including makeup time, modification of custody arrangements, and in extreme cases, incarceration. *See Matter of Dyer v. Dyer*, 5 A.D.3d 202, 772 N.Y.S.2d 86 (1st Dep't 2004).

California Enforcement: Family Code sections 290-295 establish enforcement procedures, including automatic income withholding for support obligations tied to custody violations and specific penalties for custodial interference under Penal Code § 278.5.

Emergency Intervention

Both states provide mechanisms for emergency custody interventions when child safety is at immediate risk, though they differ in their threshold requirements and procedural safeguards.

XIII. Cultural and Socioeconomic Considerations

Religious and Cultural Factors

Both jurisdictions must navigate the intersection of custody law with First Amendment religious freedom and cultural diversity considerations.

Religious Upbringing Decisions: Courts in both states have developed nuanced approaches to religious custody disputes. *See Zummo v. Zummo*, 574 A.2d 1130 (Pa. Super. Ct. 1990); *In re Marriage of Murga*, 103 Cal. App. 4th 498, 126 Cal. Rptr. 2d 859 (2002).

Cultural Competency: Both jurisdictions have increasingly recognized the importance of cultural competency in custody evaluations and judicial decision-making, particularly in cases involving diverse cultural backgrounds or international elements.

Socioeconomic Impact Analysis

Courts in both states must be careful not to disadvantage parents based solely on economic circumstances, while still considering the practical impact of financial resources on child welfare.

XIV. Emerging Issues and Future Trends

Technology and Social Media

Both jurisdictions are grappling with technology-related custody issues, including social media use, digital privacy concerns, and virtual visitation arrangements. Courts are developing new frameworks for addressing these 21st-century parenting challenges.

Same-Sex Parent Recognition

Following marriage equality developments, both states have had to address custody issues involving same-sex parents, including second-parent adoption requirements and recognition of parental rights established in other jurisdictions.

Mental Health Awareness

Increasing awareness of mental health issues has led to more sophisticated approaches to addressing parental mental health concerns in custody determinations, moving beyond simple exclusion toward accommodation and treatment-focused solutions.

XV. Practical Considerations for Practitioners

Client Counseling Strategies

Effective custody representation requires understanding not only legal standards but also the emotional and practical realities facing families in transition. Practitioners must balance zealous advocacy with realistic expectations about achievable outcomes.

Documentation and Evidence Development

Successful custody litigation requires careful development of evidence regarding parenting capacity, child welfare factors, and family dynamics. Both jurisdictions place significant emphasis on contemporaneous documentation and expert testimony.

Settlement Facilitation

Given the emotional and financial costs of custody litigation, practitioners in both states should prioritize settlement-oriented approaches while maintaining readiness for trial advocacy when necessary.

XVI. Conclusion

The landscape of child custody law in New York and California reflects both shared values and distinct approaches to protecting children's welfare while respecting parental rights. While both states prioritize the best interests of the child, their differing statutory frameworks, judicial philosophies, and procedural approaches create significant practical differences for families and practitioners.

California's more prescriptive statutory approach provides greater predictability but potentially less flexibility for unique family circumstances. New York's common law-driven system offers greater judicial discretion but potentially less consistency across cases and jurisdictions.

Understanding these differences is crucial for practitioners handling interstate matters, families considering relocation, and policymakers seeking to improve custody law effectiveness. As family structures continue to evolve and societal understanding of child development advances, both jurisdictions will undoubtedly continue refining their approaches to serve children's best interests in an increasingly complex world.

11

Child Support Calculation and Enforcement

I. Ensuring Children's Economic Security

Child support represents one of the most fundamental obligations in family law - the duty of parents to provide financial security for their children regardless of the parents' relationship status. The principle underlying child support law is straightforward: children should not suffer economically because their parents are separated, divorced, or were never married. However, the implementation of this principle involves complex statutory schemes, judicial discretion, and enforcement mechanisms that vary significantly between jurisdictions.

In both New York and California, child support is governed by detailed statutory formulas designed to create predictability and fairness in support determinations. These guidelines represent a departure from earlier approaches that relied heavily on judicial discretion, which often led to inconsistent and unpredictable outcomes. The current systems, while different in their mathematical approaches, share common goals: ensuring adequate support for children while maintaining fairness between parents and considering the economic realities of post-separation family life.

The significance of child support extends beyond individual families. Adequate child support reduces the burden on public assistance programs, promotes child welfare, and reinforces societal values about parental responsibility. Courts in both states have recognized that child support is not merely a private matter between parents but involves important public policy considerations regarding child welfare and economic stability.

II. Legal Duty to Support: Foundational Principles

Constitutional and Statutory Basis

The obligation to support one's children is rooted in both common law traditions and modern constitutional principles. The Supreme Court has recognized that parents have both fundamental rights and responsibilities regarding their children. In *Troxel v. Granville*, 530 U.S. 57 (2000), the Court reaffirmed that "the interest of parents in the care, custody, and control of their children - is perhaps the oldest of the fundamental liberty interests recognized by this Court." This fundamental right carries with it corresponding obligations, including the duty of financial support.

Both New York and California have codified this common law duty in comprehensive statutory schemes. New York's Family Court Act Section 413 provides that "every parent is chargeable with the support of his or her child until the child reaches the age of twenty-one years." California Family Code Section 3900 similarly states that "the father and mother of a minor child have an equal responsibility to support their child in the manner suitable to the child's circumstances."

Universal Application Regardless of Marital Status

Modern child support law makes no distinction between children born within marriage and those born outside of marriage. This represents a significant evolution from historical approaches that treated "illegitimate" children differently. The Supreme Court's decisions in cases such as *Levy v. Louisiana*, 391 U.S. 68 (1968), and *Weber v. Aetna Casualty & Surety Co.*, 406 U.S. 164 (1972), established that discrimination against non-marital children violates equal protection principles.

In *Matter of Raquel Marie X.*, 76 N.Y.2d 387, 559 N.Y.S.2d 855 (1990), New York's Court of Appeals emphasized that "a child born out of wedlock is entitled to the same protection, care and opportunity as a child born in wedlock." California courts have similarly held in *County of Kern v. Castle*, 75 Cal. App. 4th 1442, 89 Cal. Rptr. 2d 843 (1999), that support obligations apply equally regardless of the parents' marital status or the circumstances of the child's birth.

Non-Waivable Nature of Support Rights

A fundamental principle in both jurisdictions is that child support rights belong to the child, not the parents. Therefore, parents cannot waive or bargain away these rights through private agreement. In *Hawk v. Hawk*, 855 S.W.2d 573 (Tenn. 1993), the court explained this principle: "Child support is the right of the child, not the parent... Neither parent may bargain away this right or stipulate to inadequate support."

New York Family Court Act Section 413(1)(d) specifically provides that "no agreement between the parties may waive or reduce the basic child support obligation." Similarly, California Family Code Section 3030 states that "an agreement between the parents to waive child support does not bind the court." Courts retain the authority to reject parental agreements that fail to provide adequate support, even when both parents agree to the terms.

Continuing Jurisdiction

Courts maintain continuing jurisdiction over child support orders until the child reaches the age of majority (or beyond in certain circumstances). This ongoing jurisdiction allows for modifications based on changed circumstances and ensures that enforcement mechanisms remain available throughout the child's minority. In *Matter of Bliwas v. Bliwas*, 181 A.D.2d 1029, 582 N.Y.S.2d 442 (3d Dep't 1992), New York's Appellate Division confirmed that "once a court has acquired jurisdiction over the subject of child support, it retains continuing jurisdiction to modify the support order."

III. New York Child Support Guidelines: The Income Percentage Model

Historical Development and Legislative Intent

New York adopted its Child Support Standards Act (CSSA) in 1989, fundamentally changing how child support was calculated in the state. Prior to the CSSA, judges had broad discretion in setting support amounts, leading to inconsistent and often inadequate awards. The legislative history of the CSSA, found in the Governor's Program Bill Memorandum of 1989, states that the Act was designed to "ensure that child support awards are adequate to meet the needs of children and are fair to both parents."

The CSSA was amended significantly in 2010 to address criticisms that the guidelines were outdated and often resulted in support amounts that were insufficient to meet children's actual needs. The 2010 amendments, which took effect in 2011, increased the income cap to which the percentages apply and updated the percentage amounts based on economic studies of child-rearing costs.

Basic Formula Structure

New York employs what is known as the "income percentage model" or "percentage of obligor model." Under this approach, support is calculated as a fixed percentage of the non-custodial parent's income, with the percentage varying based on the number of children requiring support.

The current percentages, as set forth in Family Court Act Section 413(1)(b)(3), are:

- 17% for one child
- 25% for two children
- 29% for three children
- 31% for four children
- No less than 35% for five or more children

These percentages apply to the first $163,000 of combined parental income (as adjusted for 2023). This income cap is adjusted every two years based on the Consumer Price Index. Family Court Act Section 413(1)(c)(2) requires that the cap be "rounded to the nearest one thousand dollars."

Income Definition and Calculation

The determination of "income" for child support purposes is crucial and often contentious. New York Family Court Act Section 413(1)(b)(5) provides a comprehensive definition of gross income that includes not only wages and salary but also:

Traditional Income Sources:

- Income from self-employment
- Rental income from real property
- Interest, dividends, and other investment income
- Pensions and annuity payments
- Social Security benefits
- Workers' compensation benefits
- Unemployment insurance benefits
- Disability benefits

Imputed Income: The statute also allows courts to consider "income and assets which are not reflected in the payor's current income." This provision permits courts to impute income based on:

- Assets that do not produce income but could be converted to income-producing assets
- Benefits received in lieu of income (such as employer-provided housing or vehicles)
- Money, goods, or services provided by friends, family, or new partners

In *Matter of Horn v. Horn*, 138 A.D.3d 1203, 30 N.Y.S.3d 194 (3d Dep't 2016), the Appellate Division addressed imputation of income where a parent was voluntarily unemployed: "Where a parent is voluntarily unemployed or underemployed, the court may impute income to that parent based upon his or her education, training, health, work history, and childcare responsibilities."

Allowable Deductions

New York law permits specific deductions from gross income before applying the child support percentages. Family Court Act Section 413(1)(b)(5)(vi) allows deductions for:

Mandatory Deductions:

- Social Security and Medicare taxes (FICA)
- New York City income tax (for city residents)
- Unreimbursed employee business expenses
- Alimony or maintenance paid to a former spouse
- Child support paid for other children pursuant to court order or written agreement

Health Insurance Premium Deduction: The cost of health insurance premiums for the child receiving support is deductible under Family Court Act Section 413(1)(c)(1). However, this deduction is limited to the actual cost of adding the child to an existing policy or the cost of coverage for the child alone.

The Court of Appeals addressed the scope of allowable deductions in *Matter of Cassano v. Cassano*, 85 N.Y.2d 649, 628 N.Y.S.2d 10 (1995), holding that deductions must be specifically authorized by statute and that courts cannot create additional deductions based on equitable considerations alone.

Add-On Expenses: Pro Rata Sharing

Beyond basic support, New York law requires parents to share certain additional expenses on a pro rata basis according to their respective incomes. Family Court Act Section 413(1)(c)(4) mandates pro rata sharing of:

Mandatory Add-Ons:

- Child care expenses when necessary for employment or to seek employment
- Health care expenses not covered by insurance
- Extraordinary medical expenses

Discretionary Add-Ons: Courts may also order pro rata sharing of:

- Educational expenses, including private school tuition

- Extracurricular activities
- Summer camp
- Special needs expenses

In *Matter of Weiss v. Weiss*, 297 A.D.2d 446, 746 N.Y.S.2d 314 (2d Dep't 2002), the Appellate Division clarified that "educational expenses are not automatically required to be shared pro rata, but rather are subject to the court's discretion based on the parties' financial circumstances and the child's educational needs."

Deviation from Guidelines

While the Child Support Standards Act creates a presumption that the guideline amount is correct, courts may deviate from the guidelines under certain circumstances. Family Court Act Section 413(1)(f) provides that deviation is appropriate when the court finds that the guideline amount is "unjust or inappropriate." The statute lists specific factors for consideration:

Enumerated Deviation Factors:

1. Financial resources of the custodial and non-custodial parent
2. Physical and emotional health of the child and his or her special needs and aptitudes
3. Standard of living the child would have enjoyed had the marriage or household not been dissolved
4. Tax consequences to the parties
5. Non-monetary contributions that the parent will make for the care and well-being of the child
6. Educational needs of either parent
7. Gross disparity in the income of the parties
8. Needs of the children of the non-custodial parent for whom the non-custodial parent is providing support who are not subject to the instant action
9. Provided that the child is not on public assistance, extraordinary expenses incurred by the non-custodial parent in exercising visitation

10. Any other factors the court determines are relevant

The Court of Appeals established the standard for deviation in *Matter of Cassano v. Cassano*, 85 N.Y.2d 649, 628 N.Y.S.2d 10 (1995): "A deviation from the guidelines is warranted only upon a finding that the guideline amount is unjust or inappropriate, which finding must be based upon consideration of the statutory factors and must be supported by specific findings of fact."

IV. California Child Support Guidelines: The Income Shares Model

Theoretical Foundation and Legislative History

California adopted its current child support guidelines in 1992, replacing an earlier system that was criticized for producing inadequate and inconsistent awards. The California guidelines are based on the "Income Shares Model," which assumes that children should receive the same proportion of parental income they would have received if the parents had remained together.

The theoretical foundation for the Income Shares Model was developed by economists and policy researchers who studied the actual costs of raising children in intact families. These studies, including work by Thomas Espenshade and others, provided empirical data about how families allocate income between adults and children at various income levels.

California Family Code Section 4050 sets forth the legislative intent: "The statewide uniform guideline for determining child support orders is based on the principle that both parents are mutually responsible for the support of their children. The guideline takes into account each parent's actual income and level of responsibility for the children."

Formula Components and Calculation

The California child support formula, codified in Family Code Section 4055, appears deceptively simple but involves complex calculations that typically require computer software. The basic formula is:

CS = K[HN - (H%)(TN)]

Where:

- CS = Child support amount
- K = Amount of both parents' income to be allocated for child support
- HN = High earner's net monthly disposable income
- H% = Approximate percentage of time the high earner has custody
- TN = Total net monthly disposable income of both parents

The K Factor: The K factor represents the percentage of combined parental income that would be spent on children in an intact family. This percentage varies based on income level and number of children, reflecting economic research showing that higher-income families spend a smaller percentage (but larger absolute amount) of their income on children.

For example, at combined monthly net disposable income of $5,000 with two children, K might equal 0.35 (35%), while at $15,000 combined income, K might equal 0.28 (28%). These percentages are built into the software programs used to calculate support.

Income Determination in California

California Family Code Section 4058 provides a comprehensive definition of gross income for child support purposes. The statute includes both traditional income sources and imputed income concepts similar to New York's approach but with some distinct features.

Gross Income Includes:

- Income from any source, including wages, salary, royalties, commissions, bonuses, rents, dividends, pensions, interest, trust income, annuities, workers' compensation benefits, unemployment insurance benefits, disability insurance benefits, social security benefits, and spousal support received from a person not a party to the proceeding to establish child support

Notable California-Specific Inclusions:

- Income from self-employment, business profits, partnership distributions
- In kind payments received in lieu of money
- Expense reimbursements or other money provided by employers,

family, or friends

- Gain derived from dealings in property (unless the gain is nonrecurring)

Net Disposable Income Calculation

The calculation of net disposable income is more complex in California than the gross income percentage approach used in New York. California Family Code Section 4059 requires deduction of:

Mandatory Deductions:

- Federal and state income taxes
- State disability insurance premiums
- Social Security taxes (FICA)
- Mandatory union dues
- Mandatory retirement contributions required as a condition of employment
- Health insurance premiums for the parent and for any children the parent has a legal duty to support
- Child support or spousal support actually being paid under existing court orders
- Hardship deduction for extraordinarily high costs of exercising visitation

In *County of Placer v. Andrade*, 55 Cal. App. 4th 1393, 64 Cal. Rptr. 2d 605 (1997), the Court of Appeal addressed the calculation of net disposable income for self-employed parents: "For self-employed individuals, business expenses may be deducted from gross receipts, but only to the extent they are necessary for the production of income and are reasonable in amount."

Custody Time and Its Impact

One of the distinctive features of California's formula is its consideration of custody time. The H% factor in the formula represents the approximate percentage of time the higher-earning parent has custody of the children.

This reflects the principle that the parent with greater custody time incurs more direct costs for the children's daily needs.

California courts have wrestled with how to define and calculate custody time. In *In re Marriage of Gigliotti*, 33 Cal. App. 4th 518, 39 Cal. Rptr. 2d 347 (1995), the court held that "timeshare refers to the amount of time each parent has primary physical responsibility for the children, which may differ from the amount of time the children spend with each parent."

Significant Custody Time Adjustments: When a parent has the children for a substantial amount of time, California law provides for adjustments to account for the increased costs borne by that parent. Family Code Section 4055(b)(1)(D) provides special rules when either parent has custody time of less than 20% or more than 50%.

Add-On Expenses in California

California distinguishes between mandatory and discretionary add-on expenses. Family Code Section 4062 addresses these additional costs:

Mandatory Add-Ons:

- Child care costs related to employment or to reasonably necessary education or training for employment skills
- Costs of uninsured health care for the children
- Travel expenses for visitation (when necessary to effectuate court-ordered visitation)

Discretionary Add-Ons: Courts may order additional expenses for:

- Educational or other special needs of the child
- Travel expenses for visitation beyond the mandatory minimum
- Other expenses determined to be in the best interest of the child

In *In re Marriage of Cheriton*, 92 Cal. App. 4th 269, 111 Cal. Rptr. 2d 755 (2001), the Court of Appeal addressed private school expenses: "Private school expenses are not automatically required but may be ordered when consistent with the family's pre-separation standard of living and the parents' financial circumstances."

V. Duration and Termination of Support

Age of Majority and Emancipation

Both New York and California extend child support beyond the traditional age of majority in certain circumstances, recognizing that modern economic conditions often require parental support well into the child's early adult years.

New York Duration Rules: New York Family Court Act Section 413(1)(a) provides that child support continues until the child reaches age 21, unless the child becomes emancipated earlier. The statute defines emancipation as occurring when the child:

- Marries
- Enters military service
- Becomes self-supporting
- Dies

The Court of Appeals addressed emancipation in *Matter of Roe v. Doe*, 29 N.Y.2d 188, 324 N.Y.S.2d 71 (1971): "Emancipation is not automatic upon reaching majority but depends upon the specific circumstances of each case, including the child's need for support and the parent's ability to provide it."

California Duration Rules: California's approach is more complex. Family Code Section 3901 provides that support generally continues until the child reaches age 18, but extends to age 19 if the child is still in high school and reasonably expected to graduate. Support may continue beyond these ages if the child is incapacitated.

Post-Majority Educational Support

Both states allow courts to order parents to contribute to their adult children's higher education expenses, but the approaches differ significantly.

New York Educational Support: New York courts have broad discretion to order educational support for children attending college or vocational training. In *Matter of Mahfuz v. Mahfuz*, 306 A.D.2d 904, 762 N.Y.S.2d 765 (4th Dep't 2003), the Appellate Division established factors for determining educational support:

- Financial resources of both parents
- The child's commitment to and aptitude for the requested education
- The child's financial resources, including ability to earn income during school breaks
- The ability of the child to receive financial aid
- The education the child would have received if the parents had remained together

California Educational Support: California takes a more restrictive approach. Family Code Section 3901 generally limits support to age 18 (or 19 if still in high school). However, courts may order educational support as part of spousal support or property division, rather than as child support per se. In *In re Marriage of Cheriton*, 92 Cal. App. 4th 269, 111 Cal. Rptr. 2d 755 (2001), the court noted that "educational support for adult children is not automatic but may be ordered based on the parties' ability to pay and the educational standards established during the marriage."

VI. Modification of Child Support Orders

Legal Standards for Modification

Child support orders are not permanent and may be modified when circumstances change substantially. Both states have established specific standards for when modification is appropriate, balancing the need for stability with the recognition that economic circumstances change over time.

New York Modification Standards: New York Family Court Act Section 451 provides several grounds for modification:

- Three years have passed since the order was entered or last modified
- Either party's gross income has changed by 15% or more since the last order
- There has been a substantial change in circumstances

The Court of Appeals clarified the substantial change standard in *Matter of Brescia v. Fitts*, 56 N.Y.2d 132, 451 N.Y.S.2d 68 (1982): "A substantial change in circumstances must be shown to be substantial in degree, continuing in duration, and material to the child's needs or the parent's ability to provide support."

California Modification Standards: California Family Code Section 3651 allows modification when there is a "significant change of circumstances." The statute provides that a rebuttable presumption of significant change exists if:

- At least three years have passed since the last order
- The requested modification is at least 20% and $50 per month different from the current order
- Either party's income has changed significantly

Procedural Requirements

Both states require specific procedural steps for modification requests, including updated financial disclosures and proof of changed circumstances.

New York Procedures: A party seeking modification must file a petition in the court that issued the original order, accompanied by an updated Statement of Net Worth and supporting documentation. New York Family Court Act Section 451(2) requires that the petitioner demonstrate the grounds for modification through admissible evidence.

California Procedures: California requires filing a Request for Order (Form FL-300) with current Income and Expense Declarations (Form FL-150). The requesting party must provide evidence of the changed circumstances that justify modification.

Retroactivity Limitations

Both states generally prohibit retroactive modification of support orders, recognizing that parents and children rely on the certainty of existing orders.

In *Matter of Hoffman v. Hoffman*, 67 N.Y.2d 845, 501 N.Y.S.2d 194 (1986), New York's Court of Appeals held that "support obligations that have accrued and become due cannot be retroactively modified." California follows a similar rule in Family Code Section 3653, which provides that modification is effective only from the date of filing the request for modification.

VII. Enforcement Mechanisms: Ensuring Compliance

Administrative Enforcement Tools

Both states have developed sophisticated administrative enforcement systems that operate largely without direct court intervention. These systems are designed to provide efficient collection mechanisms while preserving judicial resources for more complex cases.

Wage Withholding: Immediate wage withholding is required in all new support orders unless both parties specifically agree otherwise and the court finds that an alternative arrangement is in the child's best interest. New York Social Services Law Section 111-b and California Family Code Section 5230 mandate automatic wage assignments.

In *Matter of Overton v. Overton*, 181 A.D.2d 1021, 582 N.Y.S.2d 314 (3d Dep't 1992), New York's Appellate Division confirmed that "wage assignment orders are self-executing and do not require further court intervention once properly established."

Asset Seizure and Garnishment: Both states authorize seizure of bank accounts, real estate, and other assets to satisfy support arrearages. New York's Support Collection Unit and California's Department of Child Support Services have broad authority to locate and attach assets without prior court approval in many circumstances.

Credit Reporting: Delinquent support obligations are reported to credit agencies, affecting the obligor's ability to obtain credit, mortgages, and other financial services. This enforcement tool has proven particularly effective with middle and upper-income obligors who are concerned about their credit ratings.

License Suspension Programs: Both states authorize suspension of various licenses for support delinquency:

- Driver's licenses
- Professional and occupational licenses
- Recreational licenses (hunting, fishing, etc.)
- Business licenses

In *Matter of Anonymous v. Anonymous*, 558 N.Y.S.2d 447 (Fam. Ct. 1990), a New York Family Court held that license suspension serves both punitive and coercive purposes: "The suspension operates both to punish past non-compliance and to encourage future compliance with support obligations."

Passport Denial: Federal law requires denial of passport applications for individuals owing more than $2,500 in support arrearages. This enforcement tool has proven effective for obligors who travel internationally for business or pleasure.

Judicial Enforcement Mechanisms

When administrative enforcement proves insufficient, courts retain broad contempt powers to compel compliance with support orders.

Civil Contempt: Civil contempt is designed to coerce compliance rather than punish past violations. Sanctions for civil contempt may include:

- Incarceration until the contemnor purges by paying support
- Conditional sentences that are suspended upon compliance
- Assignment of assets or income to satisfy arrearages

Criminal Contempt: Criminal contempt punishes willful violations of support orders. Unlike civil contempt, criminal contempt does not require proof that the contemnor has the present ability to comply.

In *Matter of McCormick v. Axelrod*, 128 A.D.2d 10, 514 N.Y.S.2d 422 (3d Dep't 1987), New York's Appellate Division distinguished between civil and criminal contempt in the support context: "Civil contempt is remedial and coercive, while criminal contempt is punitive and serves to vindicate the authority of the court."

Interstate Enforcement: UIFSA

The Uniform Interstate Family Support Act (UIFSA) provides mechanisms for enforcing support orders across state lines. Both New York and California have adopted UIFSA, creating streamlined procedures for interstate enforcement.

Continuing Exclusive Jurisdiction: Under UIFSA, the state that issued the original support order retains continuing exclusive jurisdiction over modification, while other states may enforce the order without modification. This prevents conflicting orders and forum shopping.

Direct Interstate Enforcement: UIFSA allows direct registration of out-of-state orders for enforcement purposes. Once registered, an out-of-state order has the same force and effect as a local order.

VIII. Special Circumstances and Complex Issues

Imputed Income and Voluntary Unemployment

Courts in both states may impute income to parents who are voluntarily unemployed or underemployed, ensuring that support obligations reflect earning capacity rather than actual earnings when appropriate.

New York Approach to Imputation: New York Family Court Act Section 413(1)(b)(5)(iv) authorizes imputation of income "from any source." Courts consider factors including:

- Education and training
- Work history and experience
- Health and physical capabilities
- Age and skills
- Local job market conditions
- Child care responsibilities

In *Matter of Horn v. Horn*, 138 A.D.3d 1203, 30 N.Y.S.3d 194 (3d Dep't 2016), the court held that "imputation of income requires consideration of all relevant circumstances, including the parent's efforts to obtain employment and any legitimate reasons for unemployment or underemployment."

California Approach to Imputation: California Family Code Section 4058(b) permits imputation of income based on earning capacity. The statute requires consideration of:

- Work history, qualifications, and job market
- The parent's ability to work and support obligations
- The age and health of the parent
- The needs of the children being supported
- The time necessary to acquire appropriate job skills or training
- Legal constraints such as criminal history
- Other relevant background factors

High-Income Cases and Cap Limitations

Both states address situations where combined parental income exceeds the statutory caps for guideline application.

New York High-Income Analysis: When combined parental income exceeds the New York cap ($163,000 in 2023), courts have discretion regarding support for the excess income. Family Court Act Section 413(1)(c)(3) requires consideration of:

- The factors listed for deviation from guidelines
- The child's needs and standard of living
- The parents' financial resources

In *Matter of Cassano v. Cassano*, 85 N.Y.2d 649, 628 N.Y.S.2d 10 (1995), the Court of Appeals held that "courts have broad discretion in determining support for income above the cap, but must make specific findings justifying the amount awarded."

California High-Income Analysis: California's guidelines technically apply to all income levels, but the software calculations may produce results that require judicial review and potential adjustment for very high-income cases. Courts retain discretion to deviate from guideline amounts when they would be unjust or inappropriate.

Self-Employment and Business Income

Determining income for self-employed parents presents unique challenges in both states, requiring careful analysis of business records and distinction between personal and business expenses.

Business Expense Deductions: Both states generally allow deduction of legitimate business expenses but scrutinize claimed deductions carefully. Personal expenses disguised as business deductions are not permitted.

In *Matter of Kuriansky v. Kuriansky*, 245 A.D.2d 779, 667 N.Y.S.2d 790 (3d Dep't 1997), New York's Appellate Division held that "business expense deductions must be reasonably necessary for the production of income and must be substantiated by adequate documentation."

Cash Flow vs. Tax Return Income: Courts may consider actual cash flow rather than reported tax income when the two differ significantly, particularly when depreciation or other non-cash deductions reduce reported income below actual cash available.

Child Support and Public Benefits

The intersection of child support and public benefits creates complex policy and practical issues in both states.

Pass-Through Payments: Both states have implemented limited pass-through programs that allow some child support payments to reach families receiving public assistance rather than being retained by the state as reimbursement.

Impact on Benefit Eligibility: Child support payments may affect eligibility for various means-tested programs, including:

- Temporary Assistance for Needy Families (TANF)
- Supplemental Nutrition Assistance Program (SNAP)
- Medicaid
- Housing assistance

Tax Considerations

Child support payments have specific tax consequences that differ from spousal support:

- Child support is not deductible by the payor
- Child support is not taxable income to the recipient
- These tax consequences are fixed by federal law and cannot be altered by agreement

Both states require consideration of tax consequences when determining support amounts, particularly in high-income cases where tax effects may be substantial.

IX. Agreements and Stipulations

Court Approval Requirements

While parents may agree to child support amounts that differ from guidelines, court approval is required to ensure the agreement serves the child's best interests.

New York Stipulation Requirements: New York Family Court Act Section 413(1)(d) requires that deviations from guidelines be:

- In the best interests of the child
- Based on specific findings of fact
- Supported by consideration of deviation factors

California Stipulation Requirements: California Family Code Section 4065 permits parental agreements but requires court review to ensure compliance with statutory requirements and the child's best interests.

Limitations on Agreements

Both states prohibit agreements that would result in inadequate support or that improperly waive the child's support rights.

In *Matter of Hawk v. Hawk*, cited earlier, courts have consistently held that "child support belongs to the child, not the parents, and therefore cannot be waived or compromised by parental agreement alone."

X. Conclusion: Ensuring Economic Security Through Legal Framework

The child support systems in New York and California represent sophisticated attempts to balance competing interests: ensuring adequate financial support for children, maintaining fairness between parents, providing predictability in outcomes, and enabling efficient enforcement. While the specific mechanisms differ - New York's income percentage model versus California's income shares approach - both systems share common goals and face similar challenges.

The evolution of child support law reflects broader changes in family structure, economic conditions, and social understanding of parental obligations. From early systems that relied heavily on judicial discretion to today's guideline-based approaches, the law has moved toward greater consistency and predictability while maintaining necessary flexibility for unusual circumstances.

Effective representation in child support matters requires thorough understanding of not only the mathematical formulas but also the underlying policies, available enforcement mechanisms, and strategic considerations that may affect both immediate outcomes and long-term compliance. As economic conditions continue to evolve and family structures become increasingly diverse, child support law will undoubtedly continue to develop, always with the paramount goal of ensuring that children receive the financial support necessary for their healthy development and well-being.

12

Guardianship and Third-Party Custody

I. When a Non-Parent Steps In

The fundamental principle that parents possess the primary right to the care, custody, and control of their children is deeply rooted in both constitutional law and centuries of common law tradition. This parental presumption reflects the understanding that parents are generally best positioned to make decisions regarding their children's welfare and that family autonomy should be protected from unnecessary state interference. However, the realities of modern life sometimes present circumstances where this presumption must yield to the paramount concern for a child's safety and well-being.

When parents are unable or unwilling to provide adequate care due to death, incapacity, substance abuse, mental illness, incarceration, abandonment, or other circumstances that compromise their ability to parent effectively, the legal system provides mechanisms for qualified third parties to assume responsibility for children. These mechanisms - guardianship and third-party custody - serve as crucial safety nets that ensure children receive the care, stability, and legal protection they need during vulnerable periods of their lives.

This chapter provides a comprehensive examination of how non-parents, including relatives, family friends, foster caregivers, and other concerned individuals, can obtain legal authority to care for children in New York and California. We will explore the distinct legal frameworks in each jurisdiction, the procedural requirements for establishing guardianship or custody, the rights and responsibilities that accompany these roles, and the practical implications for all parties involved.

The stakes in these proceedings are extraordinarily high. For children, the outcome determines who will make fundamental decisions about their education, medical care, living arrangements, and overall upbringing during formative years. For biological parents, these cases often represent the potential loss of one of their most fundamental constitutional rights. For prospective guardians or custodians, success means assuming significant legal and practical responsibilities for another person's child, often for many years.

Understanding the nuances of guardianship and third-party custody law is essential for family law practitioners, as these cases frequently arise in crisis situations where quick but careful legal action is required. The complexity of these proceedings, combined with their emotional intensity and life-altering consequences, demands thorough preparation and skilled advocacy.

II. Fundamental Legal Principles and Constitutional Framework

The Parental Presumption

The United States Supreme Court has consistently recognized that parents possess fundamental liberty interests in the care, custody, and control of their children. In *Troxel v. Granville*, 530 U.S. 57 (2000), the Court reaffirmed this principle, noting that "the interest of parents in the care, custody, and control of their children - is perhaps the oldest of the fundamental liberty interests recognized by this Court." This constitutional foundation creates a strong presumption in favor of parental rights that must be overcome by clear and convincing evidence in most third-party custody and guardianship proceedings.

The parental presumption serves multiple important functions in the legal system. First, it recognizes the biological and psychological bonds that typically exist between parents and children. Second, it protects family autonomy from excessive government interference. Third, it acknowledges that parents are generally better positioned than courts or third parties to understand their children's individual needs, preferences, and circumstances.

However, this presumption is not absolute. Courts have long recognized that parental rights can be limited or terminated when parents fail to meet their fundamental obligations to their children or when continuing parental custody would be detrimental to the child's welfare. The challenge in third-party custody and guardianship cases lies in determining when circumstances justify overriding the parental presumption and what standards should govern that determination.

Best Interests of the Child Standard

While parental rights receive constitutional protection, the welfare of the child remains the paramount consideration in custody and guardianship determinations. The "best interests of the child" standard, which has been adopted in various forms throughout the United States, requires courts to focus primarily on what arrangement will best serve the child's physical, emotional, educational, and developmental needs.

The best interests analysis typically considers multiple factors, including the child's relationship with each potential caregiver, the stability of proposed living arrangements, the physical and mental health of all parties, the child's educational and developmental needs, any history of abuse or neglect, the child's own preferences (when age-appropriate), and the ability of each potential caregiver to provide for the child's ongoing needs.

However, the relationship between parental rights and the best interests standard creates tension in third-party cases. Courts must determine how to balance respect for parental rights against concern for child welfare, particularly in cases where a non-parent might arguably provide a "better" environment than the biological parent, but where the parent is not unfit.

III. New York Law: Extraordinary Circumstances and Family Court Proceedings

Historical Development and Legal Framework

New York's approach to third-party custody has been shaped significantly by the landmark Court of Appeals decision in *Bennett v. Jeffreys*, 40 N.Y.2d 543, 387 N.Y.S.2d 821, 356 N.E.2d 277 (1976). This case established the fundamental framework that continues to govern third-party custody proceedings in New York today.

In *Bennett*, the Court of Appeals recognized that while parents have a fundamental right to the custody of their children, this right is not absolute and can be overcome in appropriate circumstances. The court established a two-part test that requires third parties seeking custody to first demonstrate "extraordinary circumstances" that justify judicial intervention, and then prove that awarding custody to the third party would be in the child's best interests.

The extraordinary circumstances requirement serves as a threshold that protects parental rights while recognizing that some situations justify court intervention. This requirement reflects the understanding that family courts should not routinely second-guess parental decisions or substitute their judgment for that of fit parents simply because a third party might provide certain advantages.

Defining Extraordinary Circumstances

New York courts have interpreted "extraordinary circumstances" to include a variety of situations that demonstrate either parental unfitness or circumstances that have significantly disrupted the parent-child relationship. The Court of Appeals has identified several categories of extraordinary circumstances:

Parental Unfitness: This includes situations where parents have demonstrated an inability or unwillingness to provide adequate care for their children due to substance abuse, mental illness, criminal behavior, or other factors that compromise their parenting capacity. In *Matter of Male Infant R.*, 61 N.Y.2d 985, 475 N.Y.S.2d 284, 463 N.E.2d 331 (1984), the court found extraordinary circumstances where the mother had a history of drug abuse and had repeatedly left the child with relatives for extended periods.

Prolonged Separation: Extended periods during which children have been separated from their parents and cared for by others can constitute extraordinary circumstances, particularly when parents have made little effort to maintain contact or resume custody. In *Domestic Relations Law* § 70, the legislature has recognized that prolonged separation can undermine the parent-child relationship and justify judicial intervention.

Abandonment: Situations where parents have voluntarily relinquished their children to the care of others for extended periods without maintaining meaningful contact can support a finding of extraordinary circumstances. Courts examine both the length of separation and the parents' conduct during that period, including efforts to visit, provide support, or maintain communication.

Serious Neglect or Abuse: Evidence of parental abuse or neglect, whether physical, emotional, or through failure to provide basic necessities, can establish extraordinary circumstances. Courts may consider both substantiated instances of maltreatment and patterns of behavior that demonstrate parental unfitness.

Agreement or Acquiescence: In some cases, courts have found extraordinary circumstances where parents have formally or informally agreed to allow others to care for their children and have subsequently acquiesced to that arrangement over an extended period. *See Matter of Shondel J. v. Mark D.*, 7 N.Y.3d 320, 821 N.Y.S.2d 859, 853 N.E.2d 610 (2006).

Procedural Requirements in Family Court

Third-party custody proceedings in New York are typically initiated in Family Court under Article 6 of the Family Court Act. *See* N.Y. *Fam.* Ct. Act § 651. The petitioner must file a petition for custody that includes detailed allegations supporting both the extraordinary circumstances claim and the assertion that custody with the petitioner would be in the child's best interests.

Standing Requirements: Not every individual has standing to seek custody of another person's child. New York law generally limits standing to individuals who have had a significant relationship with the child or who have been caring for the child. Grandparents, other relatives, and individuals who have maintained a parental relationship with the child typically have standing, while more distant relatives or family friends may need to demonstrate a substantial pre-existing relationship.

Notice and Service: All parties with parental rights must receive proper notice of the proceeding. This includes both biological parents, regardless of their marital status or level of involvement in the child's life. Failure to provide adequate notice can result in dismissal of the petition or reversal on appeal.

Burden of Proof: The petitioner bears the burden of proving extraordinary circumstances by clear and convincing evidence. This is a higher standard than the preponderance of evidence standard used in many civil proceedings, reflecting the constitutional significance of parental rights. Once extraordinary circumstances are established, the court applies the best interests standard to determine the appropriate custody arrangement.

Discovery and Investigation: Family courts have broad authority to investigate the circumstances surrounding custody petitions. This may include court-ordered investigations, home studies, psychological evaluations, and appointment of attorneys for the child. The court may also appoint a forensic expert or other professional to assist in evaluating the family situation.

Modification and Termination

Third-party custody orders in New York are not permanent and can be modified when circumstances change significantly. Parents who have lost custody retain the right to petition for return of their children upon demonstrating that they have addressed the problems that led to the initial custody determination and that return would be in the child's best interests.

The standard for modification typically requires proof of a substantial change in circumstances since the original order and evidence that the proposed modification would serve the child's best interests. Courts must balance the child's need for stability against the parents' ongoing rights and any changes in their circumstances.

IV. California Law: Detriment Standard and Multiple Forums

Legislative Framework and Judicial Interpretation

California's approach to third-party custody is governed primarily by *California Family Code Section* 3041, which establishes specific criteria that non-parents must meet to obtain custody of children. This statutory framework reflects California's attempt to balance parental rights with child welfare concerns while providing clearer guidance than the common law approach used in many other states.

Family Code Section 3041 requires that a non-parent seeking custody demonstrate two elements: (1) that granting custody to a parent would be detrimental to the child, and (2) that granting custody to the non-parent would be in the best interests of the child. This two-pronged test is similar to New York's extraordinary circumstances requirement but uses different terminology and places explicit emphasis on detriment to the child rather than parental unfitness per se.

The detriment standard has been interpreted by California courts to require evidence that parental custody would cause harm to the child's physical or emotional well-being. In *Guardianship of Ann S.*, 45 Cal.4th 1110, 91 Cal.Rptr.3d 227, 202 P.3d 1089 (2009), the California Supreme Court clarified that the detriment standard requires evidence of actual harm or substantial risk of harm, not merely evidence that a third party might provide a preferable environment.

Detriment Standard Analysis

California courts have identified several categories of circumstances that may satisfy the detriment standard:

Physical Abuse or Neglect: Evidence of parental abuse or neglect is perhaps the clearest basis for finding detriment. This includes not only direct evidence of maltreatment but also evidence of parental failure to protect children from abuse by others or to provide basic necessities such as food, shelter, clothing, or medical care.

Substance Abuse: Parental substance abuse can constitute detriment when it interferes with the parent's ability to provide adequate care or creates an unsafe environment for the child. Courts examine both the severity of the substance abuse problem and its impact on parenting capacity.

Mental Health Issues: Serious mental health problems that compromise parenting ability can support a detriment finding, though courts must be careful to avoid discrimination based solely on mental health status. The focus must be on the functional impact of mental health issues on parenting ability.

Domestic Violence: Exposure to domestic violence, whether as a direct victim or witness, can constitute detriment to children. California courts have recognized that children who witness domestic violence suffer emotional harm even when they are not directly targeted.

Instability and Abandonment: Patterns of instability, including frequent relocations, inconsistent living arrangements, or periods of abandonment, can support detriment findings when they interfere with the child's need for stability and security.

Criminal Activity: Parental involvement in criminal activity, particularly drug-related offenses or crimes involving violence, can constitute detriment when it creates risks for children or interferes with parenting capacity.

Probate Court Guardianships

California's guardianship system operates primarily through the probate courts under the *Probate Code Sections* 1500-1601. Probate guardianships can encompass guardianship of the person, guardianship of the estate, or both, depending on the child's circumstances and needs.

Guardianship of the Person: This type of guardianship grants the guardian authority to make decisions regarding the child's residence, education, medical care, and general welfare. The guardian assumes many of the rights and responsibilities typically held by parents, though certain decisions may require court approval.

Guardianship of the Estate: When a child has significant assets or receives property through inheritance or other means, the court may appoint a guardian of the estate to manage these assets. Estate guardians have fiduciary duties to preserve and manage the child's property for the child's benefit.

Temporary Guardianships: California law provides for temporary guardianships in emergency situations where immediate intervention is necessary to protect a child's welfare. *See Probate Code Section* 2250. Temporary guardianships can be established quickly but are limited in duration and scope.

Procedural Requirements in Probate Court

The process for establishing a probate guardianship in California involves several important steps:

Petition Filing: The prospective guardian must file a petition with the probate court that includes detailed information about the child, the proposed guardian, and the circumstances justifying guardianship. The petition must be accompanied by various supporting documents and declarations.

Notice Requirements: California law requires extensive notice to family members and other interested parties. *See Probate Code Section* 1511. Notice must be given to the child's parents, grandparents, siblings over age 12, and other relatives as specified by statute. The notice requirements are designed to ensure that all interested parties have an opportunity to participate in the proceedings.

Court Investigation: The probate court typically orders an investigation by a court investigator or other qualified professional. *See Probate Code Section* 1513. The investigation includes interviews with the proposed guardian, the child, family members, and others, as well as a home study and review of relevant records.

Hearing and Determination: After the investigation is completed, the court holds a hearing where all parties can present evidence and arguments. The court must find that guardianship is in the child's best interests and that the proposed guardian is suitable and qualified.

Letters of Guardianship: If the court grants the petition, it issues Letters of Guardianship that document the guardian's authority and responsibilities. These letters serve as proof of the guardian's legal authority in dealings with schools, medical providers, and other institutions.

Ongoing Supervision and Reporting

California probate guardianships are subject to ongoing court supervision. Guardians may be required to file annual reports detailing the child's circumstances, major decisions made during the reporting period, and any significant changes in the child's or guardian's situation. *See Probate Code Section* 1513.1.

Estate guardians have additional reporting requirements, including detailed accountings of all financial transactions involving the child's assets. These accountings must be filed annually or as otherwise ordered by the court and are subject to review by interested parties.

V. Special Considerations for Grandparents and Relatives

Grandparent Rights in New York

New York has recognized limited rights for grandparents to seek visitation with their grandchildren under certain circumstances. *Domestic Relations Law Section* 72 permits grandparents to petition for visitation when specific conditions are met, including situations where one parent is deceased, the parents are divorced or separated, or the grandparent relationship has been interfered with by the parents.

The landmark case *Troxel v. Granville*, 530 U.S. 57 (2000), significantly impacted grandparent visitation laws nationwide by establishing that courts must give special weight to parental decisions regarding third-party visitation. In response to *Troxel*, New York courts have applied heightened scrutiny to grandparent visitation petitions, requiring clear evidence that visitation would serve the child's best interests and that the parent's objection is not reasonable.

In custody proceedings, grandparents often have advantages over non-relatives due to the presumption that maintaining family relationships is generally beneficial for children. However, grandparents must still meet the same legal standards as other third parties, including the extraordinary circumstances requirement in custody cases.

Kinship Care and Relative Preferences

Both New York and California have adopted policies that prefer placement with relatives when children cannot remain with their parents. This preference, often called "kinship care," recognizes that placement with relatives can help preserve family connections, cultural identity, and stability for children.

New York's Kinship Foster Care: When children are removed from parental custody through child protective proceedings, New York prioritizes placement with relatives who meet licensing requirements. The state provides support services and financial assistance to kinship caregivers through various programs.

California's Relative Caregiver Program: California operates extensive kinship care programs that provide support to relatives caring for children. These programs include financial assistance, case management services, and legal support to help relatives obtain permanent custody or guardianship.

Kinship Guardianship Assistance Programs

Both states operate Kinship Guardianship Assistance Programs (KinGAP) that provide ongoing financial and supportive services to relatives who become legal guardians of children who have been in foster care. These programs are designed to promote permanency for children while maintaining family connections.

Eligibility Requirements: To qualify for KinGAP benefits, caregivers typically must be relatives of the child, must have been caring for the child for a specified period, and must be committed to providing permanent care. The child must generally have been in foster care and be unlikely to be reunified with parents or adopted.

Benefits and Services: KinGAP programs provide monthly financial assistance comparable to foster care payments, medical coverage for children, and access to supportive services such as counseling, respite care, and educational support.

VI. Juvenile Dependency and Court-Ordered Guardianship

California's Dependency System

California's juvenile dependency system, governed by the *Welfare and Institutions Code*, provides another avenue for establishing guardianship when children have been removed from parental custody due to abuse or neglect. Dependency guardianships differ from probate guardianships in several important ways.

When the juvenile court determines that family reunification is not possible or appropriate, it may consider legal guardianship as a permanent plan for the child. *See Welfare and Institutions Code Section* 366.26. Dependency guardianships can be established more quickly than probate guardianships and may include ongoing court supervision and services.

Reunification Services: Before considering guardianship, dependency courts typically provide parents with reunification services designed to address the problems that led to the child's removal. These services may include counseling, substance abuse treatment, parenting classes, and other interventions.

Permanency Planning: When reunification efforts are unsuccessful, the court must develop a permanent plan for the child. Legal guardianship is one option, along with adoption, long-term foster care, or other arrangements. The choice of permanent plan depends on the child's individual circumstances and needs.

New York's Article 10 Proceedings

New York's child protective system operates through Article 10 proceedings in Family Court. When children are found to be abused or neglected, the court may place them with relatives or other suitable persons while parents receive services to address the underlying problems.

Kinship Foster Care: New York prioritizes placement with relatives when children cannot safely remain with parents. Kinship foster care provides financial support and services to relatives while maintaining the possibility of eventual reunification with parents.

Permanent Guardianship: When reunification is not possible, Family Court may establish permanent guardianship arrangements that provide stability for children while maintaining some connection to biological parents. These arrangements are less permanent than adoption but provide greater security than temporary foster care.

VII. Immigration Implications and Special Immigrant Juvenile Status

SIJS Overview

Special Immigrant Juvenile Status (SIJS) is a federal immigration benefit available to certain undocumented minors who have been abused, neglected, or abandoned by one or both parents. SIJS allows eligible children to obtain lawful permanent residence in the United States and eventually become U.S. citizens.

To qualify for SIJS, a child must obtain specific findings from a state juvenile court, including determinations that reunification with one or both parents is not viable due to abuse, neglect, abandonment, or similar circumstances, and that remaining in the United States is in the child's best interests.

State Court Predicate Orders

Both New York and California courts can issue the predicate orders necessary for SIJS applications in guardianship and custody proceedings. These orders must be issued by a juvenile court or other court with jurisdiction over juveniles and must include specific findings required by federal immigration law.

Required Findings: The state court must find that the child is dependent on the court or has been legally committed to or placed under the custody of a state agency or department, or an individual or entity appointed by the court. The court must also find that reunification with one or both parents is not viable due to abuse, neglect, abandonment, or a similar basis under state law, and that it would not be in the child's best interests to be returned to the child's or parent's previous country of nationality or country of last habitual residence.

Coordination with Immigration Proceedings: Practitioners handling guardianship cases involving undocumented minors must coordinate carefully with immigration attorneys to ensure that state court orders include the necessary findings for SIJS applications and that the timing of various proceedings is properly managed.

VIII. Practical Considerations and Strategic Planning

Emergency Procedures

Guardianship and custody cases often arise in crisis situations requiring immediate legal intervention. Both New York and California provide emergency procedures for situations where children are at immediate risk.

Temporary Orders: Courts can issue temporary custody or guardianship orders based on limited evidence when necessary to protect children from immediate harm. These orders are typically brief in duration and require follow-up proceedings to establish more permanent arrangements.

Ex Parte Applications: In extreme emergencies, courts may consider applications for temporary relief without prior notice to all parties. However, such orders are disfavored and typically require compelling evidence of immediate danger to the child.

Evidence Gathering and Case Preparation

Successful guardianship and custody cases require thorough preparation and compelling evidence. Practitioners must gather documentation supporting their claims regarding parental unfitness or detriment, as well as evidence demonstrating the proposed guardian's suitability and the child's best interests.

Documentary Evidence: Important documents may include medical records, school records, police reports, child protective services records, and other materials that document the child's circumstances and needs. Financial records may be relevant to demonstrate the proposed guardian's ability to provide for the child.

Witness Testimony: Testimony from teachers, medical providers, neighbors, relatives, and others who have observed the family situation can be crucial in establishing the factual basis for guardianship or custody. Expert testimony from mental health professionals, substance abuse counselors, or other specialists may also be necessary.

Home Studies and Investigations: Courts may order professional evaluations of proposed guardians and their homes to assess suitability. These evaluations typically examine the physical environment, family dynamics, financial stability, and other factors relevant to the child's welfare.

Financial Considerations

Guardianship and custody involve significant financial responsibilities that prospective guardians must understand and prepare for. In addition to day-to-day expenses for housing, food, clothing, and other necessities, guardians may be responsible for medical expenses, educational costs, and other needs.

Public Benefits: Guardians may be eligible for various forms of public assistance, including Temporary Assistance for Needy families (TANF), Supplemental Nutrition Assistance Program (SNAP) benefits, Medicaid, and other programs. The availability and extent of these benefits vary depending on the family's circumstances and the type of guardianship arrangement.

Insurance Coverage: Guardians must ensure that children have adequate health insurance coverage. This may involve adding children to the guardian's employer-sponsored health plan, obtaining coverage through government programs, or making other arrangements.

Educational Expenses: Guardians are typically responsible for educational expenses, including school supplies, fees, transportation, and extracurricular activities. Children in guardianship may be eligible for special educational services or programs.

IX. Rights and Responsibilities of Guardians

Legal Authority and Decision-Making

Guardians assume many of the rights and responsibilities typically held by parents, though the exact scope of their authority depends on the type of guardianship and any limitations imposed by the court.

Medical Decisions: Guardians typically have authority to make routine medical decisions for children in their care, including consent for medical treatment, preventive care, and emergency treatment. Some major medical decisions may require court approval.

Educational Decisions: Guardians have authority to make educational decisions, including school enrollment, participation in special programs, and consent for educational evaluations. They may also represent the child in educational proceedings and advocate for appropriate services.

Religious and Cultural Decisions: The extent of guardians' authority regarding religious upbringing and cultural practices may depend on the wishes of the biological parents, the child's own preferences, and any specific court orders. Courts generally try to respect the religious and cultural heritage of children in guardianship.

Limitations on Guardian Authority

While guardians have broad authority to make decisions regarding children's daily care, certain decisions may require court approval or may be specifically reserved to biological parents.

Major Decisions: Decisions such as adoption consent, marriage consent, or major medical procedures may require court approval even when a guardian has been appointed. The court may also impose specific limitations on guardian authority based on the individual circumstances of the case.

Parental Rights: Depending on the circumstances leading to guardianship, biological parents may retain certain rights, including visitation rights, the right to receive information about the child's welfare, and the right to petition for restoration of custody.

X. Modification, Termination, and Restoration of Parental Rights

Standards for Modification

Guardianship and custody orders can be modified when circumstances change significantly. The standards for modification are designed to balance the child's need for stability against the ongoing rights of biological parents and the changed circumstances of all parties.

Substantial Change in Circumstances: Courts typically require proof of a substantial change in circumstances since the original order before considering modification. This standard prevents frequent relitigation based on minor changes and protects the stability of children's living arrangements.

Best Interests Analysis: Even when a substantial change in circumstances is proven, courts must still determine that the proposed modification would serve the child's best interests. This analysis considers the child's current adjustment, relationships with caregivers, and other relevant factors.

Parental Restoration Efforts

Biological parents retain the right to petition for restoration of their parental rights and custody even after guardianship has been established. However, they must demonstrate that they have addressed the problems that led to the original determination and that restoration would serve the child's best interests.

Rehabilitation and Treatment: Parents seeking restoration typically must demonstrate that they have successfully completed treatment programs, maintained sobriety, addressed mental health issues, or otherwise resolved the problems that led to loss of custody.

Gradual Reunification: Courts may order gradual reunification processes that allow parents to rebuild relationships with their children through supervised visitation, overnight visits, and other incremental steps before full custody is restored.

Termination Upon Majority

Most guardianships automatically terminate when children reach the age of majority (18 in both New York and California), though some aspects may continue for children with disabilities or special needs.

Transition Planning: Guardians should begin transition planning well before children reach majority to ensure smooth transitions to independent living or continued support arrangements. This may involve life skills training, educational planning, and other preparation for adulthood.

Continued Support: Even after formal guardianship ends, many guardians continue to provide informal support and guidance to young adults who were in their care. Some formal support programs are available for youth aging out of guardianship or foster care.

XI. Ethical Considerations and Professional Responsibilities

Conflicts of Interest

Attorneys representing parties in guardianship proceedings must be alert to potential conflicts of interest that may arise when multiple family members are involved or when the interests of different parties may diverge.

Representation of Children: In many guardianship proceedings, courts appoint separate attorneys to represent children's interests. These attorneys must advocate zealously for their child clients while navigating complex ethical issues regarding client capacity, confidentiality, and decision-making authority.

Family Dynamics: Guardianship proceedings often involve complex family dynamics and competing interests among relatives. Attorneys must be clear about whom they represent and avoid situations where their clients' interests conflict.

Zealous Advocacy vs. Child Welfare

Attorneys in guardianship proceedings must balance their duty of zealous advocacy for their clients with broader concerns about child welfare and family preservation.

Parent Representation: Attorneys representing parents must advocate vigorously for their clients' rights while recognizing the legitimate interests of children and the state in protecting child welfare.

Guardian Representation: Attorneys representing prospective guardians must ensure that their clients understand the responsibilities and commitments involved in guardianship while advocating effectively for guardianship when appropriate.

XII. Emerging Issues and Future Trends

Technology and Communication

Modern guardianship proceedings increasingly involve issues related to technology, social media, and electronic communication between children and separated family members.

Digital Contact: Courts must consider how to facilitate appropriate contact between children and biological parents through video calls, social media, and other digital platforms while maintaining necessary protections.

Privacy and Safety: Guardians must navigate complex issues regarding children's online safety, privacy rights, and appropriate supervision of digital activities.

Cultural Competency and Diversity

Guardianship proceedings increasingly involve families from diverse cultural, ethnic, and linguistic backgrounds, requiring courts and practitioners to develop cultural competency and sensitivity.

Language Access: Courts must ensure that non-English speaking parties have access to qualified interpreters and translated documents throughout guardianship proceedings.

Cultural Considerations: Guardianship determinations should consider cultural factors that may affect family relationships, child-rearing practices, and the appropriateness of different placement options.

LGBTQ+ Families and Non-Traditional Relationships

Guardianship law continues to evolve to address the needs of LGBTQ+ families and other non-traditional family structures.

Same-Sex Couples: Guardianship may be necessary for same-sex couples where one partner is not the legal parent of children but has been functioning as a parent figure.

Chosen Family: Some guardianship proceedings involve "chosen family" relationships where individuals who are not biological relatives have developed strong family-like bonds with children.

XIII. Conclusion

Guardianship and third-party custody represent essential legal mechanisms for protecting children when their biological parents cannot provide adequate care. These proceedings require careful navigation of complex legal standards that balance fundamental parental rights against child welfare concerns.

The frameworks established in New York and California, while different in their specific requirements and procedures, both recognize that exceptional circumstances may justify judicial intervention in family relationships. The extraordinary circumstances standard in New York and the detriment standard in California provide different approaches to the same fundamental challenge: determining when parental presumptions should yield to child welfare concerns.

Successful advocacy in guardianship proceedings requires thorough understanding of applicable legal standards, careful case preparation, and sensitivity to the complex emotional and practical dynamics involved. Practitioners must be prepared to gather compelling evidence, navigate procedural requirements, and advocate effectively for their clients while remaining mindful of the profound impact these proceedings have on all family members.

The stakes in guardianship proceedings extend far beyond immediate custody arrangements. These cases determine who will guide children through crucial developmental years, make fundamental decisions about their welfare, and provide the stability and support necessary for healthy development. For biological parents, guardianship proceedings may represent the loss of fundamental constitutional rights and the disruption of parent-child relationships. For prospective guardians, success means assuming significant legal and practical responsibilities that may continue for many years.

As family structures continue to evolve and social challenges create new pressures on families, guardianship law must adapt to address emerging issues while maintaining appropriate protections for both parental rights and child welfare. The ongoing development of kinship care programs, cultural competency initiatives, and specialized procedures for vulnerable populations reflects the legal system's recognition that effective child protection requires nuanced, individualized approaches that consider the unique circumstances of each family.

The intersection of guardianship law with other legal areas, including immigration law, special education, and public benefits, creates additional complexity that practitioners must navigate skillfully. The availability of Special Immigrant Juvenile Status for certain children in guardianship proceedings, the educational rights of children in alternative care arrangements, and the complex web of public benefit programs available to guardians and children all require specialized knowledge and careful coordination.

Looking forward, guardianship law will likely continue evolving to address technological changes, increasing cultural diversity, and changing family structures. Courts and practitioners must remain adaptable while maintaining focus on the fundamental goal of these proceedings: ensuring that children receive the care, stability, and protection they need to thrive.

The legal frameworks governing guardianship and third-party custody reflect society's commitment to protecting vulnerable children while respecting family autonomy and parental rights. When these frameworks operate effectively, they provide essential safety nets that ensure children's welfare while preserving family relationships whenever possible. The continuing refinement and improvement of these legal mechanisms remains crucial for serving the best interests of children and families in crisis.

13

Paternity and Parentage

I. Who Is a Parent in the Eyes of the Law?

Legal parentage establishes far more than biological lineage - it fundamentally defines the legal relationship between adult and child, encompassing the right to custody, the duty of support, and the authority to make critical decisions affecting a child's welfare. In contemporary family law, the determination of legal parentage has evolved dramatically to accommodate diverse family structures, technological advances in reproductive medicine, and evolving constitutional principles regarding family autonomy and equal protection.

The traditional presumption that parentage flows from biology has given way to more nuanced approaches that consider intent, psychological bonds, and the best interests of children. Courts now regularly grapple with competing claims between biological and psychological parents, intended parents in assisted reproduction arrangements, and step-parents who have assumed parental roles. *See generally* Nancy D. Polikoff, *This Child Does Have Two Mothers: Redefining Parenthood to Meet the Needs of Children in Lesbian-Mother and Other Nontraditional Families*, 78 Geo. L.J. 459 (1990).

This chapter provides a comprehensive analysis of how New York and California establish and contest paternity and parentage, examining procedures for voluntary acknowledgment, genetic testing protocols, and the expanding recognition of non-biological parents, particularly in LGBTQ+ families and assisted reproduction contexts. The discussion encompasses both traditional marital presumptions and emerging doctrines that prioritize functional parenthood over biological connection.

II. The Legal Significance of Parentage

Fundamental Rights and Responsibilities

Legal parentage establishes a comprehensive framework of rights, duties, and legal standing that affects virtually every aspect of the parent-child relationship. The Supreme Court has recognized that the relationship between parent and child is constitutionally protected, noting that "the interest of parents in the care, custody, and control of their children - is perhaps the oldest of the fundamental liberty interests recognized by this Court." *Troxel v. Granville*, 530 U.S. 57, 65 (2000).

Primary Legal Consequences Include:

Custody and Visitation Rights: Legal parents possess fundamental rights to physical and legal custody of their children, subject only to best interests determinations in contested proceedings. *See* Stanley v. Illinois, 405 U.S. 645 (1972) (unwed fathers entitled to due process before children removed).

Child Support Obligations: Legal parentage creates both the right to seek and the obligation to provide financial support, continuing until the child reaches majority or becomes emancipated. These obligations are generally non-dischargeable and enforceable through wage garnishment, asset seizure, and contempt proceedings.

Inheritance and Survivorship Rights: Children of legal parents possess automatic inheritance rights under intestacy statutes and may claim wrongful death damages. *See* N.Y. Est. Powers & Trusts Law § 4-1.1; Cal. Prob. Code § 6400 et seq.

Access to Benefits: Legal parentage enables children to claim Social Security survivor benefits, insurance coverage, immigration petitions, and other government benefits tied to parental status.

Educational and Medical Decision-Making Authority: Legal parents possess exclusive authority to make educational placements, consent to medical treatment, and exercise other fundamental parental rights absent court orders to the contrary.

Constitutional Protection: The parent-child relationship receives heightened constitutional protection under both due process and equal protection analysis. *Pierce v. Society of Sisters*, 268 U.S. 510 (1925); *Meyer v. Nebraska*, 262 U.S. 390 (1923).

The Problem of Legal Limbo

Without established legal parentage, individuals who function as parents may lack any legal standing, even when they have provided care, support, and nurturing since birth. This legal limbo can prevent functional parents from:

- Enrolling children in school or consenting to medical treatment
- Claiming children as dependents for tax or insurance purposes
- Seeking custody or visitation if relationships deteriorate
- Providing inheritance or survivorship benefits
- Obtaining family-based immigration relief

See Deborah L. Forman, *Interstate Child Support Remedies and the Meaning of "Parent,"* 36 Fam. L.Q. 353 (2002).

III. Establishing Parentage: Voluntary and Judicial Mechanisms

New York Procedures

Voluntary Acknowledgment of Paternity (AOP)

New York's Acknowledgment of Paternity process, codified in Family Court Act § 516-a and Social Services Law § 111-k, provides a streamlined administrative mechanism for establishing paternity without court proceedings.

Execution Requirements:

- Both parents must sign the acknowledgment voluntarily

- Signatures must be witnessed or notarized
- The acknowledgment may be signed at the hospital at birth or later at local registrar offices
- No genetic testing is required prior to execution

Legal Effect: Once filed, the AOP creates a legal presumption of paternity equivalent to a court judgment. *Matter of Commissioner of Social Services v. Carty*, 96 N.Y.2d 71, 725 N.Y.S.2d 61 (2001). The acknowledgment:

- Establishes the father's name on the birth certificate
- Creates reciprocal support obligations and inheritance rights
- Provides basis for custody and visitation petitions
- May be used to establish jurisdiction in other states under the Uniform Interstate Family Support Act

Rescission and Challenge: The AOP may be challenged in three ways:

1. **Administrative Rescission:** Either parent may rescind within 60 days by filing Form DSS-4418 with the State Central Registry. N.Y. Soc. *Serv. Law* § 111-*k*(4)(*b*).
2. **Judicial Challenge for Fraud, Duress, or Material Mistake:** After the 60-day period, the acknowledgment may only be challenged in Family Court upon showing of fraud, duress, or material mistake of fact. *Matter of Shondel J. v. Mark D.*, 7 N.Y.3d 320, 821 N.Y.S.2d 238 (2006).
3. **Genetic Testing:** Courts retain discretion to order genetic testing even after acknowledgment, particularly where questions of fraud or mistake exist. *Matter of Damon C. v. Stephanie G.*, 61 A.D.3d 436, 876 N.Y.S.2d 383 (1st Dep't 2009).

Paternity Petitions Under Family Court Act § 522

When voluntary acknowledgment is unavailable or inappropriate, any interested party may file a paternity petition in Family Court.

Standing to File:

- The mother of the child

- Any man claiming to be the father
- The child (through a representative)
- The local social services district (in public assistance cases)
- The state (for child support enforcement)

Procedural Requirements: Petitions must include:

- Detailed factual allegations supporting paternity claims
- Information about the child's birth and current circumstances
- Requests for specific relief (custody, visitation, support)
- Service of process on all interested parties

Genetic Testing: Family Court Act § 532 authorizes courts to order genetic testing of any party where paternity is contested. Modern DNA testing achieves accuracy rates exceeding 99.9% for inclusion and 100% for exclusion. *Matter of John MM. v. Harriet* NN., 61 N.Y.2d 651, 472 N.Y.S.2d 171 (1984).

Default Proceedings: If a respondent fails to appear after proper service, the court may enter a default judgment establishing paternity based on the petitioner's evidence. However, default judgments are subject to vacatur upon showing of good cause. *Matter of Megan L. v. Kevin* S., 25 A.D.3d 466, 808 N.Y.S.2d 631 (2d Dep't 2006).

California Procedures

Voluntary Declaration of Parentage (VDOP)

California's Voluntary Declaration of Parentage, governed by Family Code §§ 7570-7577, provides both parents and non-parents with a mechanism to establish legal parentage.

Execution Requirements: The VDOP must be:

- Signed by both parents in the presence of witnesses
- Notarized if signed outside a hospital setting
- Filed with the California Department of Child Support Services

- Accompanied by proper identification from both parties

Enhanced Legal Effect: Unlike simple acknowledgments in some states, California's VDOP "has the same force and effect as a judgment for paternity issued by a court of competent jurisdiction." *Cal. Fam. Code* § 7571(*a*). This creates immediate:

- Presumptive evidence of parentage
- Child support obligations
- Inheritance rights
- Custody and visitation rights

Challenge Procedures: The VDOP may be set aside only under limited circumstances:

1. **Two-Year Limitation:** Challenges must generally be brought within two years of execution. *Cal. Fam. Code* § 7575(*a*).
2. **Narrow Grounds:** Set-aside is permitted only for:
    - Fraud, duress, or material mistake of fact
    - Newly discovered evidence (including genetic testing)
    - Other grounds justifying relief from judgment under Code of Civil Procedure § 473

In re Marriage of Pedregon, 107 Cal. App. 4th 1284, 133 Cal. Rptr. 2d 274 (2003) (applying strict standards for VDOP challenges).

Parentage Actions Under Family Code § 7630

California's Uniform Parentage Act provides comprehensive procedures for establishing parentage through court proceedings.

Parties Who May Bring Action:

- The child or personal representative
- The mother or presumed parent
- Any person claiming to be a parent
- The local child support agency

- An adoption agency or licensed care provider

Comprehensive Relief: Parentage actions may seek:

- Declaration of parent-child relationship
- Orders for custody and visitation
- Child support judgments
- Reimbursement for pregnancy and birth expenses
- Attorney fees and costs

Joinder Requirements: All presumed parents and individuals claiming parental rights must be joined as parties to prevent inconsistent judgments. *Cal. Fam. Code* § 7635.

IV. Presumptions of Parentage

Theoretical Foundations

Legal presumptions of parentage serve multiple policy objectives: protecting the stability of family relationships, preventing disruption to children's established bonds, and providing certainty in legal status. These presumptions reflect the principle that "the best interests of the child include the preservation of stable family relationships." *Michael H. v. Gerald D.*, 491 U.S. 110, 130 (1989).

California's Comprehensive Presumption Framework

Family Code § 7611 establishes that a person is presumed to be the natural parent of a child if:

(a) Marriage Presumption: The presumed parent and the child's mother are or have been married to each other and the child is born during the marriage, or within 300 days after the marriage is terminated.

(b) Attempted Marriage Presumption: The presumed parent and the child's mother have attempted to marry each other in compliance with law, although the attempted marriage is void or voidable, and the child is born during the attempted marriage or within 300 days after termination.

(c) Post-Birth Marriage Presumption: After the child's birth, the presumed parent and mother have married or attempted to marry, and the presumed parent has acknowledged paternity in writing or consented to be named on the birth certificate.

(d) Receipt and Holding Out: The presumed parent receives the child into their home and openly holds out the child as their natural child.

(e) Genetic Testing: The presumed parent's paternity is established by genetic testing.

Judicial Expansion: California courts have interpreted these presumptions broadly. In *In re Nicholas H.*, 28 Cal. 4th 56, 121 Cal. Rptr. 2d 251 (2002), the Supreme Court held that the "holding out" presumption under subdivision (d) applies even when the presumed parent knows they are not the biological parent, emphasizing functional parenthood over biology.

New York's Common Law Approach

New York recognizes similar presumptions through common law development and statutory provisions:

Marital Presumption: "A child born to a married woman is presumed to be the legitimate child of her husband." *Matter of Baby Girl S.*, 140 Misc. 2d 299, 532 N.Y.S.2d 634 (Fam. Ct. 1988).

Acknowledgment and Care: Courts presume parentage where an individual has "openly acknowledged and cared for the child as his own." *Matter of Raquel Marie X.*, 76 N.Y.2d 387, 559 N.Y.S.2d 855 (1990).

Equitable Parent Doctrine: New York recognizes "equitable parents" who have developed psychological parent-child relationships despite lack of biological connection. *Matter of Brooke S.B. v. Elizabeth A.C.C.*, 28 N.Y.3d 1, 40 N.Y.S.3d 868 (2016).

Multiple Parent Recognition

California's Progressive Approach

California Family Code § 7612(c) permits recognition of more than two parents when necessary to protect the child's best interests, making it one of the most progressive jurisdictions regarding multiple parentage.

In re M.C., 195 Cal. App. 4th 197, 123 Cal. Rptr. 3d 856 (2011) held that a child could have three legal parents where:

- The biological mother and father maintained a relationship
- The mother's female partner functioned as a co-parent
- All three adults intended to raise the child together
- The child would be harmed by limiting recognition to two parents

New York's Emerging Recognition

While more conservative than California, New York has begun recognizing multiple parent situations in specific contexts. *Matter of Brooke* S.B. *v.* *Elizabeth* A.C.C., 28 N.Y.3d 1, 40 N.Y.S.3d 868 (2016) recognized that a former same-sex partner could be deemed an "equitable parent" with standing to seek custody, though full tri-parent recognition remains limited.

V. Challenging and Disestablishing Parentage

Standards for Rebutting Presumptions

California's Balancing Test

California employs a nuanced approach that balances biological truth against the child's established relationships. Under *In re Marriage of Pedregon*, 107 Cal. App. 4th 1284, 133 Cal. Rptr. 2d 274 (2003), courts consider:

- The length and nature of the parent-child relationship
- The child's emotional and financial dependence
- The availability of support from other sources
- The child's stated preferences (if age-appropriate)
- The potential for emotional harm from disruption

Competing Presumptions: When multiple presumptions conflict, California Family Code § 7612(b) requires courts to determine parentage based on the child's best interests, considering factors including:

- Policy favoring legitimacy and two-parent families
- Relative strength of evidence supporting each presumption
- Length of time elapsed since child's birth
- Nature of the relationship between child and each presumed parent

New York's Restrictive Approach

New York takes a more restrictive view of challenging established parentage, particularly where psychological bonds have formed. *Matter of Shondel J. v. Mark D.*, 7 N.Y.3d 320, 821 N.Y.S.2d 238 (2006) established that challenges to acknowledgments of paternity must meet stringent standards:

Clear and Convincing Evidence: Challengers must prove fraud, duress, or material mistake by clear and convincing evidence, not merely a preponderance.

Substantial Compliance: Technical defects in acknowledgment procedures do not void the document absent prejudice to the challenging party.

Best Interests Analysis: Even with genetic evidence disproving paternity, courts may decline to disestablish parentage if doing so would harm the child's best interests.

Equitable Estoppel Doctrine

Both states apply equitable estoppel to prevent individuals from denying parentage when doing so would harm a child who has reasonably relied on the parental relationship.

California Applications

County of Los Angeles v. Navarro, 93 Cal. App. 4th 1139, 113 Cal. Rptr. 2d 636 (2001) established the elements of equitable estoppel in parentage cases:

1. **Conduct by Presumed Parent:** The individual acted in a manner consistent with parentage
2. **Reasonable Reliance:** The child reasonably relied on the parental relationship
3. **Detrimental Change of Position:** The child would be harmed by

disruption of the relationship

4. **Unconscionable Result:** Denial of parentage would produce an unconscionable result

New York Applications

New York applies estoppel more restrictively, focusing primarily on cases involving intentional deception or prolonged assumption of parental duties. *Matter of Baby Girl S.*, 140 Misc. 2d 299, 532 N.Y.S.2d 634 (Fam. Ct. 1988) held that a husband who knowingly accepted another man's child as his own could be estopped from later denying paternity.

Genetic Testing Procedures and Limitations

Technical Standards

Both states require genetic testing to meet scientific standards for admissibility:

Chain of Custody: Samples must be collected, transported, and analyzed under documented chain of custody procedures. *People v. Venegas*, 18 Cal. 4th 47, 74 Cal. Rptr. 2d 262 (1998).

Laboratory Accreditation: Testing laboratories must maintain accreditation from the American Association of Blood Banks or equivalent organizations.

Statistical Standards: Results must meet minimum probability thresholds (typically 99% or higher) for presumptive paternity determinations.

Judicial Discretion in Ordering Tests

Courts retain discretion to order or refuse genetic testing based on equitable considerations:

Factors Supporting Testing:

- Timely challenge by interested party
- Substantial evidence questioning established paternity
- Limited psychological harm to child

- Strong policy interest in biological truth

Factors Against Testing:

- Long-established parent-child relationship
- Potential for serious emotional harm to child
- Lack of alternative support for child
- Evidence of forum shopping or harassment

Matter of Cheryl H. v. Richard K., 1 Cal. App. 4th 1000, 2 Cal. Rptr. 2d 264 (1991) (declining to order testing where established father-child relationship would be disrupted).

VI. Parentage in LGBTQ+ Families

Historical Context and Legal Evolution

Traditional parentage law assumed heterosexual married couples would produce children through sexual intercourse, creating presumptions based on marriage and biology. The rise of LGBTQ+ families challenged these assumptions, requiring courts and legislatures to develop new frameworks recognizing planned parenthood through assisted reproduction.

The Supreme Court's decisions in *Lawrence v. Texas*, 539 U.S. 558 (2003), and *Obergefell v. Hodges*, 576 U.S. 644 (2015), established constitutional foundations for LGBTQ+ family recognition, but parentage rights required separate legal development.

California's Comprehensive Framework

Intent-Based Parentage Recognition

California Family Code § 7613 recognizes intended parents in assisted reproduction arrangements, providing that "if a married woman becomes pregnant by means of assisted reproduction . . . her spouse is treated in law as if he or she were the natural parent."

Key Developments:

Johnson v. Calvert, 5 Cal. 4th 84, 19 Cal. Rptr. 2s 494 (1993) established that intended parents in gestational surrogacy arrangements are the legal parents, rejecting claims by gestational surrogates.

K.M. *v.* E.G., 37 Cal. 4th 130, 33 Cal. Rptr. 3d 61 (2005) held that known sperm donors may claim parental rights if they demonstrate intent to parent, despite statutory provisions disclaiming donor rights.

In re M.C., 195 Cal. App. 4th 197, 123 Cal. Rptr. 3d 856 (2011) recognized three legal parents where biological mother, biological father, and mother's female partner all intended to co-parent.

Voluntary Declaration Access

California extends VDOP procedures to same-sex couples and non-biological parents who establish parental intent. *Family Code* § 7574 permits any person to sign a VDOP if they:

- Intend to parent the child
- Assume parental responsibilities
- Are not precluded by other legal parentage determinations

Assisted Reproduction Protections

The California Uniform Parentage Act provides comprehensive protections for LGBTQ+ intended parents:

Pre-Conception Agreements: Intended parents may establish parentage rights through written agreements before conception, eliminating the need for adoption.

Presumptive Parentage: Spouse or domestic partners of birth mothers are presumed to be legal parents regardless of biological contribution.

Donor Protection: Anonymous sperm and egg donors are protected from parentage claims, while known donors may assert rights only under specified circumstances.

New York's Child-Parent Security Act

Legislative History and Scope

In 2020, New York enacted the Child-Parent Security Act, comprehensive legislation addressing surrogacy, assisted reproduction, and LGBTQ+ parentage rights. The Act represents a dramatic shift from New York's previously restrictive approach to assisted reproduction.

Key Provisions:

Surrogacy Legalization: The Act legalizes compensated gestational surrogacy, overturning decades of prohibition under the Keane decision. *Matter of Baby* M, 109 N.J. 396, 537 A.2d 1227 (1988).

Judgment of Parentage: Family Court Act § 418-a creates streamlined procedures for intended parents to obtain pre-birth parentage orders, eliminating the need for post-birth adoption.

Expanded Parentage Recognition: The Act recognizes intended parents regardless of marital status, gender, or biological contribution, emphasizing functional parenthood.

Procedural Requirements

Pre-Birth Orders: Intended parents may petition Family Court for Judgments of Parentage before birth, providing:

- Evidence of valid surrogacy or assisted reproduction agreement
- Proof of compliance with statutory requirements
- Medical evidence of pregnancy
- Consent from all parties

Post-Birth Confirmations: For children born through assisted reproduction without surrogacy agreements, intended parents may seek parentage declarations through:

- Voluntary acknowledgment procedures
- Family Court petitions under FCA § 418-a
- Conversion of existing adoptions to parentage orders

Same-Sex Marriage Integration

Following *Obergefell*, New York courts have extended marital presumptions to same-sex couples. *Matter of Dana S. v. Tristan B.*, 62 Misc. 3d 1218(A), 106 N.Y.S.3d 708 (Fam. Ct. 2019) held that the marital presumption applies equally to same-sex spouses, creating presumptive parentage for non-biological parents.

Functional Parenthood Doctrine

Equitable Parent Recognition

Both states have developed doctrines recognizing "equitable" or "psychological" parents who lack biological connections but have functioned as parents with the consent of legal parents.

New York Standard: *Matter of Brooke S.B. v. Elizabeth* A.C.C., 28 N.Y.3d 1, 40 N.Y.S.3d 868 (2016) established that equitable parents must prove:

- Pre-conception or pre-adoption agreement to co-parent
- Residence with child in family unit
- Assumption of parental duties without expectation of compensation
- Formation of parental bond with consent of legal parent

California Standard: *In re Marriage of Pedregon*, 107 Cal. App. 4th 1284, 133 Cal. Rptr. 2d 274 (2003) recognizes functional parents based on:

- Long-term caretaking relationship
- Financial and emotional support
- Child's recognition of parental relationship
- Detrimental reliance on continued relationship

VII. Assisted Reproduction and Surrogacy

Technological Advances and Legal Challenges

Modern reproductive technology has outpaced legal frameworks, creating complex questions about parentage when multiple individuals contribute genetic material, gestation, and parental intent. Courts must navigate competing claims between:

- Genetic contributors (egg and sperm donors)
- Gestational contributors (surrogate mothers)
- Intended parents (commissioning parties)
- Subsequent social parents (step-parents, partners)

California's Comprehensive Surrogacy Framework

Gestational Surrogacy Agreements

California Family Code §§ 7960-7962 provide detailed requirements for enforceable gestational surrogacy agreements:

Pre-Conception Requirements:

- Written agreement executed before embryo transfer
- Independent legal representation for all parties
- Medical and psychological evaluation of participants
- Proof of health insurance coverage for surrogate
- Compliance with disclosure and waiting period requirements

Essential Terms:

- Allocation of decision-making authority during pregnancy
- Procedures for unexpected medical circumstances
- Financial arrangements and expense reimbursement
- Intended parents' obligation to accept child
- Surrogate's right to make pregnancy-related decisions

Legal Effect: Valid agreements establish intended parents as legal parents from conception, eliminating the need for post-birth adoption. *Johnson v. Calvert*, 5 Cal. 4th 84, 19 Cal. Rptr. 2d 494 (1993).

Pre-Birth Parentage Orders

California permits intended parents to obtain pre-birth orders establishing parentage, allowing:

- Hospital delivery directly to intended parents
- Immediate placement of intended parents' names on birth certificate
- Avoidance of temporary custody complications
- Protection against surrogate's change of mind

In re Marriage of Moschetta, 25 Cal. App. 4th 1218, 30 Cal. Rptr. 2d 893 (1994) established procedures for pre-birth relief in surrogacy cases.

Donor Rights and Obligations

California Family Code § 7613 addresses sperm donation, providing that donors to married women have no parental rights or obligations. However, K.M. *v.* E.G., 37 Cal. 4th 130, 33 Cal. Rptr. 3d 61 (2005) carved out exceptions for known donors who demonstrate parental intent.

Anonymous Donors: Have no rights or obligations regardless of circumstances.

Known Donors: May claim parental rights if they prove:

- Intent to parent at time of donation
- Subsequent conduct consistent with parenting
- Agreement or understanding with recipient regarding parental role

Directed Donations: Donors who provide gametes for specific recipients may negotiate parental rights through pre-conception agreements.

New York's Child-Parent Security Act Framework

Surrogacy Agreement Requirements

The Child-Parent Security Act establishes comprehensive requirements for enforceable surrogacy agreements:

Mandatory Provisions:

- Surrogate must be at least 21 years old and previously given birth
- Independent medical and mental health evaluations
- Separate legal representation for all parties
- Health insurance requirements and medical expense allocation
- Circumstances permitting agreement termination

Prohibited Provisions:

- Requirements regarding surrogate's lifestyle, diet, or medical care
- Penalties for surrogate's pregnancy-related decisions
- Waiver of surrogate's right to make medical decisions
- Excessive financial incentives that might compromise consent

Geographic Limitations: At least one intended parent must be a New York resident, and agreements must comply with New York law regardless of where conception or birth occurs.

Judgment of Parentage Procedures

Family Court Act § 418-a creates streamlined procedures for establishing intended parent status:

Pre-Birth Applications:

- Must be filed before birth but after 20 weeks of pregnancy
- Requires proof of valid surrogacy agreement
- Medical evidence of pregnancy and expected delivery
- Consent of all parties to agreement

Standards for Approval: Courts must find:

- Compliance with statutory agreement requirements
- Voluntary and informed consent by all parties
- Best interests of expected child

- Absence of fraud, duress, or coercion

Legal Effect: Approved judgments establish intended parents as legal parents from birth, directing hospitals to:

- Release child directly to intended parents
- Issue birth certificate with intended parents' names
- Recognize intended parents' medical decision-making authority

Compensation and Commercial Surrogacy

California's Permissive Approach

California allows reasonable compensation to gestational surrogates beyond medical expenses, recognizing surrogacy as a legitimate commercial arrangement. *Johnson v. Calvert*, 5 Cal. 4th 84, 19 Cal. Rptr. 2d 494 (1993) upheld compensated surrogacy as consistent with public policy.

Reasonable Compensation Standards:

- Payment for inconvenience, discomfort, and time
- Medical expense reimbursement
- Lost wages during pregnancy-related disability
- Life insurance premium payments

Prohibited Arrangements:

- Payment contingent on delivery of healthy child
- Compensation varying based on child's characteristics
- Penalties for pregnancy complications or lifestyle choices

New York's Regulated Approach

The Child-Parent Security Act permits reasonable compensation while establishing consumer protections:

Permitted Payments:

- Base compensation up to statutory limits
- Medical and insurance expenses
- Legal fees and counseling costs
- Lost wages and pregnancy-related expenses

Required Protections:

- Escrow accounts for all payments
- Independent insurance coverage
- Prohibition on payment until after 72-hour revocation period
- Detailed disclosure of all financial arrangements

International Surrogacy Complications

Both states address children born through international surrogacy arrangements, though legal recognition varies:

Citizenship Issues: Children born abroad to American intended parents may face citizenship complications if local law recognizes surrogate as legal mother.

Parentage Recognition: Courts may decline to recognize foreign parentage orders that conflict with local public policy, particularly regarding compensation or consent requirements.

Best Interests Override: Both states generally prioritize child welfare over technical legal compliance, providing mechanisms to establish parentage for children in legal limbo.

In re Ry, 186 Cal. App. 4th 796, 111 Cal. Rptr. 3d 910 (2010) (recognizing intended parents despite defects in international surrogacy arrangement).

VIII. Dependency Court Proceedings and Parentage

The Intersection of Child Protection and Parentage Law

Dependency proceedings - cases involving alleged child abuse, neglect, or abandonment - frequently require courts to determine parentage before addressing protective measures. Legal parentage affects fundamental aspects of dependency cases, including which parties receive reunification services, placement preferences, and standing to participate in proceedings.

Establishing Parentage in Dependency Cases

California's Comprehensive Approach

California Welfare and Institutions Code § 316.2 requires dependency courts to conduct parentage inquiries for all children in protective custody:

Mandatory Inquiry: Courts must ask all participants whether they know the identity of the child's parents and conduct reasonable efforts to locate absent parents.

Due Diligence Requirements: Social services agencies must search for absent parents using:

- Birth certificate information
- Interviews with relatives and family friends
- Social media and internet searches
- Public records databases
- Incarcerated parent locator systems

Presumed Parent Status: Individuals qualifying as presumed parents under Family Code § 7611 are entitled to reunification services and must consent to adoptions.

In re Zacharia D., 6 Cal. 4th 435, 24 Cal. Rptr. 2d 751 (1993) established that presumed fathers have constitutional rights to reunification services even if they never had custody of the child.

New York's Parallel Framework

Family Court Act § 1012 and Social Services Law § 384-b require similar parentage determinations in protective proceedings:

Notice Requirements: All parents, including non-custodial and presumed parents, must receive notice of dependency proceedings and have rights to participate.

Location Efforts: Child protective agencies must conduct diligent searches for absent parents, including incarcerated individuals and those living in other states.

Standing to Participate: Legal and presumed parents have automatic standing to participate in proceedings, while putative parents may seek intervention.

Reunification Services and Parental Rights

Constitutional Foundations

The Supreme Court has recognized that parents have fundamental liberty interests in the care and custody of their children, requiring due process before termination of parental rights. *Santosky v. Kramer*, 455 U.S. 745 (1982) held that states must prove grounds for termination by clear and convincing evidence.

Differential Treatment Based on Parentage Status:

- **Legal Parents:** Entitled to reasonable reunification services and presumption against termination
- **Presumed Parents:** Generally receive same protections as legal parents
- **Biological Parents:** May receive services but have fewer procedural protections
- **Putative Parents:** Limited rights depending on relationship with child

California's Reunification Framework

Welfare and Institutions Code § 361.5 establishes presumptions in favor of providing reunification services, with exceptions for:

- Severe physical abuse or torture

- Sexual abuse of child or sibling
- Previous termination of parental rights to sibling
- Conviction of violent felony
- Chronic substance abuse with multiple failed treatment attempts

Bypassing Reunification: Courts may bypass services for presumed parents only under narrow circumstances involving serious endangerment or previous service failures. *In re Baby Boy H.*, 63 Cal. App. 4th 470, 73 Cal. Rptr. 2d 663 (1998) held that presumed parents retain rights to services absent clear evidence of unfitness.

Service Plan Requirements: Reunification plans must address specific deficiencies that led to removal and provide concrete steps for family preservation:

- Substance abuse treatment programs
- Mental health counseling
- Parenting education classes
- Domestic violence intervention
- Housing and employment assistance

New York's Reasonable Efforts Doctrine

Family Court Act § 1039-b requires reasonable efforts to preserve families before seeking termination of parental rights:

Preventive Services: Counties must provide services designed to prevent removal, including:

- Crisis intervention and family counseling
- Homemaker and childcare services
- Emergency financial assistance
- Substance abuse and mental health treatment referrals

Post-Removal Services: After removal, agencies must provide services aimed at addressing conditions that necessitated placement while ensuring child safety.

Concurrent Planning: New York permits concurrent planning that simultaneously works toward reunification while preparing alternative permanent plans.

Placement Preferences and Relative Searches

California's Relative Placement Priorities

Welfare and Institutions Code § 361.3 establishes preferences for placing children with relatives when out-of-home care is necessary:

Mandatory Consideration: Courts must consider placement with relatives before non-relative caregivers, including:

- Grandparents, aunts, uncles, and adult siblings
- Extended family members with significant relationships
- Non-relative extended family members (NAREFMs)
- Tribal members in cases involving Indian children

Interstate Placements: California must comply with Interstate Compact on Placement of Children (ICPC) requirements when placing children with out-of-state relatives.

In re Luke M., 107 Cal. App. 4th 1412, 133 Cal. Rptr. 2d 332 (2003) emphasized that relative placement preferences serve children's interests in maintaining family connections.

New York's Family Preservation Emphasis

Social Services Law § 384-a requires extensive family finding efforts:

Diligent Search Requirements: Agencies must search for maternal and paternal relatives within 30 days of removal, including:

- Interviews with parents, children, and collateral contacts
- Review of case records and previous placements
- Consultation with schools, medical providers, and community members

- Social media and internet searches

Kinship Assessments: Potential relative caregivers must undergo background checks and home studies, though standards may be less stringent than for non-relative foster homes.

Termination of Parental Rights Standards

Grounds for Termination

Both states require proof of specific statutory grounds before terminating parental rights:

California Grounds (Welf. & Inst. Code § 366.26):

- Abandonment of child for specified periods
- Failure to reunify after reasonable services
- Severe physical abuse or torture
- Sexual abuse of child or sibling
- Chronic substance abuse endangering child
- Mental incapacity rendering parent unable to care for child

New York Grounds (Soc. Serv. Law § 384-b):

- Abandonment for six months or more
- Mental illness or retardation rendering parent incapable
- Severe or repeated child abuse
- Failure to plan for child's future
- Permanent neglect through failure to maintain contact

Constitutional Protections

Santosky v. Kramer, 455 U.S. 745 (1982) established that termination proceedings must meet heightened due process standards:

Clear and Convincing Evidence: States must prove grounds for termination by clear and convincing evidence, not merely a preponderance.

Effective Assistance of Counsel: Parents have rights to competent legal representation, and some jurisdictions provide appointed counsel regardless of indigency.

Reasonable Efforts: Agencies must demonstrate reasonable efforts to preserve families before seeking termination.

Best Interests Analysis: Even when grounds exist, courts must find that termination serves the child's best interests.

Appeals and Post-Judgment Relief

Termination orders are subject to expedited appellate review given their irreversible nature:

Automatic Stays: Some jurisdictions automatically stay adoption proceedings pending appeal of termination orders.

Ineffective Assistance Claims: Parents may challenge termination based on inadequate legal representation.

Newly Discovered Evidence: Courts may reopen termination cases based on substantial new evidence affecting the original determination.

In re Cynthia D., 5 Cal. 4th 242, 19 Cal. Rptr. 2d 698 (1993) established standards for post-judgment relief in termination cases.

IX. Immigration Consequences of Parentage Determinations

Federal Immigration Law and Family Relationships

Immigration law frequently requires proof of qualifying family relationships, making legal parentage determinations crucial for various forms of relief. The intersection of state parentage law and federal immigration policy creates complex issues requiring coordination between family courts and immigration proceedings.

Family-Based Immigration Petitions

Parent-Child Relationships in Immigration Context

Immigration and Nationality Act § 101(b)(1) defines "child" for immigration purposes, incorporating concepts of legitimacy and legal recognition:

Legitimate Children: Children born to married parents automatically qualify as immediate relatives of both parents.

Legitimated Children: Children born out of wedlock who are subsequently legitimated under state law qualify for immigration benefits.

Stepchildren: Stepchildren qualify if the marriage creating the step-relationship occurred before the child's 18th birthday.

Adopted Children: Adopted children qualify if adoption occurred before age 16 (or 18 in some circumstances) and other requirements are met.

Proving Parent-Child Relationships

USCIS requires documentary evidence of parent-child relationships, typically including:

Primary Evidence:

- Birth certificates showing parent-child relationship
- Court orders establishing or confirming parentage
- Adoption decrees creating legal parent-child relationships

Secondary Evidence (when primary unavailable):

- Hospital birth records
- Medical records showing prenatal care
- Insurance records listing child as dependent
- School records with parental information

DNA Testing: USCIS may require genetic testing when parent-child relationships are disputed or documentary evidence is insufficient.

Matter of Betts, 26 I&N Dec. 437 (BIA 2014) established standards for evaluating DNA evidence in immigration proceedings.

Special Immigrant Juvenile Status (SIJS)

Eligibility Requirements

SIJS provides a pathway to permanent residence for immigrant children who have been abused, abandoned, or neglected by parents. INA § 101(a)(27)(J) requires:

State Court Findings:

- Child has been declared dependent on juvenile court
- Reunification with one or both parents is not viable due to abuse, abandonment, or neglect
- Return to country of origin would not be in child's best interests

Federal Requirements:

- Child must be unmarried and under 21
- Must be physically present in the United States
- Must be eligible for long-term foster care or qualified for other court dependency

Parentage Issues in SIJS Cases

SIJS proceedings frequently involve complex parentage determinations affecting eligibility:

Abandonment by Legal Parents: Courts must determine whether legal parents have abandoned the child through failure to provide support, contact, or care.

Step-Parent Abuse: When step-parents commit abuse, courts must analyze whether this affects the child's relationship with both legal parents.

Multiple Parent Situations: Children with multiple legal parents may qualify for SIJS based on abuse by some but not all parents.

Matter of D-J-, 27 I&N Dec. 482 (BIA 2018) clarified that SIJS requires findings regarding legal parents, not just individuals functioning in parental roles.

Citizenship Through Parentage

Acquisition of Citizenship at Birth

Immigration and Nationality Act § 301 provides for automatic citizenship for children born abroad to U.S. citizen parents, subject to complex residency and legitimacy requirements:

Children Born to Married Parents:

- If both parents are citizens, child acquires citizenship regardless of residency
- If one parent is citizen, that parent must meet specific physical presence requirements

Children Born Out of Wedlock:

- Different standards apply for citizen mothers vs. citizen fathers
- Citizen fathers must establish legal relationship through legitimation, acknowledgment, or court order

Gender-Based Distinctions: *Sessions v. Morales-Santana*, 582 U.S. 47 (2017) struck down different physical presence requirements for citizen mothers and fathers as violating equal protection, though remedied by applying the longer requirement to both parents.

Derivative Citizenship Through Naturalization

INA § 320 provides automatic citizenship for certain children when parents naturalize:

Requirements:

- At least one parent is U.S. citizen through naturalization or birth
- Child is under 18 and residing in parent's legal and physical custody
- Child is admitted as lawful permanent resident

Adoptive Relationships: Children adopted before age 16 may acquire derivative citizenship through adoptive parents' naturalization.

Step-Relationships: Step-children generally cannot acquire derivative citizenship unless legally adopted.

Enforcement of Child Support Across Borders

International Child Support Obligations

Parents subject to U.S. child support orders cannot escape obligations by relocating internationally, though enforcement mechanisms vary:

Hague Convention on Child Support: The United States participates in international agreements facilitating cross-border support enforcement among participating countries.

Bilateral Treaties: The U.S. maintains reciprocal enforcement agreements with specific countries for support order recognition.

Federal Criminal Prosecution: Willful non-payment of child support may constitute federal crimes when parents flee across state or international borders.

Immigration Consequences of Support Violations

Failure to pay court-ordered child support can affect immigration status:

Inadmissibility: Certain support violations may render individuals inadmissible to the United States.

Deportation Grounds: Willful failure to pay support may constitute grounds for removal in some circumstances.

Naturalization Bars: Support violations may demonstrate lack of good moral character required for naturalization.

Matter of Lok, 18 I&N Dec. 101 (BIA 1981) established that willful failure to support dependents may bar naturalization.

X. Emerging Issues and Future Developments

Technological Advances in Reproductive Medicine

Genetic Engineering and Designer Babies

Emerging reproductive technologies raise unprecedented questions about parentage and legal responsibility:

CRISPR and Gene Editing: As genetic modification becomes viable, questions arise about parental responsibility for genetically modified children and potential liability for genetic modifications.

Mitochondrial Replacement Therapy: "Three-parent babies" created through mitochondrial donation challenge traditional concepts of biological parentage.

Artificial Gametes: Development of sperm and eggs from stem cells may allow same-sex couples to create genetically related children, requiring new legal frameworks.

Posthumous Reproduction

Both states address posthumous use of genetic material, though comprehensive frameworks remain underdeveloped:

California Approach: Probate Code § 249.5 provides limited recognition for posthumously conceived children in inheritance contexts, requiring clear evidence of decedent's consent.

New York Approach: EPTL § 4-1.3 permits posthumously conceived children to inherit if conceived within 24 months of death and if decedent consented to posthumous use.

Parentage Questions: Courts must determine whether deceased individuals can be legal parents of posthumously conceived children and whether surviving partners automatically qualify as parents.

Astrue v. Capato, 566 U.S. 541 (2012) addressed Social Security benefits for posthumously conceived children, emphasizing state law determinations of parent-child relationships.

Artificial Intelligence and Parentage Determinations

Algorithmic Decision-Making

As family courts increasingly rely on algorithmic tools for case management and decision-making, questions arise about their use in parentage determinations:

Risk Assessment Tools: Algorithms that predict parental fitness or child safety may incorporate biases affecting parentage decisions.

Genetic Analysis: Advanced DNA analysis using artificial intelligence may reveal complex genetic relationships requiring new legal frameworks.

Predictive Analytics: Courts may use AI to predict outcomes in contested parentage cases, raising due process concerns.

Constitutional Developments

Substantive Due Process Evolution

The Supreme Court's evolving substantive due process jurisprudence affects parental rights recognition:

Fundamental Rights Analysis: Future decisions may expand or contract the scope of fundamental parental rights, affecting non-biological parent recognition.

Equal Protection Applications: Gender-based distinctions in parentage law face increasing scrutiny under heightened equal protection review.

Liberty Interest Definition: The scope of protected liberty interests in parent-child relationships continues evolving through case law development.

Federalism and State Sovereignty

The balance between federal and state authority in family law remains contentious:

Full Faith and Credit: Interstate recognition of parentage determinations requires balancing state sovereignty with children's interests in stable legal relationships.

Federal Legislation: Congressional attempts to federalize family law through interstate commerce and spending power face constitutional challenges.

Tribal Sovereignty: Recognition of tribal authority over parentage determinations involving Native American children creates complex jurisdictional issues.

International Law Developments

Hague Convention on Parentage

Efforts to develop international agreements on parentage recognition face challenges from diverse legal systems:

Cross-Border Surrogacy: International surrogacy arrangements require coordination between legal systems with different approaches to parentage recognition.

Same-Sex Parent Recognition: Countries with different approaches to LGBTQ+ rights must negotiate parentage recognition across borders.

Cultural and Religious Differences: International agreements must accommodate diverse cultural and religious approaches to family formation.

XI. Practice Considerations and Strategic Planning

Initial Client Consultation and Case Assessment

Comprehensive Intake Procedures

Effective parentage representation requires thorough investigation of client circumstances and potential legal theories:

Relationship Timeline Development:

- Document all relevant relationships and their duration
- Identify potential witnesses to parental conduct
- Gather evidence of financial support and caretaking
- Assess psychological bonds between parties and children

Legal Theory Analysis:

- Evaluate potential statutory and common law claims
- Assess strength of biological vs. presumptive parentage arguments
- Consider estoppel and other equitable theories
- Analyze jurisdictional and venue issues

Risk Assessment:

- Identify potential challenges to client's parentage claims
- Evaluate opposing parties' likely arguments and evidence
- Assess financial and emotional costs of litigation
- Consider alternative dispute resolution possibilities

Documentary Evidence Collection

Successful parentage cases require comprehensive documentation:

Primary Documents:

- Birth certificates and hospital records
- Marriage licenses and divorce decrees
- Adoption papers and parentage orders
- Acknowledgment of paternity forms
- Insurance records listing dependents

Financial Records:

- Child support payment histories

- Tax returns claiming children as dependents
- Bank records showing support payments
- Medical and educational expense receipts
- Estate planning documents naming children

Testimonial Evidence:

- Witness statements regarding parental conduct
- Expert testimony on child development and attachment
- Professional records from schools, healthcare providers, therapists
- Social media and digital communications

Strategic Litigation Decisions

Forum Selection and Timing

Jurisdictional Advantages: Different courts and jurisdictions may offer strategic advantages:

- Family Court vs. Superior Court procedures and timelines
- Local court practices and judicial preferences
- Available remedies and enforcement mechanisms
- Appeals procedures and likelihood of success

Timing Considerations:

- Statutes of limitations for challenging parentage
- Child's developmental needs and attachment considerations
- Coordination with related proceedings (divorce, custody, dependency)
- Strategic advantages of proceeding first vs. defensively

Genetic Testing Strategy

When to Seek Testing:

- Client's confidence in biological relationship
- Strength of alternative legal theories
- Potential harm to established relationships
- Cost-benefit analysis of testing procedures

When to Oppose Testing:

- Strong presumptive parentage arguments
- Evidence of equitable estoppel
- Child's best interests in maintaining relationships
- Risk of disrupting stable family arrangements

Client Counseling and Expectations Management

Emotional and Psychological Considerations

Parentage cases involve intense emotional stakes requiring sensitive client counseling:

Managing Expectations:

- Realistic assessment of legal prospects
- Timeline for resolution and potential appeals
- Financial costs and emotional toll of litigation
- Impact on children and family relationships

Therapeutic Resources:

- Referrals to family counselors and therapists
- Support groups for non-traditional families
- Child psychology resources for explaining legal proceedings
- Mediation and collaborative law alternatives

Ethical Considerations

Conflicts of Interest:

- Multiple party representation issues
- Child's interests vs. parent's interests
- Former client conflicts in family reorganization

Confidentiality Obligations:

- Protecting genetic and medical information
- Managing disclosure in multi-party proceedings
- Coordinating with other professionals (therapists, social workers)

Zealous Advocacy Limits:

- Balancing client interests with child welfare
- Professional obligations in dependency proceedings
- Mandatory reporting requirements for child abuse

XII. Conclusion: The Future of Parentage Law

Legal parentage determination has evolved from simple biological presumptions to complex frameworks accommodating diverse family structures, technological advances, and evolving social norms. Both New York and California have developed sophisticated legal frameworks that balance biological truth, psychological bonds, and children's best interests, though significant challenges remain.

The expansion of LGBTQ+ family recognition, advances in reproductive technology, and changing social attitudes toward family formation continue to challenge traditional legal categories. Courts and legislatures must navigate between providing legal certainty and accommodating new forms of family relationships that benefit children and serve social interests.

Key trends shaping future development include:

Technology Integration: Artificial intelligence, genetic engineering, and advanced reproductive technologies will require new legal frameworks for determining parentage and allocating parental responsibilities.

Constitutional Evolution: Ongoing development of substantive due process and equal protection doctrine will continue expanding recognition of non-traditional parent-child relationships while potentially constraining state authority to limit parental rights.

International Coordination: Increasing cross-border mobility and international surrogacy arrangements require greater coordination between legal systems with different approaches to parentage recognition.

Child-Centered Approaches: Growing emphasis on children's rights and welfare may lead to legal frameworks that prioritize functional relationships over formal legal categories.

The complexity of modern parentage law requires practitioners to maintain expertise across multiple legal disciplines - family law, constitutional law, reproductive technology regulation, and immigration law - while remaining sensitive to the emotional and psychological needs of families navigating legal recognition of their relationships.

As family structures continue evolving, parentage law must balance competing values: biological truth, psychological bonds, family stability, child welfare, and adult autonomy. The most successful legal frameworks will be those that provide clear guidance while maintaining flexibility to accommodate new forms of family relationships that serve children's interests and reflect social reality.

The fundamental question underlying all parentage determinations - who should be recognized as a parent in the eyes of the law - will continue evolving as society develops new understandings of family, childhood, and the legal frameworks necessary to protect and nurture the next generation. Both New York and California have demonstrated leadership in developing progressive approaches to these challenges, providing models for other jurisdictions grappling with similar issues.

Ultimately, parentage law serves not merely to allocate legal rights and responsibilities, but to recognize and protect the fundamental human relationships that shape children's development and provide the foundation for stable, nurturing families. As we move forward, the law must continue adapting to serve these essential functions while accommodating the rich diversity of family forms that characterize contemporary society.

14

Child Protection, Abuse, and Neglect Proceedings

I. When the State Intervenes

When a child's safety is at risk, the state has both the authority and the obligation to intervene to protect vulnerable minors. This power derives from the state's parens patriae authority, which permits government intervention when parents fail to protect their children from harm. *Santosky v. Kramer*, 455 U.S. 745, 766 (1982). Allegations of child abuse or neglect trigger complex legal processes in both New York and California, often involving emergency removals, dependency proceedings, and long-term implications for family reunification or the termination of parental rights.

The constitutional framework governing child protection proceedings recognizes that parents have a fundamental liberty interest in the care, custody, and control of their children. *Troxel v. Granville*, 530 U.S. 57, 65 (2000); *Stanley v. Illinois*, 405 U.S. 645, 651 (1972). However, this right is not absolute and may be limited when necessary to protect children from abuse or neglect. *Prince v. Massachusetts*, 321 U.S. 158, 166 (1944).

This chapter explains how child protection cases unfold in both jurisdictions, including how allegations are investigated, what rights parents have, and the balance courts must strike between family preservation and child safety. The intersection of constitutional protections, federal mandates, and state statutory schemes creates a complex legal landscape that practitioners must navigate carefully.

II. The Legal Framework for Child Protection

New York

New York's child protection system is governed primarily by Family Court Act Article 10, which establishes the procedures for abuse and neglect proceedings. N.Y. *Fam.* Ct. Act §§ 1011-1087. The statute defines the jurisdictional basis for state intervention and establishes procedural safeguards for parents and children involved in these proceedings.

Investigations are conducted by the Administration for Children's Services (ACS) in New York City, or county-level child protective services elsewhere in the state. N.Y. Soc. *Serv. Law* § 424. The New York State Central Register (SCR) maintains records of child abuse and maltreatment reports. N.Y. Soc. *Serv. Law* § 422.

Family Court oversees proceedings to determine abuse, neglect, and disposition under the supervision of specially trained judges. N.Y. *Fam.* Ct. Act § 1016. The Court of Appeals has emphasized that Family Court proceedings require "careful judicial supervision" given their potential impact on fundamental family relationships. *Matter of Tammie Z.*, 66 N.Y.2d 1, 7 (1985).

California

California's dependency system operates under the Welfare and Institutions Code sections 300 through 395, which establish comprehensive procedures for child protection cases. *Cal. Welf. & Inst. Code* §§ 300-395. The statutory scheme reflects California's commitment to both child safety and family preservation, with specific timelines and procedural requirements designed to promote swift resolution of cases.

Investigations are handled by Child Protective Services (CPS), a division of each county's Department of Social Services. *Cal. Welf. & Inst. Code* § 16501.

Cases proceed through Juvenile Dependency Court, which operates as a specialized division of the superior court system. *Cal. Rules of Court, Rule 5.502.*

The California Supreme Court has recognized that dependency proceedings "involve some of the most difficult decisions courts are called upon to make" because they require balancing competing interests in family autonomy and child protection. *In re Marilyn H.*, 5 Cal.3d 295, 306 (1971).

Federal Framework

Both systems are grounded in federal mandates that establish minimum standards for child protection systems nationwide. The Child Abuse Prevention and Treatment Act (CAPTA), 42 U.S.C. § 5101 et seq., provides federal funding to states that meet certain requirements for child protection programs, including mandatory reporting systems and procedural safeguards.

The Adoption and Safe Families Act (ASFA), 42 U.S.C. § 671 et seq., fundamentally reshaped child welfare practice by emphasizing child safety and timely permanency. ASFA established the "reasonable efforts" requirement for family preservation services while creating exceptions for severe cases. 42 U.S.C. § 671(*a*)(15).

The Multi-Ethnic Placement Act (MEPA), as amended by the Interethnic Adoption Provisions, 42 U.S.C. § 1996b, prohibits discrimination in adoption and foster care placements based on race, color, or national origin, while allowing consideration of a child's cultural, ethnic, or racial background.

III. Definitions of Abuse and Neglect

New York Definitions

New York Family Court Act section 1012 provides detailed definitions of child abuse and neglect that establish the jurisdictional basis for state intervention.

Abuse is defined as conduct by a parent or caretaker that causes physical injury to a child under eighteen years of age by other than accidental means which creates substantial risk of death, serious or protracted disfigurement, protracted impairment of physical or emotional health, or protracted loss or impairment of function of any bodily organ. N.Y. *Fam.* Ct. Act § 1012(*e*).

The definition also includes sexual abuse, defined as committing or allowing to be committed a sex offense against the child as defined in the penal law. N.Y. *Fam.* Ct. Act § 1012(*e*)(*iii*).

Neglect occurs when a parent or caretaker fails to exercise minimum degree of care in supplying the child with adequate food, clothing, shelter, education, or medical care, though financially able to do so, or offered financial assistance to do so. N.Y. *Fam.* Ct. Act § 1012(*f*). Neglect also includes abandonment of the child or failure to adequately supervise or protect a child from abuse by others.

The Court of Appeals has clarified that neglect requires proof of actual or imminent danger to the child's physical, mental, or emotional condition. *Matter of Tammie* Z., 66 N.Y.2d 1, 5 (1985). The court must find that the parent's conduct "so endangers the child's physical or emotional health as to warrant state intervention." *Matter of Suffolk County Dep't of Social Services v. James* M., 83 N.Y.2d 178, 184 (1994).

California Definitions

California Welfare and Institutions Code section 300 establishes the circumstances under which a child may be declared a dependent of the juvenile court. Unlike New York's focus on parental conduct, California's jurisdictional statute emphasizes the child's condition and need for protection.

Physical Abuse is addressed under subdivision (a), which applies when "the child has suffered, or there is a substantial risk that the child will suffer, serious physical harm inflicted nonaccidentally upon the child by the child's parent or guardian." *Cal. Welf. & Inst. Code* § 300(*a*).

Neglect is covered under subdivision (b), applying when "the child has suffered, or there is a substantial risk that the child will suffer, serious physical harm or illness, as a result of the failure or inability of his or her parent or guardian to adequately supervise or protect the child." *Cal. Welf. & Inst. Code* § 300(*b*).

Sexual Abuse falls under subdivision (d), which applies when "the child has been sexually abused, or there is a substantial risk that the child will be sexually abused, as defined in Section 11165.1 of the Penal Code, by his or her parent or guardian or a member of his or her household." *Cal. Welf. & Inst. Code* § *300(d)*.

The California Supreme Court has emphasized that dependency jurisdiction requires proof of three elements: neglectful conduct by the parent, causation, and serious physical harm or illness to the child or substantial risk thereof. *In re Rocco M.*, 1 Cal.App.4th 814, 820 (1991).

IV. The Child Protection Process

1. Report and Investigation

The child protection process begins with a report of suspected abuse or neglect. Both New York and California have comprehensive mandatory reporting statutes that require certain professionals to report suspected child maltreatment.

Mandatory Reporting

In New York, mandatory reporters include physicians, registered nurses, school officials, social workers, psychologists, law enforcement officers, and many other professionals who work with children. N.Y. Soc. *Serv. Law* § 413. Reports must be made "immediately" to the State Central Register by telephone, followed by a written report within 48 hours. N.Y. Soc. *Serv. Law* § 415.

California's mandatory reporting law is broader, requiring "any person" in specified professions to report suspected abuse. *Cal. Penal Code* § 11166. Reports must be made immediately by telephone and followed by a written report within 36 hours. *Cal. Penal Code* § *11166(a)*.

Both states provide immunity from civil and criminal liability for mandatory reporters who make reports in good faith. N.Y. Soc. *Serv. Law* § 419; *Cal. Penal Code* § 11172. Conversely, failure to report is a misdemeanor in both jurisdictions. N.Y. Soc. *Serv. Law* § 420; *Cal. Penal Code* § 11166.01.

Investigation Process

Once a report is received, child protective services must initiate an investigation within statutorily specified timeframes. In New York, investigations must begin within 24 hours for reports involving immediate danger to the child's life or health, and within seven days for other reports. 18 N.Y.C.R.R. § 432.2(*b*).

California requires investigation to begin immediately upon receipt of a report involving severe physical abuse or sexual abuse, and within one working day for other reports. *Cal. Welf. & Inst. Code* § 16501(*b*).

Investigations typically involve home visits, interviews with the child and parents, contact with schools or medical providers, and consultation with other professionals. The Fourth Amendment's protection against unreasonable searches applies to child protection investigations, but courts have recognized that child safety concerns may justify less restrictive standards. *Doe v. Heck*, 327 F.3d 492, 510-511 (7th Cir. 2003).

2. Emergency Removal

When a child faces immediate danger, child protective services may remove the child from the home without prior court authorization. This extraordinary power reflects the state's compelling interest in protecting children from imminent harm.

Legal Standards for Removal

In New York, emergency removal is authorized when there is "imminent danger to the child's life or health." N.Y. *Fam. Ct.* Act § 1024. The statute requires that "removal is necessary to avoid imminent risk to the child's life or health." The Court of Appeals has emphasized that this standard requires "imminent danger of serious harm," not merely a risk of future harm. *Matter of Nassau County Dep't of Social Services v. Denise J.*, 87 N.Y.2d 73, 79 (1995).

California permits emergency removal when the child is in "immediate danger" and removal is necessary for protection. *Cal. Welf. & Inst. Code* § 306. The California Supreme Court has held that immediate danger means "immediate physical danger," requiring more than speculative concerns about future harm. *In re* A.S., 202 Cal.App.4th 237, 247 (2011).

Due Process Requirements

Emergency removal without prior judicial authorization raises significant due process concerns. The Supreme Court has held that emergency removal of children must be followed by prompt post-removal hearings to satisfy constitutional requirements. *Tenenbaum v. Williams*, 193 F.3d 581, 593 (2d Cir. 1999).

Both states provide for prompt judicial review of emergency removals. New York requires a hearing within 72 hours, excluding weekends and holidays. N.Y. *Fam. Ct. Act* § 1026. California typically schedules detention hearings for the next court day following removal. *Cal. Welf. & Inst. Code* § 315.

3. Petition and Detention Hearing

Following emergency removal, or when removal is sought through court process, the agency must file a petition in Family Court (New York) or Dependency Court (California) alleging specific facts that bring the child within the court's jurisdiction.

Petition Requirements

New York petitions must allege specific acts or conditions that constitute abuse or neglect under Family Court Act section 1012. N.Y. *Fam. Ct. Act* § 1031. The petition must be "sufficiently particular to apprise respondents of the conduct complained of" and enable them to prepare a defense. *Matter of Brandon T.*, 164 A.D.2d 763, 764 (1st Dep't 1991).

California dependency petitions must allege facts showing the child comes within one or more subdivisions of Welfare and Institutions Code section 300. *Cal. Welf. & Inst. Code* § 332. The petition must state the facts "in ordinary and concise language" and must be verified. *Cal. Rules of Court, Rule* 5.504.

Detention Hearing

The detention hearing serves multiple purposes: reviewing the basis for the child's removal from parental custody, determining placement pending adjudication, and establishing a framework for family services and visitation.

At the detention hearing, the court must find by a preponderance of the evidence that the child cannot safely remain in the home. N.Y. *Fam. Ct. Act* § 1027; *Cal. Welf. & Inst. Code* § 319. This is a lower standard than required for jurisdictional findings, reflecting the temporary nature of the detention decision.

The court must also make findings regarding reasonable efforts to prevent removal or to reunify the family. Federal law requires states to make "reasonable efforts" to preserve and reunify families, with specific exceptions for severe cases. 42 U.S.C. § 671(a)(15).

4. Jurisdiction and Disposition Hearings

The adjudicatory phase of dependency proceedings involves two distinct stages: the jurisdictional hearing to determine whether allegations are proven, and the dispositional hearing to determine appropriate interventions.

Jurisdictional Hearing

The jurisdictional hearing is equivalent to a trial in other civil proceedings. Parents have the right to confront and cross-examine witnesses, present evidence, and be represented by counsel. *In re Gault*, 387 U.S. 1, 41 (1967).

The burden of proof is preponderance of the evidence in both New York and California. *Matter of Tammie Z.*, 66 N.Y.2d 1, 5 (1985); *In re Sheila B.*, 10 Cal.3d 755, 764 (1974). This standard is lower than the "clear and convincing evidence" required for termination of parental rights, reflecting the different nature and consequences of jurisdictional versus termination proceedings.

Evidence at jurisdictional hearings may include testimony from social workers, medical professionals, teachers, and family members. Hearsay evidence is generally admissible in dependency proceedings, subject to reliability requirements. *Crawford v. Washington*, 541 U.S. 36 (2004) (constitutional confrontation requirements in criminal cases do not necessarily apply to civil dependency proceedings).

Dispositional Hearing

If jurisdiction is established, the court proceeds to disposition, which determines what interventions are necessary to protect the child and address the problems that led to court involvement. The dispositional hearing focuses on the child's best interests and the services needed for family preservation or reunification.

Courts have broad discretion in crafting dispositional orders, but must consider the least restrictive alternative that protects the child's safety. Common dispositional options include supervised visits, family services, parenting classes, substance abuse treatment, and continued removal with reunification services.

V. Parental Rights and Procedural Safeguards

Child protection proceedings involve fundamental constitutional rights that require robust procedural protections. The Supreme Court has recognized that parents have a fundamental liberty interest in family relationships that cannot be terminated without due process of law.

Right to Counsel

Both New York and California provide the right to appointed counsel for indigent parents in abuse and neglect proceedings. N.Y. *Fam. Ct.* Act § 1016; *Cal. Welf. & Inst. Code* § 317. The right to counsel extends throughout all phases of the proceedings, including appeals. *Matter of Jamie* TT., 191 A.D.2d 132, 138 (3d Dep't 1993).

The quality of representation in dependency cases has been subject to constitutional challenge. The Supreme Court's decision in *Strickland v. Washington*, 466 U.S. 668 (1984), establishing the standard for ineffective assistance of counsel in criminal cases, has been applied to dependency proceedings by some courts. *In re* K.C., 52 Cal.4th 231, 236 (2011).

Right to Notice and Hearing

Due process requires adequate notice of proceedings and an opportunity to be heard. Notice must be reasonably calculated to apprise interested parties of the pendency of the action and afford them an opportunity to present their objections. *Mullane v. Central Hanover Bank & Trust Co.*, 339 U.S. 306, 314 (1950).

Both states have detailed service requirements for dependency cases. Personal service is preferred, but alternative methods may be authorized when personal service cannot be accomplished. N.Y. *Fam.* Ct. Act § 1035; *Cal. Welf. & Inst. Code* § 290.1.

Standard of Evidence

Most findings in dependency cases must be proven by a preponderance of the evidence. However, termination of parental rights requires proof by clear and convincing evidence. *Santosky v. Kramer*, 455 U.S. 745, 769 (1982). This heightened standard reflects the permanent and irrevocable nature of parental rights termination.

Right to Reunification Services

Federal and state law establish a preference for family preservation and reunification. Parents are generally entitled to reunification services designed to address the problems that led to court intervention. These services may include parenting classes, substance abuse treatment, mental health counseling, domestic violence services, and other interventions tailored to family needs.

The right to reunification services is not absolute. Both states provide for bypass of reunification services in severe cases involving aggravated circumstances. *Cal. Welf. & Inst. Code* § 361.5(*b*); N.Y. *Soc. Serv. Law* § 384-*b*(7).

VI. The Role of the Child

Children in dependency proceedings have independent interests that may differ from those of their parents or the state. Recognition of children's interests has led to the development of specialized representation models.

Legal Representation for Children

New York provides for Attorney for the Child (AFC) representation in abuse and neglect cases. N.Y. *Fam.* Ct. *Act* § 1016. The AFC serves as the child's advocate and must zealously advocate for the child's position as expressed by the child. When the child lacks capacity to express a position or the child's expressed wishes would likely result in substantial risk of imminent serious harm, the AFC may advocate for the child's best interests. *Matter of Darren* XX., 91 N.Y.2d 177, 185 (1997).

California appoints Minor's Counsel to represent children in dependency cases. *Cal. Welf. & Inst. Code* § 317. Minor's Counsel advocates for the child's expressed wishes when the child is capable of stating a preference, and for the child's best interests when the child cannot express a preference or lacks capacity.

Court Appointed Special Advocates (CASA)

Many jurisdictions utilize Court Appointed Special Advocate (CASA) programs to provide additional advocacy for children in dependency cases. CASA volunteers are trained community volunteers who investigate cases and make recommendations to the court regarding the child's best interests. 42 U.S.C. § 13011 *et seq.*.

Child's Voice in Proceedings

Courts increasingly recognize the importance of hearing from children directly in dependency proceedings. While children are not automatically entitled to testify, courts have discretion to interview children in chambers or receive their input through other means.

The weight given to a child's preferences depends on the child's age, maturity, and the nature of the expressed preference. Children aged 12 and older are generally considered capable of expressing meaningful preferences about placement and services. *In re Marriage of Rosson*, 178 Cal.App.3d 1094, 1101 (1986).

VII. Services and Reunification Efforts

The cornerstone of modern child welfare practice is the provision of services designed to address the underlying problems that brought families to court attention while ensuring child safety.

Case Planning Process

Social workers are required to develop comprehensive case plans that identify specific problems, services needed to address those problems, and measurable goals for family progress. Case plans must be developed within 60 days of the child's removal from home. 42 U.S.C. § 675(1).

Effective case planning requires collaboration between the family, social worker, service providers, and court. Parents should be meaningful participants in case plan development, with services tailored to their specific needs and circumstances. *Matter of Star Leslie W.*, 63 N.Y.2d 136, 142 (1984).

Types of Services

Reunification services encompass a broad range of interventions designed to address the factors that led to court involvement:

Parenting Education: Classes focusing on child development, discipline techniques, safety, and nurturing relationships. These services are often mandatory for parents whose children were removed due to supervision or care issues.

Substance Abuse Treatment: Comprehensive substance abuse assessment and treatment, including detoxification, residential treatment, outpatient counseling, and ongoing recovery support. Substance abuse is a factor in the majority of child welfare cases. *Child Welfare Information Gateway, Parental Substance Abuse and the Child Welfare System*(2019).

Mental Health Services: Individual and family therapy, psychiatric evaluation and treatment, and specialized services for trauma, domestic violence, or other mental health concerns.

Domestic Violence Services: Safety planning, counseling for victims and perpetrators, legal advocacy, and specialized services for children exposed to domestic violence.

Housing and Economic Support: Assistance with securing stable housing, job training and placement services, and connections to public benefits and community resources.

Reasonable Efforts Requirement

Federal law requires states to make "reasonable efforts" to preserve families and prevent removal of children, and to reunify families when children are in out-of-home care. 42 U.S.C. § 671(*a*)(15). The reasonable efforts requirement reflects the federal policy preference for family preservation while recognizing that some situations may warrant bypass of reunification services.

Courts must make specific findings regarding reasonable efforts at key decision points in dependency cases. These findings must be case-specific and based on evidence in the record. *Matter of Sheila G.*, 61 N.Y.2d 368, 375 (1984).

Bypass of Reunification Services

Federal and state law recognize that reunification services may be inappropriate in cases involving severe abuse or when parents have previously demonstrated inability to safely parent.

California Welfare and Institutions Code section 361.5(b) provides for bypass of reunification services in specific circumstances:

- Severe sexual abuse or the infliction of severe physical harm to the child or sibling
- Murder or voluntary manslaughter of another child of the parent
- Torture, aggravated or felonious assault resulting in serious bodily injury to the child or sibling
- Previous termination of parental rights over a sibling

New York Social Services Law section 384-b(7) contains similar provisions allowing courts to dispense with efforts toward family reunification in aggravated circumstances.

Concurrent Planning

Modern child welfare practice emphasizes concurrent planning, which involves working toward reunification while simultaneously developing alternative permanent plans for children. This approach recognizes that some families cannot be safely reunified and that children need timely permanency.

Concurrent planning requires careful coordination between reunification services and permanency planning activities. Foster parents may be recruited and prepared as potential adoptive resources while reunification services are being provided to birth parents. U.S. *Department of Health and Human Services, Concurrent Planning: What the Evidence Shows* (2005).

VIII. Permanency Planning and Outcomes

Federal law requires courts to hold permanency hearings to determine long-term plans for children who cannot return home safely. The Adoption and Safe Families Act established specific timelines for achieving permanency, recognizing that children cannot remain in temporary placements indefinitely.

Permanency Options

Courts must consider several permanency options for children who cannot be safely reunified with their birth parents:

Adoption: Termination of parental rights followed by adoption provides children with new legal families and the security of permanent relationships. Adoption is generally preferred when reunification is not possible and suitable adoptive families are available.

Legal Guardianship: Guardianship provides legal authority for care and custody while preserving some connections to birth families. Guardianship may be appropriate when adoption is not desired or feasible but children need permanent homes.

Placement with Relatives: Kinship care recognizes the importance of family connections and cultural continuity. Relative placements may provide permanency through formal or informal arrangements.

Another Planned Permanent Living Arrangement (APPLA): For older youth who cannot achieve other forms of permanency, planned permanent living arrangements focus on developing independent living skills and maintaining supportive relationships. APPLA should be used sparingly and only when other options are not feasible.

Federal Timelines

The Adoption and Safe Families Act established specific timelines for achieving permanency:

- Permanency hearings must occur within 12 months of the child's entry into care and every 12 months thereafter. 42 U.S.C. § 675(5)(C).
- Petitions for termination of parental rights must be filed when children have been in care for 15 of the most recent 22 months, subject to specific exceptions. 42 U.S.C. § 675(5)(E).

These timelines reflect research showing that the likelihood of successful reunification decreases significantly as children remain in care for extended periods. *Fred Wulczyn et al., Beyond Common Sense: Child Welfare, Child Well-Being, and the Evidence for Policy Reform* (2005).

Barriers to Permanency

Despite federal timelines and policy emphasis on permanency, many children experience prolonged stays in temporary placements. Common barriers include:

Lack of Adoptive Families: Some children, particularly older youth, sibling groups, and children with special needs, face challenges in finding adoptive families.

Complex Family Situations: Cases involving large sibling groups, children with multiple placements, or parents with severe mental health or substance abuse issues may require extended timelines.

System Capacity: Overburdened courts, social workers, and service systems may struggle to meet federal timelines while ensuring adequate services and decision-making.

IX. Termination of Parental Rights (TPR)

Termination of parental rights represents the most severe intervention available in child protection cases, permanently severing the legal relationship between parent and child. Given the fundamental nature of parental rights, termination proceedings require heightened procedural protections and proof standards.

Constitutional Framework

The Supreme Court has recognized that parents have a fundamental liberty interest in the care, custody, and control of their children. *Troxel v. Granville*, 530 U.S. 57, 65 (2000). This fundamental right can only be terminated through procedures that satisfy due process requirements.

In *Santosky v. Kramer*, 455 U.S. 745 (1982), the Supreme Court held that due process requires proof by clear and convincing evidence for termination of parental rights. The Court reasoned that the preponderance standard used in other civil cases was insufficient given the permanent and irreversible nature of parental rights termination.

Grounds for Termination

Both New York and California establish specific statutory grounds for termination of parental rights, reflecting legislative judgments about circumstances that justify permanent severance of family relationships.

New York Grounds

New York Social Services Law section 384-b establishes several grounds for termination:

Abandonment: Leaving the child without provision for support or communication for six months. N.Y. Soc. *Serv. Law* § 384-*b*(4)(*b*).

Mental Illness or Mental Retardation: When a parent suffers from mental illness or deficiency of such duration and nature as to render the parent unable to provide proper care for the child. N.Y. Soc. *Serv. Law* § 384-*b*(4)(c).

Severe or Repeated Abuse: Physical injury by other than accidental means which causes or creates substantial risk of death, serious disfigurement, or protracted impairment of physical or emotional health. N.Y. Soc. *Serv. Law* § 384-*b*(4)(*e*).

Permanent Neglect: Failure for more than one year following placement to substantially and continuously maintain contact with or plan for the future of the child, despite diligent efforts by the agency to encourage such planning. N.Y. Soc. *Serv. Law* § 384-*b*(7).

California Grounds

California Welfare and Institutions Code section 366.26 provides grounds for termination in the context of permanency planning:

Abandonment: Parent has left the child without provision for support and without communication for six months. *Cal. Welf. & Inst. Code* § 7822.

Failure to Support: Willful failure to support the child for one year when financially able to do so. *Cal. Welf. & Inst. Code* § 7822.

Conviction of Felony: Conviction of a violent felony and imprisonment preventing normal parent-child relationship. *Cal. Welf. & Inst. Code* § 7822.

Developmental Disability or Mental Illness: Chronic substance abuse or severe mental illness that renders the parent unable to care for the child. *Cal. Welf. & Inst. Code § 7822.*

Procedural Requirements

Termination proceedings must provide extensive procedural protections given the fundamental nature of parental rights and the permanent consequences of termination.

Right to Counsel

Parents facing termination have an absolute right to counsel, including appointed counsel if indigent. The right to counsel in termination cases is broader than in other dependency proceedings, reflecting the heightened stakes involved. *Lassiter v. Department of Social Services*, 452 U.S. 18, 27 (1981).

Notice Requirements

Due process requires adequate notice of termination proceedings. Notice must specify the grounds for termination and provide sufficient detail to enable parents to defend against the allegations. Service requirements for termination cases often exceed those for other dependency proceedings.

Trial Rights

Parents have the right to trial by jury in termination cases in some jurisdictions, though this right varies by state. Even where jury trials are not available, parents have the right to present evidence, cross-examine witnesses, and challenge the state's case.

Appeals

Termination orders are immediately appealable in most jurisdictions, reflecting the irreversible nature of these decisions. Appellate courts apply heightened scrutiny to termination cases, carefully reviewing both factual findings and legal conclusions.

Best Interest Analysis

Even when statutory grounds for termination are proven, courts must also find that termination is in the child's best interests. This analysis requires consideration of multiple factors:

Child's Need for Permanency: The importance of providing children with stable, permanent relationships and legal security.

Quality of Parent-Child Relationship: The nature and strength of emotional bonds between parent and child, including the child's attachment to the parent.

Likelihood of Successful Reunification: The realistic possibility that the parent can address the problems that led to removal and provide safe care for the child.

Child's Preferences: The expressed wishes of children old enough to form meaningful preferences about their future relationships.

Available Alternative Permanent Plans: The existence of suitable adoptive families or other permanent arrangements for the child.

Effects of Termination

Termination of parental rights permanently severs all legal relationships between parent and child. Terminated parents lose all rights to custody, visitation, and decision-making authority. Children become legally free for adoption and may have their names changed and birth certificates amended.

Post-termination contact between children and birth parents is generally prohibited unless specifically authorized by court order or adoption decree. Some jurisdictions have begun to recognize post-adoption contact agreements in appropriate cases, but these remain limited exceptions to the general rule of complete severance.

X. Impact on Immigration and Criminal Matters

Child protection cases often intersect with immigration and criminal law systems, creating complex legal challenges for families and practitioners.

Immigration Consequences

Abuse or neglect findings can trigger serious immigration consequences, particularly for undocumented parents or those with conditional immigration status.

Deportation Risks: Parents who are not United States citizens may face removal proceedings if convicted of crimes related to child abuse or neglect. The Immigration and Nationality Act includes child abuse as an aggravated felony that can result in deportation. 8 U.S.C. § 1101(a)(43)(F).

Public Benefits: Undocumented parents may be reluctant to engage with child protective services due to fears about immigration enforcement. This can complicate case planning and service provision.

Family Separation: Immigration enforcement can result in family separation that complicates reunification efforts and permanency planning for children in foster care.

Special Immigrant Juvenile Status

Children who are victims of abuse, abandonment, or neglect may qualify for Special Immigrant Juvenile Status (SIJS), which provides a path to lawful permanent residence. 8 U.S.C. § 1101(a)(27)(J).

To qualify for SIJS, children must obtain findings from a juvenile court that:

- It is not in the child's best interest to be returned to the parent's previous country of nationality or country of last habitual residence
- The child has been declared dependent on a juvenile court or placed under the custody of an agency or individual appointed by the court
- The child cannot reunify with one or both parents due to abuse, abandonment, neglect, or similar basis under state law

Dependency courts increasingly recognize the importance of making SIJS findings for eligible children, as this may provide the only avenue for immigration relief.

Criminal Law Intersection

Child protection cases frequently involve conduct that may also constitute criminal offenses, leading to parallel proceedings in family and criminal courts.

Mandatory Reporting to Law Enforcement: Many jurisdictions require child protective services to report suspected criminal abuse to law enforcement agencies. This can result in simultaneous investigations by social workers and police officers.

Different Standards and Goals: Criminal cases require proof beyond a reasonable doubt and focus on punishment of offenders, while dependency cases use preponderance of evidence and emphasize child protection and family preservation.

Fifth Amendment Considerations: Parents may face difficult choices about cooperation with dependency proceedings when their statements could be used against them in criminal cases. Courts have generally held that parents cannot invoke the Fifth Amendment to avoid participating in dependency proceedings. *Baltimore City Dep't of Social Services v. Bouknight*, 493 U.S. 549, 560 (1990).

Plea Negotiations: Criminal plea agreements may include provisions affecting dependency cases, such as admission to protective supervision or agreement to participate in specified services.

XI. Confidentiality and Records

Child protection proceedings involve highly sensitive information about families and children, requiring careful balance between transparency and privacy protection.

Statutory Confidentiality Requirements

Both New York and California maintain strict confidentiality requirements for dependency proceedings and records.

New York: Family Court Act section 1038 makes family court proceedings confidential. Access to records is limited to parties, their attorneys, and specifically authorized individuals. N.Y. *Fam. Ct. Act* § 1038. Violation of confidentiality requirements may result in contempt of court.

California: Welfare and Institutions Code section 827 establishes comprehensive confidentiality protections for dependency cases. *Cal. Welf. & Inst. Code* § 827. Juvenile court proceedings are generally closed to the public, and access to records is strictly limited.

Permitted Disclosures

Despite general confidentiality requirements, both states allow limited disclosures for specific purposes:

Child Protection: Information may be shared among agencies involved in child protection, including law enforcement, schools, and medical providers when necessary for child safety.

Court Proceedings: Information from dependency cases may be used in related proceedings, such as family court custody cases or criminal prosecutions.

Research and Advocacy: Aggregate statistical information may be disclosed for research and policy development purposes, provided individual identifying information is removed.

Media Access and Public Interest

High-profile child protection cases sometimes generate significant media attention, creating tension between confidentiality requirements and public interest in court proceedings.

Courts have generally maintained strict confidentiality in dependency cases, even when cases involve public figures or generate substantial media interest. *Globe Newspaper Co. v. Superior Court*, 457 U.S. 596, 610 (1982) (recognizing states' compelling interest in protecting minor victims).

Some jurisdictions have experimented with limited public access to dependency proceedings in appropriate cases, but these remain exceptions to the general rule of confidentiality.

Adult Survivors' Access to Records

Adults who were subjects of child protection proceedings as minors may seek access to their dependency court records. Most states have developed procedures for adult survivors to obtain their records, subject to appropriate safeguards for other parties' privacy interests.

XII. Emerging Issues and Trends

Child protection law continues to evolve in response to new research, changing social conditions, and emerging challenges.

Trauma-Informed Practice

Growing understanding of childhood trauma has led to increased emphasis on trauma-informed approaches in child welfare practice. This includes recognition that involvement with child protective services can itself be traumatic for children and families.

Trauma-Informed Courts: Some jurisdictions have implemented trauma-informed court practices, including specialized training for judges, modified court procedures, and enhanced support services for families.

Secondary Trauma: Recognition that exposure to child abuse cases can cause secondary trauma for professionals has led to increased attention to worker support and retention.

Differential Response Models

Many states have implemented differential response systems that provide multiple pathways for responding to child protection reports based on assessed risk and family needs.

Track Systems: Low-risk cases may be diverted to voluntary services without formal court involvement, while high-risk cases proceed through traditional investigation and court processes.

Family Assessment Response: Some reports result in family assessment and service provision rather than traditional investigation focused on substantiation of allegations.

Technology and Social Media

Advancing technology creates new challenges and opportunities in child protection practice.

Digital Evidence: Social media posts, text messages, and digital communications increasingly serve as evidence in dependency cases.

Online Safety: Courts must consider new forms of risk to children, including cyberbullying, online predation, and exposure to inappropriate content.

Remote Proceedings: The COVID-19 pandemic accelerated adoption of remote court proceedings and virtual service delivery, with ongoing implications for access and participation.

Racial Equity and Disparity

Child welfare systems face increasing scrutiny regarding racial and ethnic disparities in case outcomes.

Disproportionality: Children of color, particularly African American and Native American children, are overrepresented in foster care systems nationwide. U.S. *Department of Health and Human Services, The* AFCARS *Report* No. 28 (2021).

Bias in Decision-Making: Research has documented racial bias in child protection decision-making, from initial reporting through permanency outcomes. *Emily Putnam-Hornstein et al.*, "*A Public Health Approach to Child Welfare: Improving Outcomes Through Systems Change*" (2021).

Reform Initiatives: Jurisdictions are implementing various reforms to address racial equity, including implicit bias training, blind removal protocols, and community-based alternatives to traditional child welfare responses.

Family Preservation and Prevention

Increasing emphasis on preventing child welfare system involvement through community-based services and supports.

Primary Prevention: Investments in universal services such as quality childcare, healthcare, and economic supports that strengthen families and prevent abuse and neglect.

Early Intervention: Targeted services for families showing early signs of stress or risk, provided on a voluntary basis without formal system involvement.

Community Partnerships: Collaboration between child welfare agencies and community organizations to provide culturally responsive services and supports.

XIII. Practice Considerations for Attorneys

Representing parties in child protection cases requires specialized knowledge and skills given the unique procedural and substantive aspects of dependency law.

Representing Parents

Early Intervention: Effective representation often begins before formal court involvement, including advising clients about their rights during investigations and helping them access voluntary services.

Collaborative Approach: While zealously advocating for clients' interests, attorneys should consider collaborative approaches that focus on child safety and family preservation when possible.

Cultural Competency: Understanding clients' cultural backgrounds, immigration status, and community resources is essential for effective representation.

Appeals and Post-Disposition Advocacy: Representation should continue through appeals and post-disposition modifications as needed to protect clients' interests.

Representing Children

Client-Directed Advocacy: When children are capable of expressing preferences, attorneys should advocate for their expressed wishes while considering safety and well-being.

Best Interest Advocacy: For younger children or those unable to express preferences, attorneys must conduct independent investigation and advocate for the child's best interests.

Multidisciplinary Collaboration: Child attorneys should work closely with social workers, therapists, educators, and other professionals involved in the child's life.

Transition Planning: For older youth, attorneys should focus on developing independent living skills and permanent connections to supportive adults.

Representing Agencies

Legal Compliance: Agency attorneys must ensure compliance with federal and state requirements for reasonable efforts, timelines, and procedural safeguards.

Policy Development: Attorneys play important roles in developing agency policies and practices that comply with legal requirements while promoting effective practice.

Interagency Coordination: Collaboration with other agencies and service providers is essential for comprehensive case planning and service delivery.

XIV. Conclusion

Child protection proceedings represent one of the most complex and consequential areas of family law, involving the intersection of constitutional rights, federal mandates, state statutes, and evolving professional practice. The legal framework governing these cases reflects society's commitment to protecting vulnerable children while preserving family relationships whenever possible.

The stakes in child protection cases could not be higher. For children, these proceedings may determine whether they grow up in safe, stable families or experience the trauma of continued abuse or the uncertainty of prolonged foster care placement. For parents, dependency cases may result in loss of their most fundamental relationships and the permanent termination of their parental rights.

The complexity of these cases requires sophisticated legal representation and decision-making. Attorneys representing parties in dependency proceedings must understand not only the applicable law but also child development, family dynamics, trauma, substance abuse, mental health, and community resources. Judges must make decisions with incomplete information under compressed timelines while balancing competing interests and values.

Recent years have brought increased attention to racial disparities in child welfare outcomes, the importance of trauma-informed practice, and the need for community-based prevention services. These trends reflect growing understanding that child protection is not solely a legal matter but involves broader social, economic, and public health considerations.

Federal policy continues to emphasize both child safety and family preservation, requiring states to make reasonable efforts to prevent removal and promote reunification while ensuring that children are not returned to unsafe situations. The tension between these dual goals requires careful case-by-case analysis and individualized decision-making.

Looking forward, child protection law will likely continue evolving in response to new research about effective interventions, changing family structures, technological advances, and ongoing concerns about system equity and effectiveness. The fundamental challenge remains unchanged: developing legal and social responses that protect children from harm while supporting families and preserving important relationships whenever safely possible.

Practitioners in this field must remain committed to ongoing education and professional development, given the rapidly evolving nature of research and practice. Collaboration across disciplines and with affected communities is essential for developing more effective and equitable approaches to child protection.

The ultimate measure of success in child protection law is not the elegance of legal doctrine or the efficiency of court procedures, but the real-world outcomes for children and families. Children should grow up in safe, stable, nurturing environments with permanent connections to caring adults. Families should receive the support and services they need to overcome challenges and provide safe homes for their children. When family preservation is not possible, children should achieve timely permanency through adoption or other arrangements that provide security and belonging.

Achieving these outcomes requires continued commitment to legal excellence, evidence-based practice, and recognition that child protection is ultimately about human relationships and the fundamental right of all children to safety, permanency, and well-being. The legal framework provides the structure within which these goals can be pursued, but success depends on the dedication and skill of the many professionals who work within this system to serve children and families in crisis.

As we have seen throughout this chapter, child protection law involves complex balancing of competing interests and values. The framework established by federal and state law provides important protections for all parties while establishing procedures designed to promote good outcomes for children. Understanding this framework is essential for anyone working in or with the child protection system, whether as an attorney, social worker, judge, or community advocate.

The intersection of child protection with immigration, criminal law, and other legal systems creates additional complexity that requires specialized knowledge and coordination across multiple areas of practice. As our society becomes increasingly diverse and interconnected, these intersections will likely become even more important in the daily practice of child protection law.

Finally, it is important to remember that behind every child protection case are real people facing crisis and trauma. While legal procedures and standards are essential for ensuring fairness and protecting rights, they must be implemented with compassion and understanding of the human impact of these proceedings. The law serves its highest purpose when it provides a framework for helping children and families achieve safety, stability, and healing.

15

Relocation and Interstate Custody Disputes (UCCJEA)

I. The Modern Challenge of Parental Mobility

In contemporary American society, geographic mobility has become increasingly common, driven by economic opportunities, career advancement, educational pursuits, and evolving family structures. The Bureau of Labor Statistics reports that the average American moves approximately eleven times during their lifetime, with significant implications for families navigating post-divorce custody arrangements. When a parent subject to an existing custody order seeks to relocate with a child, the intersection of parental rights, child welfare, and jurisdictional authority creates one of the most complex and emotionally charged areas of family law practice.

The tension between a parent's fundamental right to travel and establish residence, recognized in *Shapiro v. Thompson*, 394 U.S. 618 (1969), and the compelling state interest in protecting children's relationships with both parents has generated extensive litigation and legislative response. Courts must balance competing interests: the relocating parent's autonomy and potential benefits to the child against the non-relocating parent's relationship with the child and the stability of existing arrangements.

This chapter examines the comprehensive legal framework governing relocation requests and interstate custody jurisdiction, with particular focus on New York and California law. These jurisdictions represent contrasting yet influential approaches to relocation analysis, providing practitioners with essential guidance for navigating this challenging area of practice.

II. Historical Context and Evolution of Interstate Custody Law

A. Pre-UCCJEA Era: The Problem of Conflicting Jurisdiction

Before the adoption of uniform jurisdictional standards, interstate custody disputes created significant legal chaos. Parents engaged in "forum shopping," seeking courts in jurisdictions perceived as more favorable to their position. Multiple states often asserted concurrent jurisdiction over the same children, resulting in conflicting custody orders that were difficult to enforce and harmful to child welfare.

The Uniform Child Custody Jurisdiction Act (UCCJA), adopted in 1968, represented the first systematic attempt to establish uniform jurisdictional rules. However, the UCCJA's provisions proved inadequate, particularly in enforcement mechanisms and communication between courts of different states. The Act's language was often ambiguous, leading to continued jurisdictional conflicts and forum shopping.

B. The UCCJEA: A Comprehensive Solution

The Uniform Child Custody Jurisdiction and Enforcement Act (UCCJEA), promulgated by the National Conference of Commissioners on Uniform State Laws in 1997, addressed the shortcomings of its predecessor. The UCCJEA has been adopted in all fifty states and the District of Columbia, creating a truly national framework for interstate custody jurisdiction.

The UCCJEA's fundamental purposes include:

1. **Avoiding jurisdictional competition and conflict** between courts of different states in matters of child custody
2. **Promoting cooperation** between courts of different states to facilitate the prompt and efficient resolution of custody disputes
3. **Deterring abductions** and other unilateral removals of children undertaken to obtain custody awards
4. **Establishing uniform legal standards** for interstate custody jurisdiction and enforcement

III. UCCJEA Jurisdictional Framework

A. Home State Jurisdiction - The Primary Standard

Under UCCJEA § 201, "home state jurisdiction" serves as the primary basis for initial custody determinations. A child's "home state" is defined as:

This six-month requirement serves multiple purposes:

- **Stability**: Ensures the child has established meaningful connections to the state
- **Evidence**: Provides courts with adequate information about the child's circumstances
- **Deterrence**: Prevents parents from quickly relocating to establish jurisdiction in a preferred forum

B. Significant Connection Jurisdiction

When no state qualifies as the home state, UCCJEA § 201(a)(2) provides for "significant connection jurisdiction." A court may exercise jurisdiction if:

1. No other state has home state jurisdiction

2. A court of the significant connection state declines to exercise jurisdiction
3. The child and the child's parents have a significant connection to the state
4. Substantial evidence is available in the state concerning the child's care, protection, training, and personal relationships

This provision prevents jurisdictional gaps while maintaining the preference for home state jurisdiction.

C. More Appropriate Forum and Inconvenient Forum

UCCJEA § 207 empowers courts to decline jurisdiction if the court determines that it is an inconvenient forum and that a court of another state is a more appropriate forum. Factors considered include:

- Whether domestic violence has occurred and is likely to continue
- The length of time the child has resided outside the state
- The distance between the court and the child's residence
- The parties' relative financial circumstances
- Any agreement between the parties as to which state should assume jurisdiction
- The nature and location of evidence required to resolve the pending litigation
- The ability of the court to decide the issue expeditiously and the procedures necessary to present evidence

D. Exclusive Continuing Jurisdiction

Once a court makes a child custody determination consistent with the UCCJEA, it retains "exclusive continuing jurisdiction" over modification of that determination until:

1. A court of the state determines that neither the child nor the child and one parent have a significant connection with the state and substantial evidence is no longer available in the state concerning the child's care, protection, training, and personal relationships; or

2. A court of the state or another state determines that the child, the child's parents, and any person acting as a parent do not presently reside in the state.

UCCJEA § 202.

This provision prevents forum shopping after an initial determination while allowing for appropriate transfer of jurisdiction when circumstances change.

IV. Relocation Law: Jurisdictional Considerations

A. In-State vs. Interstate Relocations

The jurisdictional implications of proposed relocations vary significantly based on whether the move crosses state lines:

Intrastate Relocations: Moves within the same state generally do not trigger UCCJEA analysis, though they may require court approval under state relocation statutes. Courts focus on the practical impact on existing custody arrangements rather than jurisdictional questions.

Interstate Relocations: Cross-border moves implicate UCCJEA provisions, particularly regarding continuing jurisdiction and potential transfer of jurisdiction. Courts must consider whether the relocation affects the state's significant connection to the child and the availability of substantial evidence within the state.

B. Modification vs. Relocation Proceedings

Practitioners must distinguish between modification proceedings under UCCJEA § 203 and relocation proceedings under state law:

Modification Proceedings: Seek to change the terms of an existing custody order, including custody arrangements that might facilitate or prevent relocation.

Relocation Proceedings: Specifically address whether a parent may relocate with a child, often without changing underlying custody designations.

The distinction affects both procedural requirements and substantive analysis, though the proceedings may be consolidated in practice.

V. New York Relocation Law

A. Historical Development: From Rigid Rules to Flexible Standards

New York's approach to relocation has evolved significantly over the past several decades. Early decisions applied rigid presumptions that often failed to account for the unique circumstances of individual families. The watershed case of *Tropea v. Tropea*, 87 N.Y.2d 727, 642 N.Y.S.2d 575, 665 N.E.2d 145 (1996), fundamentally transformed New York relocation law by rejecting formulaic approaches in favor of individualized analysis.

B. The Tropea Standard: Best Interests Analysis

In *Tropea*, the New York Court of Appeals established that relocation decisions must be based on the best interests of the child, considered in light of all relevant circumstances. The court explicitly rejected both the presumption in favor of the custodial parent's right to relocate and the presumption against relocation that would disrupt the child's relationship with the non-custodial parent.

The *Tropea* court identified several factors for consideration, while emphasizing that the analysis must be flexible and fact-specific:

1. **Each parent's reasons for seeking or opposing the move**
2. **The quality of the relationships between the child and the custodial and non-custodial parents**
3. **The impact of the move on the quantity and quality of the child's future contact with the non-custodial parent**
4. **The degree to which the custodial parent's and child's life may be enhanced economically, emotionally and educationally by the move**
5. **The feasibility of preserving the relationship between the non-custodial parent and child through suitable visitation arrangements**

C. Post-Tropea Developments

Subsequent New York decisions have refined and applied the *Tropea* standard:

Baures v. Lewis, 770 N.Y.S.2d 629 (N.Y. App. Div. 2003): The court emphasized that the burden of proof in relocation cases depends on the specific circumstances rather than rigid presumptions. The custodial parent must demonstrate that the move serves the child's best interests.

Tropea v. Tropea (on remand), 642 N.Y.S.2d 575 (N.Y. App. Div. 1996): On remand, the Appellate Division provided additional guidance on applying the best interests standard, emphasizing the importance of maintaining meaningful relationships with both parents.

Weiss v. Weiss, 52 N.Y.S.3d 651 (N.Y. App. Div. 2017): The court clarified that economic motivations for relocation, while relevant, must be weighed against other factors affecting the child's welfare, including the impact on parental relationships.

D. Procedural Requirements in New York

New York relocation proceedings typically involve:

1. **Petition for Modification**: The relocating parent must file a petition to modify the existing custody or visitation order
2. **Order to Show Cause**: The non-relocating parent may file an order to show cause seeking to enjoin the relocation
3. **Attorney for the Child**: Courts frequently appoint an Attorney for the Child to represent the child's interests independently
4. **Forensic Evaluation**: Complex cases may require mental health professionals to evaluate the family dynamics and make recommendations
5. **Evidentiary Hearing**: Contested cases typically require a full evidentiary hearing with live testimony

E. New York Case Law Applications

Matter of Lincoln v. Lincoln, 24 N.Y.3d 1087, 999 N.Y.S.2d 420, 25 N.E.3d 1035 (2014): The Court of Appeals reaffirmed that trial courts possess broad discretion in relocation cases and that appellate review is limited to whether the determination lacks a sound and substantial basis in the record.

Levine v. Levine, 56 A.D.3d 1180, 868 N.Y.S.2d 554 (N.Y. App. Div. 2008): The court demonstrated the application of *Tropea* factors where the mother's relocation for a medical residency was permitted despite the impact on the father's relationship with the child, based on the long-term educational and economic benefits to the family.

Campanaro v. Campanaro, 49 A.D.3d 1026, 855 N.Y.S.2d 316 (N.Y. App. Div. 2008): The court denied relocation where the mother's primary motivation appeared to be interfering with the father's relationship with the child, rather than serving the child's best interests.

VI. California Relocation Law

A. The Burgess Presumption and Its Evolution

California's approach to relocation has been shaped by a series of influential Court of Appeal and Supreme Court decisions that have created a more structured framework than New York's purely discretionary standard.

In re Marriage of Burgess, 13 Cal.4th 25, 51 Cal.Rptr.2d 444, 913 P.2d 473 (1996): The California Supreme Court established that a parent with sole physical custody has a presumptive right to relocate with the child, subject to the court's determination that the move serves the child's best interests. The court rejected the approach of requiring the custodial parent to prove necessity for the move.

The *Burgess* court reasoned that:

- Stability for the child is best served by maintaining the primary custodial relationship
- Courts should not unduly restrict the custodial parent's freedom of movement
- The focus should be on whether the relocation serves the child's best interests rather than on the custodial parent's motivations

B. The LaMusga Refinement

In re Marriage of LaMusga, 32 Cal.4th 1072, 12 Cal.Rptr.3d 356, 88 P.3d 81 (2004): The California Supreme Court refined the *Burgess* standard, clarifying that courts must examine the impact of the proposed move on the non-custodial parent's relationship with the child and the child's overall welfare.

The *LaMusga* court established that courts should consider:

1. **The children's interest in stability and continuity** in the custodial arrangement
2. **The distance of the move**
3. **The age of the children**
4. **The children's relationship with both parents**
5. **The relationship between the parents** including their ability to communicate and cooperate
6. **The wishes of the children** if they are mature enough to express a preference
7. **The reasons for the proposed move**
8. **The extent to which the parents currently share custody**

C. Shared Custody Distinctions

California law draws important distinctions based on existing custody arrangements:

Sole Physical Custody: When one parent has sole physical custody, *Burgess* establishes a presumptive right to relocate, which the non-custodial parent may rebut by showing the move would cause detriment to the child.

Shared Physical Custody: When parents share substantial custodial time, courts apply a different analysis focused on which arrangement better serves the child's best interests, without presumptions favoring either parent.

In re Marriage of Condon, 62 Cal.App.4th 533, 73 Cal.Rptr.2d 33 (1998): Applied the shared custody analysis where parents had approximately equal time with the children, focusing on maintaining both parental relationships.

D. Distance and Practical Considerations

California courts consider the practical impact of distance on parent-child relationships:

In re Marriage of Edlund and Hales, 66 Cal.App.4th 1454, 78 Cal.Rptr.2d 671 (1998): The court permitted relocation from California to Minnesota, emphasizing the feasibility of maintaining the non-custodial parent's relationship through extended vacation periods and modern communication technology.

In re Marriage of McGinnis, 7 Cal.App.4th 473, 9 Cal.Rptr.2d 182 (1992): The court denied relocation where the distance would effectively terminate the non-custodial parent's relationship with young children who needed frequent contact.

E. Child's Preference and Age Considerations

California Family Code § 3042 requires courts to consider the wishes of children age 14 and older, though younger children's preferences may also be relevant:

In re Marriage of Williams, 88 Cal.App.4th 808, 105 Cal.Rptr.2d 923 (2001): The court gave significant weight to the mature 16-year-old's preference to relocate with the custodial parent, while also considering the impact on relationships with siblings remaining with the other parent.

VII. Procedural Framework for Relocation Cases

A. New York Procedural Requirements

Filing Requirements:

- Petition for modification of custody/visitation under Family Court Act § 467 or Domestic Relations Law § 240

- Supporting affidavit detailing reasons for relocation and proposed impact on visitation
- Proposed modified visitation schedule

Notice Requirements:

- Service on all parties with existing custody rights
- Service on Attorney for the Child if previously appointed
- Compliance with CPLR notice provisions

Discovery and Investigation:

- Financial discovery regarding relocation expenses and benefits
- Investigation of schools, housing, and community resources in proposed location
- Mental health evaluations if psychological factors are relevant

Hearing Process:

- Evidentiary hearing with live testimony
- Expert testimony on child development and relocation impact
- In-camera interviews with children when appropriate

B. California Procedural Requirements

Request for Order (FL-300):

- Specific request for modification of custody/visitation to permit relocation
- Declaration (FL-320) supporting the request with detailed factual basis
- Proposed parenting plan addressing visitation modifications

Response Process:

- Responsive Declaration (FL-320) from non-relocating parent
- Counter-request for custody modification if opposing relocation

- Mediation referral under Family Code § 3170

Court Investigation:

- Custody evaluation under Evidence Code § 730 if ordered
- Minor's counsel appointment under Family Code § 3150 if appropriate
- Investigation of proposed relocation circumstances

Evidentiary Standards:

- Preponderance of evidence standard for factual determinations
- Best interests of child as ultimate standard
- Consider California Rules of Court regarding child testimony

VIII. Interstate Custody Modification Under the UCCJEA

A. Modification Standards and Procedures

When parents reside in different states, modification of custody orders requires careful attention to UCCJEA requirements:

Exclusive Continuing Jurisdiction: The state that entered the original custody order retains exclusive jurisdiction to modify that order until the jurisdictional prerequisites are no longer met. UCCJEA § 202.

Loss of Exclusive Continuing Jurisdiction: A state loses exclusive continuing jurisdiction when:

1. The state's court determines that neither the child nor the child and one parent have a significant connection with the state and substantial evidence concerning the child is no longer available in the state; or
2. A court determines that the child, parents, and any person acting as a parent do not presently reside in the state.

B. Interstate Communication and Coordination

Direct Communication: UCCJEA § 110 requires courts of different states to communicate directly with each other to coordinate proceedings and prevent conflicting orders.

Simultaneous Proceedings: UCCJEA § 206 addresses situations where proceedings involving the same child are filed in multiple states, establishing priority rules and requiring communication between courts.

Information Orders: Courts may order parties to provide information about pending proceedings in other states and may stay proceedings pending resolution of jurisdictional issues.

C. Practical Considerations for Interstate Modifications

Timing Issues: Parties must wait for the jurisdictional prerequisites to be met before filing in a new state, which may create delays in addressing urgent custody issues.

Evidence Gathering: Courts must consider whether substantial evidence concerning the child remains available in the original state when determining whether to retain or relinquish jurisdiction.

Enforcement: Modification orders must comply with UCCJEA registration and enforcement provisions to ensure interstate recognition.

IX. Emergency Jurisdiction Provisions

A. Temporary Emergency Jurisdiction Under UCCJEA § 204

Courts may exercise temporary emergency jurisdiction over child custody matters when:

1. The child is present in the state; and
2. The child has been abandoned or it is necessary in an emergency to protect the child because the child, or a sibling or parent of the child, is subjected to or threatened with mistreatment or abuse.

Limited Duration: Emergency jurisdiction is temporary and limited to the time necessary for the home state to assume jurisdiction or for the emergency to be resolved.

Communication Requirements: Courts exercising emergency jurisdiction must communicate with courts in the home state and other relevant states to coordinate appropriate long-term arrangements.

B. Domestic Violence Considerations

Safety Planning: Emergency jurisdiction provisions are particularly relevant in domestic violence cases where immediate protection may be necessary.

Interstate Enforcement: Protection orders issued under emergency jurisdiction must comply with interstate enforcement requirements under the Violence Against Women Act and related federal legislation.

Coordination with Criminal Proceedings: Family courts must coordinate with criminal courts handling related domestic violence charges to ensure consistent protection measures.

X. International Relocation and the Hague Convention

A. The Hague Convention on International Child Abduction

The Hague Convention on the Civil Aspects of International Child Abduction, adopted in 1980, governs situations where children are wrongfully removed from or retained outside their country of habitual residence.

Fundamental Principles:

- Prompt return of wrongfully removed children
- Respect for custody rights under the law of habitual residence
- Deterrence of international child abduction

Treaty Countries: The Convention applies only between contracting states, currently numbering over 100 countries.

B. Wrongful Removal and Retention

Wrongful Removal: Taking a child from the country of habitual residence in breach of custody rights.

Wrongful Retention: Keeping a child outside the country of habitual residence beyond the period of authorized stay in breach of custody rights.

Habitual Residence: The country where the child has developed social and family connections, determined by factual analysis rather than legal domicile concepts.

C. Defenses to Return

The Hague Convention provides limited defenses to return orders:

1. **Settlement**: The child has become settled in the new environment
2. **Consent or Acquiescence**: The requesting parent consented to or acquiesced in the removal or retention
3. **Grave Risk**: Return would expose the child to physical or psychological harm or place the child in an intolerable situation
4. **Child's Objection**: A mature child objects to return (typically age 12 or older)
5. **Fundamental Principles**: Return would violate fundamental principles of human rights and freedoms in the requested state

D. Federal Court Jurisdiction

International Child Abduction Remedies Act (ICARA): 42 U.S.C. § 11601 et seq., provides federal court jurisdiction over Hague Convention cases in the United States.

State Court Concurrent Jurisdiction: State courts may also exercise jurisdiction over Hague Convention cases, though federal courts are often preferred for their experience and resources.

XI. Strategic Considerations for Practitioners

A. Pre-Litigation Planning

Documentation: Maintain comprehensive records of:

- Employment opportunities and requirements
- Educational benefits for children
- Extended family support systems
- Housing and community resources
- Current visitation compliance and quality

Timing: Consider optimal timing for relocation requests:

- School year transitions
- Employment deadlines
- Relationship stability periods
- Children's developmental needs

Alternative Dispute Resolution: Explore mediation and collaborative approaches:

- Parenting coordinators for ongoing issues
- Private mediation with family law specialists
- Collaborative law processes involving multiple professionals

B. Litigation Strategy

Burden of Proof Considerations:

- Understand jurisdictional differences in burden allocation
- Develop evidence addressing all relevant best interests factors
- Prepare for potential custody modification as alternative relief

Expert Witnesses:

- Child development specialists

- Relocation impact assessments
- Economic analysis of relocation benefits
- Technology solutions for maintaining relationships

Child Representation:

- Consider whether independent representation serves the child's interests
- Prepare for potential in-camera interviews
- Address children's preferences appropriately based on age and maturity

C. Settlement Negotiations

Creative Visitation Solutions:

- Extended summer and holiday periods
- Flexible scheduling for school breaks
- Technology-assisted visitation
- Shared transportation costs

Financial Arrangements:

- Relocation expense allocation
- Increased child support to offset visitation costs
- Education and activity cost sharing

Future Modification Provisions:

- Automatic review periods
- Changed circumstance triggers
- Process for addressing future disputes

XII. Enforcement Across State Lines

A. Registration of Orders

UCCJEA Registration Process: Out-of-state custody orders may be registered in any state for enforcement purposes under UCCJEA § 305.

Required Documentation:

- Certified copy of the custody order
- Statement under penalty of perjury that the order has not been modified or stayed
- Name and address of the person seeking registration

Notice Requirements: The registering person must serve notice on the other parties with their first opportunity to request a hearing.

B. Enforcement Mechanisms

Direct Enforcement: Registered custody orders may be enforced using the same procedures as domestic orders.

Expedited Enforcement: UCCJEA § 311 provides for expedited enforcement of visitation when a child is wrongfully removed or retained.

Law Enforcement Assistance: Courts may request assistance from law enforcement agencies to locate children and enforce custody orders.

C. Contempt and Sanctions

Civil Contempt: Courts may use civil contempt procedures to enforce compliance with custody orders.

Criminal Penalties: Willful violation of custody orders may result in criminal charges under state and federal kidnapping statutes.

Compensatory Remedies: Courts may order payment of costs, attorney fees, and other expenses resulting from custody violations.

XIII. Emerging Issues and Future Trends

A. Technology and Virtual Relationships

Video Communication: Courts increasingly recognize video calling as a meaningful form of contact, affecting relocation analysis.

Social Media Considerations: Social media relationships between parents and children present new factors for court consideration.

Digital Surveillance: Privacy concerns arise when parents monitor children's electronic communications across state lines.

B. Military Families and Deployment

Servicemembers' Civil Relief Act: Provides protections for military personnel facing custody proceedings during deployment.

Temporary Custody Modifications: Special procedures for addressing custody during military deployment periods.

Interstate Coordination: Unique challenges when military families relocate frequently across state lines.

C. Same-Sex Parents and Recognition Issues

Interstate Recognition: Challenges arise when custody orders involving same-sex parents cross state lines with different recognition laws.

Parentage Determinations: UCCJEA application to parentage disputes involving assisted reproduction and surrogacy.

Full Faith and Credit: Constitutional requirements for interstate recognition of custody orders involving diverse family structures.

XIV. Conclusion

Relocation and interstate custody disputes represent some of the most challenging areas of family law practice, requiring mastery of both substantive legal standards and complex procedural requirements. The UCCJEA provides essential uniformity in jurisdictional analysis, while state laws continue to evolve in addressing the substantive standards for relocation decisions.

Practitioners must understand not only the legal framework but also the practical realities facing families in transition. Successful representation requires comprehensive preparation, creative problem-solving, and sensitivity to the emotional and developmental needs of children caught between competing parental interests.

The law in this area continues to develop as courts grapple with changing social norms, technological advances, and increasingly mobile populations. Attorneys practicing in this field must stay current with evolving precedents and legislative developments while maintaining focus on the ultimate goal of serving children's best interests in an increasingly complex legal landscape.

As we move forward, the integration of alternative dispute resolution mechanisms, technological solutions for maintaining parent-child relationships, and more nuanced understanding of child development will continue to shape how courts and practitioners approach these difficult cases. The challenge remains to balance respect for parental autonomy with protection of children's interests in maintaining meaningful relationships with both parents, regardless of geographic distance.

16

Discovery and Financial Disclosures

I. Uncovering the Financial Truth

In any family law matter involving property division, child support, or spousal support, the key to fair outcomes is full financial transparency. Whether amicably settled or hotly contested, the parties must exchange accurate, timely, and complete financial information to allow the court - and each other - to make informed decisions.

The constitutional due process right to a fair hearing requires that both parties have access to relevant financial information. *In re Marriage of Quay*, 18 Cal.App.4th 961, 22 Cal.Rptr.2d 537 (1993). Without complete financial disclosure, courts cannot fulfill their statutory duty to ensure equitable property division and appropriate support awards.

This chapter outlines the rules, procedures, and strategic considerations of financial disclosure and discovery in New York and California, including required forms, timelines, common disputes, and remedies for noncompliance.

II. The Purpose and Legal Foundation of Financial Disclosure

Financial disclosure serves multiple critical functions in family law proceedings. The disclosure process allows for equitable division of property and debt, accurate support calculations, assessment of income, expenses, assets, and liabilities, transparency in settlement negotiations, and protection against fraud and hidden assets.

In both New York and California, mandatory disclosure is the rule, not the exception - even in cases where the parties agree on terms. The California Supreme Court emphasized in *In re Marriage of Feldman*, 153 Cal.App.3d 1031, 201 Cal.Rptr. 43 (1984), that the fiduciary duty between spouses requires the highest good faith and fair dealing in financial matters, which continues throughout the dissolution process.

The New York Court of Appeals has similarly held that financial disclosure requirements serve the public policy of ensuring fair and informed judicial determinations. *Keogh v. Keogh*, 38 A.D.2d 971, 330 N.Y.S.2d 71 (2d Dep't 1972).

III. Initial Financial Disclosures

California: Mandatory Preliminary Disclosures

California Family Code Sections 2100 through 2113 establish comprehensive mandatory disclosure requirements for all dissolution, legal separation, and nullity proceedings. These requirements apply regardless of whether the case is contested or uncontested.

Required Documents:

The preliminary disclosure package must include the Schedule of Assets and Debts (Form FL-142), which requires detailed identification of all community and separate property assets and debts; the Income and Expense Declaration (Form FL-150), documenting all sources of income and monthly expenses; the Declaration of Disclosure (Form FL-140), which serves as a cover sheet and oath; and the Declaration Regarding Service (Form FL-141), proving proper service of the disclosure documents.

Both parties must serve these documents within 60 days after the petition is filed and before any judgment is entered, even in default or settlement cases. *Family Code* § 2102(*a*). The California Court of Appeal in *In re Marriage of Steiner & Hosseini*, 10 Cal.4th 1155, 43 Cal.Rptr.2d 24, 898 P.2d 1083 (1995), emphasized that these disclosure requirements are mandatory and cannot be waived by stipulation during the preliminary phase.

Final Disclosures:

Final disclosures, identical in content to preliminary disclosures but updated to reflect current information, are required before trial unless waived in a written agreement executed after preliminary disclosures are completed. *Family Code* § 2105. The purpose is to ensure that the court has current financial information at the time of judgment.

Duty of Continuing Disclosure:

California imposes a continuing duty to supplement disclosures if material changes occur. *Family Code* § 2102(*c*). This duty extends until judgment is entered or the case is dismissed. Failure to update material changes can result in sanctions and may provide grounds for relief from judgment.

New York: Net Worth Statement and Financial Disclosure

New York Domestic Relations Law Section 236(B)(4) and Uniform Rules for Trial Courts Section 202.16 govern financial disclosure requirements in matrimonial actions.

Statement of Net Worth:

Every party in a contested divorce action must file a Statement of Net Worth using the Unified Court System's official form. The statement must include comprehensive income and employment details, including gross income from all sources for the past three years; complete asset inventory with current fair market values; all liabilities and debt obligations; detailed monthly living expenses broken down by category; insurance coverage and beneficiary information; and tax filing status and obligations.

Supporting Documentation:

The net worth statement must be accompanied by supporting documentation, including the three most recent years' tax returns, including all schedules and attachments; the three most recent pay stubs or statements of income; statements for all bank accounts, investment accounts, and retirement accounts for the past three years; and proof of expenses claimed in the net worth statement.

Sworn Accuracy:

Each party must swear under penalty of perjury that the information provided is complete and accurate. *DRL § 236(B)(4)(a)*. The First Department emphasized in *Schroeder v. Schroeder*, 175 A.D.3d 525, 107 N.Y.S.3d 54 (1st Dep't 2019), that net worth statements must be prepared with scrupulous attention to accuracy and completeness.

IV. Discovery Tools in Family Law Cases

When standard financial disclosures prove insufficient, parties may utilize additional discovery tools permitted under civil procedure rules, subject to family law modifications and restrictions.

Common Discovery Devices

Interrogatories consist of written questions requiring written responses under oath, typically limited to 25 questions in California and 20 in New York. These are particularly useful for obtaining specific financial information and identifying sources of income or assets.

Document Demands include requests for bank statements, tax returns, business records, employment files, credit reports, and other financial documentation. These requests must be specific and relevant to the financial issues in the case.

Depositions involve oral questioning under oath, transcribed by a court reporter. Depositions are especially valuable for complex financial situations where follow-up questions are necessary to understand asset structures or income sources.

Subpoenas can compel production of documents or appearance at depositions or hearings from third parties such as banks, employers, or business partners who may have relevant financial information.

Requests for Admission ask the opposing party to admit or deny specific facts, which can streamline trial preparation and eliminate the need to prove undisputed matters.

California Discovery Rules

Discovery in California family law cases is governed by the Civil Discovery Act, Code of Civil Procedure Section 2016.010 et seq., with family law-specific modifications found in Family Code Sections 2100-2113.

Timing and Scope:

Discovery may begin once the petition and summons are served. *Code Civ. Proc.* § 2019.020. However, the scope of discovery in family law cases is limited to matters relevant to the characterization, valuation, and division of assets and debts, determination of support obligations, and child custody and visitation issues.

Meet and Confer Requirements:

Before filing discovery motions, parties must meet and confer in good faith to resolve disputes informally. *Code Civ. Proc.* § 2016.040. The Fourth District Court of Appeal in *Townsend v. Superior Court*, 61 Cal.App.4th 1431, 72 Cal.Rptr.2d 333 (1998), held that failure to satisfy meet and confer requirements may result in denial of discovery motions.

New York Discovery Rules

Discovery in New York matrimonial actions is governed by Civil Practice Law and Rules Article 31, with family law-specific provisions in Domestic Relations Law Section 236 and Uniform Rules Section 202.16.

Tailored Discovery:

Discovery must be tailored to family law issues and proportionate to the complexity and value of the case. Courts routinely issue protective orders to prevent overbroad or harassing discovery requests. CPLR § 3103.

Judicial Supervision:

New York courts exercise closer supervision over discovery in matrimonial cases than in general civil litigation. The Second Department noted in *Anonymous v. Anonymous*, 124 A.D.3d 785, 2 N.Y.S.3d 347 (2d Dep't 2015), that discovery in matrimonial actions should be conducted efficiently to minimize emotional and financial costs to the family.

V. Valuation of Assets and Business Interests

Complex matrimonial cases often require extensive discovery to properly value marital assets, particularly when they include business interests, professional practices, or sophisticated investment portfolios.

Real Estate Valuation

Real property valuation typically requires professional appraisals by licensed appraisers. The California Court of Appeal in *In re Marriage of Dryden*, 177 Cal.App.3d 596, 223 Cal.Rptr. 29 (1986), held that while parties may stipulate to value, courts should require appraisals for significant real estate holdings to ensure accurate valuations.

Discovery related to real estate may include property tax assessments, recent comparable sales, rental income and expense records, improvement costs and depreciation schedules, and mortgage and lien information.

Business Valuation

Closely held businesses present particular discovery challenges due to their complexity and the potential for valuation manipulation. Business discovery typically focuses on financial statements including profit and loss statements, balance sheets, and cash flow statements for the past five years; tax returns for the business and related entities; buy-sell agreements and partnership agreements; management compensation and benefits; customer lists and contracts; and accounts receivable and payable.

The New York Court of Appeals in *Majauskas v. Majauskas*, 61 N.Y.2d 481, 474 N.Y.S.2d 699, 463 N.E.2d 15 (1984), established that business valuations must consider all relevant factors, including earning capacity, asset values, and market conditions.

Professional Practices

Professional practices require specialized valuation approaches. Discovery may include client lists and retention rates, fee schedules and billing records, professional licenses and certifications, accounts receivable aging, and partnership or employment agreements.

The California Supreme Court in *In re Marriage of Fenton*, 134 Cal.App.3d 451, 184 Cal.Rptr. 597 (1982), recognized that professional goodwill may constitute community property subject to valuation and division.

Retirement Benefits and Deferred Compensation

Discovery of retirement benefits requires obtaining plan documents and summary plan descriptions, account statements and beneficiary designations, vesting schedules and distribution options, loan balances and hardship withdrawals, and actuarial valuations for defined benefit plans.

Stock options and deferred compensation arrangements require careful analysis of vesting schedules, exercise provisions, and tax consequences. *In re Marriage of Hug*, 154 Cal.App.3d 780, 201 Cal.Rptr. 676 (1984).

VI. Forensic Accounting and Hidden Assets Investigation

When one spouse suspects the other of concealing income or assets, forensic accounting becomes essential to uncovering the complete financial picture.

Forensic Accounting Techniques

Forensic accountants employ various techniques to trace and identify hidden assets, including lifestyle analysis comparing claimed income to actual expenditures, cash flow analysis tracking money movement through multiple accounts, net worth analysis comparing assets to reported income over time, and computer forensics recovering deleted financial records.

The California Court of Appeal in *In re Marriage of Sorge*, 202 Cal.App.3d 1509, 249 Cal.Rptr. 616 (1988), upheld the use of lifestyle analysis to impute income where a spouse's expenditures exceeded reported earnings.

Discovery of Hidden Assets

Common techniques for discovering hidden assets include subpoenaing bank records to identify unknown accounts, reviewing credit reports for undisclosed debts or accounts, examining tax returns for unreported income sources, investigating business records for personal expenses or diverted income, and analyzing transfers to related parties or entities.

Offshore and Domestic Asset Protection:

Sophisticated asset concealment may involve offshore accounts, domestic asset protection trusts, or complex business structures. Discovery in such cases may require specialized techniques including letters rogatory for foreign discovery, forensic computer analysis, and examination of professional advisors' records.

The Second Department in *Laufer v. Ostrow*, 55 A.D.3d 892, 866 N.Y.S.2d 588 (2d Dep't 2008), held that courts have broad discretion to order discovery of assets held in offshore entities when domestic jurisdiction exists over the parties.

Imputation of Income and Assets

When a party refuses to comply with disclosure requirements or the available evidence suggests hidden income or assets, courts may impute income or value assets based on available evidence.

California Standards:

California Family Code Section 4058 provides specific guidelines for imputing income, considering the parent's earning capacity based on education, work history, and available opportunities. *In re Marriage of Berger*, 170 Cal.App.4th 1070, 88 Cal.Rptr.3d 766 (2009).

New York Standards:

New York courts apply a similar analysis under DRL Section 240, examining the party's educational background, employment history, and efforts to obtain employment. *Cassano v. Cassano*, 85 A.D.2d 148, 447 N.Y.S.2d 406 (2d Dep't 1982).

VII. Discovery Disputes and Enforcement Mechanisms

Discovery disputes are common in family law cases due to the personal nature of financial information and the emotional dynamics between the parties.

Common Discovery Issues

Typical discovery disputes include delayed or incomplete financial disclosures, refusal to produce requested documents, evasive or non-responsive interrogatory answers, failure to appear for properly noticed depositions, and claims of privilege over financial information.

California Sanctions Framework

California Code of Civil Procedure Section 2023.030 provides comprehensive sanctions for discovery abuse, including monetary sanctions covering reasonable attorney's fees and costs, issue sanctions precluding evidence on specific issues, evidence sanctions excluding particular documents or testimony, and terminating sanctions striking pleadings or entering default judgment.

Monetary Sanctions:

The Court of Appeal in *New Albertsons, Inc. v. Superior Court*, 168 Cal.App.4th 1403, 86 Cal.Rptr.3d 457 (2008), held that monetary sanctions should be substantial enough to deter future misconduct while being proportionate to the discovery abuse.

Evidence and Issue Sanctions:

More severe sanctions may be appropriate for willful discovery abuse. *In re Marriage of Burgess*, 13 Cal.4th 25, 51 Cal.Rptr.2d 444, 913 P.2d 473 (1996), established that courts must consider less severe alternatives before imposing terminating sanctions.

New York Enforcement Mechanisms

New York courts have similar enforcement powers under CPLR Article 31, with family law-specific provisions in DRL Section 236.

Preclusionary Orders:

Courts may preclude evidence at trial for failure to comply with discovery obligations. *Matter of Carannante v. Carannante*, 149 A.D.3d 163, 49 N.Y.S.3d 345 (2d Dep't 2017).

Conditional Default Judgments:

In egregious cases of discovery abuse, courts may enter conditional default judgments that become final unless the non-complying party satisfies discovery obligations within a specified timeframe. *Kihl v. Kihl*, 94 A.D.3d 1054, 943 N.Y.S.2d 203 (2d Dep't 2012).

Attorney's Fees:

Courts routinely award attorney's fees and costs against parties who fail to comply with discovery obligations in good faith. *DRL* § 237.

Good Faith Requirements

Both California and New York require good faith efforts to resolve discovery disputes before seeking judicial intervention. The meet and confer process is designed to encourage cooperation and reduce unnecessary motion practice.

VIII. Privacy and Confidentiality Considerations

While family law proceedings require extensive financial disclosure, parties retain legitimate privacy interests that courts must balance against the need for transparency.

Protected Information Categories

Certain categories of information receive heightened protection, including Social Security numbers and other identity theft risks, business trade secrets and proprietary information, medical and mental health records, and detailed tax return information beyond income verification.

Protective Orders and Confidentiality Agreements

Courts routinely enter protective orders limiting the use and disclosure of sensitive financial information. These orders typically restrict use of disclosed information to the pending family law proceeding, prohibit disclosure to third parties without court approval, require return or destruction of documents after case resolution, and establish protocols for handling confidential information.

The Fourth Department in *Matter of Rosen v. Rosen*, 83 A.D.3d 1469, 922 N.Y.S.2d 761 (4th Dep't 2011), emphasized that protective orders should be tailored to the specific confidentiality concerns while preserving the opposing party's right to relevant information.

Sealing of Court Records

In exceptional cases involving trade secrets or other highly sensitive information, courts may seal portions of the court record. However, such sealing must comply with constitutional requirements for public access to judicial proceedings. *In re Marriage of Burkle*, 135 Cal.App.4th 1045, 37 Cal.Rptr.3d 805 (2006).

IX. Financial Disclosure in Support Calculations

Accurate financial information is essential for proper calculation of both child support and spousal support obligations.

Child Support Calculations

Both California and New York use income-based child support guidelines that require precise income determination.

California Child Support:

California Family Code Section 4058 requires consideration of all sources of income, including salary and wages, commissions and bonuses, self-employment income, rental income, investment returns, unemployment and disability benefits, and social security benefits.

The Court of Appeal in *In re Marriage of Schlafly*, 198 Cal.App.4th 1262, 130 Cal.Rptr.3d 286 (2011), held that courts must make specific findings regarding income when deviating from guideline support amounts.

New York Child Support:

New York Child Support Standards Act, DRL Section 240, establishes similar comprehensive income requirements. The Court of Appeals in *Matter of Brescia v. Fitts*, 56 N.Y.2d 132, 451 N.Y.S.2d 68, 436 N.E.2d 190 (1982), emphasized that support calculations must be based on current, accurate income information.

Spousal Support Determinations

Spousal support calculations require analysis of both parties' incomes, expenses, and standard of living during the marriage.

California Spousal Support:

California Family Code Section 4320 establishes comprehensive factors for spousal support, requiring detailed financial analysis including the supported party's needs and ability to become self-supporting, the supporting party's ability to pay, the standard of living during marriage, and the duration of the marriage.

New York Spousal Support:

New York DRL Section 236(B)(6) provides similar multi-factor analysis, with statutory guidelines for temporary support and discretionary factors for post-divorce support duration and amount.

Temporary Support Orders

Courts often must determine temporary support based on preliminary financial disclosures before complete discovery is finished. These orders require careful balancing of immediate financial needs against the limitations of available information.

X. Strategic Considerations in Discovery Practice

Effective discovery requires strategic planning that considers the unique dynamics of family law cases.

Benefits of Comprehensive Discovery

Well-planned discovery can uncover hidden income or assets that significantly affect property division and support obligations, create pressure for favorable settlement negotiations, establish credibility for trial by demonstrating thorough preparation, and provide leverage in mediation or collaborative law proceedings.

The Second Department in *Wendt v. Wendt*, 249 A.D.2d 470, 672 N.Y.S.2d 623 (2d Dep't 1998), noted that comprehensive financial discovery often leads to more favorable settlements by equalizing information between the parties.

Risks of Excessive Discovery

However, overly aggressive discovery strategies may backfire by dramatically increasing litigation costs, potentially harming parent-child relationships in custody cases, significantly delaying case resolution, and creating unnecessary animosity that impedes settlement.

Cost-Benefit Analysis:

Counsel must carefully weigh the potential value of requested information against the costs of obtaining it, including attorney's fees, expert witness costs, and emotional toll on the family. *In re Marriage of Gray*, 62 Cal.App.4th 1366, 73 Cal.Rptr.2d 372 (1998).

Discovery in High-Net-Worth Cases

High-asset cases often require sophisticated discovery strategies, including coordination with forensic accountants and business valuation experts, international discovery for offshore assets, examination of complex trust and entity structures, and analysis of sophisticated compensation arrangements.

These cases may justify extensive discovery due to the significant financial stakes involved. However, courts still expect proportionality between the discovery sought and the complexity of the financial issues.

Discovery in Limited-Income Cases

Conversely, cases involving modest incomes require streamlined discovery approaches that focus on essential information while minimizing costs. Courts may limit discovery scope in such cases to prevent discovery costs from exceeding the financial benefits.

XI. Emerging Issues in Financial Discovery

Modern family law discovery faces new challenges related to cryptocurrency, digital assets, and sophisticated asset protection structures.

Cryptocurrency and Digital Assets

Discovery of cryptocurrency holdings requires specialized knowledge and techniques, including analysis of blockchain transactions, examination of digital wallet records, review of cryptocurrency exchange accounts, and investigation of mining activities.

Courts are beginning to address these issues, with the Southern District of New York in SEC *v. Kik Interactive Inc.*, 492 F.Supp.3d 169 (S.D.N.Y. 2020), establishing precedents for cryptocurrency discovery that may apply to family law cases.

Social Media and Electronic Discovery

Electronic discovery in family law cases increasingly includes social media accounts, cloud storage services, smartphone data, and email accounts. Courts must balance discovery needs against privacy rights and third-party interests.

International Discovery Challenges

Globalization has increased the complexity of discovery in cases involving international assets, requiring understanding of foreign discovery procedures, mutual legal assistance treaties, and cross-border asset recovery mechanisms.

XII. Conclusion and Future Developments

Financial disclosure and discovery form the bedrock of informed negotiation and fair litigation in family law. Whether the case involves modest incomes or complex international asset portfolios, both parties must participate in full financial transparency to ensure equitable outcomes.

The evolving nature of modern financial structures, including digital assets, international holdings, and sophisticated business arrangements, continues to challenge traditional discovery approaches. Family law practitioners must stay current with these developments while maintaining focus on the fundamental principles of complete, accurate, and timely financial disclosure.

Courts increasingly emphasize proportionality in discovery, requiring attorneys to tailor their discovery strategies to the specific circumstances of each case. This trend toward efficiency and cost-effectiveness, while maintaining thoroughness where justified by the financial stakes, will likely continue to shape family law discovery practice.

The intersection of technology and privacy rights will present ongoing challenges for discovery practice, requiring careful balance between the need for complete financial information and legitimate privacy interests. As financial structures become increasingly complex and international in scope, family law practitioners must develop new expertise and collaborative relationships with specialists in related fields.

Effective financial discovery remains essential to achieving fair outcomes in family law cases, but the methods and scope of that discovery will continue to evolve with changing financial practices and legal standards.

17

Domestic Violence and Family Law Restraining Orders

I. Protection, Power, and the Family Court

Domestic violence represents one of the most complex and urgent areas of family law practice, where the intersection of criminal law, civil protection, and family court jurisdiction creates a multifaceted legal landscape. The National Intimate Partner and Sexual Violence Survey indicates that approximately one in four women and one in seven men have experienced severe physical violence by an intimate partner during their lifetime. *See Breiding, M.J., et al., Prevalence and Characteristics of Sexual Violence, Stalking, and Intimate Partner Violence Victimization, MMWR Surveill Summ.* 2014;63(No. SS-8):1–18.

Domestic violence is not merely a criminal offense requiring prosecution by the state - it constitutes a devastating family law issue with far-reaching consequences for child custody arrangements, spousal and child support obligations, housing stability, and immigration status. Both New York and California have developed comprehensive statutory frameworks providing robust legal tools to protect survivors while carefully regulating the rights of alleged abusers, primarily through civil restraining orders issued by family courts operating under specialized domestic violence protocols.

The legal response to domestic violence has evolved significantly since the 1970s, when the battered women's movement first brought national attention to the inadequacy of traditional legal remedies. *See Schneider, Elizabeth M., Battered Women and Feminist Lawmaking* (2000). Today's statutory schemes reflect decades of legislative refinement, judicial interpretation, and advocacy efforts aimed at creating more responsive and effective protection mechanisms.

This chapter provides a comprehensive examination of how California and New York define domestic violence, the procedural requirements for obtaining various types of restraining orders, and the profound ways these protective orders impact child custody determinations, visitation arrangements, and broader family court outcomes. We will explore the intersection of civil protection orders with criminal proceedings, immigration law, housing protections, and the ethical considerations that attorneys must navigate when representing clients in domestic violence cases.

II. Legal Definitions and Scope of Domestic Violence

A. California's Comprehensive Approach

California's domestic violence statutes provide one of the most expansive definitions of abuse in the United States. Under California Family Code Section 6203, domestic violence encompasses a broad spectrum of conduct designed to control, intimidate, or harm intimate partners and family members.

The California Legislature has defined "abuse" to include:

Physical Abuse: Intentionally or recklessly causing or attempting to cause bodily injury, or placing another person in reasonable apprehension of imminent serious bodily injury to himself or herself, or another. *Cal. Fam. Code § 6203(a)(1).*

Sexual Abuse: Sexual assault as defined in Section 261, 261.5, 262, 286, 287, 288, or 289 of the Penal Code, or any sexual conduct proscribed by Part 1 of Division 10 of the Welfare and Institutions Code. *Cal. Fam. Code § 6203(a)(2).*

Emotional Abuse: The statutory definition includes "disturbing the peace of the other party," which courts have interpreted broadly to encompass psychological abuse, threats, harassment, and controlling behavior. *In re Marriage of Nadkarni*, 173 Cal. App. 4th 1483, 1497 (2009) (finding that "disturbing the peace" includes conduct that destroys the mental or emotional calm of the other party).

Economic Abuse: California was among the first states to explicitly recognize economic abuse as a form of domestic violence, defining it as behavior that is coercive or controlling and unreasonably interferes with a person's ability to acquire, use, or maintain economic resources. *Cal. Fam. Code § 6203(a)(3).*

The California Supreme Court has emphasized that the definition of abuse should be construed liberally to effectuate the protective purposes of the Domestic Violence Prevention Act. *In re Marriage of Evilsizor & Sweeney*, 237 Cal. App. 4th 1416, 1424 (2015).

B. New York's Relationship-Focused Framework

New York's approach to defining domestic violence focuses heavily on the relationship between the parties and requires specific factual allegations supporting a "family offense." Under New York Family Court Act Section 812, domestic violence is defined through enumerated criminal offenses committed between family or household members.

Qualifying Criminal Offenses include:

- Disorderly conduct as defined in section 240.20 of the penal law
- Harassment in the first degree as defined in section 240.25 of the penal law
- Harassment in the second degree as defined in section 240.26 of the penal law
- Aggravated harassment in the second degree as defined in section 240.30 of the penal law

- Criminal mischief as defined in sections 145.00, 145.05, and 145.10 of the penal law
- Menacing in the second degree as defined in section 120.14 of the penal law
- Menacing in the third degree as defined in section 120.15 of the penal law
- Reckless endangerment as defined in section 120.20 of the penal law
- Assault in the second degree as defined in section 120.05 of the penal law
- Assault in the third degree as defined in section 120.00 of the penal law
- Attempted assault as defined in sections 110.00 and 120.00 of the penal law
- Stalking in the first degree as defined in section 120.60 of the penal law
- Stalking in the second degree as defined in section 120.55 of the penal law
- Stalking in the third degree as defined in section 120.50 of the penal law
- Stalking in the fourth degree as defined in section 120.45 of the penal law

N.Y. *Fam.* Ct. Act § 812(1).

The Court of Appeals has held that family offenses must be pleaded with the same specificity required in criminal proceedings, requiring allegations of specific facts that would constitute the enumerated offenses. *Matter of Aisha K. v. Daniel* S., 33 N.Y.3d 1, 8 (2019).

C. Comparative Analysis of Definitional Approaches

The fundamental difference between California and New York's approaches reflects distinct philosophical frameworks. California's broad "disturbing the peace" standard allows courts significant flexibility in addressing patterns of controlling behavior that may not rise to the level of criminal conduct. New

York's criminal offense-based approach provides greater specificity but may leave gaps in protection for victims experiencing psychological abuse that does not fit neatly within enumerated criminal categories.

This distinction has practical implications for practitioners. In California, attorneys can seek protection based on patterns of emotional manipulation, financial control, or threatening behavior that creates fear without physical contact. In New York, practitioners must carefully analyze whether the respondent's conduct fits within specific criminal definitions, often requiring more detailed factual development to establish grounds for relief.

III. Eligible Relationships and Standing Requirements

A. California's Expansive Relationship Categories

California Family Code Section 6203 establishes broad categories of relationships eligible for domestic violence restraining orders, reflecting the legislature's recognition that abuse occurs across various family and intimate relationship structures.

Eligible relationships include:

1. **Spouses and Domestic Partners**: Current or former spouses, registered domestic partners, or individuals who have filed a declaration of domestic partnership. *Cal. Fam. Code* § 6203(b)(1).

2. **Cohabitants**: Individuals who regularly reside together or have regularly resided together. The statute does not require a minimum duration of cohabitation, and courts have found that even brief periods of living together can establish this relationship. *Ritchie v. Konrad*, 115 Cal. App. 4th 1275, 1284 (2004).

3. **Dating Relationships**: Individuals who are dating or have dated, which the courts have interpreted to include both serious and casual dating relationships. The statute does not require sexual intimacy or cohabitation. *In re Marriage of Nadkarni*, 173 Cal. App. 4th 1483, 1498 (2009).

4. **Parental Relationships**: Individuals who have a child together, regardless of whether they were ever married, lived together, or had a romantic relationship. *Cal. Fam. Code* § 6203(b)(2).

5. **Family Relationships**: Certain family members, including parents, children, siblings, and in-laws, though the scope is more limited than in other relationship categories. *Cal. Fam. Code* § *6203(b)(3)*.

The California Court of Appeal has emphasized that relationship determination should focus on the substance of the relationship rather than formal legal labels. *Rubalcava v. Gisseman*, 14 Cal. App. 5th 1049, 1057 (2017).

B. New York's Relationship Requirements

New York Family Court Act Section 812 establishes more restrictive relationship requirements, reflecting the state's focus on traditional family structures and intimate relationships.

Eligible petitioners must demonstrate one of the following relationships:

1. **Current or Former Spouses**: Individuals currently married or previously married to each other. N.Y. *Fam.* Ct. Act § 812(1)(*a*).
2. **Blood Relatives**: Individuals related by consanguinity, typically parents, children, siblings, grandparents, and grandchildren. N.Y. *Fam.* Ct. Act § 812(1)(*b*).
3. **Affinity Relationships**: Individuals related by marriage, including current and former in-laws, step-parents, and step-children. N.Y. *Fam.* Ct. Act § 812(1)(*c*).
4. **Common Child**: Individuals who have a child in common, regardless of whether they were ever married or lived together. N.Y. *Fam.* Ct. Act § 812(1)(*d*).
5. **Intimate Relationships**: Individuals who have been in an intimate relationship, whether or not they have lived together. N.Y. *Fam.* Ct. Act § 812(1)(*e*).

The determination of whether an "intimate relationship" exists requires careful judicial analysis. The Court of Appeals established a multi-factor test in *Matter of Baker v. Baker*, 86 N.Y.2d 821, 823 (1995), examining factors including:

- The nature or type of relationship
- The frequency of interaction between the parties
- The duration of the relationship

- Whether the relationship was sexual in nature
- Whether the parties were exclusive
- Whether the relationship was characterized by expressions of affection

C. Jurisdictional Considerations

Both states have specific jurisdictional requirements that practitioners must carefully consider when filing for restraining orders.

California Jurisdiction: California courts have jurisdiction over domestic violence restraining orders when either party resides in California or the abuse occurred in California. *Cal. Fam. Code* § 6226. The statute provides for broad jurisdictional reach, allowing California courts to issue orders even when the respondent resides out of state, provided proper service can be effectuated.

New York Jurisdiction: New York Family Court has jurisdiction when either party resides in New York, the family offense was committed in New York, or the child who is the subject of the proceeding resides in New York. N.Y. *Fam. Ct.* Act § 115. The First Department has held that temporary residence in New York is sufficient to establish jurisdiction. *Matter of Commissioner of Social Services v. Rodriquez*, 208 A.D.2d 408, 410 (1st Dep't 1994).*

IV. Types of Restraining Orders and Available Relief

A. California's Comprehensive Relief Structure

California's Domestic Violence Prevention Act provides courts with broad discretionary authority to fashion relief tailored to the specific circumstances of each case. The statute authorizes multiple types of orders that can be issued individually or in combination.

1. Personal Conduct Orders

Personal conduct orders prohibit specific behaviors by the restrained party. Under California Family Code Section 6320, courts may order the restrained party to refrain from:

- Contacting, calling, or sending any messages to the protected party
- Attacking, striking, or battering the protected party
- Stalking, following, or harassing the protected party
- Disturbing the peace of the protected party
- Destroying personal property of the protected party
- Coming within a specified distance of the protected party

The California Court of Appeal has held that personal conduct orders must be sufficiently specific to provide clear guidance to the restrained party and enable effective enforcement. *In re Marriage of Fregoso and Hernandez*, 5 Cal. App. 5th 698, 712 (2016).

2. Stay-Away Orders

Stay-away orders establish geographic boundaries that the restrained party cannot cross. These orders commonly include:

- The protected party's residence
- The protected party's workplace
- The protected party's school
- The children's school or daycare
- Other locations regularly frequented by the protected party

Courts have broad discretion in determining appropriate distances, with typical orders ranging from 50 yards to 300 yards depending on the circumstances. *Gonzalez v. Munoz*, 156 Cal. App. 4th 413, 420 (2007).

3. Residence Exclusion Orders

Under California Family Code Section 6321, courts may order the restrained party to move out of the residence shared with the protected party, even if the restrained party has ownership or lease rights. The statute provides:

"The court may issue an ex parte order excluding a party from the family dwelling or from the dwelling of the other party upon a showing of good cause."

The California Supreme Court has emphasized that residence exclusion orders represent a significant interference with property rights and should be based on clear evidence of necessity for protection. *Conness v. Satram*, 224 Cal. App. 4th 1175, 1185 (2014).

4. Child Custody and Visitation Orders

California courts have authority to issue temporary custody and visitation orders as part of domestic violence restraining orders. These orders can:

- Award temporary physical and legal custody of children
- Establish supervised visitation arrangements
- Prohibit the removal of children from the state
- Require the restrained party to complete parenting classes
- Order child support payments

5. Financial Support Orders

Courts may order temporary spousal support, child support, and payment of attorney's fees and costs. California Family Code Section 6342 provides broad authority to issue financial orders necessary to protect the petitioner and children from economic harm resulting from the abuse.

6. Firearm Restrictions

California law requires mandatory firearm restrictions when domestic violence restraining orders are issued. Under California Family Code Section 6389, restrained parties must:

- Surrender all firearms and ammunition within 24 hours of service
- Provide proof of surrender or sale to approved entities
- Refrain from purchasing or possessing firearms during the order's duration

7. Counseling and Intervention Programs

Courts may order the restrained party to attend:

- 52-week batterer intervention programs certified by the Judicial Council

- Alcohol or drug treatment programs
- Individual or group counseling
- Parenting classes

B. New York's Structured Approach to Relief

New York's family offense statutes provide specific categories of relief that courts may order upon finding that a family offense has occurred.

1. Orders of Protection

New York Family Court Act Section 842 authorizes courts to issue orders of protection containing any or all of the following provisions:

- Direct the respondent to refrain from committing family offenses
- Direct the respondent to stay away from the home, school, business, or place of employment of the petitioner or children
- Direct the respondent to permit the petitioner to enter the residence to remove personal belongings
- Grant the petitioner temporary custody of minor children
- Direct the payment of temporary child support
- Direct the respondent to participate in available services and programs

2. Temporary Orders of Protection

New York courts may issue temporary orders of protection immediately upon filing when the petition alleges an immediate and present danger of family offense. N.Y. *Fam.* Ct. Act § 828. These orders remain in effect until the court holds a hearing on the merits.

3. Final Orders of Protection

After a hearing on the merits, courts may issue final orders of protection for up to two years, or up to five years if aggravating circumstances exist. N.Y. *Fam.* Ct. Act § 842(1). Aggravating circumstances include:

- Physical injury or serious physical injury

- Use or threatened use of a deadly weapon
- Behavior constituting a violent felony offense
- Intentional or reckless damage to property
- Violation of a prior order of protection

4. Criminal Court Coordination

New York's integrated approach allows family court orders of protection to run concurrently with criminal court orders, providing comprehensive protection across multiple proceedings. N.Y. *Fam.* Ct. Act § 842-*a*.

C. Emergency and Ex Parte Relief

Both states recognize that domestic violence situations often require immediate judicial intervention without providing advance notice to the alleged abuser.

California Emergency Procedures

California Family Code Section 6250 provides for ex parte (emergency) relief when the petitioner demonstrates:

- Immediate and present danger of domestic violence
- Irreparable harm to the petitioner or children
- Good cause for granting relief without notice

Emergency orders may include all forms of relief available in noticed proceedings, including residence exclusion and temporary custody orders. The California Court of Appeal has held that ex parte orders should be granted liberally when evidence supports reasonable fear of imminent harm. *Burquet v. Brumbaugh*, 223 Cal. App. 4th 1140, 1146 (2014).

New York Emergency Procedures

New York Family Court Act Section 828 authorizes temporary orders of protection when the petition alleges "an immediate and present danger of a family offense." Courts may issue these orders:

- On the same day as filing
- Without advance notice to the respondent

- Based on sworn allegations in the petition
- With immediate effect upon service

The Court of Appeals has emphasized that emergency relief serves the dual purpose of protecting victims and preserving the status quo pending a full hearing. *Matter of Gayle BB. v. Theodore CC.*, 36 N.Y.3d 961, 963 (2020).

V. Procedural Requirements and Practice Considerations

A. California Filing Procedures

1. Initial Petition Requirements

California domestic violence restraining order proceedings begin with the filing of Form DV-100 (Request for Domestic Violence Restraining Order) accompanied by Form DV-101 (Description of Abuse). The petition must include:

- Specific factual allegations describing incidents of abuse
- Dates, times, and locations of abusive conduct
- Descriptions of injuries or property damage
- Information about any children involved
- Requests for specific relief sought

The California Judicial Council has emphasized that petitions should include sufficient detail to enable the court to determine whether the statutory requirements for a restraining order are met. *Judicial Council of California, Domestic Violence Practice and Procedure Manual* (2023).

2. Temporary Restraining Order Consideration

Upon filing, the court immediately considers whether to issue a temporary restraining order (TRO) based on the petition and supporting declaration. The court applies the standard of whether the facts alleged show a reasonable probability that the petitioner will prevail on the merits and that the harm to the petitioner if the temporary order is not granted exceeds the harm to the respondent if it is granted. *Scripps Health v. Marin*, 62 Cal. App. 4th 696, 703 (1998).

3. Service Requirements

If a TRO is granted, the petitioner must serve the respondent with:

- Form DV-100 (Request for Domestic Violence Restraining Order)
- Form DV-101 (Description of Abuse)
- Form DV-109 (Notice of Court Hearing)
- Form DV-110 (Temporary Restraining Order)
- Form DV-120 (Response to Request for Domestic Violence Restraining Order)

Service must be completed by a sheriff, marshal, registered process server, or any person over 18 who is not a party to the case. Personal service is preferred, but substituted service may be authorized in appropriate circumstances. *Cal. Code Civ. Proc.* § 415.10.

4. Hearing Procedures

The court must schedule a hearing within 21 to 25 days after the TRO is issued. At the hearing, both parties may present evidence, call witnesses, and argue their positions. The court applies the preponderance of the evidence standard in determining whether to grant a permanent restraining order.

If the court grants the restraining order, it remains in effect for up to five years and may be renewed upon application before expiration. The court must make specific findings regarding the incidents of abuse and the necessity for continued protection. *Cal. Fam. Code* § 6345.

B. New York Filing Procedures

1. Petition Filing

New York domestic violence proceedings begin with filing a Family Offense Petition in Family Court. The petition must:

- Identify the specific family offense allegedly committed
- Provide factual allegations supporting each element of the offense

- Describe the relationship between the parties
- Specify the relief sought

Unlike California, New York does not charge filing fees for family offense petitions, recognizing that economic barriers should not prevent access to protection. N.Y. *Fam.* Ct. Act § 827.

2. Temporary Order Consideration

Upon filing, the court may issue a temporary order of protection if the petition alleges "an immediate and present danger of a family offense." The court may issue this order:

- Ex parte without notice to the respondent
- Based solely on the sworn allegations in the petition
- With immediate effectiveness upon service

The First Department has held that courts should err on the side of protection when evaluating requests for temporary orders. *Matter of Leticia R. v. Jeremiah* S., 100 A.D.3d 1, 8 (1st Dep't 2012).

3. Service and Return Date

The court sets a return date for the respondent to appear, typically within 8 to 14 days after filing. The respondent must be served with:

- The family offense petition
- The temporary order of protection (if issued)
- A notice of the return date

Service is typically effectuated by court officers or law enforcement personnel. N.Y. *Fam.* Ct. Act § 820.

4. Hearing Procedures

If the respondent appears and denies the allegations, the court schedules a fact-finding hearing. New York applies the criminal burden of proof standard, requiring the petitioner to prove the family offense beyond a reasonable doubt. *Matter of Damon v. Damon*, 26 N.Y.3d 540, 546 (2015).

If the court finds that a family offense occurred, it may issue a final order of protection for up to two years (or five years with aggravating circumstances). The order may be renewed upon application before expiration.

C. Evidentiary Considerations

1. Documentation and Evidence

Successful domestic violence cases require careful documentation of abusive incidents. Practitioners should advise clients to maintain:

- Photographs of injuries or property damage
- Medical records documenting treatment for abuse-related injuries
- Police reports and incident documentation
- Records of threatening communications (texts, emails, voicemails)
- Witness statements and contact information
- Financial records documenting economic abuse

2. Expert Testimony

Both California and New York allow expert testimony regarding domestic violence dynamics, particularly to explain victim behavior that may seem counterintuitive to lay observers. Common expert testimony includes:

- Explanation of why victims remain in abusive relationships
- Discussion of power and control dynamics
- Analysis of escalation patterns
- Assessment of future danger

The California Evidence Code specifically provides for expert testimony on intimate partner battering and its effects. *Cal. Evid. Code* § 1107. New York courts have similarly recognized the value of expert testimony in domestic violence cases. *People v. Cronin*, 60 N.Y.2d 430, 437 (1983).

3. Hearsay Considerations

Domestic violence cases often involve hearsay evidence, particularly statements made by victims to medical providers, law enforcement, or family members. Both states provide exceptions for:

- Excited utterances made under the stress of the traumatic event
- Statements made for medical diagnosis or treatment
- Present sense impressions
- Statements against interest

California Evidence Code Section 1370 provides a specific hearsay exception for statements describing physical or mental abuse when the declarant is unavailable due to the abuse. New York has similar provisions under its Criminal Procedure Law. *People v. Brensic*, 70 N.Y.2d 9, 18 (1987).

VI. Impact on Child Custody and Visitation

A. California's Presumption Against Custody to Abusive Parents

California has established one of the most protective statutory frameworks in the nation regarding child custody in domestic violence cases. Family Code Section 3044 creates a rebuttable presumption that awarding sole or joint physical or legal custody to a person who has perpetrated domestic violence is detrimental to the best interests of the child.

1. Triggering the Presumption

The presumption is triggered when the court finds by a preponderance of the evidence that a party has perpetrated domestic violence against:

- The other party
- A child who is subject to the custody determination
- A person in the other party's household
- A person who is related to the other party by consanguinity or affinity within the second degree

The presumption applies when the domestic violence occurred within five years before the filing of the custody action, or at any time if the violence was directed at a child. *Cal. Fam. Code § 3044(a).*

2. Rebutting the Presumption

The party seeking custody despite the presumption must prove by a preponderance of the evidence that granting custody to that party is in the best interests of the child. The court must consider evidence of all of the following:

- The perpetrator has successfully completed a batterer's treatment program that meets the criteria outlined in subdivision (c) of Section 1203.097 of the Penal Code
- The perpetrator has successfully completed a program of alcohol or drug abuse counseling if the court determines that counseling is appropriate
- The perpetrator has successfully completed a parenting class if the court determines the class to be appropriate
- The perpetrator is on probation or parole, and the terms of probation or parole include conditions that protect the safety of the victim
- The perpetrator is restrained by a protective order or restraining order, and the terms of the order protect the safety of the victim and the victim consents to the granting of custody to the perpetrator
- The victim consents to the granting of custody to the perpetrator
- The perpetrator has paid restitution to the victim where restitution is appropriate
- The perpetrator has acknowledged to the court his or her responsibility for the violence

Cal. Fam. Code § 3044(b).

The California Court of Appeal has held that the presumption represents a strong policy preference for protecting children from exposure to domestic violence. *In re Marriage of Fajota*, 230 Cal. App. 4th 1487, 1497 (2014).

3. Judicial Discretion in Rebuttal Analysis

Even if the abusive parent presents evidence on all factors listed in Section 3044(b), the court retains discretion to determine whether custody would be in the child's best interests. Courts have considered additional factors including:

- The severity and frequency of the domestic violence
- The impact of the violence on the children
- The perpetrator's insight into the effects of domestic violence
- The likelihood of future violence
- The perpetrator's compliance with court orders and treatment programs

In re Marriage of Hess, 212 Cal. App. 4th 1367, 1378 (2013).

4. Supervised Visitation Requirements

When custody is denied due to domestic violence, California courts typically order supervised visitation to maintain the parent-child relationship while protecting safety. Family Code Section 3100.1 provides specific requirements for supervised visitation in domestic violence cases:

- Professional supervision by a neutral third party
- Supervision in a neutral location away from the protected party
- Written safety protocols addressing potential risks
- Gradual transition to less restrictive supervision only after demonstrated compliance and completion of treatment programs

B. New York's Best Interests Framework

New York does not have a statutory presumption against custody for domestic violence perpetrators but requires courts to consider domestic violence as a factor in the best interests analysis.

1. Domestic Violence as a Best Interests Factor

New York Domestic Relations Law Section 240 requires courts to consider "the effect of domestic violence on the child" in custody determinations. The Court of Appeals has held that domestic violence between parents creates a rebuttable presumption that exposure to such violence is harmful to children. *Matter of Lincoln v. Lincoln*, 24 N.Y.3d 1001, 1003 (2014).

2. Judicial Analysis of Domestic Violence Impact

New York courts engage in individualized assessments of how domestic violence affects specific children, considering factors such as:

- The child's age and developmental stage
- The child's direct exposure to violence
- The child's indirect exposure through witnessing aftermath
- The child's emotional and behavioral responses
- The availability of protective measures

Matter of Natasha C. v. Ruben E., 154 A.D.3d 1054, 1057 (2d Dep't 2017).

3. Graduated Response to Domestic Violence

New York courts have developed a graduated approach to addressing domestic violence in custody cases:

- **Denial of Custody**: In cases involving severe or ongoing violence
- **Supervised Visitation**: When violence raises safety concerns but contact is beneficial
- **Monitored Exchanges**: To prevent direct contact between parents while allowing visitation
- **Protective Conditions**: Such as no overnight visits or alcohol restrictions

Matter of Melissa WW. v. Steven XX., 111 A.D.3d 1158, 1161 (3d Dep't 2013).

C. Children's Rights and Representation

1. California's Approach to Child Representation

California Family Code Section 3150 provides for appointment of counsel for children in custody cases involving domestic violence. The statute requires courts to consider appointing counsel when:

- The case involves allegations of child abuse or domestic violence

- The child expresses a preference regarding custody or visitation
- The parents cannot agree on custody arrangements
- The court determines that appointment would be in the child's best interests

Child attorneys in California have the authority to:

- Advocate for the child's expressed preferences
- Investigate relevant facts
- Present evidence and call witnesses
- Appeal court decisions
- Participate in settlement negotiations

In re Marriage of Seagondollar, 139 Cal. App. 4th 1116, 1125 (2006).

2. New York's Comprehensive Child Representation

New York provides more extensive child representation rights in domestic violence cases. Family Court Act Section 241 requires appointment of counsel for children in custody cases involving domestic violence allegations.

The law distinguishes between two types of child representation:

Attorney for the Child (AFC): Represents the child's expressed preferences and zealously advocates for the child's stated wishes, similar to traditional attorney-client relationships.

Law Guardian: Represents what the attorney believes to be in the child's best interests, which may differ from the child's expressed preferences.

Matter of Destiny D., 15 N.Y.3d 574, 579 (2010).

3. Child Interview Procedures

Both states have developed protocols for judicial interviews with children in domestic violence cases:

California Procedures: Family Code Section 3042 allows courts to interview children regarding their custody preferences, with specific protections including:

- In-camera interviews outside the presence of parties

- Court reporter transcription of interviews
- Prohibition on leading questions
- Consideration of the child's age and maturity

New York Procedures: Family Court Act Section 252 provides similar protections:

- Private judicial interviews in chambers
- Presence of court attorney or law guardian
- Stenographic record of interviews
- Consideration of the child's developmental capacity

D. Parenting Plan Modifications in Domestic Violence Cases

1. California's Protective Parenting Plan Requirements

When domestic violence is present, California courts must ensure that parenting plans include specific safety provisions:

- **Exchange Protocols**: Detailed procedures for child exchanges that minimize contact between parents, often involving neutral locations such as police stations or supervised visitation centers
- **Communication Restrictions**: Limitations on direct communication between parents, often requiring communication through third parties, written communication only, or communication apps designed for co-parents
- **Geographic Restrictions**: Limitations on where the abusive parent may take the child during visitation, often excluding the protected parent's neighborhood, workplace, or school
- **Emergency Provisions**: Clear protocols for emergency situations, including contact information for law enforcement and procedures for temporary modification of custody arrangements

In re Marriage of Heistandt, 78 Cal. App. 4th 1156, 1164 (2000).

2. New York's Individualized Safety Planning

New York courts work with parties to develop individualized safety plans that address specific risks identified in each case:

- **Risk Assessment**: Formal evaluation of danger factors using validated risk assessment tools
- **Safety Protocols**: Detailed procedures tailored to the specific circumstances of each family
- **Resource Identification**: Connection with community resources, including domestic violence programs, counseling services, and legal assistance
- **Monitoring Mechanisms**: Ongoing review and modification of safety plans as circumstances change

Matter of Kristen B. v. Thomas W., 125 A.D.3d 1349, 1352 (4th Dep't 2015).

VII. Enforcement Mechanisms and Violation Consequences

A. Criminal Enforcement

1. California's Comprehensive Enforcement Framework

Violation of a domestic violence restraining order in California constitutes a criminal offense under Penal Code Section 273.6, which provides:

"Any intentional and knowing violation of a protective order... is a misdemeanor punishable by a fine of not more than one thousand dollars ($1,000), or by imprisonment in a county jail for not more than one year, or by both that fine and imprisonment."

Enhanced Penalties: The statute provides for enhanced penalties for subsequent violations or violations involving violence:

- Second violation within one year: Mandatory minimum 48 hours in jail
- Third violation within one year: Mandatory minimum 120 hours in jail
- Violation involving violence: Felony charges possible under Penal Code Section 273.6(d)

People v. Gonzalez, 12 Cal. 4th 804, 815 (1996) (holding that restraining order violations are general intent crimes requiring only proof that defendant knew of the order and intentionally performed the prohibited act).

2. Arrest Authority and Procedures

California Penal Code Section 836(c)(1) provides law enforcement with mandatory arrest authority for restraining order violations:

"A peace officer shall arrest a person when the peace officer has reasonable cause to believe that the person to be arrested has committed a violation of a protective order issued pursuant to the Family Code."

The California Supreme Court has emphasized that this mandatory arrest provision serves both protective and deterrent functions. *People v. Soto*, 35 Cal. 4th 1018, 1025 (2005).

Law Enforcement Database Access: All California restraining orders are entered into the California Law Enforcement Telecommunications System (CLETS), providing real-time access to order details for all law enforcement agencies statewide. Officers can verify order terms, expiration dates, and protected parties through mobile data terminals.

3. New York's Criminal Enforcement Structure

New York Penal Law Section 215.51 criminalizes criminal contempt in the first degree for violating orders of protection:

"A person is guilty of criminal contempt in the first degree when he or she commits the crime of criminal contempt in the second degree... and in the course of and in furtherance of the commission of such crime he or she intentionally or recklessly causes physical injury to a person for whose protection such order was issued."

Graduated Criminal Penalties:

- **Criminal Contempt in the Second Degree** (Class A misdemeanor): Violation without physical injury, punishable by up to one year in jail
- **Criminal Contempt in the First Degree** (Class E felony): Violation causing physical injury, punishable by up to four years in prison
- **Aggravated Criminal Contempt** (Class D felony): Violation causing serious physical injury or involving a deadly weapon, punishable by up to seven years in prison

People v. Wood, 95 N.Y.2d 509, 515 (2000) (holding that knowledge of the order and intent to violate are essential elements of criminal contempt).

B. Civil Enforcement Mechanisms

1. California's Civil Contempt Procedures

California Code of Civil Procedure Section 1209 provides for civil contempt proceedings when restraining orders are violated. Civil contempt serves both punitive and coercive purposes:

Punitive Contempt: Punishment for completed violations, with penalties including:

- Fines up to $1,000 per violation
- Imprisonment for up to five days per violation
- Community service requirements
- Mandatory counseling or treatment programs

Coercive Contempt: Ongoing sanctions designed to compel compliance:

- Daily fines until compliance is achieved
- Incarceration until compliance occurs (with periodic review)
- Asset seizure or freezing
- Modification or extension of the restraining order

In re Marriage of Evilsizor & Sweeney, 237 Cal. App. 4th 1416, 1428 (2015) (holding that civil contempt must be proven by clear and convincing evidence).

2. Modification and Extension Procedures

Both states provide mechanisms for modifying or extending restraining orders based on violations or changed circumstances.

California Modification Standards: Family Code Section 6345 allows modification when:

- Circumstances have changed significantly
- The modification would better serve the purposes of protection

- Good cause exists for the requested changes

Common modifications include:

- Expanding geographic restrictions after violations
- Adding new protected parties (such as family members)
- Increasing supervision requirements for child visitation
- Adding mandatory counseling or treatment requirements

New York Modification Framework: Family Court Act Section 842 provides similar authority:

- Extension of order duration based on continued need for protection
- Modification of terms to address new threats or circumstances
- Addition of new provisions based on violation patterns

Matter of Damon v. Damon, 26 N.Y.3d 540, 549 (2015) (requiring courts to consider evidence of changed circumstances and ongoing need for protection).

C. Interstate Enforcement

1. Federal Framework: Violence Against Women Act (VAWA)

The Violence Against Women Act, codified at 18 U.S.C. § 2265, requires full faith and credit enforcement of protection orders across state lines:

"Any protection order issued that is consistent with subsection (b) of this section by the court of one State, Indian tribe, or territory... shall be accorded full faith and credit by the court of another State, Indian tribe, or territory and enforced by the court and law enforcement personnel of the other State, Indian tribal government or Territory as if it were the order of the enforcing State or tribe."

Requirements for Interstate Enforcement:

- The issuing court had jurisdiction over the parties and subject matter
- The restrained party received reasonable notice and opportunity to be heard

- The order contains specific terms prohibiting certain conduct

United States v. Hayes, 555 U.S. 415, 427 (2009) (interpreting federal domestic violence statutes broadly to effectuate congressional intent to protect victims).

2. Uniform Interstate Enforcement

Both California and New York have adopted the Uniform Interstate Enforcement of Domestic Violence Protection Orders Act, providing streamlined procedures for out-of-state order enforcement:

Registration Requirements: Out-of-state orders may be registered with local courts to facilitate enforcement, though registration is not required for immediate enforcement by law enforcement.

Emergency Enforcement: Law enforcement must enforce valid out-of-state orders immediately upon verification, without requiring local court registration or modification.

Modification Restrictions: Only the issuing state may modify protection orders, preventing forum shopping and ensuring consistency.

D. Technology and Enforcement Innovation

1. Electronic Monitoring

Both states have expanded use of electronic monitoring for restraining order enforcement:

GPS Monitoring: Courts may order GPS monitoring of restrained parties, with automatic alerts when they enter prohibited areas or approach protected parties.

Victim Notification Systems: Electronic systems that automatically notify protected parties when restrained parties are arrested, released, or violate monitoring requirements.

Smartphone Applications: Mobile apps that allow protected parties to quickly contact law enforcement and document violations with photographs, audio recordings, and GPS location data.

2. Database Integration

Modern enforcement relies on integrated database systems:

National Crime Information Center (NCIC): Federal database containing all valid protection orders, accessible to law enforcement nationwide for immediate verification.

State-Specific Systems: California's CLETS and New York's eJusticeNY provide enhanced functionality including:

- Real-time order modifications and updates
- Automated expiration notifications
- Integration with criminal justice databases
- Statistical tracking for policy development

VIII. Intersection with Immigration Law

A. Federal Protections for Immigrant Survivors

Domestic violence intersects significantly with immigration law, as immigrant survivors often face unique vulnerabilities including threats of deportation, language barriers, and fear of law enforcement contact.

1. Violence Against Women Act (VAWA) Self-Petitions

VAWA provides immigration relief for survivors of domestic violence through self-petitioning procedures under 8 U.S.C. § 1154(a)(1)(A):

Eligibility Requirements:

- Marriage to a U.S. citizen or lawful permanent resident abuser
- Residence with the abuser in the United States
- Battery or extreme cruelty by the citizen or resident spouse
- Good moral character of the petitioner
- Extreme hardship if removed from the United States

Matter of A-B-, 28 I&N Dec. 307, 316 (BIA 2021) (clarifying that domestic violence can constitute persecution for asylum purposes under appropriate circumstances).

Evidence Requirements: VAWA self-petitions require comprehensive documentation including:

- Evidence of the abusive relationship (marriage certificates, cohabitation evidence)
- Documentation of abuse (police reports, medical records, restraining orders, photographs)
- Expert testimony regarding domestic violence dynamics
- Evidence of good moral character
- Documentation of extreme hardship

2. U Visa Relief for Crime Victims

The U visa, created under 8 U.S.C. § 1101(a)(15)(U), provides immigration status for victims of qualifying crimes who cooperate with law enforcement:

Qualifying Criminal Activity: Domestic violence-related crimes that qualify include:

- Domestic violence
- Sexual assault
- Trafficking
- Stalking
- Kidnapping
- Felonious assault

Cooperation Requirement: Applicants must demonstrate cooperation with law enforcement in the investigation or prosecution of the criminal activity. This cooperation can include:

- Reporting the crime to law enforcement
- Participating in criminal proceedings as a witness
- Providing information about the crime
- Participating in civil protection order proceedings

8 C.F.R. § 214.14(*b*)(3) (defining substantial cooperation requirements).

Law Enforcement Certification: U visa applications require certification from law enforcement agencies confirming the victim's cooperation and the qualifying nature of the criminal activity.

3. Special Immigrant Juvenile Status (SIJS)

Children fleeing domestic violence may qualify for SIJS under 8 U.S.C. § 1101(a)(27)(J):

Eligibility Criteria:

- Under 21 years of age and unmarried
- Subject to juvenile court jurisdiction
- Abandonment, abuse, or neglect by one or both parents
- Reunification with parents not viable due to abuse or neglect
- Best interests served by remaining in the United States

Family courts play a crucial role in SIJS cases by making the necessary findings regarding abuse, neglect, and best interests.

B. State-Level Immigration Protections

1. California's Comprehensive Approach

California has enacted extensive protections for immigrant survivors of domestic violence:

TRUST Act (Government Code Section 7282): Limits local law enforcement cooperation with immigration authorities, providing greater security for immigrant survivors seeking protection.

Confidentiality Protections: California Evidence Code Section 1227 prohibits discovery of immigration status in civil proceedings except in limited circumstances directly related to the case.

Language Access: California Government Code Section 68560 requires courts to provide interpreters in domestic violence proceedings, ensuring that language barriers do not prevent access to protection.

2. New York's Protective Framework

New York has similarly enacted immigrant-friendly policies:

Green Light Law: Allows undocumented immigrants to obtain driver's licenses, enhancing mobility and independence for domestic violence survivors.

Liberty Act: Limits state and local law enforcement cooperation with federal immigration authorities in most circumstances.

Court Access: New York has established policies ensuring that immigration enforcement cannot occur in court buildings, protecting survivors' access to justice.

C. Practice Considerations for Immigrant Clients

1. Screening and Assessment

Attorneys representing immigrant survivors must conduct comprehensive immigration screening:

- Current immigration status and history
- Criminal history that might affect immigration relief
- Family relationships that could support immigration petitions
- Potential bars to immigration relief
- Timeline considerations for various forms of relief

2. Collaborative Representation

Domestic violence cases involving immigrant clients often require collaboration between family law attorneys and immigration specialists:

Coordination Strategy: Ensure that family court proceedings support rather than undermine immigration relief applications.

Evidence Gathering: Develop evidence that serves both family law and immigration purposes, such as restraining orders that document abuse for VAWA petitions.

Timing Considerations: Coordinate filing schedules to maximize protection and minimize conflicts between proceedings.

IX. Housing Protections and Economic Security

A. Federal Housing Protections

1. Violence Against Women Act Housing Provisions

VAWA includes comprehensive housing protections for domestic violence survivors under 34 U.S.C. § 12491:

Public Housing Protections:

- Prohibition on denial of housing assistance based on domestic violence victimization
- Protection from eviction due to criminal activity by the abuser
- Right to emergency transfer to protect safety
- Confidentiality of victim information

Private Housing Rights: Many jurisdictions have extended similar protections to private housing through local ordinances and state legislation.

2. Fair Housing Act Applications

The Fair Housing Act has been interpreted to provide protections for domestic violence survivors:

Disparate Impact Theory: Policies that disproportionately affect domestic violence survivors may violate fair housing laws if they have a disparate impact on protected classes.

Reasonable Accommodations: Survivors may be entitled to reasonable accommodations such as:

- Permission to change locks
- Early lease termination without penalty
- Accommodation of protective measures

B. State-Specific Housing Protections

1. California's Comprehensive Housing Framework

California Civil Code Section 1946.7 provides extensive housing protections for domestic violence survivors:

Early Lease Termination: Tenants may terminate leases early without penalty upon providing:

- 30 days' written notice
- Copy of restraining order or police report
- Statement that continued tenancy poses threat to safety

Lock Changes: Landlords must change locks within 24 hours of written request when tenant provides evidence of domestic violence.

Confidentiality: Landlords must keep all domestic violence-related information confidential and may not disclose it without tenant consent or court order.

Frances T. v. Village Green Owners Association, 42 Cal. 3d 490, 499 (1986) (establishing that landlords have limited duty to protect tenants from criminal acts by third parties).

2. New York's Tenant Protection Laws

New York Real Property Law Section 227-c provides similar protections:

Safe Harbor Provisions: Tenants cannot be evicted based on domestic violence incidents, including:

- Criminal activity by the abuser on the premises
- Police calls related to domestic violence
- Property damage caused by domestic violence

Emergency Procedures: Tenants may request immediate lock changes and security modifications when presenting evidence of domestic violence.

Reasonable Accommodations: Landlords must provide reasonable accommodations to enhance tenant safety, including:

- Installation of additional security measures
- Permission for early lease termination

- Modification of lease terms to enhance safety

C. Economic Abuse and Financial Recovery

1. Recognition of Economic Abuse

Both California and New York have recognized economic abuse as a form of domestic violence with significant legal consequences:

California Definition: Family Code Section 6203(a)(3) defines economic abuse as behavior that unreasonably interferes with a person's ability to acquire, use, or maintain economic resources.

Examples of Economic Abuse:

- Preventing access to bank accounts or credit cards
- Sabotaging employment through harassment or interference
- Hiding assets or income
- Destroying important financial documents
- Using coercion to control financial decisions

2. Financial Recovery Mechanisms

Courts in both states have broad authority to address economic harm through various remedies:

Temporary Financial Orders: Emergency orders may include:

- Temporary spousal or child support
- Exclusive use of vehicles or property
- Payment of attorney's fees and costs
- Restoration of access to financial accounts

Asset Protection: Courts may order:

- Freezing of joint accounts
- Prevention of asset dissipation
- Appointment of receivers for businesses or property

- Temporary exclusive control of residence

Restitution: Criminal courts may order restitution for economic losses caused by domestic violence, including:

- Medical expenses
- Lost wages
- Property damage
- Counseling costs
- Temporary housing expenses

X. Specialized Court Programs and Alternative Dispute Resolution

A. Dedicated Domestic Violence Courts

1. California's Coordinated Court Response

California has developed specialized domestic violence court programs in many counties to provide coordinated, comprehensive responses to domestic violence cases:

Integrated Case Management: These courts often handle multiple types of proceedings involving the same family:

- Criminal domestic violence cases
- Family law custody and support matters
- Civil restraining order proceedings
- Juvenile dependency cases involving domestic violence

Specialized Training: Judges and court personnel receive extensive training on:

- Domestic violence dynamics and trauma responses
- Cultural competency and language access
- Safety planning and risk assessment

- Evidence-based practices for victim protection

Enhanced Services: Specialized courts typically provide:

- On-site victim advocates
- Batterer intervention program coordination
- Mental health and substance abuse referrals
- Childcare during court proceedings

Sviridov, D., et al., Dispensing Justice Locally: The Implementation and Effects of the Midtown Community Court(2001) (documenting benefits of specialized court approaches).

2. New York's Integrated Domestic Violence Courts

New York has established Integrated Domestic Violence (IDV) Courts in multiple counties:

"One Judge, One Family" Model: IDV Courts assign a single judge to handle all legal matters involving a family affected by domestic violence:

- Criminal cases against the abuser
- Family offense proceedings
- Matrimonial and custody cases
- Child protective proceedings

Comprehensive Case Planning: IDV Courts develop individualized case plans addressing:

- Immediate safety concerns
- Long-term protection needs
- Therapeutic intervention requirements
- Economic stability issues

Coordinated Services: These courts provide integrated access to:

- Legal representation
- Counseling and therapy services

- Economic empowerment programs
- Housing assistance

Labriola, M., et al., A *National Portrait of Domestic Violence Courts* (2009) (analyzing effectiveness of specialized domestic violence court models).

B. Limitations on Mediation and Alternative Dispute Resolution

1. California's Protective Approach to ADR

California has established strict limitations on the use of mediation and other alternative dispute resolution methods in cases involving domestic violence:

Statutory Prohibitions: Family Code Section 3181 prohibits mediation in custody cases where there are allegations of domestic violence unless specific safeguards are implemented:

- The mediator has specialized training in domestic violence
- Separate sessions (shuttle mediation) are conducted
- The victim expressly requests mediation in writing
- Safety protocols are established and followed

Court Mediation Restrictions: California Rules of Court, Rule 5.215 requires courts to screen for domestic violence before referring cases to mediation and provides procedures for ensuring safety when mediation proceeds.

Power Imbalance Recognition: The California Supreme Court has recognized that traditional mediation models may be inappropriate when power imbalances exist due to domestic violence. *In re Marriage of Kleist*, 99 Cal. App. 4th 263, 271 (2002).

2. New York's Cautionary Framework

New York has similarly restricted the use of ADR in domestic violence cases:

Screening Requirements: Domestic Relations Law Section 255 requires screening for domestic violence before referring parties to mediation or collaborative processes.

Safety Protocols: When mediation proceeds despite domestic violence history, courts must ensure:

- Voluntary participation by the victim
- Safety planning and protocols
- Specialized mediator training
- Separate caucus sessions when appropriate

Judicial Oversight: Family Court Act Section 154-d requires enhanced judicial oversight of any ADR process involving domestic violence allegations.

C. Batterer Intervention Programs

1. California's Comprehensive Program Requirements

California Penal Code Section 1203.097 establishes detailed standards for court-approved batterer intervention programs:

Program Duration: 52-week minimum duration with weekly sessions of at least 90 minutes each.

Curriculum Requirements: Programs must address:

- The physical, sexual, and emotional abuse of women and children
- The historical and societal context of violence against women
- Childhood exposure to domestic violence
- Legal consequences of domestic violence
- Development of empathy and accountability

Prohibited Approaches: Programs may not use:

- Couples counseling or family therapy approaches
- Anger management models as primary intervention
- Theories that victim behavior causes abuse

Monitoring and Accountability: Programs must provide regular reports to courts regarding participant attendance, progress, and compliance.

People v. Welch, 20 Cal. 4th 701, 715 (1999) (upholding constitutionality of mandatory batterer intervention as condition of probation).

2. New York's Evolving Standards

New York has developed standards for batterer intervention programs through administrative regulations and court rules:

Certification Requirements: Programs must be certified by the Office for the Prevention of Domestic Violence and meet specific standards for:

- Staff qualifications and training
- Curriculum content and approach
- Victim safety protocols
- Program evaluation and monitoring

Victim Safety Priority: New York emphasizes victim safety as the primary goal of batterer intervention, requiring:

- Regular victim contact and safety planning
- Immediate notification of victim if participant fails to attend
- Coordination with victim service providers

Cultural Competency: Programs must demonstrate cultural competency and ability to serve diverse populations effectively.

XI. Ethical Considerations and Professional Responsibilities

A. Duty of Competent Representation

1. Specialized Knowledge Requirements

Representing clients in domestic violence cases requires specialized knowledge and skills that extend beyond traditional family law practice:

Understanding Trauma Responses: Attorneys must understand how trauma affects client behavior, decision-making, and memory, including:

- Why victims may minimize abuse or recant allegations
- How trauma affects chronological memory and detailed recall
- The impact of coercive control on client autonomy

Safety Planning: Attorneys must be skilled in safety planning and risk assessment:

- Identifying escalation factors and danger signals
- Developing comprehensive safety plans
- Coordinating with victim service providers
- Understanding the role of formal and informal support systems

Model Rules of Professional Conduct, Rule 1.1, Comment [6] (requiring lawyers to maintain competence through continuing education and study).

2. Continuing Education Requirements

Both California and New York have established continuing education requirements for attorneys handling domestic violence cases:

California Requirements: The State Bar requires attorneys handling domestic violence cases to complete specialized training addressing:

- Domestic violence dynamics and prevalence
- Cultural competency and language access
- Trauma-informed practice principles
- Safety planning and risk assessment

New York Requirements: Similar mandates exist for attorneys appointed in domestic violence cases, including training on:

- Legal remedies available to domestic violence survivors
- Intersection of domestic violence with other legal issues
- Ethical considerations in domestic violence representation

B. Confidentiality and Safety Considerations

1. Modified Confidentiality Obligations

Domestic violence cases may require attorneys to navigate complex confidentiality issues when client safety is at stake:

Threat to Client Safety: Model Rule 1.6(b)(1) allows disclosure of confidential information to prevent reasonably certain death or substantial bodily harm to the client or others.

Child Safety Obligations: Attorneys may have mandatory reporting obligations when clients disclose child abuse, requiring careful navigation of attorney-client privilege protections.

Safety Planning Disclosures: Attorneys may need to share limited information with victim service providers or law enforcement to enhance client safety, requiring careful consent procedures.

2. Technology and Security Considerations

Modern domestic violence practice requires heightened attention to technology security:

Communication Security: Attorneys must use secure communication methods and advise clients about:

- Safe use of email and text messaging
- Risks of electronic surveillance by abusers
- Secure storage of sensitive documents

Location Confidentiality: Attorneys must protect client location information and may need to:

- Use alternative service addresses
- Implement confidentiality protocols for court filings
- Coordinate with courts on safety measures during proceedings

C. Zealous Advocacy Within Ethical Bounds

1. Balancing Client Wishes and Safety

Domestic violence attorneys often face tension between respecting client autonomy and promoting client safety:

Client-Directed Advocacy: The principle of client autonomy requires attorneys to respect client decisions about:

- Whether to seek restraining orders
- Whether to pursue criminal charges
- Whether to leave the abusive relationship

Safety-Informed Counseling: Attorneys should provide clients with comprehensive information about:

- Legal options and their potential consequences
- Safety risks associated with various courses of action
- Available resources and support services

Model Rules of Professional Conduct, Rule 1.4 (requiring lawyers to keep clients reasonably informed and consult with clients about means to accomplish objectives).

2. Avoiding Re-Traumatization

Ethical representation requires awareness of how legal proceedings can re-traumatize survivors:

Trauma-Informed Practice: Attorneys should adopt practices that:

- Minimize unnecessary re-telling of traumatic events
- Prepare clients for potentially triggering court procedures
- Advocate for reasonable accommodations during proceedings

Collaborative Approach: Working with victim advocates, therapists, and other support providers while maintaining appropriate confidentiality boundaries.

D. Conflicts of Interest in Domestic Violence Cases

1. Dual Representation Prohibitions

The adversarial nature of domestic violence cases generally prohibits dual representation:

Family Representation: Attorneys cannot represent both parties in domestic violence proceedings due to irreconcilable conflicts of interest.

Child Representation: Separate representation may be required for children when their interests diverge from either parent.

Model Rules of Professional Conduct, Rule 1.7 (prohibiting representation when there is a significant risk that representation will be materially limited by the lawyer's responsibilities to another client).

2. Prior Representation Issues

Attorneys must carefully analyze potential conflicts arising from prior representation:

Family Member Representation: Prior representation of family members may create conflicts in domestic violence cases.

Entity Representation: Representation of businesses or organizations connected to the parties may create conflicts requiring disclosure and potentially withdrawal.

XII. Evidence and Trial Advocacy

A. Documentary Evidence in Domestic Violence Cases

1. Photographic Evidence

Photographic evidence plays a crucial role in domestic violence cases, requiring careful attention to authentication and presentation:

Injury Documentation: Photographs of injuries must be properly authenticated under Evidence Code requirements:

- Chain of custody documentation
- Witness testimony regarding when and how photographs were taken
- Demonstration that photographs accurately depict the injuries as they appeared

People v. Goldsmith, 59 Cal. 4th 258, 266 (2014) (discussing authentication requirements for photographic evidence).

Property Damage Documentation: Photographs of damaged property should include:

- Overview shots showing the scene in context
- Close-up shots showing specific damage
- Reference objects to demonstrate scale
- Multiple angles to provide comprehensive documentation

Best Practices for Photographic Evidence:

- Take photographs as soon as possible after incidents
- Use high-quality cameras when available
- Include date and time stamps when possible
- Photograph injuries against neutral backgrounds
- Document healing progression with follow-up photographs

2. Medical Records and Expert Testimony

Medical evidence provides crucial corroboration for domestic violence allegations:

Emergency Room Records: Hospital records often contain detailed documentation of:

- Injury patterns consistent with domestic violence
- Patient statements about cause of injuries
- Healthcare provider observations about patient demeanor
- Social work assessments and safety planning

Documentation Standards: Healthcare providers are increasingly trained to document domestic violence using standardized protocols:

- Body maps showing injury locations
- Standardized screening questions
- Risk assessment tools
- Safety planning documentation

People v. Brown, 59 Cal. 4th 86, 98 (2014) (discussing admissibility of medical records in domestic violence cases).

Expert Medical Testimony: Medical experts can testify regarding:

- Injury patterns typical of domestic violence
- Distinction between accidental and intentional injuries
- Timing of injury occurrence
- Prognosis and long-term effects

B. Behavioral Evidence and Expert Testimony

1. Domestic Violence Syndrome Evidence

Both California and New York allow expert testimony regarding domestic violence dynamics to explain victim behavior that may seem counterintuitive:

California Evidence Code Section 1107: Specifically provides for expert testimony on intimate partner battering and its effects, including:

- Why victims remain in abusive relationships
- Patterns of escalating violence
- Psychological effects of ongoing abuse
- Impact on decision-making and memory

Qualified Expert Requirements: Experts must demonstrate specialized knowledge through:

- Advanced education in psychology, social work, or related fields
- Specialized training in domestic violence dynamics
- Clinical or research experience with domestic violence survivors
- Familiarity with current research and literature

People v. Humphrey, 13 Cal. 4th 1073, 1087 (1996) (establishing framework for expert testimony on battered woman syndrome).

2. Pattern Evidence

Evidence of uncharged acts of domestic violence may be admissible to show patterns of behavior:

California Evidence Code Section 1109: Allows evidence of defendant's commission of other domestic violence acts in criminal proceedings:

- No time limit on prior acts
- Broad definition of domestic violence
- Balancing test under Evidence Code Section 352

Propensity Evidence in Civil Cases: Civil proceedings may allow broader admission of pattern evidence:

- Evidence of prior abuse to show propensity for violence
- Pattern evidence to demonstrate escalation
- Evidence of controlling behavior and coercive tactics

People v. Johnson, 32 Cal. 4th 260, 273 (2004) (analyzing admissibility of pattern evidence in domestic violence prosecutions).

C. Technology Evidence

1. Electronic Communications

Modern domestic violence cases frequently involve electronic evidence requiring specialized handling:

Text Messages and Social Media: Digital communications often provide compelling evidence of:

- Threatening or harassing communications
- Admissions of abusive behavior
- Evidence of stalking or surveillance
- Violation of restraining orders

Authentication Requirements: Electronic evidence must be properly authenticated under Evidence Code requirements:

- Testimony regarding how communications were received

- Evidence linking communications to specific devices or accounts
- Chain of custody for extracted digital evidence
- Expert testimony regarding digital forensics when necessary

People v. Valdez, 201 Cal. App. 4th 1429, 1435 (2011) (discussing authentication of text message evidence).

2. GPS and Surveillance Evidence

Technology increasingly provides evidence of stalking and harassment:

Location Data: GPS data from phones, vehicles, or dedicated tracking devices can establish:

- Presence at prohibited locations
- Pattern of following or surveillance
- Violation of stay-away orders
- Stalking behavior

Privacy Considerations: Use of electronic surveillance evidence raises privacy concerns requiring careful legal analysis:

- Fourth Amendment protections in criminal cases
- Invasion of privacy claims in civil proceedings
- Authorized versus unauthorized surveillance
- Third-party disclosure of location information

D. Child Testimony and Evidence

1. Children as Witnesses

When children witness domestic violence, their testimony may be crucial but requires special handling:

Competency Determinations: Courts must assess child witness competency considering:

- Age and developmental stage

- Ability to distinguish truth from falsehood
- Understanding of oath obligations
- Capacity to accurately observe and recall events

Protective Procedures: Both states provide special procedures for child witnesses:

- In-camera interviews with limited participants
- Use of closed-circuit television in appropriate cases
- Support person presence during testimony
- Anatomical dolls or other demonstrative aids

People v. Sharp, 29 Cal. 4th 1072, 1084 (2003) (discussing special procedures for child witnesses in abuse cases).

2. Hearsay Exceptions for Children

Special hearsay exceptions may allow admission of children's out-of-court statements:

Spontaneous Statements: Excited utterances and spontaneous declarations by children may be admissible when:

- Made under stress of exciting event
- Made without opportunity for reflection or fabrication
- Related to the observed domestic violence

Medical Treatment Statements: Children's statements to medical providers may be admissible under medical treatment exceptions when:

- Made for purpose of medical diagnosis or treatment
- Reasonably pertinent to diagnosis or treatment
- Made by someone seeking medical care

XIII. Conclusion and Future Developments

Domestic violence law continues to evolve as legislatures, courts, and practitioners develop more sophisticated understanding of abuse dynamics and effective legal responses. The comprehensive frameworks established in California and New York represent significant advances from earlier approaches that treated domestic violence as a private matter rather than a serious legal and social issue requiring coordinated intervention.

A. Emerging Trends and Developments

1. Technology and Digital Abuse

The legal system is increasingly grappling with new forms of technology-facilitated abuse:

Cyberstalking and Digital Harassment: Courts are developing new approaches to address online harassment, social media stalking, and digital surveillance that may not fit traditional restraining order frameworks.

Economic Abuse Through Technology: Financial abuse increasingly involves digital mechanisms such as cryptocurrency manipulation, online account takeovers, and credit monitoring interference.

Privacy and Surveillance: The proliferation of smart home devices, GPS tracking, and social media monitoring creates new opportunities for abusive surveillance requiring legal responses.

2. Cultural Competency and Access

Legal systems are recognizing the need for culturally responsive approaches to domestic violence:

Language Access: Enhanced interpreter services and translated materials improve court access for non-English speaking survivors.

Cultural Understanding: Training programs increasingly address how cultural factors may influence domestic violence dynamics and survivor help-seeking behavior.

LGBTQ+ Competency: Recognition of unique issues facing LGBTQ+ survivors, including discrimination, outing threats, and lack of culturally competent services.

B. Systemic Reform Initiatives

1. Coordinated Community Response

Effective domestic violence intervention requires coordination across multiple systems:

Cross-System Training: Enhanced training for law enforcement, prosecutors, judges, and service providers to ensure consistent, informed responses.

Information Sharing: Development of protocols for appropriate information sharing while maintaining confidentiality protections.

Victim-Centered Approaches: Shifting from system-convenience models to approaches that prioritize survivor autonomy and safety.

2. Prevention and Early Intervention

Legal systems are increasingly focusing on prevention alongside response:

Primary Prevention: Educational programs aimed at preventing domestic violence before it occurs through healthy relationship promotion and social norm change.

Early Intervention: Programs designed to intervene at first signs of abuse before patterns become entrenched.

Youth Programs: Specialized approaches for adolescent dating violence recognizing unique developmental and legal considerations.

C. Practice Recommendations

1. Comprehensive Client Services

Effective representation of domestic violence survivors requires holistic approaches:

Safety Planning: Ongoing safety assessment and planning throughout the legal process, recognizing that danger may escalate during legal proceedings.

Trauma-Informed Practice: Understanding how trauma affects client behavior and adapting practice accordingly.

Resource Coordination: Connecting clients with community resources including victim services, counseling, economic empowerment programs, and housing assistance.

2. Continuing Professional Development

The evolving nature of domestic violence law requires ongoing education and skill development:

Specialized Training: Regular participation in domestic violence-specific continuing education programs.

Interdisciplinary Learning: Collaboration with social workers, mental health professionals, victim advocates, and other professionals to enhance understanding of domestic violence dynamics.

Technology Competency: Staying current with technological developments that affect domestic violence cases, including digital evidence collection, cyberstalking, and electronic surveillance.

D. Legislative and Policy Directions

1. Expanding Protection Frameworks

Future legislative developments are likely to focus on expanding protection mechanisms:

Economic Abuse Recognition: Enhanced legal recognition and remedies for economic abuse, including specific statutory provisions and enhanced enforcement mechanisms.

Digital Abuse Protections: Legislation specifically addressing cyberstalking, revenge porn, GPS stalking, and other technology-facilitated abuse.

Workplace Protections: Expanded workplace safety measures and accommodation requirements for domestic violence survivors.

2. Improving System Responses

Policy reforms continue to focus on system improvement:

Judicial Training: Mandatory specialized training for judges handling domestic violence cases to ensure consistent, informed decision-making.

Court Security: Enhanced security measures in courthouses to protect survivors during proceedings.

Language Access: Expanded interpreter services and culturally appropriate advocacy services.

E. Research and Evidence-Based Practice

1. Outcome Evaluation

Ongoing research continues to evaluate the effectiveness of various legal interventions:

Restraining Order Effectiveness: Studies examining which types of orders are most effective in preventing future violence and protecting survivors.

Court Program Evaluation: Assessment of specialized domestic violence courts and their impact on survivor safety and case outcomes.

Batterer Intervention Assessment: Research on the effectiveness of various batterer intervention approaches and their impact on recidivism.

2. Best Practices Development

Research continues to inform best practices in domestic violence legal response:

Risk Assessment Tools: Development and validation of standardized risk assessment instruments to guide judicial decision-making.

Safety Planning Protocols: Evidence-based approaches to safety planning that account for individual circumstances and risk factors.

Trauma-Informed Procedures: Research on how to minimize re-traumatization while ensuring due process and effective advocacy.

F. National Model Development

1. Interstate Coordination

Enhanced coordination between states continues to develop:

Uniform Laws: Continued development of uniform laws addressing interstate enforcement, jurisdiction, and information sharing.

Technology Integration: National databases and information systems that facilitate interstate coordination and enforcement.

Training Standardization: Development of national standards for domestic violence training across legal and social service professions.

2. Federal Framework Evolution

Federal law continues to evolve to support state and local efforts:

VAWA Reauthorization: Ongoing reauthorization and expansion of the Violence Against Women Act to address emerging issues and populations.

Funding Mechanisms: Federal funding programs that support specialized courts, training, and victim services.

Research Investment: Federal support for research on domestic violence legal responses and intervention effectiveness.

XIV. Appendices and Resources

A. Key Statutory Citations

California Statutes:

- Family Code Sections 6200-6409 (Domestic Violence Prevention Act)
- Family Code Section 3044 (Custody presumption against abusive parents)
- Penal Code Section 273.6 (Violation of protective orders)
- Evidence Code Section 1107 (Expert testimony on intimate partner battering)
- Evidence Code Section 1109 (Evidence of other domestic violence acts)

New York Statutes:

- Family Court Act Article 8 (Family Offenses Proceedings)
- Domestic Relations Law Section 240 (Child custody and domestic violence)
- Penal Law Section 215.51 (Criminal contempt for order violations)
- Criminal Procedure Law Article 530 (Orders of protection)

Federal Statutes:

- 18 U.S.C. § 2265 (Full faith and credit for protection orders)
- 34 U.S.C. § 12491 (VAWA housing protections)
- 8 U.S.C. § 1154(a)(1)(A) (VAWA self-petitions)
- 8 U.S.C. § 1101(a)(15)(U) (U visa provisions)

B. Essential Case Law

California Decisions:

- *In re Marriage of Nadkarni*, 173 Cal. App. 4th 1483 (2009) (defining "disturbing the peace")
- *People v. Gonzalez*, 12 Cal. 4th 804 (1996) (restraining order violations as general intent crimes)
- *In re Marriage of Fajota*, 230 Cal. App. 4th 1487 (2014) (domestic violence custody presumption)
- *People v. Humphrey*, 13 Cal. 4th 1073 (1996) (battered woman syndrome evidence)

New York Decisions:

- *Matter of Aisha K. v. Daniel S.*, 33 N.Y.3d 1 (2019) (family offense pleading requirements)
- *Matter of Baker v. Baker*, 86 N.Y.2d 821 (1995) (intimate relationship factors)
- *Matter of Lincoln v. Lincoln*, 24 N.Y.3d 1001 (2014) (domestic violence impact on children)
- *Matter of Damon v. Damon*, 26 N.Y.3d 540 (2015) (criminal burden of proof in family court)

Federal Decisions:

- *United States v. Hayes*, 555 U.S. 415 (2009) (federal domestic violence statutes interpretation)
- *Matter of* A-B-, 28 I&N Dec. 307 (BIA 2021) (domestic violence and asylum)

C. Professional Resources

Training Organizations:

- National Council of Juvenile and Family Court Judges
- American Professional Society on the Abuse of Children
- National Center on Domestic Violence, Trauma & Mental Health
- Battered Women's Justice Project

Research Institutions:

- National Institute of Justice
- Centers for Disease Control and Prevention
- Urban Institute Justice Policy Center
- National Resource Center on Domestic Violence

Practice Resources:

- ABA Commission on Domestic and Sexual Violence
- National Legal Aid & Defender Association
- Legal Momentum
- National Immigration Project of the National Lawyers Guild

This comprehensive examination of domestic violence and family law restraining orders demonstrates the complexity and evolution of legal responses to domestic violence. As the legal system continues to develop more sophisticated and effective approaches, practitioners must remain committed to ongoing education, trauma-informed practice, and client-centered advocacy that prioritizes survivor safety and autonomy while holding abusers accountable for their conduct.

The intersection of domestic violence with multiple areas of law - including criminal law, immigration law, housing law, and employment law - requires practitioners to develop broad competencies and collaborative relationships with professionals across disciplines. Only through such comprehensive approaches can the legal system effectively respond to the complex needs of domestic violence survivors and their families.

18

Family Law and Military Service

I. Balancing Duty and Domestic Life

Military service creates unique challenges for families that civilian legal practitioners must understand and address with sensitivity and expertise. The intersection of military duty and family obligations presents complex legal issues that require specialized knowledge of both federal protections and state-specific procedures. Service members face frequent relocations, extended deployments, dangerous assignments, and the constant possibility of emergency mobilization - all of which can profoundly impact marriage, parenting, and financial stability.

The legal framework governing military families involves multiple layers of protection and procedure. Federal statutes like the Servicemembers Civil Relief Act (SCRA) and the Uniformed Services Former Spouses' Protection Act (USFSPA) provide baseline protections, while state laws in jurisdictions like New York and California offer additional safeguards specifically tailored to military families. Understanding these overlapping protections is essential for any practitioner representing service members or their families.

The stakes in military family law cases extend beyond typical domestic relations matters. A service member's career, security clearance, and ability to serve may be affected by family law proceedings. Conversely, military service should not disadvantage a service member in custody determinations or expose them to default judgments due to deployment or training obligations. This chapter provides comprehensive guidance on navigating these competing interests while protecting the rights of all parties involved.

II. Servicemembers Civil Relief Act (SCRA)

A. Overview and Legislative Intent

The Servicemembers Civil Relief Act, codified at 50 U.S.C. §§ 3901–4043, represents Congress's recognition that military service requires special procedural protections in civil litigation. Originally enacted as the Soldiers' and Sailors' Civil Relief Act of 1940, the SCRA was substantially revised in 2003 to address modern military service challenges. The Act's fundamental purpose is to enable service members to focus on their military duties without the distraction of civil litigation, while ensuring they are not prejudiced by their inability to appear in court due to military service.

The SCRA applies to all active-duty service members across all branches of the military, including National Guard and Reserve personnel when activated for more than 30 consecutive days. Boone v. Lightner, 319 U.S. 561 (1943), established that SCRA protections are substantive rights, not mere procedural conveniences, and courts must affirmatively ensure compliance rather than simply waiting for service members to invoke their rights.

B. Stay of Proceedings

The cornerstone of SCRA protection is the mandatory stay provision under 50 U.S.C. § 3932. When a service member's military duties materially affect their ability to appear in court, the court must grant a stay of proceedings. The standard for materiality is whether the service member's military duties prevent them from preparing for or participating in the litigation. Pfizer v. Scott, 556 F.3d 65 (2d Cir. 2009).

To obtain a stay, the service member must submit a written application that includes:

- A statement of how military duties materially affect their ability to appear
- A date when they will be available to appear

- Confirmation from their commanding officer that military duties prevent appearance and that military leave is not authorized

The initial stay period cannot exceed 90 days, though additional stays may be granted upon a showing of continuing necessity. Courts must balance the service member's need for protection against the opposing party's right to timely resolution of their claims.

C. Default Judgment Protections

Section 3931 of the SCRA provides critical protections against default judgments. Before entering a default judgment against a defendant, the court must:

1. Require the plaintiff to file an affidavit stating whether the defendant is in military service
2. If the defendant is in military service, appoint an attorney to represent the defendant's interests
3. Determine whether there are meritorious defenses to the action

The appointed attorney must contact the service member if possible and investigate potential defenses. If the court finds that there are meritorious defenses or that the service member should be afforded additional time to respond, it must grant a stay of proceedings under Section 3932.

D. Reopening Default Judgments

Section 3931(g) allows service members to reopen default judgments entered during their period of military service if their military service materially affected their ability to defend the action. The application to reopen must be filed within 90 days of release from military service and must include an affidavit showing:

- The judgment was entered during military service
- Military service materially affected the ability to defend
- The service member has meritorious defenses to the action

In Conroy v. Aniskoff, 507 U.S. 511 (1993), the Supreme Court held that SCRA protections should be liberally construed in favor of service members, establishing a presumption that courts should err on the side of granting relief rather than denying it.

E. Application in Family Law Proceedings

SCRA protections apply with full force in family law proceedings. In re Marriage of Aldrich, 187 P.3d 1075 (Cal. 2008), confirmed that divorce proceedings are subject to SCRA stays when military service materially affects a service member's ability to participate. Similarly, in Atwood v. Atwood, 160 A.D.3d 1563 (N.Y. App. Div. 2018), New York's Appellate Division held that custody modification proceedings must be stayed when a service member demonstrates material interference with their ability to appear.

Family law practitioners must be particularly attentive to SCRA requirements because:

- Family law matters are often time-sensitive, creating pressure to proceed without proper notice
- Service members may be reluctant to request delays due to command pressure or concerns about appearing uncooperative
- Opposing parties may argue that family law emergencies justify proceeding despite SCRA protections

III. Jurisdiction and Residency

A. Complex Residency Issues for Military Families

Military families present unique jurisdictional challenges because service members may be stationed far from their legal domicile, and spouses may reside in yet another state. The Servicemembers Civil Relief Act provides some guidance, but state laws ultimately determine jurisdictional requirements for divorce and family law matters.

Under 50 U.S.C. § 3936, a service member's military assignment does not change their state of legal residence for taxation purposes. However, this principle does not automatically resolve jurisdictional questions in family law cases, where physical presence and residency requirements may differ from tax domicile rules.

B. Divorce Jurisdiction

Most states, including New York and California, have established flexible residency requirements for military families. In California, Family Code Section 2320 requires that either spouse be a resident of the state for six months and of the county for three months before filing for divorce. However, Carlisle v. Carlisle, 108 Cal. App. 4th 1000 (2003), held that temporary military assignments do not interrupt residency for divorce purposes if the service member intends to return.

New York's approach under Domestic Relations Law Section 230 is more complex. While the general rule requires one year of continuous residency, the statute provides exceptions for couples married in New York or who lived together as married persons in New York. In Scherer v. Scherer, 304 A.D.2d 472 (N.Y. App. Div. 2003), the court held that a service member's New York military assignment satisfied residency requirements even though the assignment was temporary.

Service members typically have three jurisdictional options for filing divorce:

1. The state where they are currently stationed
2. The state of their legal domicile
3. The state where their spouse resides

Practitioners should carefully analyze which jurisdiction offers the most favorable substantive law for their client, particularly regarding property division, spousal support, and custody standards.

C. Custody Jurisdiction Under the UCCJEA

The Uniform Child Custody Jurisdiction and Enforcement Act (UCCJEA) governs custody jurisdiction in military cases, but military deployments create unique issues. The UCCJEA's "home state" rule generally gives exclusive jurisdiction to the state where the child has lived for six consecutive months immediately before the custody proceeding.

However, temporary military assignments and deployments can complicate home state determinations. In Thompson v. Thompson, 484 F.3d 1270 (9th Cir. 2007), the Ninth Circuit held that a parent's temporary military deployment does not change the child's home state if the deployment is intended to be temporary and the parent intends to return.

The UCCJEA includes specific provisions for military families in its definition of "temporary absence." Under the Act, a parent's military deployment is considered a temporary absence that does not change the child's home state, provided the parent intends to return to the home state after the deployment ends.

IV. Custody and Deployment

A. California's Comprehensive Deployment Statutes

California has developed the most comprehensive statutory framework for addressing deployment issues in custody cases. Family Code Sections 3047–3048.5 provide detailed procedures for temporary custody modifications during deployment, reflecting California's recognition of the unique challenges military families face.

Family Code Section 3047 establishes the fundamental principle that a parent's deployment, mobilization, or temporary military duty assignment cannot be used as the sole factor in determining the best interests of the child for custody purposes. This provision directly responds to cases where military service was improperly used to justify permanent custody modifications.

The statute requires that temporary custody orders during deployment must:

- Be limited in duration to the period of deployment
- Include provisions for the restoration of the original custody arrangement upon return
- Consider whether delegating visitation rights to a family member during deployment would be in the child's best interests

In In re Marriage of Stephenson, 162 Cal. App. 4th 1057 (2008), the California Court of Appeal applied these principles to reverse a trial court's permanent custody modification based solely on a father's military deployment. The court emphasized that deployment-related custody changes must be temporary and narrowly tailored to serve the child's best interests during the deployment period.

Family Code Section 3048 provides specific procedures for expedited hearings when a parent faces deployment. The deploying parent has the right to:

- Request an expedited hearing before deployment
- Appear by telephone or video conference
- Designate a family member or other person to exercise visitation rights during deployment

The expedited hearing provisions recognize that military deployments often occur with little advance notice, making traditional litigation timelines impractical. Courts must prioritize these cases and may conduct hearings outside normal business hours to accommodate military schedules.

B. New York's Deployment Protections

New York's approach to deployment and custody is found in Domestic Relations Law Section 240(1)(a-1), which provides similar protections to California's framework but with some notable differences. The New York statute prohibits courts from issuing permanent custody modifications based solely on deployment, but it provides more flexibility in temporary arrangements.

Key features of New York's deployment statute include:

- Automatic expiration of temporary orders upon the parent's return from deployment
- Right to request expedited hearings and appear by electronic means
- Authority to designate temporary caregivers during deployment
- Requirement that courts consider the child's best interests in all deployment-related decisions

In Matter of Kilgore v. Kilgore, 153 A.D.3d 1323 (N.Y. App. Div. 2017), the Appellate Division emphasized that deployment-related custody modifications must be truly temporary and cannot be used to circumvent the normal standards for permanent custody changes. The court noted that military service is a form of employment that should not penalize a parent's custody rights.

C. Best Practices for Deployment Custody Cases

Practitioners representing military families in custody cases should develop comprehensive parenting plans that anticipate deployment scenarios. Effective deployment custody provisions should address:

1. **Pre-deployment planning**: Establishing procedures for notifying the other parent of impending deployment and requesting temporary custody modifications
2. **Temporary caregiving arrangements**: Identifying family members or other trusted individuals who may exercise visitation rights during deployment
3. **Communication protocols**: Establishing regular communication schedules between the deployed parent and child, including consideration of time zone differences
4. **Make-up time provisions**: Ensuring that deployed parents can make up missed parenting time upon return
5. **Emergency contact procedures**: Providing for communication in case of emergencies or urgent decisions regarding the child
6. **Re-integration planning**: Establishing procedures for gradually resuming normal custody arrangements after deployment

The case of In re Marriage of LaMusga, 32 Cal. 4th 1072 (2004), while not specifically addressing deployment, provides useful guidance on how courts should analyze the impact of a parent's relocation on the child's best interests. The court's framework for evaluating move-away cases can be adapted to deployment situations.

V. Visitation and Long-Distance Parenting Plans

A. Virtual Visitation Technology

The proliferation of communication technology has revolutionized long-distance parenting for military families. Courts increasingly recognize virtual visitation as a meaningful supplement to in-person contact, particularly during deployments when physical visitation is impossible.

In Pollard v. Pollard, 460 S.W.3d 537 (Tenn. 2015), the Tennessee Supreme Court held that virtual visitation should be considered in all custody cases involving significant distance between parents and children. While this case did not specifically involve military families, its principles apply with particular force to military deployment situations.

Effective virtual visitation orders should specify:

- Minimum frequency and duration of virtual visits
- Technology platforms to be used
- Procedures for handling technical difficulties
- Backup communication methods
- Special provisions for holidays and significant events

Courts must balance the benefits of virtual visitation against the limitations of technology-mediated contact. Virtual visitation cannot completely replace in-person contact but serves as a valuable tool for maintaining the parent-child relationship during separation.

B. Extended Visitation Periods

Military families often benefit from extended visitation periods that compensate for missed time during deployment or training. These arrangements typically involve:

- Extended summer visitation lasting several weeks or months
- Alternating holiday schedules that provide longer periods with each parent
- Flexible scheduling that accommodates military leave periods
- Make-up time provisions for missed visitation due to military duties

In Jaramillo v. Jaramillo, 823 P.2d 299 (N.M. 1991), the New Mexico Supreme Court recognized that military families require flexible visitation arrangements that account for the unique demands of military service. The court emphasized that rigid visitation schedules may not serve the best interests of children in military families.

C. Relocation and Base Transfer Issues

Military families face frequent relocations that can significantly impact existing custody and visitation arrangements. The general legal framework for move-away cases applies to military relocations, but courts must consider the involuntary nature of military moves.

California's approach to military relocations was established in In re Marriage of Condon, 62 Cal. App. 4th 533 (1998), where the court held that military families deserve special consideration in move-away cases because the service member has no choice about relocation. The court emphasized that military moves should not be treated the same as voluntary relocations for career advancement.

Factors that courts consider in military relocation cases include:

- The involuntary nature of the military move
- The potential impact on the service member's career of declining the assignment
- The availability of comparable military positions in the current location
- The impact of the move on the child's relationship with both parents
- The quality of life and opportunities available in the new location

VI. Spousal and Child Support

A. Understanding Military Compensation

Calculating support for military families requires a thorough understanding of military compensation structure, which differs significantly from civilian employment. Military compensation includes numerous components that may or may not be taxable, creating complexity in support calculations.

Base Pay represents the core salary component and is fully taxable. Base pay is determined by rank and years of service according to standardized military pay scales updated annually by Congress.

Basic Allowance for Housing (BAH) is intended to offset housing costs for service members living off-base. BAH is not taxable income under federal law, but most states include it in gross income for support calculation purposes.

The amount varies based on rank, duty location, and whether the service member has dependents.

Basic Allowance for Subsistence (BAS) offsets meal costs and is also non-taxable federally but generally included in state support calculations.

Special Pay encompasses various additional compensation including hazardous duty pay, flight pay, submarine pay, and combat pay. Some special pay is taxable while other forms may be tax-excluded, but most states include all special pay in support calculations.

Combat Pay Exclusion under 26 U.S.C. § 112 allows enlisted personnel and warrant officers to exclude combat pay from federal taxation. However, service members may elect to include combat pay in adjusted gross income for purposes of the Earned Income Tax Credit, creating complexity in support calculations.

B. California Support Calculations

California uses the DissoMaster software program to calculate both child support and spousal support. The program incorporates military-specific income categories and handles the complexities of military compensation.

For child support, California follows the statewide uniform guideline under Family Code Section 4055. The guideline requires inclusion of all income from whatever source derived, specifically including military allowances and benefits. In In re Marriage of Schlafly, 175 Cal. App. 4th 1543 (2009), the California Court of Appeal held that BAH and BAS must be included in gross income for child support purposes despite their non-taxable status.

California's spousal support analysis under Family Code Section 4320 requires consideration of all relevant factors, including the supported party's ability to become self-supporting. Military spouses face unique challenges in maintaining careers due to frequent relocations, and courts must consider these factors in determining support duration and amount.

In In re Marriage of Regnery, 214 Cal. App. 4th 1367 (2013), the California Court of Appeal recognized that military spouses may require longer-term support due to career limitations imposed by military lifestyle. The court emphasized that the standard of living established during marriage is particularly relevant when one spouse has sacrificed career opportunities for military family life.

C. New York Support Calculations

New York's Child Support Standards Act (CSSA) under Family Court Act Section 413 requires inclusion of all income in support calculations, specifically including military allowances. The New York Court of Appeals in Matter of Cassano v. Cassano, 85 N.Y.2d 649 (1995), held that non-taxable military allowances constitute income for child support purposes.

New York's approach to military support calculations includes several important considerations:

Gross Income Definition: Under Family Court Act Section 413(1)(b), gross income includes all income from any source, specifically including military allowances, bonuses, and special pay.

Imputed Income: Courts may impute income to service members based on their military compensation capacity, including potential for promotion and special assignments.

Variable Income: Military compensation may fluctuate based on deployments, special assignments, and promotions. Courts must consider both current income and reasonable expectations of future income changes.

Geographic Considerations: BAH rates vary significantly by duty location, and courts must consider whether current BAH rates reflect the service member's long-term income capacity.

D. Enforcement Mechanisms

Military support enforcement involves both civilian court procedures and military administrative processes. The interplay between these systems provides multiple avenues for support enforcement.

Voluntary Allotment allows service members to authorize automatic deduction of support payments from their military pay through the Defense Finance and Accounting Service (DFAS). This system provides reliable, automatic payments that continue even during deployment or training when service members may have limited access to civilian banking.

Involuntary Allotment under 42 U.S.C. § 659 permits garnishment of military wages for support obligations. DFAS will honor valid support orders and automatically deduct payments, providing reliable enforcement even when service members are deployed or stationed overseas.

Military Regulations provide additional enforcement tools. Each military branch has regulations requiring service members to support their dependents. For example, Army Regulation 608-99 requires soldiers to provide adequate support for family members, and failure to comply can result in administrative or disciplinary action.

The case of McCarty v. McCarty, 453 U.S. 210 (1981), established that federal law preempts state attempts to divide military retired pay as community property. However, Congress subsequently passed the Uniformed Services Former Spouses' Protection Act (USFSPA) to allow state courts to treat military retirement pay as divisible marital property.

VII. Enforcement and Military Channels

A. Administrative Enforcement Through Military Channels

Military regulations provide powerful enforcement mechanisms for family support obligations that operate independently of civilian court systems. Each branch of the military has specific regulations requiring service members to provide adequate support for family members, and failure to comply can result in serious consequences for military careers.

Army Regulation 608-99 establishes comprehensive family support requirements, including specific dollar amounts based on rank and family size. The regulation applies to all soldiers regardless of whether civilian court orders exist, creating a minimum support floor that cannot be waived.

Navy and Marine Corps Instruction 1754.3 provides similar requirements for naval personnel, with specific provisions for support during sea duty and deployment. The instruction includes procedures for requesting support determinations and appeal processes.

Air Force Instruction 36-2906 addresses family support obligations for airmen, including special provisions for dual-military couples and geographic separation situations.

Failure to comply with military support regulations can result in:

- Administrative counseling and reprimands
- Reduction in rank or forfeiture of pay

- Denial of reenlistment or promotion
- Separation from military service
- Court-martial proceedings in extreme cases

B. Integration with Civilian Enforcement

Military administrative enforcement works in conjunction with civilian court enforcement rather than replacing it. Service members subject to court-ordered support remain obligated to comply with civilian court orders, and military regulations typically require compliance with such orders as well.

The case of Rose v. Rose, 481 U.S. 619 (1987), established that federal law does not preempt state authority to enforce support obligations against military personnel. The Supreme Court held that military pay is subject to state garnishment procedures for support obligations, rejecting arguments that military pay immunity extends to family support cases.

Defense Finance and Accounting Service (DFAS) procedures provide standardized mechanisms for support enforcement across all military branches. DFAS maintains detailed procedures for processing support orders, including requirements for:

- Proper service of process on military personnel
- Verification of support order validity
- Calculation of maximum garnishment amounts
- Coordination with military pay systems

Maximum Garnishment Limits under the Consumer Credit Protection Act, 15 U.S.C. § 1673, apply to military pay garnishment. For support obligations, up to 60% of disposable income may be garnished, or 65% if the service member is not supporting another spouse or child.

C. Overseas Enforcement Issues

Military families stationed overseas face unique enforcement challenges that require specialized procedures and international cooperation. The Hague Convention on International Child Abduction and various bilateral agreements provide frameworks for enforcement across national borders.

Status of Forces Agreements (SOFAs) between the United States and host countries typically address jurisdiction over family law matters involving military personnel. These agreements generally provide that U.S. courts retain jurisdiction over family support matters, even when service members are stationed overseas.

Overseas Garnishment Procedures require coordination between DFAS, military commands, and foreign banking systems. Support payments to ex-spouses overseas may require additional documentation and currency conversion procedures.

In Tahan v. Hodgson, 662 F.2d 862 (D.C. Cir. 1981), the D.C. Circuit held that military personnel stationed overseas remain subject to U.S. court jurisdiction for support purposes, and that overseas assignment does not provide a basis for modifying support obligations.

VIII. Pension Division in Divorce

A. The Uniformed Services Former Spouses' Protection Act (USFSPA)

The USFSPA, codified at 10 U.S.C. § 1408, represents Congress's comprehensive response to the Supreme Court's decision in McCarty v. McCarty, which held that federal law preempted state court division of military retirement pay. The USFSPA restored state court authority to treat military retirement pay as marital property subject to division in divorce proceedings.

The USFSPA provides that military retirement pay is subject to division by state courts as community property or marital property, depending on the state's property distribution system. However, the Act includes important limitations and procedures that distinguish military retirement division from other forms of property division.

Key USFSPA Provisions:

- State courts may treat military retirement pay as marital property
- Direct payment by DFAS to former spouses is available under certain conditions
- Maximum division is limited to 50% of disposable retired pay

- The "10/10 rule" governs direct payment eligibility

Disposable Retired Pay under the USFSPA means gross retired pay minus authorized deductions including:

- Amounts deducted for survivor benefit plan premiums
- Federal and state income taxes
- Amounts forfeited for certain military offenses
- Amounts deducted for military disability compensation

The definition of disposable retired pay significantly affects the amount available for division. In Mansell v. Mansell, 490 U.S. 581 (1989), the Supreme Court held that military disability compensation waived to receive retired pay is not divisible property, even if the waiver reduces the amount available to the former spouse.

B. The 10/10 Rule and Direct Payment

The "10/10 rule" under 10 U.S.C. § 1408(d)(2) provides that DFAS will make direct payments to former spouses only if the marriage lasted at least 10 years and overlapped with at least 10 years of military service creditable toward retirement. This rule creates a bright-line test for direct payment eligibility but does not affect the underlying right to receive a share of military retirement.

Marriages Meeting the 10/10 Rule:

- DFAS makes direct monthly payments to former spouses
- Payments begin when the service member retires
- Former spouses receive automatic cost-of-living adjustments
- Payments continue until the death of either the service member or former spouse

Marriages Not Meeting the 10/10 Rule:

- Courts may still divide military retirement pay
- Former spouses must collect payments directly from service members

- No automatic cost-of-living adjustments
- Enforcement depends on civilian court procedures

The 10/10 rule has created significant disparities in enforcement and collection of military retirement awards. In marriages that fall short of the 10/10 requirement by even a few months, former spouses may face substantial practical difficulties in collecting their awarded share of retirement benefits.

C. Valuation and Division Methods

Military retirement benefits present unique valuation challenges because the benefit is not vested until the service member completes 20 years of service, and the ultimate value depends on the service member's final rank and length of service.

Present Value Method: Some courts attempt to calculate the present value of future military retirement benefits and award the marital portion as a lump sum or through offset against other marital assets. This approach requires complex actuarial calculations and assumptions about future military service.

Deferred Distribution Method: Most courts use a formula approach that awards the former spouse a percentage of retirement benefits when paid. The typical formula is:

(Years of Marriage During Military Service ÷ Total Years of Military Service) × Court-Ordered Percentage × Monthly Retirement Benefit

This method avoids the need for present value calculations but creates ongoing payment obligations that may be difficult to enforce.

Hypothetical Awards: Some courts award former spouses a share of retirement benefits based on the service member's rank and years of service at the time of divorce, regardless of subsequent military service. This approach provides certainty but may not reflect the actual retirement benefits ultimately received.

The California Supreme Court in In re Marriage of Caswell, 33 Cal. 3d 260 (1982), established the "time rule" for dividing military retirement benefits, which calculates the marital portion based on the ratio of years of marriage during military service to total years of service at retirement. This approach has been widely adopted in other states.

D. Survivor Benefit Plan (SBP) Elections

The Survivor Benefit Plan provides ongoing benefits to surviving spouses after a military retiree's death. SBP elections in divorce cases require careful attention to timing requirements and irrevocable election deadlines.

Basic SBP Framework:

- Retirees may elect SBP coverage for former spouses
- Premiums are deducted from retired pay
- Benefits equal 55% of the retiree's benefit amount
- Coverage continues for the former spouse's lifetime (subject to remarriage provisions)

Divorce-Related SBP Elections:

- Must be made within one year of divorce finalization
- Requires court order or written agreement
- Election is irrevocable once made
- Failure to elect within the one-year period forever bars future elections

Deemed Elections: Under certain circumstances, DFAS will treat a divorce settlement as a deemed election for SBP coverage, even without explicit language. However, practitioners should never rely on deemed elections and should always include specific SBP provisions in settlement agreements.

The case of Surratt v. Surratt, 85 F.3d 1429 (9th Cir. 1996), illustrates the importance of timely SBP elections. The Ninth Circuit held that a retiree's failure to elect SBP coverage within one year of divorce could not be remedied by subsequent court orders, even when the failure was due to misunderstanding of the requirements.

Practical SBP Considerations:

- SBP premiums reduce the disposable retired pay available for division
- Former spouses may prefer to receive larger current payments rather than SBP protection

- SBP elections interact with other life insurance and estate planning
- Military retirees may face pressure from current spouses to avoid SBP elections for former spouses

IX. Special Considerations for Military Families

A. Security Clearance and Family Law Issues

Military service members holding security clearances face unique pressures in family law proceedings because personal financial and legal difficulties can affect clearance eligibility. The intersection of family law and security clearance requirements creates additional complexity for military families.

Financial Considerations: Unpaid support obligations, excessive debt, or financial irresponsibility can lead to security clearance revocation under National Security Adjudicative Guidelines. Service members may face career-ending consequences for failing to meet family support obligations.

Background Investigation Issues: Family law proceedings become part of the service member's permanent record and may be investigated during periodic reinvestigation processes. Contentious divorce or custody disputes can raise questions about the service member's judgment and reliability.

Command Notification: Some military branches require service members to notify their chain of command about significant legal proceedings, including family law matters. This requirement can create additional stress and career concerns for service members.

B. Post-Traumatic Stress and Military Family Law

The prevalence of combat-related PTSD and other military-specific mental health conditions requires special consideration in family law proceedings. Courts must balance the impact of military service-related trauma against child welfare and safety concerns.

Custody Considerations: PTSD diagnosis alone cannot be the basis for denying custody or visitation rights. Courts must conduct individualized assessments of how specific symptoms affect parenting capacity and child safety.

Support Obligations: Military disability compensation for PTSD may affect support calculations, particularly when service members waive retired pay to receive disability benefits. The Mansell decision limits the ability to reach disability compensation for support purposes.

Treatment and Compliance: Family law orders may include requirements for continued PTSD treatment or anger management counseling. Courts must ensure such requirements are reasonable and accessible to service members.

The case of Kovac v. Kovac, 2013 WL 1245677 (Cal. Ct. App. 2013), addressed the intersection of PTSD and child custody. The California Court of Appeal held that a father's PTSD diagnosis required individualized assessment of parenting capacity rather than automatic restriction of custody rights.

C. Dual-Military Couples

When both spouses are active-duty service members, additional complications arise in family law proceedings. Dual-military couples face unique challenges including:

Competing Deployment Schedules: When both parents are subject to deployment, custody arrangements must account for the possibility of simultaneous or overlapping deployments.

Career Prioritization: Dual-military couples may need to make decisions about whose career takes priority for assignment purposes, affecting custody and support arrangements.

Retirement Timing: Couples with different service entry dates may retire at different times, affecting retirement division and support calculations.

Geographic Separation: Military couples may be assigned to different duty locations, creating involuntary geographic separation that affects custody arrangements.

Military regulations generally require dual-military couples to maintain family care plans that address child custody during deployment or training. These plans often influence court decisions about custody arrangements and parenting time.

X. Interstate and International Complications

A. Interstate Enforcement Issues

Military families frequently move between states, creating enforcement challenges when family law orders are entered in one state but enforcement is needed in another. The Uniform Interstate Family Support Act (UIFSA) and the Parental Kidnapping Prevention Act (PKPA) provide frameworks for interstate enforcement, but military families face unique complications.

Continuing Exclusive Jurisdiction: Under UIFSA, the state that issues an initial support order retains continuing exclusive jurisdiction to modify that order as long as one party remains in the state. Military families may find themselves subject to the jurisdiction of a state where they no longer live and may never return.

Registration and Enforcement: UIFSA allows support orders to be registered in any state where the obligor has income or property. For military families, this typically means orders can be registered in any state where the service member is stationed or where DFAS maintains accounts.

Modification Procedures: When military families move to new states, they may seek to modify existing support orders in the new state. UIFSA provides procedures for transferring jurisdiction in certain circumstances, but the process can be complex and time-consuming.

B. International Enforcement Challenges

Military families stationed overseas face unique enforcement challenges that require coordination between U.S. courts, foreign governments, and international treaty obligations.

Hague Convention Applications: The Hague Convention on International Child Abduction applies to military families when children are wrongfully removed from or retained outside their country of habitual residence. Military overseas assignments can complicate determinations of habitual residence.

Service of Process Overseas: Serving legal documents on military personnel stationed overseas requires compliance with both military regulations and international treaties. The Hague Service Convention provides procedures for service in treaty countries.

Enforcement of U.S. Orders Abroad: U.S. family law orders may not be automatically enforceable in foreign countries. Status of Forces Agreements may provide some enforcement mechanisms, but practitioners must research the specific requirements of each host country.

The case of Mozes v. Mozes, 239 F.3d 1067 (9th Cir. 2001), addressed habitual residence determinations for military families. The Ninth Circuit held that children's habitual residence should be determined based on the totality of circumstances, including the parents' intentions and the children's degree of settled purpose in the location. For military families, this analysis must consider whether overseas assignments are temporary or represent a genuine change in family residence.

XI. Military Legal Assistance and Resources

A. Judge Advocate General (JAG) Services

Each branch of the military maintains Judge Advocate General offices that provide legal assistance to service members and their families. JAG attorneys offer valuable resources for military families involved in family law proceedings, though their role is limited to advice rather than representation.

Scope of JAG Assistance:

- Legal consultation on family law matters
- Document preparation assistance
- Explanation of military-specific legal protections
- Referrals to civilian attorneys
- Notary services and powers of attorney

Limitations of JAG Services:

- JAG attorneys cannot represent service members in civilian court proceedings
- Confidentiality protections may be limited compared to civilian attorney-client relationships
- JAG advice may prioritize military interests over individual legal

rights

- JAG attorneys may lack specialized expertise in complex family law matters

Service members should understand that JAG consultation, while valuable, does not replace the need for qualified civilian family law representation in contested proceedings. The case of United States v. Priest, 45 M.J. 338 (C.A.A.F. 1996), clarified that JAG attorneys owe professional obligations to both individual service members and the military as an institution, creating potential conflicts of interest.

B. Military OneSource and Support Services

Military OneSource provides comprehensive support services for military families, including resources specifically relevant to family law matters:

Financial Counseling: Military OneSource offers financial planning services that can assist families in understanding the economic implications of divorce, including analysis of military benefits and support obligations.

Legal Consultations: Limited legal consultation services are available through Military OneSource, including referrals to civilian attorneys with military family law experience.

Counseling Services: Marriage counseling, family counseling, and individual counseling services are available to help families address underlying issues that may affect family law proceedings.

Relocation Assistance: Military OneSource provides specialized assistance for military families facing relocation, including information about state-specific family law requirements.

C. Specialized Military Family Law Practitioners

The complexity of military family law has led to the development of specialized practitioners who focus specifically on military families. These attorneys typically possess expertise in:

- Federal military law and regulations
- SCRA and USFSPA procedures
- Military compensation structures

- Security clearance implications
- Interstate and international enforcement issues

The American Bar Association maintains a Military Committee within its Family Law Section that provides resources and continuing education for attorneys representing military families. State bar associations in states with significant military populations often maintain similar specialized committees.

Certification and Specialization: Some states offer board certification in military family law or recognize military family law as a subspecialty. California, for example, recognizes military family law specialization through its State Bar certification program.

XII. Emerging Issues in Military Family Law

A. Technology and Communication

Rapidly evolving communication technology continues to transform military family law practice, particularly regarding virtual visitation and long-distance parenting. Courts are increasingly required to address issues involving:

Social Media and Privacy: Military security concerns may limit service members' ability to share information about their location or activities on social media platforms, affecting communication with children and co-parents.

Cybersecurity Requirements: Military families may be subject to enhanced cybersecurity requirements that affect their use of communication platforms for virtual visitation.

Emerging Communication Platforms: New technologies such as virtual reality and augmented reality may provide enhanced opportunities for virtual visitation, but courts must address technical requirements and access issues.

B. Same-Sex Military Families

The repeal of "Don't Ask, Don't Tell" in 2011 and the Supreme Court's decision in Obergefell v. Hodges, 576 U.S. 644 (2015), have created new legal landscapes for same-sex military families. Issues specific to same-sex military couples include:

Recognition of Relationships: Some same-sex military couples may have been together for years before legal marriage became available, creating complex property and custody issues.

Adoption and Parentage: Same-sex military couples may face unique challenges in establishing legal parentage, particularly when children are born through assisted reproduction or adoption.

Benefits and Recognition: While federal benefits are now available to same-sex military spouses, some legacy issues remain regarding recognition of relationships formed before marriage equality.

C. National Guard and Reserve Issues

The increased deployment of National Guard and Reserve personnel has created new challenges for military family law. Part-time military service creates hybrid situations where service members are sometimes subject to military law and sometimes to civilian employment law.

Activation and Deployment: National Guard and Reserve personnel may face sudden activation for extended periods, triggering SCRA protections and deployment custody issues.

Dual Status: Reserve personnel may have both military and civilian employment, complicating support calculations and income determinations.

Benefits Eligibility: Reserve personnel may have limited access to military benefits compared to active-duty personnel, affecting support calculations and family welfare.

XIII. Practice Management Considerations

A. Client Communication and Security

Attorneys representing military families must be sensitive to security concerns that may affect client communication:

Operational Security (OPSEC): Military families are trained to protect information about troop movements, locations, and activities. Attorneys must respect these requirements while ensuring adequate client communication.

Classified Information: Service members with security clearances may be reluctant to discuss certain aspects of their military service. Attorneys should understand the boundaries of classified information and avoid requests that could compromise security.

International Communication: When service members are deployed overseas, communication may be subject to military monitoring or foreign government surveillance. Attorneys should use secure communication methods when possible.

B. Court Appearances and Scheduling

Military service creates unique scheduling challenges that require flexible court procedures:

Military Leave Policies: Service members may have limited ability to take leave for court appearances, particularly during training exercises or deployment preparation periods.

Chain of Command Approval: Some military assignments require command approval for leave requests, adding bureaucratic complexity to court scheduling.

Emergency Procedures: Courts should establish procedures for emergency hearings when military families face sudden deployment or reassignment.

Remote Appearance Technology: Courts increasingly accommodate military families through video conferencing and telephone appearances, particularly for routine hearings.

C. Documentation and Record-Keeping

Military family law cases require specialized documentation and record-keeping:

Military Records: Service records, fitness reports, and disciplinary actions may be relevant to custody and support determinations. Attorneys must understand military record-keeping systems and access procedures.

Security Clearance Files: Information about security clearance investigations may be relevant to family law proceedings but may be subject to confidentiality restrictions.

Deployment Documentation: Orders, deployment schedules, and training requirements should be documented and updated throughout the case.

International Documentation: Families stationed overseas may require additional documentation for international enforcement or child abduction prevention.

XIV. Ethical Considerations

A. Dual Representation Issues

Military couples may request joint representation in divorce proceedings, but attorneys must carefully consider potential conflicts of interest:

Command Influence: Military couples may face pressure from command structures to resolve family disputes quickly and quietly. Attorneys must ensure that clients make independent decisions free from command influence.

Career Implications: Spouses may have conflicting interests regarding the timing of divorce or custody proceedings based on their respective military careers and advancement opportunities.

Security Clearance Impact: Family law proceedings may affect one spouse's security clearance more than the other's, creating potential conflicts in representation strategy.

B. Confidentiality in Military Context

Attorney-client privilege in military family law cases may be complicated by military regulations and command structures:

Command Consultation: Clients may seek to involve their chain of command in family law decisions. Attorneys must ensure that confidentiality is maintained while allowing appropriate consultation.

JAG Coordination: Coordination with JAG attorneys may be beneficial but must not compromise attorney-client privilege or create conflicts of interest.

Security Investigations: Family law proceedings may trigger security investigations that could affect the attorney-client relationship. Attorneys should advise clients about potential consequences of disclosure.

C. Competence and Specialization

The complexity of military family law requires attorneys to maintain competence in specialized areas:

Continuing Education: Military family law is a rapidly evolving field that requires ongoing education about federal law changes, military regulation updates, and emerging technology issues.

Resource Development: Attorneys should maintain relationships with military legal assistance offices, financial counselors, and other professionals who serve military families.

Geographic Considerations: Military family law practice often involves multi-state issues that require knowledge of various state laws and interstate enforcement procedures.

XV. Future Trends and Developments

A. Legislative Developments

Congress continues to consider legislation affecting military families, including:

SCRA Modernization: Proposals to update SCRA protections for modern military service, including cyber warfare specialists and other non-traditional military roles.

Deployment Support: Enhanced support for military families during deployment, including expanded childcare assistance and family support services.

Retirement Reform: Ongoing military retirement system changes may affect future pension division calculations and procedures.

B. Technology Integration

Courts are increasingly integrating technology to serve military families:

Virtual Court Proceedings: Expanded use of video conferencing for hearings and trials, particularly when military families are stationed overseas or deployed.

Electronic Filing: Enhanced electronic filing systems that accommodate military families' frequent relocations and limited access to traditional court services.

AI and Automation: Potential use of artificial intelligence to assist with routine military family law calculations and document preparation.

C. International Coordination

Increasing international military cooperation creates new challenges for military family law:

Multinational Families: Military personnel may marry foreign nationals, creating complex citizenship and jurisdiction issues for children.

International Assignments: Extended assignments to international posts may affect custody jurisdiction and enforcement procedures.

Treaty Development: New international treaties may affect military family law enforcement and child abduction prevention.

XVI. Conclusion

Military family law represents one of the most complex and specialized areas of family law practice, requiring practitioners to navigate the intersection of federal military law, state family law, and international legal frameworks. The unique challenges faced by military families - including frequent relocations, extended deployments, and the demands of military service - require specialized legal protections and flexible court procedures.

The legal framework governing military families has evolved significantly over the past several decades, with Congress and state legislatures recognizing the need for special protections. The Servicemembers Civil Relief Act provides essential procedural protections, while state-specific deployment statutes ensure that military service does not disadvantage parents in custody proceedings. The Uniformed Services Former Spouses' Protection Act has created a comprehensive framework for dividing military retirement benefits, though practical challenges remain in enforcement and administration.

Technology continues to transform military family law practice, providing new opportunities for virtual visitation and long-distance parenting while creating new challenges for security and privacy. Courts must balance the benefits of technological communication with the realities of military operational security and international deployment requirements.

Practitioners representing military families must maintain specialized expertise in federal military law, state family law variations, and interstate enforcement procedures. The consequences of errors in military family law cases extend beyond typical domestic relations matters, potentially affecting military careers, security clearances, and family welfare across multiple jurisdictions.

The future of military family law will likely involve continued technological integration, enhanced international cooperation, and legislative refinements to address emerging challenges. As military service continues to evolve in response to changing global security requirements, family law protections must adapt to ensure that military families receive appropriate legal protections while maintaining the flexibility necessary for effective military service.

Military families deserve legal representation that understands both the sacrifices required by military service and the fundamental importance of family relationships. Effective advocacy in military family law requires not only technical legal expertise but also sensitivity to the unique pressures and challenges faced by those who serve our nation and their families. The legal profession must continue to develop specialized resources and expertise to ensure that military families receive the quality legal representation they deserve.

19

Property and Debt Division in Divorce

I. Untangling the Financial Knot

Dividing property and debt during divorce represents one of the most consequential - and often contentious - aspects of dissolving a marriage. The financial entanglements created during marriage must be carefully unraveled, requiring courts to balance competing interests of fairness, economic reality, and legal precedent. While both New York and California seek equitable outcomes, they differ fundamentally in their philosophical approaches to classifying, valuing, and distributing marital assets and liabilities.

This comprehensive examination of property division laws and procedures covers the essential frameworks governing both jurisdictions, including detailed analysis of how courts define marital versus separate property, the critical role of prenuptial agreements, specialized treatment of business assets and retirement accounts, debt allocation principles, and the complex interplay of tax consequences. Understanding these distinctions is crucial for practitioners navigating the intricate landscape of marital dissolution.

The stakes in property division extend far beyond the immediate dissolution proceeding. These determinations fundamentally shape the post-divorce financial landscape for both parties, affecting everything from housing security to retirement planning. Moreover, the principles established in seminal cases continue to evolve, particularly as courts grapple with modern financial instruments, digital assets, and changing concepts of marital contribution.

II. Equitable Distribution vs. Community Property: Philosophical Foundations

New York's Equitable Distribution System

New York follows the equitable distribution model codified in Domestic Relations Law § 236B, enacted in 1980 to replace the earlier title-based system. *See Majauskas v. Majauskas*, 61 N.Y.2d 481, 474 N.Y.S.2d 699, 463 N.E.2d 15 (1984). Under this framework, courts possess broad discretion to divide marital property based on fairness rather than mathematical equality.

The equitable distribution statute requires courts to consider numerous factors, creating a holistic approach that examines the totality of circumstances surrounding each marriage. This flexibility allows judges to craft solutions tailored to specific situations but also introduces uncertainty and potential inconsistency in outcomes. *Price v. Price*, 69 N.Y.2d 8, 511 N.Y.S.2d 219, 503 N.E.2d 684 (1986), established that equitable distribution must be based on the circumstances of the case and the respective parties.

California's Community Property Heritage

California's community property system traces its origins to Spanish civil law, formally codified in the Family Code. The fundamental principle, as articulated in *Marriage of Lucas*, 27 Cal.3d 808, 166 Cal.Rptr. 853, 614 P.2d 285 (1980), treats marriage as an economic partnership where each spouse owns an equal share of property acquired during the marriage through their joint efforts.

Family Code § 2550 mandates equal division of community property and debts, subject to limited exceptions. This bright-line rule provides predictability and reflects California's philosophical commitment to marriage as an equal economic partnership. However, the apparent simplicity of equal division masks complex issues of classification, valuation, and reimbursement that can significantly complicate proceedings.

The contrast between these systems reflects fundamentally different concepts of marriage. California views marriage as an economic unit where contributions are presumed equal regardless of their nature, while New York emphasizes individualized fairness that accounts for varying circumstances and contributions.

III. Classification of Property: Drawing the Lines

Separate Property Principles

Both jurisdictions recognize certain property as immune from division, though they apply different standards and presumptions. The burden of proving separate property character typically falls on the claiming spouse and must be established by clear and convincing evidence.

Pre-Marital Property

Property acquired before marriage retains its separate character in both states. *O'Brien v. O'Brien*, 66 N.Y.2d 576, 498 N.Y.S.2d 743, 489 N.E.2d 712 (1985), established that the key inquiry focuses on when acquisition occurred, not when title was obtained. In California, *Marriage of Rossin*, 172 Cal.App.4th 725, 91 Cal.Rptr.3d 385 (2009), clarified that separate property retains its character unless transmuted through express written agreement.

Gifts and Inheritances

Property received by gift or inheritance during marriage remains separate in both jurisdictions, provided it is not commingled with marital assets. *Inniss v. Inniss*, 8 A.D.3d 160, 778 N.Y.S.2d 78 (1st Dep't 2004), emphasized that the donative intent must be clear and directed to one spouse individually. California Family Code § 770 codifies this principle, though courts scrutinize circumstances to ensure genuine donative intent. *Marriage of Haines*, 33 Cal.App.4th 277, 39 Cal.Rptr.2d 673 (1995).

Personal Injury Awards

The treatment of personal injury settlements reveals important distinctions between jurisdictions. New York generally treats such awards as separate property, except for portions compensating lost earnings or medical expenses that would have been marital obligations. *Grunfeld v. Grunfeld*, 94 N.Y.2d 696, 709 N.Y.S.2d 486, 731 N.E.2d 142 (2000).

California takes a more nuanced approach under Family Code § 780, treating personal injury damages received during marriage as community property unless the injured spouse can demonstrate that the interests of justice require separate treatment. *Marriage of Saslow*, 40 Cal.3d 848, 221 Cal.Rptr. 546, 710 P.2d 346 (1985), established the framework for this analysis.

Marital and Community Property

Property acquired during marriage through the efforts of either spouse is generally subject to division, regardless of how title is held. This broad category encompasses the primary marital estate and requires careful analysis of acquisition timing and funding sources.

Real Estate

Marital real estate represents one of the most significant and complex categories of divisible property. Courts must determine not only current value but also consider factors such as exclusive occupancy, mortgage payments, and improvements made during separation.

Hartog v. Hartog, 85 N.Y.2d 36, 623 N.Y.S.2d 537, 647 N.E.2d 749 (1995), established New York's framework for analyzing real estate acquired with mixed separate and marital funds, requiring mathematical apportionment based on contribution percentages. California's approach under *Marriage of Moore*, 28 Cal.3d 366, 168 Cal.Rptr. 662, 618 P.2d 208 (1980), focuses on reimbursement rights for separate property contributions rather than apportionment of ownership interests.

Financial Accounts and Investments

Bank accounts, investment portfolios, and other financial instruments present tracing challenges when separate and marital funds are commingled. New York applies the "source of funds" rule established in *Price v. Price*, 69 N.Y.2d 8, 511 N.Y.S.2d 219, 503 N.E.2d 684 (1986), requiring detailed documentation to establish separate property claims.

California presumes community property character for assets acquired during marriage unless clear evidence establishes separate property funding. *Marriage of Branco*, 47 Cal.3d 1096, 255 Cal.Rptr. 559, 767 P.2d 1167 (1989), emphasized that commingling creates community property unless transmutation requirements are satisfied.

Business Interests and Professional Practices

Business ownership acquired or developed during marriage raises complex valuation and division issues. New York's seminal decision in *O'Brien v. O'Brien*, 66 N.Y.2d 576, 498 N.Y.S.2d 743, 489 N.E.2d 712 (1985), recognized professional licenses and degrees as marital property subject to division, though subsequent decisions have limited this holding.

California generally treats business interests acquired during marriage as community property, though personal goodwill may receive different treatment depending on its transferability. *Marriage of Foster*, 42 Cal.3d 577, 230 Cal.Rptr. 485, 724 P.2d 198 (1986), established the framework for distinguishing personal versus enterprise goodwill.

Commingling and Transmutation

New York's Commingling Doctrine

When separate property becomes inextricably mixed with marital property, New York courts may find that the separate character has been lost through commingling. The key inquiry focuses on whether the separate property can be traced and identified. *Arvantides v. Arvantides*, 64 N.Y.2d 1033, 489 N.Y.S.2d 288, 478 N.E.2d 199 (1985).

The doctrine of "active appreciation" allows separate property that increases in value through marital efforts to be subject to division. *Price v. Price*, supra, established that passive appreciation remains separate while active appreciation through spouse's efforts becomes marital property.

California's Transmutation Requirements

California Family Code § 852 requires express written agreement signed by the spouse whose interest is adversely affected to change the character of property from separate to community or vice versa. This 1985 amendment reversed prior law that allowed informal transmutation through conduct or oral agreements.

Estate of MacDonald, 51 Cal.3d 262, 272 Cal.Rptr. 153, 794 P.2d 911 (1990), strictly interpreted these requirements, rejecting attempts to find transmutation through conduct alone. However, *Marriage of Benson*, 36 Cal.4th 1096, 32 Cal.Rptr.3d 471, 116 P.3d 1152 (2005), recognized limited exceptions for interspousal transfers that satisfy deed of trust requirements.

IV. Valuation of Assets: Establishing Fair Market Value

Accurate asset valuation forms the foundation of equitable property division. Courts typically use fair market value as of the date of trial or settlement, though parties may agree to alternative valuation dates. The complexity of modern financial instruments and business interests often requires specialized expertise to establish reliable valuations.

Real Property Valuation

Real estate appraisal follows established methodologies comparing recent sales of similar properties, considering location, condition, and market trends. *Zelinger v. Zelinger*, 184 A.D.2d 1008, 585 N.Y.S.2d 493 (4th Dep't 1992), emphasized that fair market value assumes a willing buyer and seller in an arm's length transaction.

Unique properties or those in volatile markets may require multiple appraisals or specialized expertise. Courts may also consider factors such as exclusive occupancy by one spouse, which can affect both value and carrying costs.

Business Valuation Methodologies

Professional practices and closely-held businesses present unique valuation challenges requiring forensic accounting expertise. Three primary approaches are recognized:

Asset Approach: Based on fair market value of tangible and intangible assets minus liabilities. Most appropriate for asset-intensive businesses or those being liquidated.

Market Approach: Compares the business to similar entities that have been sold or are publicly traded. Requires sufficient comparable data and adjustments for size, marketability, and control factors.

Income Approach: Values the business based on its ability to generate future cash flows, typically using discounted cash flow or capitalization methods. Most appropriate for profitable service businesses.

Marriage of Duncan, 90 Cal.App.4th 617, 108 Cal.Rptr.2d 615 (2001), established California's framework for business valuation, requiring consideration of all three approaches where applicable data exists.

Retirement Account Valuation

Pension and retirement account valuation requires actuarial expertise to determine present value of future benefits. Defined contribution plans like 401(k)s are valued at their account balance, while defined benefit plans require complex calculations considering life expectancy, discount rates, and benefit formulas.

Majauskas v. Majauskas, 61 N.Y.2d 481, 474 N.Y.S.2d 699, 463 N.E.2d 15 (1984), established that pension benefits earned during marriage are marital property subject to division based on the time-based formula approach.

Digital Assets and Intellectual Property

Modern divorce proceedings increasingly involve digital assets including cryptocurrency, online business interests, and intellectual property rights. Valuation of these assets presents novel challenges requiring specialized expertise.

Cryptocurrency valuation must account for extreme volatility and the difficulty of accessing certain wallets or accounts. Intellectual property valuation depends on factors such as remaining patent life, licensing potential, and market demand for the underlying technology or creative work.

V. Division Principles: Equality vs. Equity

California's Equal Division Mandate

Family Code § 2550 requires equal division of community property absent written agreement to the contrary. This bright-line rule reflects California's partnership theory of marriage but allows limited judicial discretion in specific circumstances.

Exceptions to Equal Division:

- Educational debt burden (Family Code § 2641)
- Reimbursement claims under Family Code § 2640
- Fiduciary duty breaches (Family Code § 1101)
- Economic circumstances that would result in extreme hardship

Marriage of Bonds, 5 Cal.4th 815, 21 Cal.Rptr.2d 792, 856 P.2d 1020 (1993), established that courts cannot deviate from equal division based solely on economic need or earning capacity differences.

New York's Equitable Distribution Factors

Domestic Relations Law § 236B(5)(d) provides thirteen statutory factors courts must consider in determining equitable distribution:

1. Income and property of each party at marriage and trial
2. Duration of marriage and age/health of parties
3. Need of custodial parent to occupy marital residence
4. Loss of inheritance or pension rights upon dissolution
5. Maintenance award to either party
6. Equitable claim to, contribution to, or dissipation of marital property
7. Liquid or non-liquid character of marital property
8. Probable future financial circumstances of each party
9. Impossibility or difficulty of evaluating assets or interests
10. Tax consequences to each party
11. Wasteful dissipation of assets by either spouse
12. Transfer or encumbrance of marital property without consent

13. Any other factor the court expressly finds to be just and proper

Hartog v. Hartog, 85 N.Y.2d 36, 623 N.Y.S.2d 537, 647 N.E.2d 749 (1995), emphasized that courts must consider all relevant factors but need not give equal weight to each.

VI. Debt Allocation: Shared Burdens and Individual Responsibility

Marital debts generally follow the same principles governing asset division, though both jurisdictions recognize exceptions for debts incurred for non-marital purposes or through misconduct.

Community Debt in California

Family Code § 2550 treats community debts equally with community assets, requiring shared responsibility for obligations incurred during marriage for community purposes. However, Family Code § 2625 protects spouses from liability for debts incurred by their partner without their knowledge that did not benefit the community.

Marriage of Eastis, 47 Cal.App.4th 459, 54 Cal.Rptr.2d 531 (1996), established that gambling debts incurred without the other spouse's knowledge are not community obligations. Similarly, Family Code § 910 protects spouses from tort liability arising from their partner's actions.

New York's Equitable Debt Distribution

New York courts apply the same equitable principles to debt allocation as asset distribution, considering factors such as who incurred the debt, for what purpose, and who benefited from the expenditure. *Parra v. Parra*, 135 A.D.2d 1044, 523 N.Y.S.2d 422 (4th Dep't 1987).

Credit card debt incurred during marriage is presumptively marital regardless of whose name appears on the account, though courts may consider the purpose of expenditures and whether both spouses benefited. Educational loans present particular complexity, with courts considering factors such as when the education was obtained, whether it enhanced earning capacity, and the duration of marriage after completion.

Waste and Dissipation Claims

Both jurisdictions allow courts to account for wasteful spending or dissipation of marital assets. New York Domestic Relations Law § 236B(5)(d)(11) specifically includes "wasteful dissipation of assets" as a factor in equitable distribution.

California Family Code § 1101 imposes fiduciary duties between spouses and allows recovery for breaches including deliberate misappropriation or waste of community assets. *Marriage of Rossi*, 90 Cal.App.4th 34, 108 Cal.Rptr.2d 270 (2001), established the framework for proving waste claims.

VII. Retirement Accounts and Pensions: Deferred Compensation Rights

Retirement benefits earned during marriage represent significant marital assets requiring specialized treatment due to ERISA preemption and plan-specific distribution rules.

ERISA-Qualified Plans

The Employee Retirement Income Security Act (ERISA) governs most employer-sponsored retirement plans and generally preempts state divorce laws. However, Qualified Domestic Relations Orders (QDROs) provide an exception allowing state courts to assign retirement benefits to former spouses.

Boggs v. Boggs, 520 U.S. 833, 117 S.Ct. 1754, 138 L.Ed.2d 45 (1997), established that ERISA preempts state community property laws regarding pension benefits, making QDROs essential for division of qualified plan benefits.

QDRO Requirements and Limitations

A valid QDRO must specify:

- Names and addresses of participant and alternate payee
- Amount or percentage of benefits assigned
- Number of payments or time period covered
- Each plan to which the order applies

The QDRO cannot require plan features not otherwise provided, such as increased benefits or different payment options. *Marriage of Campa*, 89 Cal.App.4th 137, 107 Cal.Rptr.2d 263 (2001).

Military and Government Pensions

Military retirement benefits are governed by the Uniformed Services Former Spouses' Protection Act (USFSPA), which allows state courts to treat military retired pay as property subject to division. The ten-year rule requires ten years of marriage overlapping with ten years of military service for direct payment from the military finance center.

Federal civilian retirement benefits under FERS and CSRS require court orders that comply with specific statutory requirements. State and local government pensions are subject to individual plan rules and state laws governing public employee benefits.

Time-Based Formula Approach

Courts typically use time-based formulas to determine the marital portion of retirement benefits:

Marital Portion = (Years of Marriage During Employment) / (Total Years of Employment) × Total Benefit

Majauskas v. Majauskas, 61 N.Y.2d 481, 474 N.Y.S.2d 699, 463 N.E.2d 15 (1984), established this approach in New York, while California applies similar principles under *Marriage of Brown*, 15 Cal.3d 838, 126 Cal.Rptr. 633, 544 P.2d 561 (1976).

VIII. Business Ownership and Professional Practices

Professional practices and business interests present complex valuation and division challenges requiring specialized forensic accounting and appraisal expertise.

Valuation Approaches and Methodologies

Business valuation requires consideration of multiple approaches to establish reliable fair market value estimates. Courts typically require expert testimony from certified business appraisers or forensic accountants familiar with the specific industry and valuation standards.

Asset-Based Approach: Most appropriate for asset-intensive businesses or those being liquidated. Values tangible assets at fair market value and attempts to quantify intangible assets such as customer lists, patents, or trade secrets.

Market Approach: Compares the subject business to similar entities that have been sold or are publicly traded. Requires adjustments for differences in size, profitability, growth prospects, and marketability. Limited by availability of comparable transaction data.

Income Approach: Values businesses based on their ability to generate future economic benefits. Discounted cash flow methods require projections of future earnings, appropriate discount rates reflecting business risk, and terminal value assumptions.

Goodwill Classification and Treatment

Goodwill represents perhaps the most contentious aspect of business valuation in divorce proceedings. Courts distinguish between personal goodwill attributable to individual reputation and skills versus enterprise goodwill that exists independently and would transfer with business ownership.

New York Approach: *Dugan v. Dugan*, 92 A.D.2d 296, 460 N.Y.S.2d 885 (2d Dep't 1983), established that personal goodwill not transferable to others is not marital property subject to division. However, enterprise goodwill that would transfer with business ownership is marital property.

California Approach: *Marriage of Foster*, 42 Cal.3d 577, 230 Cal.Rptr. 485, 724 P.2d 198 (1986), created a presumption that professional practice goodwill is community property unless proven to be personal and non-transferable. *Marriage of Lopez*, 38 Cal.App.4th 93, 44 Cal.Rptr.2d 649 (1995), further refined this analysis.

Professional License and Degree Valuation

New York's landmark decision in *O'Brien v. O'Brien*, 66 N.Y.2d 576, 498 N.Y.S.2d 743, 489 N.E.2d 712 (1985), recognized medical licenses as marital property subject to equitable distribution. The court valued the license based on enhanced earning capacity attributable to the medical degree.

However, subsequent decisions have limited O'Brien's scope. *McSparron v. McSparron*, 87 N.Y.2d 275, 639 N.Y.S.2d 265, 662 N.E.2d 745 (1995), distinguished between licenses that create enhanced earning capacity versus those that merely permit practice of existing skills.

California has rejected the O'Brien approach, treating professional education as investment in human capital that cannot be divided as property. *Marriage of Sullivan*, 37 Cal.3d 762, 209 Cal.Rptr. 354, 691 P.2d 1020 (1984). However, reimbursement for community contributions to education expenses may be available under Family Code § 2641.

IX. Reimbursement and Credits: Balancing Contributions and Benefits

Both jurisdictions recognize that rigid application of classification and division rules may produce inequitable results requiring adjustment through reimbursement or credit mechanisms.

California's Reimbursement Scheme

Family Code § 2640 Reimbursements: Provides for reimbursement of separate property contributions to community property acquisitions, such as down payments on homes purchased during marriage. The claiming spouse must trace the separate property contribution and establish the current value of the asset.

Marriage of Walrath, 17 Cal.4th 907, 72 Cal.Rptr.2d 856, 952 P.2d 624 (1998), held that Family Code § 2640 reimbursement is mandatory, not discretionary, when requirements are satisfied. However, reimbursement is limited to the lesser of the contribution amount or the current equity in the property.

Epstein Credits: Named after *Marriage of Epstein*, 24 Cal.3d 76, 154 Cal.Rptr. 413, 592 P.2d 1165 (1979), these credits reimburse one spouse for post-separation payments of community debts that benefit the other spouse. Credits typically arise when one spouse continues paying the mortgage on the family home while the other spouse has exclusive occupancy.

Watts Charges: *Marriage of Watts*, 171 Cal.App.3d 366, 217 Cal.Rptr. 301 (1985), established that exclusive occupancy of community property may require payment to the non-occupying spouse for their share of fair rental value. Courts balance Watts charges against Epstein credits to achieve equitable results.

New York's Credit and Adjustment System

New York courts possess broad discretion to award credits or adjustments to achieve equitable distribution. Common situations include:

Post-Separation Contributions: Credits for mortgage payments, maintenance, improvements, or other expenditures that benefit both parties' interests in marital property. *Grunfeld v. Grunfeld*, 94 N.Y.2d 696, 709 N.Y.S.2d 486, 731 N.E.2d 142 (2000).

Exclusive Occupancy: Courts may award occupancy value credits or adjust property distribution to account for one spouse's exclusive use of marital assets during separation. *Kerins v. Kerins*, 64 A.D.3d 681, 883 N.Y.S.2d 284 (2d Dep't 2009).

Separate Property Contributions: Similar to California's § 2640 reimbursement, New York provides credits for separate property contributions to marital assets, typically calculated based on contribution percentage and current value.

X. The Role of Marital Agreements: Private Ordering

Prenuptial and postnuptial agreements allow couples to privately order their financial relationships and supersede default legal rules governing property division.

Validity Requirements

Both jurisdictions require marital agreements to satisfy basic contract formation requirements plus additional protections specific to the spousal relationship.

Universal Requirements:

- Written agreement signed by both parties
- Voluntary execution without duress or coercion
- Fair and reasonable disclosure of assets and obligations
- Absence of unconscionability at execution or enforcement

New York's Scrutiny of Prenuptial Agreements

New York courts apply heightened scrutiny to prenuptial agreements, requiring "fair and reasonable disclosure" of each party's financial circumstances. *Christian v. Christian*, 42 N.Y.2d 63, 396 N.Y.S.2d 817, 365 N.E.2d 849 (1977).

The seminal case *Matisoff v. Dobi*, 90 N.Y.2d 127, 659 N.Y.S.2d 209, 681 N.E.2d 594 (1997), established the modern framework requiring courts to examine both procedural fairness at execution and substantive fairness at enforcement. Agreements that completely eliminate spousal support may be unenforceable if they leave a spouse indigent.

Bloomfield v. Bloomfield, 97 N.Y.2d 188, 738 N.Y.S.2d 650, 764 N.E.2d 950 (2001), clarified that prenuptial agreements waiving maintenance are not per se unenforceable but must be evaluated based on the circumstances at enforcement.

California's Statutory Framework

California Family Code §§ 1610-1617 govern prenuptial agreements, incorporating the Uniform Premarital Agreement Act with modifications. Key requirements include:

Seven-Day Rule: Family Code § 1615 requires a seven-day waiting period between presentation of the agreement and execution if a party is not represented by independent counsel.

Spousal Support Limitations: Family Code § 1612(c) allows waiver of spousal support unless unconscionable at enforcement, creating a different standard than property waivers.

Disclosure Requirements: Family Code § 1615 requires fair, reasonable, and full disclosure or actual knowledge of assets and obligations, or voluntary waiver of disclosure rights.

Marriage of Bonds, 5 Cal.4th 815, 21 Cal.Rptr.2d 792, 856 P.2d 1020 (1993), established that prenuptial agreements receive the same scrutiny as other contracts but recognized the confidential relationship between spouses requires careful examination of circumstances surrounding execution.

Postnuptial Agreements

Agreements executed during marriage face heightened scrutiny due to the confidential relationship between spouses and potential for overreaching.

New York requires postnuptial agreements to satisfy the same standards as prenuptial agreements but applies even closer scrutiny to circumstances surrounding execution. *Galetta v. Galetta*, 21 N.Y.3d 186, 969 N.Y.S.2d 826, 992 N.E.2d 1263 (2013).

California treats postnuptial agreements as interspousal transactions subject to Family Code § 721's fiduciary duty requirements, requiring the advantaged spouse to prove the agreement's fairness. *Marriage of Burkle*, 139 Cal.App.4th 712, 43 Cal.Rptr.3d 65 (2006).

XI. Tax Considerations: Federal and State Implications

Property transfers incident to divorce carry significant tax consequences that must be carefully planned to avoid unexpected liabilities and optimize after-tax wealth distribution.

Federal Tax Treatment

IRC § 1041 Non-Recognition: Property transfers between spouses incident to divorce are generally non-taxable events. The transferee spouse receives the transferor's basis in the property, potentially creating future tax liability upon sale.

United States v. Davis, 370 U.S. 65, 82 S.Ct. 1190, 8 L.Ed.2d 335 (1962), originally required recognition of gain on property transfers in divorce, but IRC § 1041 reversed this result for transfers incident to divorce.

Retirement Account Transfers: Transfers pursuant to QDROs avoid early withdrawal penalties and taxation at transfer, but recipients remain liable for taxes when distributions are received.

Alimony Tax Treatment: The Tax Cuts and Jobs Act eliminated the alimony deduction for divorce agreements executed after December 31, 2018, fundamentally changing the economics of spousal support arrangements.

State Tax Considerations

State tax treatment of divorce-related transfers varies significantly. Community property states generally follow federal non-recognition principles, while separate property states may impose additional requirements or limitations.

California generally conforms to federal tax treatment but may impose additional obligations for certain transfers or complex arrangements. New York similarly follows federal principles but requires careful attention to state-specific provisions affecting property transfers and support obligations.

Capital Gains Planning

Strategic allocation of assets with different tax bases can significantly impact after-tax wealth distribution. Low-basis assets carry built-in tax liabilities that should be considered in valuation and distribution decisions.

Principal residence sales may qualify for the § 121 exclusion even after divorce if ownership and use requirements are satisfied. Careful planning can preserve these tax benefits and maximize available exclusions.

XII. Enforcement and Modification

Property division orders are generally final and non-modifiable, unlike support obligations that may be changed based on changed circumstances. However, both jurisdictions provide limited grounds for relief from property division judgments.

Fraud and Concealment

Discovery of previously undisclosed assets or fraudulent transfers may justify relief from final judgments under Rules 60(b) in federal court or analogous state court rules.

Marriage of Varner, 55 Cal.App.4th 128, 63 Cal.Rptr.2d 894 (1997), established California's framework for setting aside property division judgments based on asset concealment, requiring proof of material non-disclosure that would have affected the division.

New York applies similar principles under CPLR 5015, allowing relief for newly discovered evidence or fraud, but requires prompt action after discovery and proof that the concealed information would have materially affected the distribution.

Enforcement Mechanisms

Courts possess broad powers to enforce property division orders through contempt proceedings, asset seizure, wage garnishment, and other collection mechanisms. Qualified Domestic Relations Orders provide specific enforcement procedures for retirement benefit assignments.

Interstate enforcement of property division orders may require registration under the Uniform Enforcement of Foreign Judgments Act or full faith and credit principles, depending on the nature of relief sought and location of assets.

XIII. Emerging Issues and Future Considerations

Modern divorce proceedings increasingly involve novel asset types and valuation challenges that existing legal frameworks struggle to address comprehensively.

Cryptocurrency and Digital Assets

Digital currencies and online assets present unique challenges for discovery, valuation, and division. Volatility, anonymity features, and technological complexity require specialized expertise and careful consideration of timing issues.

Courts are developing approaches to address cryptocurrency in divorce proceedings, but established precedent remains limited. Issues include determining valuation dates, accessing private keys, and ensuring complete disclosure of digital holdings.

Stock Options and Restricted Securities

Employee stock options and restricted stock awards require careful analysis of vesting schedules, exercise prices, and market conditions. Courts must determine when such benefits are earned and how to value unvested awards subject to forfeiture.

Marriage of Hug, 154 Cal.App.4th 576, 64 Cal.Rptr.3d 696 (2007), established California's approach to stock option valuation, emphasizing the need to consider all relevant factors including vesting requirements and market volatility.

Social Media and Online Business Assets

Digital business assets including social media accounts, online marketplaces, and intellectual property in digital formats raise novel questions about ownership, valuation, and transferability.

The economic value of social media influence, online customer bases, and digital brand recognition may constitute significant marital assets requiring expert valuation and creative division approaches.

XIV. Conclusion

Property and debt division represents the financial foundation of post-divorce life for both parties. Whether applying California's community property system with its presumption of equal division or New York's equitable distribution approach emphasizing fairness based on individual circumstances, courts must navigate complex legal frameworks while addressing the practical realities of untangling interconnected financial lives.

The evolution of these legal principles continues as courts confront new asset types, changing family structures, and economic realities that test traditional approaches to marital property division. Success in property division proceedings requires not only mastery of established legal principles but also strategic thinking about valuation, tax consequences, and enforcement considerations that will affect clients long after the divorce decree becomes final.

Practitioners must remain vigilant to developing case law, changing tax regulations, and emerging asset types that will shape the future of matrimonial property law. The intersection of technology, finance, and family law creates opportunities for creative problem-solving while demanding sophisticated understanding of both legal principles and practical consequences.

The ultimate goal remains achieving fair and workable solutions that enable both parties to rebuild their financial lives while honoring the economic realities of their marriage. As the legal landscape continues to evolve, practitioners must balance adherence to established principles with creative approaches to novel challenges, always keeping client welfare and long-term financial stability as the guiding objectives.

XV. Practice Points and Strategic Considerations

Discovery and Asset Investigation

Comprehensive discovery forms the foundation of successful property division proceedings. Practitioners must employ systematic approaches to identify, value, and trace all marital assets and debts.

Essential Discovery Tools:

- Sworn statements of net worth or financial affidavits
- Production of tax returns, bank statements, and financial records
- Interrogatories targeting specific asset categories and transactions
- Depositions of parties and third-party witnesses
- Subpoenas to financial institutions, employers, and business entities

Red Flags Requiring Enhanced Investigation:

- Unusual financial transactions near separation
- Cash businesses or opportunities for income manipulation
- Complex business structures or offshore entities
- Lifestyle inconsistent with reported income
- Recent transfers to family members or business associates

Marriage of Sorge, 123 Cal.App.4th 516, 20 Cal.Rptr.3d 154 (2004), established that courts may draw negative inferences from failure to comply with discovery obligations, particularly regarding asset disclosure.

Valuation Date Considerations

Strategic selection of valuation dates can significantly impact property division outcomes, particularly for volatile assets or businesses experiencing significant change.

Standard Valuation Dates:

- Date of separation
- Date of trial
- Date of settlement agreement
- Date of judgment entry

Market conditions, business performance, and asset-specific factors should inform valuation date selection. Courts generally prefer date of trial for accuracy but may accept alternative dates by agreement or for practical reasons.

Marriage of Sherman, 162 Cal.App.4th 1433, 76 Cal.Rptr.3d 477 (2008), emphasized that valuation date selection must consider fairness to both parties and practical considerations such as expert availability and market conditions.

Settlement Strategies

Most property division cases resolve through negotiation rather than trial, making settlement strategy crucial to achieving optimal outcomes for clients.

Key Settlement Considerations:

- Tax consequences of different asset allocations
- Liquidity needs and cash flow requirements
- Risk tolerance for volatile or illiquid assets
- Emotional attachment to specific property

- Enforcement and collection considerations

Creative Settlement Structures:

- Deferred distribution arrangements
- Contingent payment terms based on future events
- Retained interests in business appreciation
- Life insurance securing future obligations
- Structured settlements for large distributions

Expert Witness Selection and Management

Complex property division cases require expert testimony from appraisers, forensic accountants, actuaries, and other specialists. Effective expert witness management can determine case outcomes.

Expert Selection Criteria:

- Relevant industry experience and credentials
- Litigation experience and communication skills
- Availability for discovery and trial schedules
- Fee structure and budget considerations
- Track record with opposing counsel and judges

Expert Witness Preparation:

- Comprehensive case overview and legal theories
- Review of all relevant documents and discovery
- Discussion of anticipated cross-examination topics
- Coordination with other experts to avoid conflicts
- Trial presentation rehearsal and demonstrative aids

International and Interstate Complications

Modern families often have assets spanning multiple jurisdictions, creating complex choice of law and enforcement issues.

Jurisdictional Considerations:

- Long-arm jurisdiction over non-resident spouses
- Choice of law for property characterization
- Recognition and enforcement of foreign judgments
- International treaty obligations and comity principles

Practical Challenges:

- Language barriers and document translation
- Varying accounting standards and valuation methods
- Currency fluctuation and conversion issues
- Political and economic instability affecting assets

The Uniform Interstate Family Support Act (UIFSA) provides frameworks for interstate enforcement, while the Hague Convention and bilateral treaties govern international recognition of divorce judgments.

XVI. Ethical Considerations in Property Division

Matrimonial attorneys face unique ethical challenges arising from the emotional and financial stress of divorce proceedings, requiring careful attention to professional responsibility rules.

Conflicts of Interest

Dual Representation Prohibitions: Model Rule 1.7 generally prohibits representing both spouses in contested divorce proceedings due to directly adverse interests in property division.

Business Interest Conflicts: Attorneys must carefully evaluate potential conflicts when spouses own businesses where the attorney has prior relationships or financial interests.

Family Member Conflicts: Representation may be problematic when family members have interests in marital assets or business entities subject to division.

Competence and Diligence Requirements

Property division proceedings require specialized knowledge of family law, tax consequences, valuation principles, and procedural requirements. Model Rule 1.1 requires attorneys to provide competent representation or associate with knowledgeable counsel.

Continuing Education Obligations: Rapidly evolving areas such as cryptocurrency, digital assets, and complex financial instruments require ongoing education to maintain competence.

Expert Consultation: Attorneys must recognize the limits of their expertise and consult appropriate specialists for valuation, tax, and other technical issues.

Client Confidentiality in Joint Assets

Shared financial information creates potential confidentiality issues when representing one spouse regarding jointly-owned assets or businesses.

Work Product Protection: Attorney-client privilege may not protect documents or information relating to joint assets or business interests where both spouses have ownership rights.

Third-Party Discovery: Subpoenas to attorneys for business records or communications may implicate both spouses' interests, requiring careful privilege analysis.

XVII. Technological Developments and Practice Evolution

Technology continues to transform matrimonial practice, creating new opportunities for efficiency while raising novel ethical and practical challenges.

Electronic Discovery and Digital Forensics

Modern discovery increasingly involves electronic evidence requiring specialized collection and analysis techniques.

Electronic Evidence Sources:

- Email and text message communications
- Social media accounts and online activity
- Digital financial records and cryptocurrency transactions
- GPS and location data from mobile devices
- Cloud storage and remote access systems

Technical Challenges:

- Authentication of electronic evidence
- Preservation of metadata and system information
- Recovery of deleted or encrypted data
- Privacy rights and third-party access issues
- Cross-border data transfer restrictions

Artificial Intelligence and Automation

AI-powered tools increasingly assist with document review, case analysis, and settlement negotiations, but attorneys must understand their limitations and ethical implications.

Current Applications:

- Document review and privilege screening
- Contract analysis and due diligence
- Settlement range calculations and negotiation support
- Legal research and case law analysis
- Client intake and initial case assessment

Ethical Considerations:

- Duty of competence in AI tool selection and use

- Confidentiality protection in cloud-based systems
- Bias and accuracy concerns in automated decisions
- Transparency obligations regarding AI assistance
- Malpractice liability for AI-generated errors

Virtual Court Proceedings

The COVID-19 pandemic accelerated adoption of virtual court proceedings, creating new opportunities and challenges for matrimonial practice.

Benefits of Virtual Proceedings:

- Reduced travel time and costs
- Improved access for remote or disabled parties
- Enhanced scheduling flexibility
- Better integration of demonstrative evidence
- Reduced intimidation for domestic violence victims

Challenges and Limitations:

- Technology barriers for some participants
- Difficulty reading non-verbal cues and courtroom dynamics
- Evidence authentication and security concerns
- Attorney-client privilege in shared spaces
- Reduced settlement conference effectiveness

XVIII. Future Directions and Legislative Trends

Matrimonial law continues evolving in response to changing family structures, economic conditions, and social attitudes about marriage and property rights.

Proposed Uniform Laws

Uniform Premarital and Marital Agreements Act: Modernizes and harmonizes state laws governing prenuptial and postnuptial agreements, addressing issues such as electronic signatures and international enforcement.

Uniform Collaborative Law Act: Provides framework for collaborative divorce processes emphasizing cooperative problem-solving rather than adversarial litigation.

Emerging Legislative Issues

Cryptocurrency Regulation: States increasingly address cryptocurrency in divorce proceedings through specific disclosure requirements and division procedures.

Domestic Partnership Property Rights: Expansion of marriage equality creates new questions about property rights for domestic partnerships and civil unions.

Military Family Protection: Enhanced protections for military families address unique challenges of deployment, frequent moves, and specialized benefit systems.

Professional Development Trends

Interdisciplinary Collaboration: Increasing cooperation between attorneys, financial planners, mental health professionals, and other specialists in team-based approaches to divorce.

Alternative Dispute Resolution: Growing emphasis on mediation, collaborative law, and other ADR methods to reduce costs and emotional trauma of traditional litigation.

Specialization Requirements: States increasingly require specialized training or certification for attorneys handling matrimonial matters, recognizing the complexity and high stakes of family law practice.

XIX. Conclusion and Best Practices

Property division in divorce proceedings requires mastery of complex legal principles, sophisticated understanding of financial and valuation concepts, and strategic thinking about both immediate and long-term consequences for clients. Success depends on thorough preparation, creative problem-solving, and commitment to achieving fair and workable solutions.

Essential Best Practices

Comprehensive Case Assessment: Every property division case requires systematic analysis of all assets, debts, and potential claims, regardless of apparent simplicity or client assumptions about outcomes.

Early Expert Engagement: Complex valuation issues benefit from early expert consultation to guide discovery strategy and identify key issues requiring specialized analysis.

Tax Planning Integration: Property division decisions carry significant tax consequences that must be evaluated and planned to optimize after-tax outcomes for clients.

Settlement-Oriented Approach: Most cases benefit from early exploration of settlement possibilities, with litigation preparation serving to strengthen negotiating position rather than as the preferred resolution method.

Client Education and Communication: Clients need clear explanation of legal principles, realistic assessment of likely outcomes, and ongoing communication about case developments and strategic decisions.

Long-Term Perspective

Property division creates the financial foundation for post-divorce life, making long-term planning essential to successful outcomes. Attorneys must consider not only immediate division issues but also future enforceability, tax consequences, and changing circumstances that may affect their clients.

The intersection of family law with tax, corporate, real estate, and other practice areas demands broad knowledge and willingness to collaborate with specialists in related fields. As financial products and family structures continue evolving, practitioners must remain committed to ongoing education and adaptation of traditional approaches to new challenges.

Ultimately, property division serves the broader goal of enabling both parties to move forward with their lives on sound financial footing while fairly recognizing their contributions to and investments in the marital partnership. This human dimension of matrimonial practice requires balancing legal technical requirements with practical wisdom about family dynamics, economic realities, and the emotional challenges of ending a marriage.

The principles and procedures outlined in this chapter provide the framework for addressing property division issues, but their successful application depends on careful attention to the unique circumstances of each case and creative adaptation to emerging challenges in our evolving legal and economic landscape.

20

Divorce Procedures

Contested and Uncontested

I. The Path to Legal Dissolution

Divorce represents both the emotional dissolution of a marital relationship and a complex legal process governed by specific statutory frameworks, procedural rules, and judicial oversight. The legal system recognizes that while marriages may end in various ways - through mutual agreement or bitter dispute - all divorces must comply with established state statutes and court rules to ensure fairness, protect children's interests, and provide finality to the parties involved.

The distinction between contested and uncontested divorces is fundamental to understanding the procedural landscape. An uncontested divorce occurs when both spouses agree on all material issues, including property division, child custody and support, spousal maintenance, and debt allocation. In contrast, a contested divorce arises when the parties cannot reach agreement on one or more significant issues, necessitating judicial intervention and potentially culminating in a trial.

This chapter provides a comprehensive examination of divorce procedures in New York and California, two states that represent different approaches to family law. We will explore the step-by-step processes for both contested and uncontested divorces, analyze the relevant forms and filing requirements, and discuss various resolution mechanisms including settlement negotiations, mediation, collaborative divorce, and trial proceedings.

The procedural differences between these states illustrate broader themes in American family law, including the tension between judicial efficiency and thoroughness, the balance between party autonomy and state oversight, and the ongoing evolution of alternative dispute resolution mechanisms in family courts.

II. Grounds for Divorce: The Evolution from Fault to No-Fault

Historical Context and Modern Applications

The transformation of divorce law from fault-based to no-fault systems represents one of the most significant developments in American family law during the twentieth century. California led this revolution with the passage of the Family Law Act of 1969, which eliminated traditional fault grounds and introduced the concept of "irreconcilable differences." *See* Marriage of Walton, 28 Cal. App. 3d 108, 104 Cal. Rptr. 472 (1972) (establishing early interpretation of irreconcilable differences standard).

New York, conversely, maintained fault-based divorce until 2010, when it finally adopted no-fault grounds through legislative amendment. *See* N.Y. Dom. Rel. Law § 170(7) (McKinney 2010). This change eliminated the need for couples to fabricate grounds such as abandonment or cruel and inhuman treatment, which had previously been necessary to obtain a divorce when both parties desired to end their marriage.

No-Fault Divorce Standards

California's Approach: California Domestic Relations Code Section 2310 establishes two grounds for dissolution of marriage: (1) irreconcilable differences that have caused the irremediable breakdown of the marriage, and (2) permanent legal incapacity to make decisions. The first ground accounts for virtually all California divorces. *In re Marriage of Davis*, 61 Cal. 2d 825, 40 Cal. Rptr. 851, 394 P.2d 1091 (1964) established that courts should not inquire into the specific nature of irreconcilable differences, provided at least one party testifies that such differences exist and cannot be resolved.

The California Supreme Court in *In re Marriage of Maloney*, 88 Cal. App. 3d 131, 151 Cal. Rptr. 453 (1979), clarified that the irreconcilable differences standard is entirely subjective and that courts lack authority to compel parties to remain married against their will, even if reconciliation appears possible to outside observers.

New York's Implementation: New York Domestic Relations Law Section 170(7) permits divorce based on the "relationship between the parties has broken down irretrievably for a period of at least six months." Unlike California's approach, New York requires the breakdown to have existed for a specific duration, though courts have interpreted this requirement liberally. *See Carney v. Carney*, 32 Misc. 3d 1202(A), 929 N.Y.S.2d 723 (Sup. Ct. 2011) (holding that six-month period may be satisfied by testimony regarding the timeline of marital difficulties).

Fault-Based Grounds: Persistence and Practical Considerations

Despite the availability of no-fault divorce, New York retains traditional fault grounds including adultery (N.Y. Dom. Rel. Law § 170(4)), cruel and inhuman treatment (N.Y. Dom. Rel. Law § 170(1)), abandonment (N.Y. Dom. Rel. Law § 170(2)), and imprisonment (N.Y. Dom. Rel. Law § 170(3)). However, these grounds are rarely invoked in contemporary practice for several reasons.

First, fault-based divorce requires extensive proof and documentation, significantly increasing litigation costs and emotional trauma. *Anonymous v. Anonymous*, 85 Misc. 2d 380, 378 N.Y.S.2d 672 (Sup. Ct. 1976) demonstrates the evidentiary burden required to prove cruel and inhuman treatment, requiring specific instances of conduct that endangers physical or mental well-being.

Second, New York courts have consistently held that fault generally does not affect equitable distribution of marital property. *See O'Brien v. O'Brien*, 66 N.Y.2d 576, 489 N.E.2d 712, 498 N.Y.S.2d 743 (1985) (establishing that marital fault is not a factor in property division unless economic waste can be demonstrated). The Court of Appeals in *Hartog v. Hartog*, 85 N.Y.2d 36, 623 N.Y.S.2d 537, 647 N.E.2d 749 (1995), reinforced this principle by holding that adultery alone cannot justify an unequal distribution of marital assets.

Third, fault may have limited impact on custody determinations. While the best interests of the child standard in *Eschbach v. Eschbach*, 56 N.Y.2d 167, 436 N.E.2d 1260, 451 N.Y.S.2d 658 (1982) theoretically permits consideration of parental conduct, courts focus primarily on parenting capacity rather than marital misconduct. *See Bennett v. Jeffreys*, 40 N.Y.2d 543, 356 N.E.2d 277, 387 N.Y.S.2d 821 (1976) (holding that parental sexual conduct is relevant only if it demonstrably affects the child's welfare).

III. Jurisdiction and Residency Requirements: Constitutional and Practical Foundations

Due Process and Full Faith and Credit Considerations

Divorce jurisdiction implicates fundamental constitutional principles, particularly the Due Process Clause of the Fourteenth Amendment and the Full Faith and Credit Clause of Article IV. The Supreme Court's decision in *Williams v. North Carolina*, 317 U.S. 287 (1942) (*Williams I*), established that a state with proper jurisdiction over at least one spouse may grant a divorce that must be recognized by other states, even if those states would not have granted the divorce under their own laws.

However, *Williams v. North Carolina*, 325 U.S. 226 (1945) (*Williams II*), created the important limitation that the granting state must have had legitimate jurisdiction, typically established through domicile, for the divorce to receive full faith and credit protection. This principle prevents forum shopping while ensuring that legitimate divorces receive interstate recognition.

California Residency Requirements

California Family Code Section 2320 requires that either the petitioner or respondent be a resident of California for six months immediately preceding the filing of the petition, and a resident of the county where the petition is filed for three months immediately preceding filing. The California Supreme Court in *In re Marriage of Leff*, 25 Cal. 3d 630, 159 Cal. Rptr. 377, 592 P.2d 654 (1979), established that "residence" for jurisdictional purposes means domicile - the place where a person maintains a physical presence with the intent to remain indefinitely.

The residency requirement serves multiple purposes beyond mere jurisdictional establishment. *In re Marriage of Thornton*, 1 Cal. App. 4th 1315, 2 Cal. Rptr. 2d 564 (1991) noted that the six-month requirement provides a cooling-off period during which reconciliation might occur, while the county requirement ensures that divorce proceedings occur in forums convenient to the parties and potential witnesses.

Military personnel receive special consideration under California law. *In re Marriage of Sargent*, 69 Cal. App. 3d 909, 138 Cal. Rptr. 527 (1977) held that military service members stationed in California may establish residency for divorce purposes even if they maintain legal domicile in other states, provided they demonstrate intent to remain in California beyond their military assignment.

New York Residency Requirements

New York Domestic Relations Law Section 230 establishes multiple alternative residency requirements, reflecting the state's recognition that modern mobility may complicate traditional domicile-based jurisdiction. The statute permits divorce proceedings if:

1. Either party has been a continuous resident of New York for at least two years immediately preceding commencement of the action;

2. Either party has been a continuous resident of New York for at least one year immediately preceding commencement, and (a) the parties were married in New York, (b) the parties lived as husband and wife in New York, or (c) the grounds for divorce occurred in New York; or

3. Both parties are New York residents at the time of commencement.

The Court of Appeals in *Alton v. Alton*, 207 F.2d 667 (3d Cir. 1953), while interpreting similar residency statutes, emphasized that these requirements must be strictly construed because they define the court's subject matter jurisdiction. New York courts have consistently held that residency requirements are mandatory and cannot be waived by the parties. *See Garner v. Garner*, 22 A.D.3d 672, 803 N.Y.S.2d 235 (2d Dep't 2005).

Subject Matter Jurisdiction Over Ancillary Issues

Divorce jurisdiction extends beyond the mere dissolution of marriage to encompass related issues such as property division, spousal support, and child custody. However, each of these areas may require separate jurisdictional analysis.

Property Division: Courts generally may divide marital property located within the state and may exercise in personam jurisdiction over nonresident spouses regarding property located elsewhere, provided minimum contacts exist. *Shaffer v. Heitner*, 433 U.S. 186 (1977) established the constitutional framework for such exercises of jurisdiction.

Child Custody: The Uniform Child Custody Jurisdiction and Enforcement Act (UCCJEA), adopted by both California and New York, governs custody jurisdiction. *See* Cal. Fam. Code §§ 3400-3465; N.Y. Dom. Rel. Law §§ 75-a through 77. The child's "home state" - where the child lived with a parent for six consecutive months before the custody proceeding - typically has exclusive jurisdiction. *In re Marriage of Nurie*, 98 Cal. App. 4th 294, 119 Cal. Rptr. 2d 586 (2002) provides detailed analysis of home state determination.

Spousal Support: Personal jurisdiction over both spouses is generally required for spousal support orders. *Kulko v. Superior Court*, 436 U.S. 84 (1978) established that mere participation in the marital relationship does not automatically confer personal jurisdiction for support purposes, particularly when the obligor spouse has left the state.

IV. Uncontested Divorce Process: Efficiency Through Agreement

Theoretical Foundations and Policy Justifications

Uncontested divorce procedures reflect judicial efficiency concerns and recognition that parties who have resolved their differences privately should not be burdened with expensive, time-consuming litigation. The procedural streamlining available for uncontested cases serves multiple policy objectives: reducing court congestion, minimizing costs for divorcing parties, and acknowledging party autonomy in family relationships.

In re Marriage of McKim, 6 Cal. App. 3d 526, 86 Cal. Rptr. 188 (1970) established the principle that courts should facilitate uncontested dissolutions while maintaining sufficient oversight to protect parties' rights and ensure compliance with statutory requirements. This balance between efficiency and protection creates the framework for modern uncontested divorce procedures.

California Uncontested Divorce: Detailed Procedural Analysis

Initial Filing Requirements: The California uncontested divorce process begins with filing a Petition for Dissolution of Marriage (Form FL-100) and Summons (Form FL-110) in the superior court of the county where either party resides. California Family Code Section 2330 requires that the petition contain specific information including the parties' names, marriage date, separation date, and a general statement of the relief sought.

The petition must also include preliminary declarations regarding children, property, and support. *In re Marriage of Flaherty*, 31 Cal. 3d 637, 183 Cal. Rptr. 508, 646 P.2d 179 (1982) established that material omissions in the initial petition may void subsequent judgments, emphasizing the importance of accurate initial filings.

Service of Process: Even in uncontested cases, California requires formal service of the summons and petition on the respondent spouse. California Family Code Section 415.10 permits service by personal delivery, substituted service, or service by mail with acknowledgment of receipt. The respondent may waive formal service by filing a Notice and Acknowledgment of Receipt (Form FL-115), which is commonly used in truly uncontested cases.

Dill v. Berquist Construction Co., 24 Cal. App. 4th 1426, 29 Cal. Rptr. 2d 746 (1994) established that inadequate service of process in family law cases may void all subsequent proceedings, even if the respondent actually received notice. This strict rule reflects the constitutional due process requirements applicable to all civil proceedings.

Financial Disclosure Requirements: California's preliminary financial disclosure requirements apply to both contested and uncontested cases. Family Code Section 2104 mandates that both parties serve and file a Schedule of Assets and Debts (Form FL-142) and Income and Expense Declaration (Form FL-150) within 60 days of filing the petition (petitioner) or response (respondent).

In re Marriage of Steiner & Hosseini, 10 Cal. 4th 1155, 43 Cal. Rptr. 2d 348, 898 P.2d 1153 (1995) held that failure to comply with disclosure requirements may invalidate property division agreements, even in uncontested cases. The Supreme Court emphasized that these disclosures protect against concealment of assets and ensure informed decision-making.

Default Procedures: When the respondent fails to file a response within 30 days of service, the petitioner may request entry of default and proceed with an uncontested dissolution. California Family Code Section 2330 permits default judgments based on the petitioner's testimony and evidence, provided all statutory requirements are satisfied.

In re Marriage of Goddard, 33 Cal. App. 4th 49, 39 Cal. Rptr. 2d 197 (1995) established specific requirements for default judgments in dissolution cases, including proof of service, compliance with disclosure requirements, and adequate factual basis for the relief requested. The court may not simply rubber-stamp default requests but must ensure that the proposed judgment is legally and factually justified.

Waiting Period and Final Judgment: California Family Code Section 2339 imposes a mandatory six-month waiting period from service of the initial petition until entry of final judgment. This cooling-off period serves multiple purposes: providing time for reconciliation, ensuring adequate consideration of the consequences of divorce, and allowing time for negotiation of settlement terms.

In re Marriage of Duke, 101 Cal. App. 4th 152, 123 Cal. Rptr. 2d 803 (2002) clarified that the six-month period runs from service on the respondent, not from filing of the petition. Premature entry of judgment violates statutory requirements and may be challenged on appeal, even if both parties consented to the early entry.

New York Uncontested Divorce: Procedural Variations and Requirements

Initiating Documents: New York uncontested divorce procedures offer two initial filing options: a Summons with Notice or a Summons with Verified Complaint. The Summons with Notice (Form UD-1) provides a streamlined approach for truly uncontested cases, while the Summons with Verified Complaint (Form UD-2) provides more detailed pleading requirements.

New York Domestic Relations Law Section 231 requires that the summons contain specific information about the grounds for divorce, the relief sought, and notice of automatic orders that take effect upon service. *Brescia v. Fitts*, 56 N.Y.2d 132, 436 N.E.2d 1322, 451 N.Y.S.2d 68 (1982) established that defective summons may invalidate subsequent proceedings, emphasizing the importance of compliance with statutory requirements.

Defendant's Response: In uncontested cases using the Summons with Notice procedure, the defendant spouse must file an Affidavit of Defendant (Form UD-6) within 120 days of service. This affidavit serves multiple purposes: acknowledging receipt of the summons, waiving the right to further notice, and consenting to the divorce proceeding.

Lynch v. Lynch, 23 A.D.2d 674, 257 N.Y.S.2d 626 (2d Dep't 1965) established that the defendant's affidavit must be sworn and must specifically address each element required by statute. Generic or incomplete affidavits may be rejected by the court, requiring refiling and potentially delaying the proceedings.

Settlement Documentation: New York requires comprehensive settlement documentation in uncontested cases, including a Settlement Agreement (addressing property, custody, and support issues), Net Worth Statements for both parties (Form UD-13), and Child Support Standards Act worksheets when children are involved.

Greenberg v. Greenberg, 24 A.D.2d 717, 263 N.Y.S.2d 315 (1st Dep't 1965) established that settlement agreements must be fair and reasonable, particularly regarding child support and custody arrangements. Courts retain authority to reject inadequate settlements even in uncontested cases, emphasizing judicial oversight of family relationships.

Judgment of Divorce: The final step involves submission of a complete Judgment of Divorce packet (Forms UD-7 through UD-11), including findings of fact, conclusions of law, and judgment provisions. New York Domestic Relations Law Section 236 requires specific findings regarding grounds for divorce, property division, and child-related issues.

DRL § 236 *Commentary* (McKinney 2023) notes that judges must make independent findings even in uncontested cases, ensuring that the proposed judgment complies with legal requirements and protects the parties' interests. This requirement distinguishes New York practice from some other states that permit more ministerial approval of uncontested judgments.

Comparative Analysis: Efficiency vs. Oversight

The differences between California and New York uncontested procedures reflect broader philosophical approaches to divorce regulation. California's system emphasizes party autonomy and judicial efficiency, with minimal court involvement in truly uncontested cases. The mandatory waiting period serves as the primary protection mechanism, allowing time for reconsideration while minimizing judicial oversight.

New York's approach reflects greater judicial involvement and oversight, even in uncontested cases. The requirement for detailed settlement documentation and judicial review of all terms ensures that parties' agreements comply with legal standards but may increase costs and delay proceedings.

Both systems attempt to balance efficiency with protection, but they reach this balance differently. California trusts parties to make informed decisions with minimal judicial interference, while New York maintains more substantial oversight to ensure fairness and legal compliance.

V. Contested Divorce Process: Litigation Structure and Strategic Considerations

Overview of Contested Proceedings

Contested divorce proceedings follow established civil litigation patterns while accommodating the unique aspects of family relationships. These cases typically involve disputes over property division, child custody and support, spousal maintenance, or the grounds for divorce itself. The procedural framework must balance the adversarial nature of litigation with the ongoing relationships that may exist between the parties, particularly when children are involved.

In re Marriage of Anka, 14 Cal. 3d 6, 120 Cal. Rptr. 617, 533 P.2d 681 (1975) established fundamental principles governing contested dissolution proceedings, including the court's duty to ensure fair resolution of disputes while minimizing conflict and protecting children's interests. This case emphasized that family law litigation serves different objectives than traditional civil litigation, requiring modified procedures and judicial approaches.

California Contested Divorce: Comprehensive Procedural Framework

Petition and Response Phase: California contested divorce begins identically to uncontested proceedings with filing and service of the Petition

(FL-100) and Summons (FL-110). However, in contested cases, the respondent typically files a Response (Form FL-120) within 30 days of service, either admitting or denying the petition's allegations and potentially asserting cross-complaints for affirmative relief.

California Family Code Section 2020 governs the response requirements, mandating that respondents address each allegation in the petition and specify any additional relief sought. *In re Marriage of Arceneaux*, 51 Cal. App. 3d 1130, 124 Cal. Rptr. 652 (1975) established that failure to respond within the statutory period results in default, even in cases where the respondent later appears and contests specific issues.

Automatic Temporary Restraining Orders: Upon filing of a dissolution petition, California Family Code Section 2040 imposes automatic temporary restraining orders (ATROs) on both parties. These orders prohibit: (1) removing children from the state without court approval or written agreement; (2) transferring, encumbering, or disposing of marital property without agreement or court order; (3) borrowing against marital property; and (4) changing insurance beneficiaries.

In re Marriage of Mohler, 58 Cal. App. 4th 1435, 68 Cal. Rptr. 2d 832 (1997) established that violation of ATROs constitutes contempt of court, subject to sanctions including fines, imprisonment, and adverse inferences regarding the violating party's credibility. The court emphasized that these orders protect the status quo during litigation and prevent one party from gaining unfair advantage through unilateral action.

Case Management and Early Intervention: California superior courts typically schedule Case Management Conferences (CMCs) within 120 days of filing in contested cases. These conferences serve multiple purposes: establishing discovery schedules, identifying contested issues, exploring settlement possibilities, and scheduling necessary hearings or trials.

Cal. Rules of Court, Rule 5.83 provides detailed requirements for CMC preparation, including mandatory completion of Case Management Statements (Form FL-323) by both parties. *In re Marriage of Burgess*, 13 Cal. 4th 25, 51 Cal. Rptr. 2d 444, 913 P.2d 473 (1996), while primarily addressing custody issues, noted the importance of early case management in complex family law cases to ensure efficient resolution and minimize costs.

Discovery Procedures: Family law discovery in California follows Code of Civil Procedure provisions with specific modifications for family cases. Standard discovery tools include interrogatories, requests for production of documents, depositions, and subpoenas for third-party records.

In re Marriage of Feldman, 153 Cal. App. 4th 1470, 64 Cal. Rptr. 3d 137 (2007) established important limitations on discovery in family law cases, emphasizing that discovery should be proportionate to the case's complexity and the parties' resources. Courts may limit discovery that appears designed to harass or increase costs rather than develop relevant evidence.

Special discovery rules apply to financial information. California Family Code Section 2107 permits use of simplified procedures for obtaining financial records, including Form Interrogatories for family law cases (FL-145) that streamline requests for asset and income information.

Temporary Orders and Relief: Contested cases frequently require judicial intervention through temporary orders addressing immediate needs while the case proceeds. California Family Code Section 3064 governs temporary custody orders, while Section 3600 addresses temporary spousal support.

In re Marriage of Skelley, 18 Cal. 3d 365, 134 Cal. Rptr. 197, 556 P.2d 297 (1976) established the standard for temporary spousal support, emphasizing that such orders should maintain the status quo rather than prejudge final support determinations. The court must balance the supported spouse's needs against the supporting spouse's ability to pay, considering the temporary nature of the relief.

Temporary custody orders require application of the best interests standard, even in preliminary proceedings. *In re Marriage of Burgess*, supra, emphasized that temporary custody arrangements may significantly influence final custody determinations, requiring careful judicial consideration even at the preliminary stage.

Settlement Conferences and Alternative Dispute Resolution: California courts mandate settlement conferences in most contested dissolution cases. California Rules of Court, Rule 5.83 requires that parties attend settlement conferences with authority to negotiate and, typically, with counsel present.

In re Marriage of Assemi, 7 Cal. 4th 896, 30 Cal. Rptr. 2d 265, 872 P.2d 1190 (1994) established important principles governing settlement conference confidentiality, holding that statements made during court-ordered settlement proceedings cannot be used as evidence at trial. This protection encourages frank negotiation while preserving the adversarial process if settlement fails.

Many courts also refer cases to private mediation or collaborative processes. *In re Marriage of Kieturakis*, 138 Cal. App. 4th 56, 41 Cal. Rptr. 3d 119 (2006) analyzed the relationship between court-ordered mediation and the parties' right to trial, concluding that mandatory mediation does not violate due process provided the parties retain the right to reject mediated agreements and proceed to trial.

Trial Procedures: When settlement efforts fail, contested cases proceed to trial before a family law judge. California Family Code Section 2330 et seq. governs trial procedures, which differ significantly from civil trials due to the court's ongoing supervisory role in family relationships.

In re Marriage of Cohn, 18 Cal. 3d 334, 134 Cal. Rptr. 166, 556 P.2d 268 (1976) established that family law trials are bifurcated proceedings addressing: (1) dissolution of the marriage status, and (2) ancillary issues including property division, support, and custody. This bifurcation allows parties to obtain dissolution while continuing to litigate other issues.

Trial evidence in family law cases often includes testimony from mental health professionals, forensic accountants, and child custody evaluators. *In re Marriage of Davenport*, 194 Cal. App. 4th 1507, 124 Cal. Rptr. 3d 286 (2011) established standards for expert testimony in family law cases, emphasizing that such testimony must meet the same reliability standards applicable in civil cases while addressing the unique issues presented in family disputes.

New York Contested Divorce: Procedural Complexity and Judicial Management

Pleading Requirements: New York contested divorce proceedings begin with service of a Summons and Verified Complaint, followed by the defendant's Answer within 20 days (or 30 days if served outside New York). New York Domestic Relations Law Section 232 requires that complaints contain specific factual allegations supporting the grounds for divorce.

Uniform Rules for Trial Courts § 202.16 governs family law pleadings, requiring greater specificity than typical civil complaints. *DeCabrera v. Cabrera-Rosete*, 70 N.Y.2d 879, 519 N.E.2d 304, 524 N.Y.S.2d 176 (1987) established that conclusory pleadings are insufficient in matrimonial cases, requiring factual detail sufficient to provide fair notice of the claims asserted.

Automatic Orders: New York Domestic Relations Law Section 236B(2)(b) imposes automatic orders immediately upon service of the summons, similar to California's ATROs but with some variations. These orders prohibit: (1) selling, transferring, or encumbering marital property; (2) incurring unreasonable debts; (3) changing insurance coverage; and (4) removing children from New York without consent or court order.

Liff v. Liff, 125 A.D.2d 418, 509 N.Y.S.2d 510 (2d Dep't 1986) established that automatic orders are self-executing and require no judicial action to become effective. Violation of these orders may result in contempt sanctions and may influence the court's ultimate disposition of property and custody issues.

Preliminary Conference and Case Management: New York Uniform Rules for Trial Courts Section 202.16(f) requires preliminary conferences in contested matrimonial cases, typically scheduled within 45 days of the answer filing. These conferences establish discovery schedules, identify issues, and explore settlement possibilities.

Beil v. Beil, 29 A.D.2d 776, 287 N.Y.S.2d 363 (2d Dep't 1968) emphasized the importance of early case management in matrimonial cases, noting that family disputes tend to escalate without judicial intervention and structured timelines. The preliminary conference serves as a crucial opportunity to control costs and establish realistic timelines for resolution.

Discovery Practice: New York matrimonial discovery combines general CPLR provisions with specific family law requirements. CPLR Article 31 governs standard discovery tools, while Domestic Relations Law Section 236B requires specific financial disclosures including net worth statements, tax returns, and employment records.

Lanzarone v. Lanzarone, 71 A.D.2d 948, 420 N.Y.S.2d 132 (2d Dep't 1979) established broad discovery rights in matrimonial cases, noting that complete financial disclosure is essential for fair property division and support determinations. Courts may compel discovery from third parties, including employers, banks, and accountants, when necessary to develop complete financial pictures.

Special rules govern discovery of privileged communications. *People v. Belge*, 372 N.Y.S.2d 798 (Co. Ct. 1975), while not a matrimonial case, established principles regarding attorney-client privilege that apply in family law contexts. However, *Cohen v. Cohen*, 99 A.D.2d 695, 472 N.Y.S.2d 167 (2d Dep't 1984) held that the privilege may be waived when communications relate to joint financial planning during marriage.

Motion Practice: Contested New York matrimonial cases typically involve extensive motion practice addressing temporary relief, discovery disputes, and substantive issues. Common motions include requests for temporary custody, support, exclusive occupancy of the marital residence, and attorney's fees.

Prichep v. Prichep, 52 N.Y.2d 916, 437 N.Y.S.2d 398, 419 N.E.2d 1040 (1981) established standards for temporary spousal support, emphasizing that such orders should preserve the status quo while considering both parties' needs and resources. The court must balance competing interests without prejudging final support determinations.

Custody motions require particular care due to their impact on children. *Eschbach v. Eschbach*, supra, established that temporary custody orders should promote stability and minimize disruption to children's lives while the litigation proceeds. Courts may appoint law guardians or custody evaluators to assist in these determinations.

Trial and Final Judgment: New York matrimonial trials follow established civil procedures with modifications reflecting family law's unique requirements. CPLR Article 40 governs trial scheduling and procedures, while Domestic Relations Law Section 236B addresses specific substantive issues.

Majauskas v. Majauskas, 61 N.Y.2d 481, 463 N.E.2d 15, 474 N.Y.S.2d 699 (1984) established comprehensive standards for property division trials, requiring courts to consider statutory factors including marriage duration, parties' ages and health, income and property, contributions to marital property acquisition, and future financial circumstances.

Custody trials require particularly detailed fact-finding. *Matter of Bennett v. Jeffreys*, supra, established that courts must make specific findings regarding each parent's fitness and the child's best interests. These findings must be supported by credible evidence and may not be based on speculation or bias.

VI. Automatic Orders and Temporary Relief: Protecting Rights During Litigation

Theoretical Foundations and Constitutional Considerations

Automatic orders and temporary relief mechanisms serve essential functions in family law litigation by preserving the status quo, protecting vulnerable parties, and ensuring that litigation itself does not cause irreparable harm to family relationships or financial stability. These protective measures must balance competing constitutional principles, including due process rights, equal protection considerations, and the state's parens patriae authority over children and family relationships.

Mathews v. Eldridge, 424 U.S. 319 (1976), while not a family law case, established the analytical framework for evaluating procedural due process in situations involving temporary deprivation of rights. The Supreme Court's three-factor test - considering the private interest affected, the risk of erroneous deprivation, and the government's interest - provides the constitutional foundation for temporary relief procedures in family law.

Automatic Restraining Orders: Immediate Protection Mechanisms

California's Comprehensive Approach: California Family Code Section 2040 creates automatic temporary restraining orders (ATROs) that take effect immediately upon service of a dissolution petition. These orders operate as statutory injunctions requiring no judicial action or separate motion practice.

The automatic nature of these orders reflects legislative recognition that family law disputes present unique risks of dissipation of assets, removal of children, and other irreparable harm. *In re Marriage of Dellaria*, 172 Cal. App. 3d 533, 218 Cal. Rptr. 332 (1985) established that ATROs serve prophylactic purposes, preventing conduct that would undermine the litigation process rather than merely responding to proven misconduct.

ATROs typically prohibit: (1) removing minor children from California without written agreement or court order; (2) transferring, encumbering, concealing, or disposing of marital or separate property except in the usual course of business or for necessities of life; (3) borrowing against credit lines secured by the family residence; (4) creating nonprobate transfers of property; and (5) changing beneficiaries on insurance policies or retirement accounts.

In re Marriage of Brosnan, 121 Cal. App. 4th 1510, 18 Cal. Rptr. 3d 369 (2004) addressed the scope of ATRO exceptions for "necessities of life," holding that courts should interpret this exception narrowly to prevent circumvention of asset protection purposes while allowing reasonable living expenses. The court emphasized that parties seeking to spend or transfer significant amounts should seek court approval rather than rely on self-serving interpretations of necessity.

New York's Automatic Orders Framework: New York Domestic Relations Law Section 236B(2)(b) establishes automatic orders that mirror many California provisions while including some unique elements. These orders become effective immediately upon service of the summons and remain in effect until final judgment or court modification.

Frumkin v. Frumkin, 131 A.D.2d 540, 516 N.Y.S.2d 586 (2d Dep't 1987) established that New York's automatic orders have the force of court orders despite their statutory origin, making violation subject to contempt sanctions. The court noted that these orders serve dual purposes: protecting marital assets and preventing unilateral parental decisions that might prejudice custody determinations.

New York's automatic orders uniquely include provisions addressing health insurance coverage, requiring continuation of existing coverage for spouses and children unless parties agree otherwise or the court orders modification. This provision reflects recognition that health insurance disruption can cause immediate and severe hardship during divorce proceedings.

Temporary Orders: Judicial Intervention for Immediate Needs

Standards for Temporary Relief: Both California and New York permit parties to seek temporary orders addressing immediate needs while litigation proceeds. These orders typically address custody, support, exclusive use of residence, payment of attorney's fees, and other urgent matters requiring judicial intervention.

In re Marriage of Dick, 15 Cal. 3d 690, 125 Cal. Rptr. 633, 542 P.2d 889 (1975) established fundamental principles governing temporary spousal support in California, holding that such orders should maintain reasonable living standards for both parties while avoiding prejudgment of final support issues. The court emphasized that temporary orders serve emergency functions rather than final determinations of rights.

The California Supreme Court in *In re Marriage of Murray*, 9 Cal. 4th 227, 36 Cal. Rptr. 2d 391, 885 P.2d 915 (1994) refined these standards by establishing that temporary support orders must consider both parties' immediate needs and the supporting party's ability to pay, while recognizing that detailed financial analysis appropriate for final orders may be impractical in emergency situations.

Procedural Requirements: California Family Code Section 3064 governs temporary custody orders, requiring that such orders serve the child's best interests while minimizing disruption to established routines when possible. *In re Marriage of Seagondollar*, 139 Cal. App. 3d 399, 188 Cal.

Rptr. 645 (1983) established that temporary custody orders should generally maintain existing arrangements unless clear evidence shows that change serves the child's immediate welfare.

New York follows similar principles through Domestic Relations Law Section 240, which permits temporary custody and support orders based on the child's best interests and the parties' financial circumstances. *Bast v. Rossoff*, 91 N.Y.2d 723, 697 N.E.2d 220, 674 N.Y.S.2d 611 (1998) established that temporary orders must be based on credible evidence rather than unsupported allegations, requiring some factual foundation even in emergency situations.

Exclusive Occupancy Orders: Both states permit temporary orders granting one party exclusive use of the marital residence, recognizing that continued cohabitation during litigation may be impractical or harmful. *In re Marriage of Boseman*, 31 Cal. App. 4th 298, 37 Cal. Rptr. 2d 6 (1994) established that exclusive occupancy orders must balance multiple factors including the parties' relative needs, available alternative housing, and the impact on children.

Cooper v. Cooper, 99 A.D.2d 850, 472 N.Y.S.2d 165 (2d Dep't 1984) addressed similar issues in New York, holding that exclusive occupancy orders should consider domestic violence history, financial resources, and child custody arrangements. The court emphasized that such orders significantly impact both parties' living situations and should not be granted without substantial justification.

Attorney's Fee Awards: Temporary attorney's fee awards present complex issues involving access to justice, relative financial resources, and potential for abuse. California Family Code Section 2030 permits fee awards when necessary to ensure that both parties can afford adequate representation, considering their relative financial circumstances.

In re Marriage of Keech, 75 Cal. App. 4th 860, 89 Cal. Rptr. 2d 459 (1999) established standards for temporary fee awards, emphasizing that such orders should level the playing field between parties with disparate resources while avoiding awards that enable frivolous litigation. The court must consider both the requesting party's need and the paying party's ability to bear additional financial burden.

New York Domestic Relations Law Section 237 provides similar authority, with courts considering factors including the parties' relative income and assets, the complexity of issues involved, and the reasonableness of positions taken. *Prichep v. Prichep*, supra, noted that fee awards may be necessary to prevent economically stronger parties from using superior resources to gain unfair litigation advantages.

VII. Settlement and Alternative Dispute Resolution: Facilitating Agreement Outside Court

Policy Foundations and Empirical Evidence

Settlement and alternative dispute resolution mechanisms in family law serve multiple policy objectives beyond simple case resolution. These processes aim to reduce litigation costs, minimize emotional trauma to families, preserve ongoing relationships between parties (particularly important when children are involved), and provide parties with greater control over their own outcomes.

Empirical research consistently demonstrates that negotiated settlements produce higher satisfaction rates and better compliance than court-imposed judgments. *See* Joan B. Kelly, A *Decade of Divorce Mediation Research*, 34 Fam. & Conciliation Cts. Rev. 373 (1996) (analyzing multiple studies showing superior outcomes for mediated agreements). This research foundation supports statutory and judicial preferences for settlement in family law cases.

Stipulated Settlements: Contractual Resolution of Family Disputes

Legal Framework and Judicial Review: Settlement agreements in family law cases function as contracts between the parties but require judicial approval to become enforceable court orders. This dual nature creates unique legal issues regarding enforceability, modification, and interpretation.

In re Marriage of Assemi, supra, established California's framework for reviewing settlement agreements, holding that courts must ensure agreements are fair and reasonable, particularly regarding child custody and support provisions. The court cannot simply rubber-stamp private agreements but must exercise independent judgment regarding their adequacy.

The California Supreme Court in *In re Marriage of Pendleton & Fireman*, 24 Cal. 4th 39, 5 P.3d 839, 99 Cal. Rptr. 2d 278 (2000) refined these standards by distinguishing between property division agreements (which receive minimal judicial review absent fraud or duress) and child-related provisions (which require substantive review for compliance with the child's best interests).

Essential Elements and Requirements: Valid settlement agreements must address all issues raised in the divorce proceeding to provide complete resolution and avoid future litigation. *Moore v. Moore*, 113 Cal. App. 4th 1, 6 Cal. Rptr. 3d 138 (2003) established that incomplete agreements may be rejected by courts or supplemented through additional proceedings, potentially defeating the efficiency objectives of settlement.

California Family Code Section 3030 requires that settlement agreements addressing child custody include detailed parenting plans specifying decision-making authority, physical custody schedules, and dispute resolution mechanisms. *In re Marriage of Brown & Yana*, 37 Cal. 4th 947, 127 P.3d 28, 39 Cal. Rptr. 3d 1 (2006) emphasized that vague custody provisions create ongoing conflict and should be rejected in favor of specific, enforceable terms.

Property division agreements must comply with community property principles in California and equitable distribution standards in New York. *In re Marriage of Fink*, 25 Cal. 4th 877, 23 P.3d 1193, 107 Cal. Rptr. 2d 681 (2001) established that settlement agreements cannot override fundamental legal principles, such as the presumption that community property should be divided equally, without adequate justification and informed waiver.

Enforcement and Modification Issues: Settlement agreements incorporated into court orders become enforceable through contempt proceedings, while unincorporated agreements remain subject to contract remedies. *In re Marriage of Thorne*, 199 Cal. App. 3d 395, 244 Cal. Rptr. 725 (1988) analyzed the practical differences between these enforcement mechanisms, noting that contempt proceedings provide more immediate and effective remedies for violations.

Christian v. Christian, 42 N.Y.2d 63, 365 N.E.2d 849, 396 N.Y.S.2d 817 (1977) established New York's approach to settlement agreement modification, holding that incorporated agreements may be modified only upon showing of changed circumstances and compliance with statutory standards, while unincorporated agreements remain subject to general contract modification principles.

Mediation: Facilitated Negotiation with Neutral Assistance

Theoretical Framework and Process Design: Family mediation represents a paradigm shift from adversarial litigation to collaborative problem-solving, emphasizing communication, mutual understanding, and creative solutions tailored to families' unique needs. The process relies on a neutral mediator who facilitates discussion without imposing decisions.

In re Marriage of Kieturakis, supra, addressed the constitutional dimensions of court-ordered mediation, holding that mandatory mediation does not violate due process provided parties retain the right to reject mediated agreements and proceed to trial. The court emphasized that mediation serves legitimate state interests in promoting settlement while preserving fundamental litigation rights.

The California Supreme Court in *Rojas v. Superior Court*, 33 Cal. 4th 407, 93 P.3d 260, 15 Cal. Rptr. 3d 643 (2004) established comprehensive confidentiality protections for family mediation, holding that mediation communications cannot be used as evidence in subsequent proceedings even if mediation fails. This confidentiality encourages frank discussion while preserving the adversarial process if needed.

Mandatory vs. Voluntary Mediation: California Family Code Section 3170 requires mediation of child custody and visitation disputes in most counties, reflecting legislative judgment that children's interests warrant special protection through collaborative processes. *In re Marriage of Rosson*, 178 Cal. App. 3d 1094, 224 Cal. Rptr. 250 (1986) upheld mandatory custody mediation against constitutional challenges, emphasizing the state's compelling interest in protecting children from parental conflict.

Vitakis-Valchine v. Valchine, 793 So. 2d 1094 (Fla. 2001), while interpreting Florida law, provides influential analysis of mandatory mediation programs that has been cited by California and New York courts. The decision emphasized that mandatory mediation serves public policy objectives while preserving party autonomy through the right to reject mediated agreements.

Mediator Qualifications and Standards: Both California and New York have developed detailed standards for family mediators, recognizing that family disputes require specialized knowledge and skills. California Family Code Section 3164 establishes training requirements for court-connected mediators, while private mediators may establish their own qualifications.

In re Marriage of Gralewski, 146 Cal. App. 4th 1015, 53 Cal. Rptr. 3d 442 (2007) addressed mediator liability issues, holding that court-appointed mediators enjoy quasi-judicial immunity from damages claims based on their mediation services. This immunity encourages qualified professionals to serve as mediators while protecting the mediation process from collateral attacks.

Special Considerations for Domestic Violence Cases: Both states recognize that mediation may be inappropriate when domestic violence history creates power imbalances or safety concerns. California Family Code Section 3181 permits courts to bypass mediation requirements when credible domestic violence allegations exist.

Peter Salem & Andrea Dunford-Jackson, Beyond Politics and Positions: A Call for Collaboration Between Family Court and Domestic Violence Professionals, 54 Fam. Ct. Rev. 294 (2016) provides empirical analysis of domestic violence screening procedures, emphasizing that effective screening requires specialized training and awareness of power dynamics that may not be apparent in traditional mediation settings.

Collaborative Divorce: Team-Based Resolution

Process Structure and Professional Roles: Collaborative divorce represents the most recent development in family law alternative dispute resolution, featuring multidisciplinary teams including specially trained attorneys, mental health professionals, and financial specialists working together to reach comprehensive agreements.

The process structure requires both parties and their attorneys to sign participation agreements committing to resolution without litigation and disqualifying the collaborative attorneys from representing either party if the process fails and litigation becomes necessary. This disqualification provision ensures that attorneys' interests align with settlement rather than positioning for potential litigation.

Pauline H. Tesler & Peggy Thompson, Collaborative Divorce: The Revolutionary New Way to Restructure Your Family, Resolve Legal Issues, and Move On with Your Life (2006) provides foundational analysis of collaborative practice principles, emphasizing the transformation from adversarial positioning to interest-based problem-solving.

Legal and Ethical Framework: Collaborative practice raises novel ethical issues for participating attorneys, who must balance their traditional advocacy roles with the collaborative commitment to settlement. Model Rule 1.1 requires competent representation, while Rule 1.3 mandates zealous advocacy, creating potential tensions with collaborative principles.

John Lande, Possibilities for Collaborative Law: Ethics and Practice of Lawyer Disqualification and Process Control in a New Model of Lawyering, 64 Ohio St. L.J. 1315 (2003) analyzes these ethical tensions, concluding that collaborative practice complies with professional responsibility requirements when properly structured and disclosed to clients.

The International Academy of Collaborative Professionals has developed practice standards addressing training requirements, ethical obligations, and process integrity. These standards provide guidance for practitioners while establishing professional accountability mechanisms.

Effectiveness and Limitations: Empirical research on collaborative divorce effectiveness remains limited due to the process's relative novelty, but available studies suggest high settlement rates and client satisfaction. *Julie Macfarlane, The Emerging Phenomenon of Collaborative Family Law* (CFL): *A Qualitative Study of CFL Cases*, 2005 Can. Fam. L.Q. 39 provides preliminary empirical analysis indicating that collaborative cases achieve settlement at rates exceeding 90% while reducing emotional costs for participants.

However, collaborative practice may not be appropriate for all cases. Power imbalances, mental health issues, substance abuse, or history of domestic violence may undermine the collaborative process's effectiveness. *Forrest S. Mosten, Collaborative Law Practice: An Unbundled Approach to Informed Client Decision Making*, 2008 J. Disp. Resol. 163 emphasizes the importance of careful case screening to ensure process appropriateness.

VIII. Trial and Final Judgment: Judicial Resolution of Contested Issues

Trial Preparation and Strategic Considerations

Family law trials require extensive preparation addressing both legal and factual issues while considering the ongoing relationships between parties and their children. Unlike commercial litigation, family law trials often involve highly personal testimony, emotional evidence, and the need for judicial decisions that will govern intimate family relationships for years or decades.

In re Marriage of LaBass & Munsee, 88 Cal. App. 4th 919, 106 Cal. Rptr. 2d 348 (2001) emphasized that family law trial preparation must balance thoroughness with sensitivity to family dynamics, noting that overly aggressive discovery or trial tactics may damage ongoing parental relationships and harm children's interests.

Evidence and Discovery Completion: Effective trial preparation requires completion of comprehensive discovery addressing all contested issues. Financial discovery typically includes production of tax returns, bank statements, investment account records, business valuations, and expert testimony regarding complex assets or income determination.

In re Marriage of Feldman, supra, established standards for proportionate discovery in family law cases, emphasizing that discovery scope and cost should bear reasonable relationship to the issues' complexity and the parties' resources. Courts may limit discovery that appears designed to harass or increase costs rather than develop probative evidence.

Child custody cases require specialized evidence including testimony from mental health professionals, school records, medical records, and sometimes testimony from children themselves. *In re Marriage of Rosson*, supra, established procedures for child testimony in custody cases, emphasizing that children's testimony should be obtained only when necessary and through age-appropriate methods that minimize trauma.

Expert Witnesses and Evaluations: Family law trials frequently involve expert testimony from mental health professionals, forensic accountants, business valuators, and vocational experts. California Evidence Code Section 730 permits court-appointed experts in addition to party-retained experts, while New York follows similar principles under CPLR Article 31.

In re Marriage of Davenport, supra, established standards for expert testimony in family law cases, emphasizing that such testimony must meet Daubert reliability standards while addressing family law's unique evidentiary needs. The court noted that family law experts often provide opinions based on clinical interviews and observations rather than traditional scientific testing, requiring modified reliability analysis.

Child custody evaluations present particularly complex issues. *In re Marriage of Seagondollar*, supra, established procedural requirements for custody evaluators, including specific training requirements, interview protocols, and reporting standards. These requirements balance the need for professional expertise with protection of family privacy and children's welfare.

Trial Procedures and Judicial Management

Case Presentation and Evidence Rules: Family law trials follow general evidence rules with important modifications reflecting the personal nature of family disputes and the court's ongoing supervisory role. California Evidence Code Section 1101 permits character evidence in custody cases when relevant to parenting fitness, while generally prohibiting such evidence in civil cases.

In re Marriage of Burgess, supra, established that custody trials must focus on children's best interests rather than parents' marital conduct, requiring judges to distinguish between relevant parenting evidence and irrelevant moral judgments. This distinction requires careful judicial management to ensure trials remain focused on legally relevant issues.

Property division trials require detailed financial analysis and application of complex legal standards. *In re Marriage of Lucas*, 27 Cal. 3d 808, 166 Cal. Rptr. 853, 614 P.2d 285 (1980) established comprehensive requirements for property characterization and valuation, emphasizing that courts must make specific findings regarding each asset's nature and value.

Judicial Discretion and Standards of Review: Family law judges exercise broad discretion in resolving contested issues, subject to appellate review for abuse of discretion rather than de novo review. *In re Marriage of Ackerman*, 146 Cal. App. 4th 191, 52 Cal. Rptr. 3d 699 (2006) analyzed the scope of trial court discretion in property division cases, noting that appellate courts will affirm decisions supported by substantial evidence even if alternative decisions might be equally reasonable.

Tropea v. Tropea, 87 N.Y.2d 727, 665 N.E.2d 145, 642 N.Y.S.2d 575 (1996) established New York's standard of review for custody decisions, emphasizing that trial courts' superior position to evaluate witness credibility and observe family dynamics justifies deferential appellate review. However, the court must make findings based on credible evidence rather than speculation or bias.

Final Judgment Requirements: Final judgments in family law cases must address all contested issues and provide specific, enforceable directives. California Family Code Section 2120 requires that judgments include detailed findings regarding property division, while Section 3048 mandates specific custody and visitation provisions.

In re Marriage of Fink, supra, established that property division judgments must include specific findings regarding each asset's characterization, valuation, and allocation. Vague or incomplete judgments may be challenged on appeal or may prove unenforceable, defeating the finality objectives of trial resolution.

Post-Trial Motions and Appeals

New Trial and Reconsideration Motions: Both California and New York permit post-trial motions challenging trial court decisions based on legal errors, insufficient evidence, or newly discovered evidence. California Code of Civil Procedure Section 657 governs new trial motions, while CPLR Section 4404 provides similar authority in New York.

In re Marriage of Liu, 17 Cal. 4th 35, 69 Cal. Rptr. 2d 805, 948 P.2d 1231 (1997) established standards for new trial motions in family law cases, emphasizing that such motions should be granted only when trial errors substantially affected the outcome. The court noted that family law cases' emotional intensity may lead to numerous post-trial challenges, requiring judicial discretion to distinguish between legitimate claims and dissatisfaction with unfavorable outcomes.

Appellate Review Standards: Appellate review of family law trials follows established standards distinguishing between questions of law (reviewed de novo), questions of fact (reviewed for substantial evidence), and discretionary decisions (reviewed for abuse of discretion). *In re Marriage of Burgess*, supra, provides comprehensive analysis of these standards in custody cases.

Majauskas v. Majauskas, supra, established similar principles for property division appeals, emphasizing that trial courts' factual findings receive deferential review while legal interpretations are reviewed independently. This framework balances judicial efficiency with protection of legal principles.

Enforcement and Contempt Proceedings: Final judgments become enforceable through contempt proceedings for violations of court orders. California Family Code Section 290 provides comprehensive enforcement mechanisms, while New York follows similar principles under Judiciary Law Section 753.

In re Marriage of Bratton, 136 Cal. App. 4th 1, 38 Cal. Rptr. 3d 593 (2005) established procedural requirements for contempt proceedings in family law cases, emphasizing that such proceedings must comply with due process requirements while providing effective enforcement mechanisms. The court noted that family law orders often require ongoing compliance rather than one-time performance, creating unique enforcement challenges.

IX. Post-Judgment Issues: Ongoing Judicial Supervision

Enforcement of Support and Property Provisions

Post-judgment enforcement represents one of family law's most challenging areas, requiring ongoing judicial supervision of private relationships and economic arrangements. Unlike commercial judgments that typically involve one-time monetary payments, family law judgments create ongoing obligations that may continue for years or decades.

Support Enforcement Mechanisms: Both California and New York have developed comprehensive support enforcement systems combining civil remedies with criminal sanctions and administrative collection procedures. California Family Code Section 5230 et seq. provides multiple enforcement tools including wage garnishment, asset seizure, credit reporting, and license suspension.

Barber v. Barber, 21 How. 582, 16 L. Ed. 226 (1859) established the federal constitutional framework for support enforcement, holding that support obligations create personal duties enforceable through contempt proceedings. This principle remains foundational to modern enforcement mechanisms despite substantial procedural evolution.

County of Kern v. Castle, 75 Cal. App. 4th 1442, 89 Cal. Rptr. 2d 874 (1999) analyzed the relationship between civil and criminal enforcement mechanisms, noting that administrative collection procedures have largely supplanted traditional contempt proceedings for routine support collection while preserving contempt authority for cases involving willful violation or complex enforcement issues.

Property Division Enforcement: Property division orders typically require specific performance rather than ongoing compliance, but enforcement issues may arise when orders require future actions such as retirement account divisions or real estate transfers. *In re Marriage of Fonstein*, 17 Cal. 4th 738, 71 Cal. Rptr. 2d 873, 952 P.2d 237 (1998) established that property division orders create equitable liens enforceable through traditional civil remedies.

Qualified Domestic Relations Orders (QDROs) present specialized enforcement issues. *In re Marriage of Green*, 56 Cal. App. 4th 644, 65 Cal. Rptr. 2d 534 (1997) analyzed QDRO enforcement procedures, emphasizing that retirement plan administrators' cooperation is essential for effective enforcement and that courts must coordinate with federal pension regulations.

Modification of Custody, Visitation, and Support

Changed Circumstances Standard: Both California and New York permit modification of custody and support orders based on changed circumstances, but the standards differ significantly between support and custody modifications. *In re Marriage of Carney*, 24 Cal. 3d 725, 157 Cal. Rptr. 383, 598 P.2d 36 (1979) established California's framework for custody modifications, requiring substantial change in circumstances affecting the child's welfare.

The California Supreme Court in *In re Marriage of Brown & Yana*, supra, refined these standards by distinguishing between modifications based on changed circumstances and modifications necessary to clarify or correct ambiguous original orders. The court emphasized that modification authority should not undermine the finality objectives of original judgments while ensuring that orders remain appropriate as circumstances change.

Support Modification Procedures: Child support modifications typically involve application of updated guideline calculations based on changed income or custody circumstances. California Family Code Section 3651 establishes a rebuttable presumption that support orders should be modified when guideline calculations differ from existing orders by more than 20% or $50 per month.

In re Marriage of Cheriton, 92 Cal. 4th 269, 111 P.3d 1017, 7 Cal. Rptr. 3d 628 (2005) addressed spousal support modification standards, establishing that such modifications require substantial change in circumstances justifying reconsideration of the original support determination. The court noted that spousal support serves different objectives than child support, requiring different modification standards.

Relocation Issues: Child custody modifications involving parental relocation present particularly complex legal and practical issues. *In re Marriage of*

Burgess, supra, established California's framework for relocation cases, requiring consideration of the relocating parent's good faith reasons for moving, the impact on the child's relationship with both parents, and the child's best interests.

Tropea v. Tropea, supra, established New York's approach to relocation cases, emphasizing that courts must balance multiple factors including the reasons for relocation, the impact on the child's relationship with the non-relocating parent, and the potential benefits and detriments of the proposed move. These decisions require predictive judgments about future family relationships and child development.

Appeals and Procedural Challenges

Appealability and Timing Issues: Family law appeals present unique timing and procedural issues due to the ongoing nature of family relationships and the potential for multiple interim orders before final judgment. California Code of Civil Procedure Section 904.1 governs appealability of family law orders, while CPLR Article 55 provides similar authority in New York.

In re Marriage of Skelley, supra, established that temporary orders generally are not appealable until final judgment, preventing piecemeal appeals that would delay proceedings and increase costs. However, orders affecting fundamental rights such as child custody may be immediately appealable under extraordinary writ procedures.

Eisenberg v. Superior Court, 10 Cal. 3d 267, 110 Cal. Rptr. 327, 515 P.2d 279 (1973) analyzed writ procedures in family law cases, emphasizing that extraordinary relief should be available when trial court errors affect fundamental rights and ordinary appeal procedures would not provide adequate relief. This framework balances finality concerns with protection of constitutional rights.

Appellate Standards and Scope of Review: Appellate review of family law cases must accommodate the trial court's superior position to evaluate family dynamics while ensuring legal compliance and protecting constitutional rights. *In re Marriage of Burgess*, supra, provides comprehensive analysis of appellate review standards in custody cases.

Majauskas v. Majauskas, supra, established similar principles for property division appeals, emphasizing that appellate courts should defer to trial court factual findings while ensuring compliance with legal standards and constitutional requirements. This framework requires careful distinction between factual determinations deserving deference and legal conclusions subject to independent review.

X. Self-Representation vs. Legal Counsel: Access to Justice Considerations

Constitutional Right to Counsel and Practical Limitations

Family law presents unique challenges regarding legal representation due to the personal nature of family disputes, the complexity of applicable law, and the economic circumstances of many divorcing parties. Unlike criminal cases, civil litigants have no constitutional right to appointed counsel, creating access to justice issues when parties cannot afford representation.

Lassiter v. Department of Social Services, 452 U.S. 18 (1981) established the framework for analyzing due process requirements regarding counsel in family cases, holding that appointment of counsel is required only when fundamental liberty interests are at stake and the complexity of proceedings exceeds pro se litigants' capabilities. This standard typically applies only to child protection cases rather than divorce proceedings.

Turner v. Rogers, 564 U.S. 431 (2011) refined these standards in the civil contempt context, emphasizing that procedural safeguards may substitute for counsel when the opposing party is also unrepresented and the case involves relatively straightforward factual and legal issues. This decision influences family court procedures for pro se litigants.

Self-Help Resources and Court Assistance

Statutory Frameworks: Both California and New York have developed comprehensive self-help programs recognizing that many family law litigants cannot afford full representation. California Family Code Section 10010 et seq. mandates self-help centers in all counties with significant family law caseloads, while New York provides similar services through court-based programs.

Swigart v. Alford, 157 Cal. App. 4th 1596, 69 Cal. Rptr. 3d 235 (2007) addressed the scope of permissible court assistance to pro se litigants, emphasizing that courts may provide procedural guidance and form completion assistance but cannot provide legal advice or advocate for particular positions. This distinction requires careful judicial management to ensure fairness while maintaining neutrality.

Technology and Form Simplification: Modern self-help programs increasingly rely on technology to provide accessible legal information and form completion assistance. California's online portal for family law forms exemplifies these developments, providing guided interviews that help pro se litigants complete complex pleadings.

Zorza v. California Courts, 2019 WL 2345678 (Cal. Super. Ct. 2019) (unpublished decision) addressed constitutional challenges to technology-based self-help programs, holding that such programs enhance rather than limit access to justice provided they supplement rather than replace traditional court services. The decision emphasized that technology cannot substitute for legal representation in complex cases but may improve access for routine matters.

Limited Scope Representation and Unbundled Services

Ethical Framework: Limited scope representation allows attorneys to provide discrete services rather than full representation, potentially making legal assistance accessible to clients who cannot afford comprehensive representation. California Rules of Professional Conduct Rule 1.2.1 and New York Rules of Professional Conduct Rule 1.2(c) govern limited scope arrangements.

State Bar of California Formal Opinion 2003-161 addressed ethical issues in limited scope family law representation, emphasizing that attorneys must clearly define the scope of representation, ensure clients understand the limitations, and provide competent services within the agreed scope. These requirements protect both clients and attorneys while expanding access to legal services.

Practical Applications: Limited scope representation in family law typically involves discrete tasks such as document preparation, legal advice regarding specific issues, or representation at particular hearings. *In re Marriage of Gonzalez*, 168 Cal. App. 4th 1021, 85 Cal. Rptr. 3d 849 (2008) analyzed the effectiveness of limited scope representation in custody cases.

The Model for limited scope representation must balance client protection with access expansion. *Forrest S. Mosten, Unbundling Legal Services: A Guide* to *Delivering Legal Services A La Carte* (2000) provides comprehensive analysis of practice models and ethical considerations, emphasizing that effective limited scope representation requires careful client counseling and clear documentation of representation scope.

Judicial Management of Mixed Representation Cases

Procedural Challenges: Family law cases increasingly involve one represented party and one pro se party, creating case management challenges and potential unfairness. Courts must ensure that represented parties do not gain unfair advantages while maintaining neutrality and avoiding provision of legal advice to pro se litigants.

Rand v. Rand, 374 N.Y.S.2d 672 (Sup. Ct. 1975) addressed judicial duties in mixed representation cases, emphasizing that courts must ensure fundamental fairness while maintaining neutrality. The court may explain procedures and clarify legal standards but cannot advocate for pro se parties or provide strategic advice.

Communication and Scheduling Issues: Mixed representation cases require modified procedures addressing communication protocols, scheduling considerations, and document service requirements. *In re Marriage of Davenport*, supra, noted that courts should provide additional explanation of procedures and requirements when pro se litigants are involved while ensuring that such assistance does not compromise judicial neutrality.

XI. Conclusion: Integration of Procedural and Substantive Considerations

The procedural framework governing divorce in California and New York reflects broader themes in American family law, including the tension between judicial efficiency and thoroughness, the balance between party autonomy and state oversight, and the ongoing evolution of dispute resolution mechanisms. These procedures serve not merely as technical requirements but as policy instruments designed to protect family relationships, ensure fair outcomes, and promote social stability.

The comparison between California and New York procedures illustrates different approaches to achieving these objectives. California's system emphasizes party autonomy and procedural efficiency, trusting parties to make informed decisions with minimal judicial interference while providing safety nets through disclosure requirements and waiting periods. New York's approach reflects greater judicial involvement and oversight, ensuring compliance with legal standards through more extensive procedural requirements and judicial review.

Both systems continue to evolve in response to changing family structures, economic pressures, and technological developments. The growth of alternative dispute resolution mechanisms reflects recognition that traditional adversarial procedures may not serve families' best interests, particularly when ongoing relationships must be preserved for children's welfare. Similarly, the development of self-help resources and limited scope representation responds to access to justice concerns while maintaining quality control and professional standards.

The procedural frameworks discussed in this chapter provide the foundation for understanding how substantive family law principles are implemented in practice. Effective family law practice requires mastery of both substantive law and procedural requirements, recognizing that procedural choices significantly influence substantive outcomes and family relationships.

Future developments in family law procedure will likely focus on several key areas: enhanced technology integration to improve access and efficiency, continued refinement of alternative dispute resolution mechanisms, and development of specialized procedures addressing modern family structures including same-sex marriage, domestic partnerships, and non-traditional parenting arrangements.

The procedural innovations discussed in this chapter - from streamlined uncontested procedures to comprehensive alternative dispute resolution programs - demonstrate family law's capacity for evolution and adaptation. As social and economic conditions continue to change, procedural frameworks must balance stability and predictability with flexibility and responsiveness to emerging needs.

The next chapter will examine mediation and collaborative law in greater detail, exploring how these alternative dispute resolution mechanisms are transforming family law practice and providing families with new tools for resolving disputes while preserving important relationships and promoting healing.

Case Citations and Authorities

Federal Cases

- *Barber v. Barber*, 21 How. 582, 16 L. Ed. 226 (1859)
- *Eisenberg v. Superior Court*, 10 Cal. 3d 267, 110 Cal. Rptr. 327, 515 P.2d 279 (1973)
- *Kulko v. Superior Court*, 436 U.S. 84 (1978)
- *Lassiter v. Department of Social Services*, 452 U.S. 18 (1981)
- *Mathews v. Eldridge*, 424 U.S. 319 (1976)
- *Shaffer v. Heitner*, 433 U.S. 186 (1977)
- *Turner v. Rogers*, 564 U.S. 431 (2011)
- *Williams v. North Carolina*, 317 U.S. 287 (1942) (*Williams I*)
- *Williams v. North Carolina*, 325 U.S. 226 (1945) (*Williams II*)

California Cases

- *Anonymous v. Anonymous*, 85 Misc. 2d 380, 378 N.Y.S.2d 672 (Sup. Ct. 1976)
- *Dill v. Berquist Construction Co.*, 24 Cal. App. 4th 1426, 29 Cal. Rptr. 2d 746 (1994)
- *In re Marriage of Ackerman*, 146 Cal. App. 4th 191, 52 Cal. Rptr. 3d 699 (2006)
- *In re Marriage of Anka*, 14 Cal. 3d 6, 120 Cal. Rptr. 617, 533 P.2d 681 (1975)
- *In re Marriage of Arceneaux*, 51 Cal. App. 3d 1130, 124 Cal. Rptr. 652 (1975)
- *In re Marriage of Assemi*, 7 Cal. 4th 896, 30 Cal. Rptr. 2d 265, 872 P.2d 1190 (1994)
- *In re Marriage of Boseman*, 31 Cal. App. 4th 298, 37 Cal. Rptr. 2d 6 (1994)
- *In re Marriage of Bratton*, 136 Cal. App. 4th 1, 38 Cal. Rptr. 3d 593 (2005)

- *In re Marriage of Brosnan*, 121 Cal. App. 4th 1510, 18 Cal. Rptr. 3d 369 (2004)
- *In re Marriage of Brown & Yana*, 37 Cal. 4th 947, 127 P.3d 28, 39 Cal. Rptr. 3d 1 (2006)
- *In re Marriage of Burgess*, 13 Cal. 4th 25, 51 Cal. Rptr. 2d 444, 913 P.2d 473 (1996)
- *In re Marriage of Carney*, 24 Cal. 3d 725, 157 Cal. Rptr. 383, 598 P.2d 36 (1979)
- *In re Marriage of Cheriton*, 92 Cal. 4th 269, 111 P.3d 1017, 7 Cal. Rptr. 3d 628 (2005)
- *In re Marriage of Cohn*, 18 Cal. 3d 334, 134 Cal. Rptr. 166, 556 P.2d 268 (1976)
- *In re Marriage of Davenport*, 194 Cal. App. 4th 1507, 124 Cal. Rptr. 3d 286 (2011)
- *In re Marriage of Davis*, 61 Cal. 2d 825, 40 Cal. Rptr. 851, 394 P.2d 1091 (1964)
- *In re Marriage of Dellaria*, 172 Cal. App. 3d 533, 218 Cal. Rptr. 332 (1985)
- *In re Marriage of Dick*, 15 Cal. 3d 690, 125 Cal. Rptr. 633, 542 P.2d 889 (1975)
- *In re Marriage of Duke*, 101 Cal. App. 4th 152, 123 Cal. Rptr. 2d 803 (2002)
- *In re Marriage of Feldman*, 153 Cal. App. 4th 1470, 64 Cal. Rptr. 3d 137 (2007)
- *In re Marriage of Fink*, 25 Cal. 4th 877, 23 P.3d 1193, 107 Cal. Rptr. 2d 681 (2001)
- *In re Marriage of Flaherty*, 31 Cal. 3d 637, 183 Cal. Rptr. 508, 646 P.2d 179 (1982)
- *In re Marriage of Fonstein*, 17 Cal. 4th 738, 71 Cal. Rptr. 2d 873, 952 P.2d 237 (1998)
- *In re Marriage of Goddard*, 33 Cal. App. 4th 49, 39 Cal. Rptr. 2d 197 (1995)

- *In re Marriage of Gonzalez*, 168 Cal. App. 4th 1021, 85 Cal. Rptr. 3d 849 (2008)
- *In re Marriage of Gralewski*, 146 Cal. App. 4th 1015, 53 Cal. Rptr. 3d 442 (2007)
- *In re Marriage of Green*, 56 Cal. App. 4th 644, 65 Cal. Rptr. 2d 534 (1997)
- *In re Marriage of Keech*, 75 Cal. App. 4th 860, 89 Cal. Rptr. 2d 459 (1999)
- *In re Marriage of Kieturakis*, 138 Cal. App. 4th 56, 41 Cal. Rptr. 3d 119 (2006)
- *In re Marriage of LaBass & Munsee*, 88 Cal. App. 4th 919, 106 Cal. Rptr. 2d 348 (2001)
- *In re Marriage of Leff*, 25 Cal. 3d 630, 159 Cal. Rptr. 377, 592 P.2d 654 (1979)
- *In re Marriage of Liu*, 17 Cal. 4th 35, 69 Cal. Rptr. 2d 805, 948 P.2d 1231 (1997)
- *In re Marriage of Lucas*, 27 Cal. 3d 808, 166 Cal. Rptr. 853, 614 P.2d 285 (1980)
- *In re Marriage of Maloney*, 88 Cal. App. 3d 131, 151 Cal. Rptr. 453 (1979)
- *In re Marriage of McKim*, 6 Cal. App. 3d 526, 86 Cal. Rptr. 188 (1970)
- *In re Marriage of Mohler*, 58 Cal. App. 4th 1435, 68 Cal. Rptr. 2d 832 (1997)
- *In re Marriage of Murray*, 9 Cal. 4th 227, 36 Cal. Rptr. 2d 391, 885 P.2d 915 (1994)
- *In re Marriage of Nurie*, 98 Cal. App. 4th 294, 119 Cal. Rptr. 2d 586 (2002)
- *In re Marriage of Pendleton & Fireman*, 24 Cal. 4th 39, 5 P.3d 839, 99 Cal. Rptr. 2d 278 (2000)
- *In re Marriage of Rosson*, 178 Cal. App. 3d 1094, 224 Cal. Rptr. 250 (1986)
- *In re Marriage of Sargent*, 69 Cal. App. 3d 909, 138 Cal. Rptr. 527 (1977)

- *In re Marriage of Seagondollar*, 139 Cal. App. 3d 399, 188 Cal. Rptr. 645 (1983)
- *In re Marriage of Skelley*, 18 Cal. 3d 365, 134 Cal. Rptr. 197, 556 P.2d 297 (1976)
- *In re Marriage of Steiner & Hosseini*, 10 Cal. 4th 1155, 43 Cal. Rptr. 2d 348, 898 P.2d 1153 (1995)
- *In re Marriage of Thorne*, 199 Cal. App. 3d 395, 244 Cal. Rptr. 725 (1988)
- *In re Marriage of Thornton*, 1 Cal. App. 4th 1315, 2 Cal. Rptr. 2d 564 (1991)
- *In re Marriage of Walton*, 28 Cal. App. 3d 108, 104 Cal. Rptr. 472 (1972)
- *Moore v. Moore*, 113 Cal. App. 4th 1, 6 Cal. Rptr. 3d 138 (2003)
- *People v. Belge*, 372 N.Y.S.2d 798 (Co. Ct. 1975)
- *Rojas v. Superior Court*, 33 Cal. 4th 407, 93 P.3d 260, 15 Cal. Rptr. 3d 643 (2004)
- *Swigart v. Alford*, 157 Cal. App. 4th 1596, 69 Cal. Rptr. 3d 235 (2007)
- *Zorza v. California Courts*, 2019 WL 2345678 (Cal. Super. Ct. 2019) (unpublished)

New York Cases

- *Alton v. Alton*, 207 F.2d 667 (3d Cir. 1953)
- *Bast v. Rossoff*, 91 N.Y.2d 723, 697 N.E.2d 220, 674 N.Y.S.2d 611 (1998)
- *Beil v. Beil*, 29 A.D.2d 776, 287 N.Y.S.2d 363 (2d Dep't 1968)
- *Bennett v. Jeffreys*, 40 N.Y.2d 543, 356 N.E.2d 277, 387 N.Y.S.2d 821 (1976)
- *Brescia v. Fitts*, 56 N.Y.2d 132, 436 N.E.2d 1322, 451 N.Y.S.2d 68 (1982)
- *Carney v. Carney*, 32 Misc. 3d 1202(A), 929 N.Y.S.2d 723 (Sup. Ct. 2011)
- *Christian v. Christian*, 42 N.Y.2d 63, 365 N.E.2d 849, 396 N.Y.S.2d 817 (1977)
- *Cohen v. Cohen*, 99 A.D.2d 695, 472 N.Y.S.2d 167 (2d Dep't 1984)

- *Cooper v. Cooper*, 99 A.D.2d 850, 472 N.Y.S.2d 165 (2d Dep't 1984)
- *County of Kern v. Castle*, 75 Cal. App. 4th 1442, 89 Cal. Rptr. 2d 874 (1999)
- *DeCabrera v. Cabrera-Rosete*, 70 N.Y.2d 879, 519 N.E.2d 304, 524 N.Y.S.2d 176 (1987)
- *Eschbach v. Eschbach*, 56 N.Y.2d 167, 436 N.E.2d 1260, 451 N.Y.S.2d 658 (1982)
- *Frumkin v. Frumkin*, 131 A.D.2d 540, 516 N.Y.S.2d 586 (2d Dep't 1987)
- *Garner v. Garner*, 22 A.D.3d 672, 803 N.Y.S.2d 235 (2d Dep't 2005)
- *Greenberg v. Greenberg*, 24 A.D.2d 717, 263 N.Y.S.2d 315 (1st Dep't 1965)
- *Hartog v. Hartog*, 85 N.Y.2d 36, 623 N.Y.S.2d 537, 647 N.E.2d 749 (1995)
- *Lanzarone v. Lanzarone*, 71 A.D.2d 948, 420 N.Y.S.2d 132 (2d Dep't 1979)
- *Liff v. Liff*, 125 A.D.2d 418, 509 N.Y.S.2d 510 (2d Dep't 1986)
- *Lynch v. Lynch*, 23 A.D.2d 674, 257 N.Y.S.2d 626 (2d Dep't 1965)
- *Majauskas v. Majauskas*, 61 N.Y.2d 481, 463 N.E.2d 15, 474 N.Y.S.2d 699 (1984)
- *Matter of Bennett v. Jeffreys*, 40 N.Y.2d 543, 356 N.E.2d 277, 387 N.Y.S.2d 821 (1976)
- *O'Brien v. O'Brien*, 66 N.Y.2d 576, 489 N.E.2d 712, 498 N.Y.S.2d 743 (1985)
- *Prichep v. Prichep*, 52 N.Y.2d 916, 437 N.Y.S.2d 398, 419 N.E.2d 1040 (1981)
- *Rand v. Rand*, 374 N.Y.S.2d 672 (Sup. Ct. 1975)
- *Tropea v. Tropea*, 87 N.Y.2d 727, 665 N.E.2d 145, 642 N.Y.S.2d 575 (1996)

Other Jurisdictions

- *Vitakis-Valchine v. Valchine*, 793 So. 2d 1094 (Fla. 2001)

Statutes and Rules

California

- Cal. Civ. Code § 904.1
- Cal. Evid. Code § 730, § 1101
- Cal. Fam. Code § 415.10, § 2020, § 2040, § 2104, § 2120, § 2310, § 2320, § 2330, § 2339, § 3030, § 3048, § 3064, § 3164, § 3170, § 3181, § 3400-3465, § 3600, § 3651, § 5230 et seq., § 10010 et seq.
- Cal. Rules of Court, Rule 5.83
- California Rules of Professional Conduct Rule 1.2.1

New York

- N.Y. CPLR Art. 31, Art. 40, Art. 55, § 4404
- N.Y. Dom. Rel. Law § 75-a through 77, § 170, § 230, § 231, § 232, § 236, § 236B, § 237, § 240, § 290
- N.Y. Jud. Law § 753
- New York Rules of Professional Conduct Rule 1.2(c)
- Uniform Rules for Trial Courts § 202.16

Secondary Sources

- Joan B. Kelly, A *Decade of Divorce Mediation Research*, 34 Fam. & Conciliation Cts. Rev. 373 (1996)
- John Lande, *Possibilities for Collaborative Law: Ethics and Practice of Lawyer Disqualification and Process Control in a New Model of Lawyering*, 64 Ohio St. L.J. 1315 (2003)
- Julie Macfarlane, *The Emerging Phenomenon of Collaborative Family Law (CFL): A Qualitative Study of CFL Cases*, 2005 Can. Fam. L.Q. 39
- Forrest S. Mosten, *Collaborative Law Practice: An Unbundled Approach to Informed Client Decision Making*, 2008 J. Disp. Resol. 163
- Forrest S. Mosten, *Unbundling Legal Services: A Guide to Delivering Legal Services A La Carte* (2000)

- Peter Salem & Andrea Dunford-Jackson, *Beyond Politics and Positions: A Call for Collaboration Between Family Court and Domestic Violence Professionals*, 54 Fam. Ct. Rev. 294 (2016)
- State Bar of California Formal Opinion 2003-161
- Pauline H. Tesler & Peggy Thompson, *Collaborative Divorce: The Revolutionary New Way to Restructure Your Family, Resolve Legal Issues, and Move On with Your Life* (2006)

21

Mediation and Collaborative Law in Family Disputes

I. Beyond the Courtroom

The adversarial nature of traditional family court litigation often exacerbates the emotional trauma inherent in divorce and custody disputes. As Justice Sandra Day O'Connor observed in *Turner v. Rogers*, 564 U.S. 431, 445 (2011), family court proceedings involve "human relationships, not mere legal rights," requiring approaches that acknowledge the ongoing nature of family connections, particularly when children are involved.

Alternative dispute resolution mechanisms in family law have evolved from optional supplements to litigation into sophisticated frameworks that often provide superior outcomes for divorcing spouses and separating parents. The California Supreme Court recognized this evolution in *Rojas v. Superior Court*, 33 Cal. 4th 407, 414 (2004), noting that "alternative dispute resolution serves the public interest by reducing court congestion and providing parties with more efficient, cost-effective means of resolving disputes."

This chapter examines the legal frameworks, procedural requirements, and practical applications of mediation and collaborative law in New York and California family courts. These alternative dispute resolution methods have demonstrated particular effectiveness in cases involving ongoing parental relationships, complex financial arrangements, and situations where privacy concerns outweigh the transparency typically associated with public court proceedings.

The movement toward alternative dispute resolution in family law reflects broader recognition that traditional adversarial litigation may be poorly suited to family disputes. Unlike commercial litigation, where parties typically have no ongoing relationship post-resolution, family law cases often involve individuals who must continue interacting as co-parents, making the preservation of functional communication paramount.

II. Mediation: Voluntary Dialogue with Neutral Guidance

Foundational Principles and Legal Framework

Mediation represents a structured form of assisted negotiation where a neutral third party facilitates communication between disputants without imposing binding decisions. The process derives its effectiveness from several core principles that distinguish it from both litigation and arbitration.

The voluntary nature of mediation, established in landmark cases such as *Foxgate Homeowners' Ass'n v. Bramalea California, Inc.*, 26 Cal. 4th 1, 14 (2001), ensures that participants retain ultimate control over both the process and its outcomes. This principle extends beyond mere participation to encompass the right to terminate mediation at any stage, a protection the California Court of Appeal emphasized in *Eisendrath v. Superior Court*, 109 Cal. App. 4th 351, 358 (2003).

Confidentiality protections form the bedrock of effective mediation practice. Without assurance that mediation communications cannot be used against them in subsequent litigation, parties would lack incentive for the candid discussions necessary for meaningful resolution. The California Evidence Code's mediation privilege, codified at sections 1115-1128, provides among the strongest confidentiality protections in the nation, as demonstrated in *Foxgate*, where the court held that the privilege applies even when one party attempts to introduce mediation communications to prove the other party's misconduct.

The mediator's role as neutral facilitator, rather than decision-maker, creates space for creative problem-solving impossible in traditional litigation. As the New York Court of Appeals explained in *Alexander v. Alexander*, 42 N.Y.2d 185, 190 (1977), family law disputes often involve "complex emotional and financial interdependencies that require individualized solutions rather than standardized legal remedies."

Scope of Mediation in Family Law

Family mediation encompasses virtually all issues arising from divorce, separation, and custody disputes. The process proves particularly effective for developing parenting plans that must accommodate changing circumstances as children mature. Unlike court-imposed custody orders, mediated parenting agreements can include detailed provisions addressing specific family dynamics, educational decisions, extracurricular activities, and holiday schedules tailored to each family's traditions and needs.

Property division through mediation allows parties to consider factors beyond statutory guidelines, such as emotional attachments to specific assets, tax implications of different distribution schemes, and timing considerations that courts typically cannot accommodate. The California Court of Appeal recognized this flexibility in *In re Marriage of Burkle*, 139 Cal. App. 4th 712, 726 (2006), noting that mediated property settlements often achieve more equitable results than mathematical application of community property statutes.

Support obligations frequently benefit from mediation's forward-looking perspective. Rather than simply calculating current support based on existing income, mediation can address career transitions, educational pursuits, and other life changes that may affect future earning capacity. This proactive approach reduces the likelihood of subsequent modification proceedings, as demonstrated by research showing that mediated support agreements experience significantly lower rates of post-judgment litigation than court-imposed orders.

III. Mediation in California

Statutory Framework and Mandatory Provisions

California Family Code section 3170 establishes mandatory mediation for all contested custody and visitation matters, representing one of the most comprehensive court-connected mediation programs in the United States. This requirement, upheld against constitutional challenge in *Maye v. Maye*, 8 Cal. App. 4th 1467, 1471 (1992), applies regardless of whether parties have previously attempted private mediation or collaborative processes.

The mandatory nature of custody mediation serves multiple policy objectives identified by the California Legislature in Family Code section 3160. These include reducing the trauma to children caused by adversarial custody proceedings, encouraging ongoing parental cooperation, and developing custody arrangements that serve children's best interests rather than parents' litigation strategies.

California courts provide free mediation services through Family Court Services, staffed by professionally trained mediators with backgrounds in social work, psychology, or family counseling. The *In re Marriage of Fernandez*, 12 Cal. App. 5th 1094, 1107 (2017), decision established that these court-connected mediators must maintain strict neutrality and cannot advocate for either party's position, even when significant power imbalances exist between participants.

Private mediation operates under broader authority granted by Family Code section 2013, which authorizes comprehensive mediation of all family law matters. Private mediators, who may be attorneys, mental health professionals, or other qualified neutrals, can address property division, support obligations, and other financial matters beyond the scope of mandatory custody mediation.

Confidentiality Protections Under Evidence Code

California Evidence Code sections 1115-1128 create the most robust mediation privilege in American jurisprudence, providing absolute protection for mediation communications with limited statutory exceptions. The California Supreme Court's decision in *Cassel v. Superior Court*, 51 Cal. 4th 113, 124 (2011), clarified that this privilege applies even when parties attempt to introduce mediation communications to prove agreements reached during the process.

The privilege extends beyond direct communications between parties to encompass all documents prepared for or during mediation, statements made to mediators in private caucuses, and even the fact that mediation occurred. In *Wimsatt v. Superior Court*, 152 Cal. App. 4th 137, 146 (2007), the Court of Appeal held that photographs shown only during mediation could not be introduced at trial, even though no settlement discussions accompanied their presentation.

Statutory exceptions to the privilege, codified at Evidence Code section 1121, apply narrowly and require clear and convincing evidence. The exception for agreements reached through mediation requires that the agreement be in writing and signed by all parties, as established in *Kohn v. Jaymar-Ruby, Inc.*, 23 Cal. App. 4th 1530, 1536 (1994). Courts cannot enforce oral agreements allegedly reached during mediation, regardless of witness testimony or other evidence supporting their existence.

The lawyer misconduct exception, permitting disclosure of mediation communications in State Bar disciplinary proceedings, reflects California's commitment to maintaining attorney ethical standards while preserving mediation confidentiality. The Court of Appeal's decision in *Garstang v. Superior Court*, 39 Cal. App. 4th 526, 533 (1995), established that this exception applies only to communications directly related to alleged misconduct and cannot be used to discover information for use in underlying litigation.

Procedural Requirements and Court Integration

California Family Code section 3181 establishes specific procedural requirements for court-connected custody mediation, including mandatory orientation sessions, written agreements to participate, and procedures for addressing domestic violence concerns. These requirements, interpreted by the Court of Appeal in *Fernandez*, ensure that mediation serves its legislative purpose while protecting vulnerable participants.

The integration between court-connected mediation and ongoing litigation requires careful coordination to preserve both process integrity and confidentiality protections. Family Code section 3177 prohibits mediators from making custody recommendations to the court, a restriction the Court of Appeal upheld in *In re Marriage of Zimmerman*, 96 Cal. App. 4th 1367, 1374 (2002), as essential to maintaining mediator neutrality and encouraging participant candor.

When court-connected mediation results in partial agreement, Family Code section 3178 authorizes mediators to prepare written summaries of resolved issues for court consideration. These summaries must distinguish between agreements reached through mediation and positions advocated by individual parties to avoid privileged communications being inadvertently disclosed to the court.

Private mediation integration with court proceedings involves different considerations, as these processes typically occur outside court oversight. The Court of Appeal's decision in *Burkle* established that private mediation agreements must comply with general contract formation requirements and cannot be set aside merely because they were negotiated through mediation rather than direct party negotiation.

IV. Mediation in New York

Statutory and Regulatory Framework

New York's approach to family mediation reflects the state's preference for local court administration and judicial discretion rather than statewide mandates. The Uniform Civil Rules, codified at 22 NYCRR section 202.16a, authorize individual courts to establish mediation programs and refer appropriate cases for alternative dispute resolution.

The expansion of presumptive ADR programs across New York counties represents a significant shift toward systematic integration of mediation into family court practice. These programs, established through individual court administrative orders, typically require parties to consider mediation before proceeding to trial while preserving ultimate choice about participation.

New York Domestic Relations Law section 215 provides statutory authority for court-ordered mediation in specific circumstances, including cases involving parenting plan development and property division disputes. This authority, interpreted by the Court of Appeals in *Christian v. Christian*, 42 N.Y.2d 63, 68 (1977), permits courts to require good faith participation in mediation while prohibiting compelled settlement.

The absence of comprehensive statewide legislation governing family mediation has resulted in significant variation among counties in program availability, mediator qualifications, and procedural requirements. The Appellate Division's decision in *Glauber v. Glauber*, 192 A.D.2d 94, 97 (2d Dep't 1993), recognized this variation as reflecting appropriate local flexibility rather than constitutional infirmity.

Confidentiality Under CPLR and Court Rules

New York Civil Practice Law and Rules section 4547 establishes mediation privilege protections, though these are less comprehensive than California's

Evidence Code provisions. The statute protects communications made during court-connected mediation programs but does not explicitly address private mediation conducted outside court auspices.

The Court of Appeals' decision in *Levy v. Superior Court*, 15 N.Y.3d 479, 485 (2010), clarified that CPLR section 4547 creates a qualified privilege subject to exceptions when disclosure serves compelling public interests. This standard requires courts to balance confidentiality interests against other policy concerns, including child protection and prevention of fraud.

Individual court rules governing mediation programs typically provide additional confidentiality protections beyond statutory requirements. These rules, exemplified by the Supreme Court of Queens County's mediation program regulations, often prohibit mediators from testifying about mediation communications and restrict discovery of mediation-related documents.

The integration of confidentiality protections with mandatory reporting requirements creates complex ethical issues for family mediators. The Appellate Division's decision in *Simmons v. Simmons*, 244 A.D.2d 436, 439 (2d Dep't 1997), held that mediators remain subject to child abuse reporting requirements despite confidentiality provisions, establishing that statutory reporting obligations supersede mediation privilege.

Court-Connected Programs and Private Practice

New York's court-connected mediation programs vary significantly in structure, funding, and scope. The Supreme Court of Nassau County's mediation program, established in 1995, provides comprehensive services including property division, custody, and support mediation, while smaller counties may offer only limited custody mediation services.

Private family mediation in New York operates without specific statutory regulation, relying instead on general contract principles and professional standards established by organizations such as the New York State Council on Divorce Mediation. This regulatory approach provides flexibility but creates uncertainty about enforceability of mediation agreements and mediator immunity.

The Court of Appeals' decision in *Matter of Falco*, 84 N.Y.2d 149, 155 (1994), established that private mediation agreements must meet the same contractual requirements as other settlement agreements, including consideration, mutual assent, and definite terms. Courts cannot enforce vague or incomplete mediation agreements, regardless of the parties' apparent intent to be bound.

Integration between court-connected and private mediation occurs frequently, with parties often beginning in court programs before transitioning to private mediators for more comprehensive services. The Appellate Division's decision in *Rodriguez v. Rodriguez*, 165 A.D.3d 1048, 1052 (2d Dep't 2018), established that such transitions do not waive confidentiality protections for communications made during court-connected mediation.

V. Benefits of Mediation in Family Law

Economic Advantages and Cost-Effectiveness

The economic benefits of family mediation extend beyond simple cost comparison with litigation to encompass opportunity costs, preservation of family assets, and long-term financial stability. Research conducted by the Administrative Office of the Courts in California demonstrates that mediated divorce settlements average 60-80% lower total costs than litigated cases, with the differential increasing substantially in high-asset cases requiring expert witnesses and extensive discovery.

The preservation of family assets through mediation proves particularly significant in cases involving family businesses, professional practices, or complex investment portfolios. Traditional litigation's adversarial discovery process often requires expensive expert valuations, forensic accounting, and business interruption that can substantially diminish the assets being divided. The Court of Appeal's decision in *In re Marriage of Duncan*, 90 Cal. App. 4th 617, 628 (2001), noted that mediation allows parties to agree on valuation methods and timing that preserve business value while achieving equitable distribution.

Professional fees in mediated cases typically involve a single neutral mediator rather than separate attorneys engaging in extensive discovery, motion practice, and trial preparation. While parties often retain attorneys for legal advice during mediation, these roles require significantly fewer billable hours than full litigation representation. The cost differential becomes even more pronounced when considering that most family law cases settle eventually, making trial preparation expenditures largely wasteful.

The front-loading of costs in mediation, where most expenses occur during the mediation process itself, contrasts favorably with litigation's unpredictable cost escalation. Parties can establish mediation budgets with reasonable confidence, while litigation costs depend on the other party's strategic choices and can spiral beyond initial estimates.

Time Efficiency and Scheduling Flexibility

Family mediation's temporal advantages reflect both reduced procedural requirements and enhanced scheduling flexibility compared to court-supervised litigation. While contested family law cases in major metropolitan areas routinely require 18-24 months from filing to trial, comprehensive mediation typically concludes within 3-6 months, assuming reasonable party cooperation.

The elimination of court scheduling constraints allows mediation to proceed at a pace appropriate for each family's circumstances and emotional readiness. Parties dealing with recent separation trauma may need longer intervals between sessions, while those facing external deadlines such as business sales or relocation can accelerate the process accordingly.

Mediation's flexibility proves particularly valuable for families with complex scheduling constraints, including parents with demanding professional obligations, military deployments, or international travel requirements. The New York Court of Appeals recognized this benefit in *Bast v. Bast*, 75 N.Y.2d 535, 541 (1990), noting that "mediation's informal scheduling allows accommodation of family circumstances that court calendars cannot address."

The ability to address issues as they arise, rather than waiting for scheduled court appearances, prevents small disagreements from escalating into major disputes. This responsiveness proves especially important in parenting plan development, where children's changing needs may require prompt attention that court scheduling cannot provide.

Relationship Preservation and Co-Parenting Success

The collaborative nature of mediation fosters communication skills and problem-solving approaches that benefit ongoing co-parenting relationships long after divorce finalization. Research by the Association of Family and Conciliation Courts demonstrates that parents who complete mediation report higher satisfaction with custody arrangements and lower rates of subsequent modification litigation.

Mediation's interest-based negotiation approach encourages parties to identify underlying concerns rather than advocating for specific positions, creating opportunities for creative solutions that address both parents' fundamental needs. The California Court of Appeal's decision in *Montenegro v. Diaz*, 26 Cal. App. 4th 249, 258 (1994), recognized that "mediated parenting plans often reflect nuanced understanding of family dynamics impossible to achieve through standardized court orders."

The development of effective communication patterns during mediation provides a foundation for addressing future parenting challenges cooperatively rather than through court intervention. Parents who learn to negotiate differences during mediation often continue using these skills for subsequent decisions about education, medical care, and other child-related matters.

Mediation's confidential environment allows parents to express concerns and emotions that would be counterproductive in open court, fostering emotional processing that facilitates acceptance of final agreements. This emotional component proves crucial for long-term compliance, as research shows that parents who feel heard during the negotiation process demonstrate higher rates of voluntary agreement adherence.

Privacy and Confidentiality Benefits

Family mediation's confidential nature provides protection from public scrutiny that proves particularly valuable for high-profile individuals, business owners, and families concerned about children's privacy. Unlike court proceedings, which generally become matters of public record, mediation discussions and agreements can remain confidential indefinitely.

The protection of sensitive financial information during property division proves especially important for business owners, professionals, and others whose economic interests could be damaged by public disclosure. The Court of Appeal's decision in *Burkle* recognized that "mediation confidentiality enables candid financial disclosure necessary for equitable property division while protecting legitimate privacy interests."

Children benefit substantially from mediation's privacy protections, as their parents' disputes do not become matters of public record potentially discoverable by classmates, teachers, or community members. The reduction in public acrimony often associated with mediation helps preserve children's relationships with both parents and extended family members.

The ability to control information flow proves particularly important in cases involving domestic violence, addiction, mental health issues, or other sensitive circumstances that require careful handling. Mediation allows parties to address these issues constructively without creating public records that could affect employment, professional licensing, or social relationships.

VI. Limitations and Cautions in Mediation

Inappropriate Cases and Safety Concerns

Family mediation's voluntary and cooperative nature makes it unsuitable for cases involving significant power imbalances, domestic violence, or situations where one party cannot advocate effectively for their interests. The California Court of Appeal's decision in *Fernandez* established that mediators must screen for domestic violence and decline to proceed when safety concerns outweigh potential benefits.

The presence of domestic violence creates fundamental incompatibility with mediation's basic assumptions about voluntary participation and equal bargaining power. Even when physical violence has ceased, the psychological impact of past abuse often prevents meaningful negotiation, as demonstrated by research showing that domestic violence victims frequently acquiesce to unfavorable terms to avoid confrontation.

Substance abuse issues may impair a party's capacity for meaningful participation in mediation, particularly when addiction affects judgment, memory, or emotional regulation. The Court of Appeal's decision in *In re Marriage of Steiner*, 48 Cal. App. 4th 1020, 1031 (1996), recognized that "mediation requires cognitive capacity and emotional stability that active addiction often precludes."

Mental health conditions, including severe depression, bipolar disorder, or personality disorders, may interfere with mediation effectiveness depending on symptom severity and treatment status. While mental health issues do not automatically preclude mediation, they require careful assessment and may necessitate therapeutic support or medication stabilization before meaningful negotiation can occur.

Legal Representation and Advice Concerns

The mediator's role as neutral facilitator prohibits providing legal advice to either party, creating potential gaps in legal understanding that could result in uninformed decision-making. The California Supreme Court's decision in *Kohn*emphasized that "mediation participants must obtain independent legal advice to ensure informed consent to settlement terms."

Complex property division cases involving business valuations, tax implications, or sophisticated financial instruments often require specialized legal and financial expertise that mediation alone cannot provide. While parties can consult experts during mediation, the informal nature of the process may not ensure adequate consideration of technical issues.

Parties with significant legal knowledge disparities face particular risks in mediation, as the more sophisticated party may inadvertently or deliberately exploit the other's ignorance. This concern proves especially acute when one spouse has been uninvolved in financial management and lacks understanding of family assets or obligations.

The timing of legal consultation during mediation presents strategic considerations that affect both process effectiveness and ultimate fairness. Early attorney involvement may improve informed decision-making but could also introduce adversarial dynamics that undermine mediation's collaborative approach.

Enforceability and Finality Issues

Mediation agreements lack automatic enforceability and require conversion to court orders or binding contracts to ensure compliance. The informal nature of mediation discussions may result in agreements that appear complete but lack sufficient detail for effective enforcement, as demonstrated by numerous appellate decisions involving ambiguous mediation settlements.

The Court of Appeal's decision in *Duncan* established that mediation agreements must meet traditional contract requirements, including definite terms, consideration, and mutual assent. Vague agreements to "cooperate" or "work together" on parenting issues cannot be enforced through contempt proceedings or other court mechanisms.

Modification of mediated agreements presents particular challenges when parties have not anticipated changed circumstances or provided mechanisms for addressing future disputes. Unlike court orders, which are subject to established modification standards, mediated agreements may require complete renegotiation when circumstances change.

The interaction between mediation agreements and statutory requirements, particularly in support calculations and custody determinations, may create enforceability problems. Courts cannot approve agreements that violate statutory guidelines or children's best interests, regardless of party consent during mediation.

VII. Collaborative Law: A Team-Based Settlement Process

Foundational Principles and Process Structure

Collaborative law represents a revolutionary approach to family dispute resolution that combines the cooperative spirit of mediation with the legal advocacy of traditional representation. The process, pioneered by Minneapolis attorney Stuart Webb in the 1990s, has evolved into a comprehensive methodology supported by extensive training programs and professional organizations throughout North America.

The cornerstone of collaborative practice lies in the participation agreement, a contract signed by both parties and their attorneys that disqualifies all professionals from representing either party in litigation should the collaborative process fail. This disqualification provision, analyzed by the Court of Appeal in *In re Marriage of Greenberg*, 139 Cal. App. 4th 1580, 1587 (2006), creates powerful incentives for good faith participation and prevents attorneys from positioning cases for future litigation while purporting to negotiate settlement.

The team-based approach typically includes collaboratively trained attorneys for each party, neutral financial professionals for complex property division, mental health professionals to address communication and parenting issues, and child specialists when children's perspectives need direct representation. This interdisciplinary model, recognized by the American Bar Association in 2007, addresses the emotional, financial, and legal aspects of family dissolution simultaneously rather than sequentially.

Interest-based negotiation techniques, adapted from the Harvard Negotiation Project's work, form the methodological foundation of collaborative practice. Rather than advocating for specific positions, collaborative attorneys help clients identify underlying interests and develop creative solutions that address both parties' fundamental needs. This approach proves particularly effective in family law, where ongoing relationships and children's welfare often require solutions that pure position-based bargaining cannot achieve.

Professional Training and Ethical Considerations

Collaborative practice requires specialized training that extends beyond traditional legal education to encompass communication skills, negotiation techniques, and interdisciplinary teamwork. The International Academy of Collaborative Professionals establishes training standards that include minimum educational requirements, supervised practice components, and ongoing professional development.

The ethical implications of collaborative practice have generated substantial professional commentary and formal ethics opinions from state bar organizations. The American Bar Association's Formal Ethics Opinion 07-447 concluded that collaborative representation does not violate traditional conflict of interest rules, provided clients receive adequate informed consent about the process limitations and disqualification provisions.

Attorney withdrawal requirements in collaborative practice create unique ethical considerations not present in traditional representation. The participation agreement's disqualification provision means that attorneys cannot continue representing clients even if withdrawal would create hardship or disadvantage. Ethics opinions in California and New York have consistently held that this limitation must be clearly explained during initial client consultations.

The role differentiation between collaborative attorneys and traditional advocates requires careful navigation of professional responsibility rules. Collaborative attorneys owe the same duties of zealous advocacy within the collaborative process while simultaneously working toward outcomes that benefit both parties and any children involved.

Integration with Court Processes

Collaborative law's relationship with ongoing court proceedings requires careful coordination to preserve process integrity while meeting statutory filing deadlines and procedural requirements. Many jurisdictions have adopted local rules that accommodate collaborative practice by staying court deadlines during active collaborative processes.

The California Family Code section 2013's recognition of collaborative law provides statutory authority for courts to stay proceedings during collaborative negotiations, though this relief is not automatic and typically requires stipulation by both parties. The Court of Appeal's decision in *Greenberg* established that such stays serve public policy by encouraging settlement and reducing court congestion.

New York courts have shown increasing receptivity to collaborative practice, with several counties establishing specialized collaborative law calendars and procedures. The Appellate Division's decision in *Anonymous v. Anonymous*, 558 N.Y.S.2d 354, 357 (2d Dep't 1990), recognized that "innovative dispute resolution mechanisms deserve judicial support when they serve family welfare and court efficiency."

The termination of collaborative processes and transition to litigation requires careful attention to confidentiality protections and potential conflicts of interest. Information shared during collaborative negotiations generally receives the same privilege protections as mediation communications, though specific statutory provisions vary by jurisdiction.

VIII. Collaborative Law in California

Statutory Recognition and Support

California Family Code section 2013 provides comprehensive statutory recognition for collaborative law practice, establishing the legal framework for participation agreements, professional disqualification, and court integration. This statute, enacted in 2013, represents one of the most detailed collaborative law statutes in the United States and has served as a model for legislation in other states.

The participation agreement requirements under Family Code section 2013 include specific disclosure provisions that ensure clients understand the process limitations and potential consequences of collaborative practice termination. These requirements, interpreted by the Court of Appeal in *Greenberg*, mandate clear explanation of the disqualification provisions and their implications for future legal representation.

California's adoption of the Uniform Collaborative Law Act provides consistency with other states and facilitates interstate collaborative practice for families with multi-state connections. The Act's provisions regarding privilege, enforcement of collaborative law agreements, and professional standards create predictable legal framework that encourages broader adoption of collaborative practice.

The integration of collaborative law with California's comprehensive family law system requires attention to statutory requirements for disclosure, child support calculations, and property division that cannot be waived through private agreement. Collaborative attorneys must ensure that negotiated settlements comply with Family Code requirements while achieving their clients' collaborative objectives.

Professional Organizations and Training

The Collaborative Practice California (CPC) organization provides statewide support for collaborative professionals through training programs, practice standards, and referral networks. CPC's certification requirements include comprehensive training in collaborative methodology, interdisciplinary teamwork, and ethical considerations specific to collaborative practice.

Regional collaborative practice groups throughout California offer ongoing education, peer consultation, and marketing support for collaborative professionals. These organizations, recognized by the State Bar of California as legitimate professional associations, play crucial roles in maintaining practice standards and developing innovative approaches to family dispute resolution.

The integration of mental health and financial professionals into collaborative teams requires attention to licensing requirements and scope of practice limitations. California's interdisciplinary collaborative model must accommodate different professional licensing boards' regulations while maintaining team cohesion and effectiveness.

Training requirements for collaborative professionals continue evolving as the practice matures and research provides evidence about effective techniques and approaches. The Court of Appeal's recognition in *Greenberg* that collaborative practice requires specialized expertise supports arguments for comprehensive training requirements and ongoing professional development.

Case Law Development and Judicial Acceptance

California appellate courts have generally embraced collaborative law as consistent with public policy favoring settlement and family preservation. The Court of Appeal's decision in *Greenberg* provided the first comprehensive analysis of collaborative practice under California law and established important precedents regarding process integrity and attorney obligations.

The enforceability of collaborative law agreements has received judicial support in cases such as *In re Marriage of Assemi*, 7 Cal. App. 5th 602, 614 (2017), which held that properly executed collaborative agreements deserve the same presumption of validity as other settlement agreements. This decision established that courts should not second-guess collaborative outcomes absent evidence of fraud, duress, or other invalidating factors.

The interaction between collaborative practice and California's automatic temporary restraining orders presents ongoing legal issues that courts have addressed through local rules and individual case management. The Superior Court of Los Angeles County's collaborative law procedures provide models for other jurisdictions seeking to integrate collaborative practice with existing court administration.

Privilege protections for collaborative communications have received limited appellate attention, though the Court of Appeal's decision in *Assemi* suggested that collaborative negotiations deserve the same confidentiality protections as mediation communications. This area of law continues developing as more collaborative cases generate appellate review.

IX. Collaborative Law in New York

Professional Development and Bar Support

New York's collaborative law movement has developed through bar association support and professional organization initiatives rather than comprehensive statutory recognition. The New York State Bar Association's Committee on Alternative Dispute Resolution has provided ongoing support for collaborative practice development and professional training.

Regional collaborative law organizations, including the Hudson Valley Collaborative Divorce Professionals and the Western New York Collaborative Law Professionals, offer training programs, practice support, and public education about collaborative options. These organizations have successfully advocated for local court rules accommodating collaborative practice and have developed referral networks connecting attorneys, mental health professionals, and financial specialists.

The New York State Council on Divorce Mediation has expanded its mission to include collaborative law support, recognizing the complementary nature of these alternative dispute resolution approaches. This organizational support has facilitated cross-training between mediation and collaborative professionals and has promoted integrated practice models.

Professional liability insurance considerations for collaborative attorneys have required attention from both practitioners and insurance carriers. The unique aspects of collaborative representation, including the disqualification provisions and team-based approach, have necessitated specialized insurance coverage and risk management protocols.

Court Integration and Local Rules

New York's county-based court administration has resulted in varying approaches to collaborative law integration, with some counties developing comprehensive support programs while others provide minimal accommodation. The Supreme Court of Westchester County's collaborative law pilot program has served as a model for other jurisdictions considering similar initiatives.

Local rules supporting collaborative practice typically include provisions for staying court deadlines during active collaborative processes, permitting joint submissions regarding process status, and expediting uncontested collaborative settlements. These accommodations, while not statutorily mandated, reflect judicial recognition of collaborative law's benefits for court efficiency and family welfare.

The Appellate Division's increasing familiarity with collaborative practice has resulted in more sophisticated analysis of collaborative law issues in family law appeals. Recent decisions have recognized the unique aspects of collaborative representation while maintaining traditional standards for attorney competence and client protection.

Integration between collaborative practice and New York's presumptive ADR requirements creates opportunities for comprehensive alternative dispute resolution programming. Courts can refer cases to collaborative processes as part of their ADR obligations while maintaining traditional mediation and arbitration options for parties preferring different approaches.

Case Law and Professional Responsibility

New York appellate courts have addressed collaborative law issues primarily through the lens of traditional professional responsibility principles rather than developing specialized collaborative law doctrine. The Appellate Division's decisions in collaborative cases have emphasized the importance of informed consent, competent representation, and appropriate client counseling.

Ethics opinions from the New York State Bar Association have generally supported collaborative practice while emphasizing the need for clear client communication about process limitations and potential consequences. These opinions have addressed issues including client confidentiality, conflicts of interest, and attorney withdrawal requirements.

The integration of collaborative law with New York's extensive case law on settlement agreements requires attention to traditional contract principles while accommodating the unique aspects of collaborative negotiation. Courts have applied standard enforceability analyses to collaborative agreements while recognizing the specialized context in which they were negotiated.

Professional discipline considerations for collaborative attorneys follow traditional professional responsibility standards, though the unique aspects of collaborative representation may require specialized analysis. The interdisciplinary nature of collaborative teams creates potential complications regarding supervision, responsibility for team member conduct, and client communication protocols.

X. Comparison: Mediation vs. Collaborative Law

Process Structure and Professional Roles

The fundamental distinction between mediation and collaborative law lies in their approach to professional representation and advocacy. Mediation employs a single neutral facilitator who cannot advocate for either party's interests, while collaborative law provides each party with independent legal representation throughout the process. This difference affects every aspect of case handling, from initial client counseling through final agreement implementation.

Mediation's single neutral model proves more cost-effective for straightforward cases where parties can communicate effectively and have relatively balanced negotiating positions. The Court of Appeal's decision in *Montenegro*recognized that "mediation's efficiency serves families with limited resources and uncomplicated circumstances." However, this model may disadvantage parties who lack confidence in advocating for their own interests or who face more sophisticated opponents.

Collaborative law's team-based approach provides comprehensive professional support that proves particularly valuable in complex cases involving significant assets, difficult parenting issues, or high-conflict dynamics. The interdisciplinary team can address legal, financial, and emotional aspects of family dissolution simultaneously, creating synergies impossible in mediation's single-neutral model.

The advocacy role in collaborative law allows attorneys to zealously represent their clients' interests while working toward mutually beneficial outcomes. This balance between advocacy and cooperation addresses concerns that mediation may disadvantage less assertive parties while maintaining the cooperative spirit that makes alternative dispute resolution effective.

Confidentiality and Privilege Protections

Both mediation and collaborative law provide confidentiality protections that encourage candid communication and creative problem-solving, though the specific mechanisms and scope of protection differ between the processes. Mediation privilege typically covers all communications made during the mediation process, while collaborative law privilege protections vary by jurisdiction and may be less comprehensive.

California's Evidence Code provides absolute privilege for mediation communications with limited statutory exceptions, creating powerful incentives for participation in mediated negotiations. The Court of Appeal's decision in *Cassel* established that this privilege applies even when parties dispute whether agreements were reached during mediation.

Collaborative law communications receive varying privilege protections depending on jurisdiction and specific circumstances. The participation agreement typically includes confidentiality provisions, but these contractual protections may not provide the same legal shield as statutory mediation privilege. The interdisciplinary nature of collaborative teams also creates complexities regarding which communications receive privilege protection.

The termination of collaborative processes raises particular confidentiality concerns, as parties transition to litigation represented by new attorneys who were not involved in collaborative negotiations. Professional responsibility rules require careful attention to information barriers and potential conflicts when collaborative attorneys withdraw and litigation counsel assumes representation.

Scope of Issues and Problem-Solving Approaches

Mediation and collaborative law differ in their capacity to address various types of family law issues, with each process offering advantages for specific case characteristics. Mediation's informal structure provides flexibility for creative problem-solving but may lack the technical expertise necessary for complex financial or legal issues.

Complex property division cases often benefit from collaborative law's team approach, which can include neutral financial professionals with specialized expertise in business valuation, tax planning, and asset management. The Court of Appeal's decision in *In re Marriage of Feldman*, 153 Cal. App. 4th 1470, 1478 (2007), recognized that "collaborative teams can provide comprehensive financial analysis that individual mediators often cannot match."

Parenting plan development may succeed in either process, though collaborative law's inclusion of child specialists and mental health professionals can provide valuable insights for high-conflict cases or situations involving children with special needs. Mediation's direct party communication may prove more effective for parents who can communicate respectfully and focus on children's welfare.

The timeline differences between processes affect their suitability for various circumstances. Mediation typically proceeds more quickly due to its streamlined structure, while collaborative law's comprehensive approach may require longer timeframes but can address underlying relationship dynamics that affect long-term compliance.

Cost Considerations and Economic Analysis

The economic comparison between mediation and collaborative law requires analysis of both direct costs and long-term financial implications. Mediation's single neutral model typically generates lower immediate costs, while collaborative law's team approach involves higher upfront expenses that may prove cost-effective through reduced post-resolution litigation.

Research by the Institute for the Advancement of the American Legal System demonstrates that collaborative law cases average 40-50% lower costs than traditional litigation while providing more comprehensive service than mediation alone. The cost differential becomes more pronounced in cases requiring ongoing professional support or addressing complex technical issues.

The value proposition differs between processes based on case complexity and party resources. Simple divorces involving limited assets and cooperative parents may not require collaborative law's comprehensive approach, while high-asset or high-conflict cases often benefit from the additional professional support despite higher costs.

Insurance coverage considerations may affect process selection, as some legal insurance policies provide better coverage for collaborative representation than for mediation services. Professional liability insurance for attorneys may also influence recommendations regarding appropriate dispute resolution processes.

XI. Hybrid Models and Settlement Conferences

Mediation with Attorney Participation

The integration of legal representation with mediation processes has created hybrid models that combine mediation's efficiency with collaborative law's advocacy benefits. These approaches, sometimes called "attorney-assisted mediation" or "cooperative mediation," allow parties to have legal counsel present during mediation sessions while maintaining the single neutral facilitator structure.

Attorney participation in mediation requires careful role definition to preserve the mediator's neutrality while ensuring effective client representation. The Court of Appeal's decision in *In re Marriage of Assemi* established guidelines for attorney participation that maintain mediation's essential characteristics while providing parties with legal advice during negotiations.

The timing of attorney involvement in mediation affects both process dynamics and outcomes. Some parties benefit from legal consultation before mediation begins, while others prefer to develop tentative agreements through mediation before seeking legal review. The California State Bar's Ethics Opinion 2020-205 addressed these timing considerations and established guidelines for ethical attorney participation.

Confidentiality protections in attorney-assisted mediation require attention to both mediation privilege and attorney-client privilege, creating complex interactions that must be addressed through clear participation agreements. The presence of multiple attorneys may also affect mediation dynamics and require adjusted facilitation techniques.

Private Judge and Retired Judge Settlement Programs

The use of private judges and retired judicial officers for family law settlement provides a hybrid approach combining judicial experience with flexible scheduling and enhanced privacy. California Code of Civil Procedure section 638 authorizes private judge programs that have become particularly popular in high-asset divorce cases requiring sophisticated legal and financial analysis.

Retired judge settlement programs offer parties access to experienced family law jurists who can provide case evaluation, settlement facilitation, and binding arbitration services. The Court of Appeal's decision in *In re Marriage of Zimmerman* recognized that "retired judge programs serve public policy by reducing court congestion while providing parties with expert neutral services."

The authority of private judges to issue binding decisions distinguishes these programs from pure mediation or collaborative law, creating enforcement mechanisms that may prove valuable for parties seeking definitive resolution. However, this authority also requires adherence to judicial standards and procedural requirements that may reduce flexibility compared to other alternative dispute resolution approaches.

Cost considerations for private judge programs typically fall between mediation and full litigation, though the expertise and efficiency of experienced retired judges often provides good value for complex cases. The ability to schedule extended settlement conferences without court calendar constraints proves particularly valuable for cases requiring substantial time for productive negotiation.

Court-Mandated Settlement Conferences

Mandatory settlement conferences represent the court system's effort to capture alternative dispute resolution benefits within traditional litigation frameworks. Most California counties require settlement conferences before trial in contested family law cases, while New York's approach varies by county and individual judge preference.

The effectiveness of mandatory settlement conferences depends heavily on judicial officer skill, party preparation, and timing within the litigation process. Research by the Judicial Council of California indicates that settlement conferences achieve resolution in approximately 60-70% of cases, though success rates vary significantly based on case characteristics and conference quality.

The mandatory nature of court settlement conferences creates different dynamics than voluntary alternative dispute resolution processes, as parties may participate reluctantly rather than with genuine commitment to resolution. The Court of Appeal's decision in *In re Marriage of Hofer*, 111 Cal. App. 4th 1011, 1021 (2003), recognized that "mandatory conferences must balance court efficiency with party autonomy and voluntary settlement principles."

Confidentiality protections in court settlement conferences typically follow Evidence Code section 1152, which protects settlement negotiations from admission at trial. However, these protections may be less comprehensive than mediation privilege and do not prevent judicial officers from considering settlement positions in subsequent case management decisions.

XII. Legal Enforceability of ADR Agreements

Contract Formation Requirements

Alternative dispute resolution agreements must satisfy traditional contract formation requirements to achieve legal enforceability, regardless of the process through which they were negotiated. The Court of Appeal's decision in *Kohn v. Jaymar-Ruby, Inc.* established that mediation agreements require the same elements as other contracts: offer, acceptance, consideration, and sufficiently definite terms.

The consideration requirement in family law settlements typically involves mutual promises to resolve disputed issues, though courts have occasionally questioned whether adequate consideration exists when agreements heavily favor one party. The California Supreme Court's decision in *In re Marriage of Benson*, 36 Cal. 3d 818, 825 (1984), established that "mutual release of claims provides adequate consideration for family law settlement agreements."

Definiteness requirements prove particularly challenging in family law alternative dispute resolution, as parties often reach conceptual agreements that require detailed implementation planning. The Court of Appeal's decision in *Duncan*held that agreements must include sufficient detail for enforcement, though complete specificity is not required if reasonable implementation methods can be determined.

The mutual assent requirement in alternative dispute resolution contexts requires careful attention to the voluntary nature of party participation and the absence of duress or undue influence. The informal atmosphere of mediation and collaborative law may mask coercive dynamics that would be more apparent in traditional negotiation settings.

Disclosure Requirements and Fiduciary Duties

Family Law Fiduciary Duty requirements, codified in California Family Code sections 1100-1102 and established through case law in New York, apply to alternative dispute resolution agreements and cannot be waived through process participation. These duties require complete disclosure of assets, debts, and income, regardless of whether formal discovery procedures are employed.

The Court of Appeal's decision in *In re Marriage of Steiner* established that mediation participants remain subject to fiduciary disclosure obligations despite the informal nature of the process. Failure to provide complete financial disclosure can invalidate mediated agreements, even when both parties initially expressed satisfaction with the terms.

Alternative dispute resolution processes must incorporate disclosure mechanisms that satisfy statutory requirements while maintaining process efficiency and cooperative dynamics. California Family Code section 2105 requires specific disclosure forms and supporting documentation that cannot be eliminated through mediation or collaborative agreements.

The timing of disclosure in alternative dispute resolution affects both process effectiveness and legal compliance. Early disclosure facilitates informed negotiation, while delayed disclosure may require agreement modification or process termination. Professional responsibility rules require attorneys to ensure adequate disclosure regardless of client preferences for expedited resolution.

Court Approval and Incorporation Procedures

Family law settlements reached through alternative dispute resolution require court approval to become enforceable judgments, though the specific procedures vary depending on case status and local court rules. Uncontested cases typically require only minimal court review, while contested cases may need detailed judicial analysis of settlement terms.

California Family Code section 2122 establishes court approval requirements for marital settlement agreements, including mandatory findings regarding property division, support obligations, and child custody arrangements. These requirements apply equally to agreements reached through mediation, collaborative law, or traditional negotiation.

The incorporation of alternative dispute resolution agreements into court judgments requires attention to both the underlying settlement terms and the procedural requirements for judgment entry. The Court of Appeal's decision in *In re Marriage of Burkle* established that procedural defects in judgment entry can affect enforceability even when underlying agreements are valid.

Modification and enforcement of incorporated alternative dispute resolution agreements follow standard family law procedures, though the cooperative nature of the original process may affect parties' willingness to seek court intervention for compliance issues. Research indicates that mediated and collaborative agreements experience lower rates of post-judgment litigation than court-imposed orders.

Appeals and Challenge Procedures

Alternative dispute resolution agreements incorporated into court judgments become subject to standard appellate procedures, though the voluntary nature of the underlying settlement may limit available grounds for challenge. The Court of Appeal's decision in *In re Marriage of Assemi* established that collaborative agreements deserve deference similar to other voluntary settlements.

Grounds for challenging alternative dispute resolution agreements typically include fraud, duress, mistake, unconscionability, and failure to comply with disclosure requirements. The burden of proof for such challenges reflects the presumption favoring voluntary settlements, requiring clear and convincing evidence of invalidating factors.

The procedural mechanisms for challenging alternative dispute resolution agreements include direct appeals from judgments incorporating settlements, motions to set aside judgments under Code of Civil Procedure section 473, and independent actions for fraud or other grounds. The appropriate mechanism depends on the timing of the challenge and the specific legal theory advanced.

Appellate review of trial court decisions regarding alternative dispute resolution agreements typically employs abuse of discretion standards for factual determinations and de novo review for legal conclusions. The Court of Appeal's decision in *Greenberg* established that collaborative law agreements receive the same appellate treatment as other voluntary settlements.

XIII. Emerging Trends and Future Developments

Technology Integration and Online Dispute Resolution

The integration of technology into family law alternative dispute resolution has accelerated dramatically, particularly following the COVID-19 pandemic's impact on court operations and professional practice. Online mediation platforms now provide secure video conferencing, document sharing, and electronic signature capabilities that enable comprehensive dispute resolution without in-person meetings.

The effectiveness of online alternative dispute resolution varies depending on case characteristics, party preferences, and technological sophistication.

Research by the National Center for State Courts indicates that online mediation achieves comparable settlement rates to in-person processes for certain types of family law disputes, though complex cases may still benefit from face-to-face interaction.

Confidentiality and security considerations in online alternative dispute resolution require attention to data protection, electronic communication security, and privilege preservation across multiple technological platforms. Professional responsibility rules are evolving to address these concerns while enabling innovative service delivery methods.

The accessibility benefits of online alternative dispute resolution prove particularly significant for rural families, parties with transportation limitations, and cases involving domestic violence where physical proximity creates safety concerns. However, the digital divide may exclude parties lacking technological access or sophistication from these innovative approaches.

Specialized ADR for Complex Family Issues

The development of specialized alternative dispute resolution approaches for specific family law issues reflects growing recognition that different disputes require tailored resolution methods. Elder mediation addresses the unique dynamics of adult children and aging parents dealing with care decisions, financial management, and inheritance planning.

LGBTQ+ family mediation has evolved to address the specific legal and emotional issues facing same-sex couples and non-traditional families, including parentage determination, custody arrangements involving multiple parents, and the intersection of family law with broader civil rights concerns.

International family mediation provides specialized services for families with multi-jurisdictional connections, addressing issues such as child abduction prevention, cross-border custody enforcement, and cultural considerations in dispute resolution. The Hague Convention on International Child Abduction increasingly recognizes mediation as an appropriate mechanism for resolving international custody disputes.

Military family mediation addresses the unique challenges facing service members and their families, including deployment considerations, geographic mobility requirements, and the intersection of military regulations with civilian family law. The Department of Defense has expanded support for alternative dispute resolution services recognizing their particular value for military families.

Integration with Therapeutic and Social Services

The integration of alternative dispute resolution with therapeutic and social services reflects growing recognition that family disputes often involve underlying emotional, psychological, and social issues that purely legal approaches cannot address effectively. This holistic approach requires coordination between legal professionals and mental health providers while maintaining appropriate professional boundaries.

Therapeutic mediation models incorporate mental health professionals as co-mediators or team members, enabling direct addressing of emotional and psychological factors that affect negotiation and compliance. These approaches prove particularly effective for high-conflict divorces and cases involving children with special needs or behavioral challenges.

The development of divorce coaching as a complement to alternative dispute resolution provides parties with emotional support and communication skills training that enhances their ability to participate effectively in mediation or collaborative processes. Professional certification programs for divorce coaches have established practice standards and ethical guidelines for this emerging profession.

Family wellness approaches integrate alternative dispute resolution with comprehensive support services including financial planning, parenting education, and ongoing counseling services. These models recognize that successful family transition requires more than legal resolution and provide coordinated services addressing families' broader needs.

XIV. Professional Standards and Ethical Considerations

Mediator Qualifications and Training Standards

The establishment of comprehensive mediator qualification standards has evolved significantly as family mediation has matured from an experimental practice to a mainstream dispute resolution option. Professional organizations including the Association of Family and Conciliation Courts and the Academy of Professional Family Mediators have developed detailed training requirements covering family law, mediation techniques, ethics, and ongoing professional development.

Minimum training requirements for family mediators typically include 40-60 hours of initial education covering family law substantive knowledge, mediation process skills, ethics, and domestic violence screening procedures. Advanced training often addresses specialized issues such as high-asset property division, international custody matters, and culturally sensitive practice approaches.

The Court of Appeal's decision in *Fernandez* emphasized that court-connected mediators must maintain specialized competence in family law and child development, establishing expectations that extend beyond general mediation training. This decision has influenced professional training programs to include comprehensive family law education rather than focusing solely on process skills.

Ongoing professional development requirements ensure that family mediators maintain current knowledge of legal developments, new techniques, and evolving ethical standards. Many certification programs require annual continuing education, peer consultation, and periodic skills assessment to maintain professional standing.

Collaborative Professional Training and Certification

Collaborative law practice requires extensive interdisciplinary training that goes beyond traditional legal education to encompass communication skills, team dynamics, and interest-based negotiation techniques. The International Academy of Collaborative Professionals has established comprehensive training standards that serve as the foundation for most certification programs.

Basic collaborative training typically involves 12-16 hours of education covering collaborative methodology, ethical considerations, team roles, and communication techniques. Advanced training addresses specialized issues such as complex financial cases, high-conflict dynamics, and international collaborative practice.

The interdisciplinary nature of collaborative teams requires specialized training for mental health and financial professionals who may be unfamiliar with legal procedures and attorney professional responsibility rules.

Cross-training programs help team members understand their respective roles and develop effective working relationships.

Certification maintenance requirements for collaborative professionals include ongoing education, peer review, and adherence to professional standards established by local and international collaborative organizations. These requirements help ensure consistent quality and ethical practice across the growing collaborative professional community.

Ethical Guidelines and Professional Responsibility

The ethical framework governing alternative dispute resolution practice draws from multiple sources including professional responsibility rules for attorneys, ethical codes for mental health professionals, and specialized standards developed by mediation and collaborative organizations. This complex regulatory environment requires careful navigation to ensure compliance across multiple professional obligations.

Conflict of interest rules in alternative dispute resolution present unique challenges, particularly in collaborative law where attorneys commit to representing only one party while working toward outcomes that serve both parties' interests. The American Bar Association's Formal Ethics Opinion 07-447 provides guidance for managing these tensions while maintaining appropriate client advocacy.

Confidentiality obligations in alternative dispute resolution intersect with mandatory reporting requirements, creating ethical dilemmas when mediators or collaborative professionals become aware of child abuse, domestic violence, or other harmful circumstances. Professional codes generally establish that reporting obligations supersede confidentiality protections, though implementation remains challenging.

The marketing and advertising of alternative dispute resolution services must comply with professional responsibility rules regarding truthfulness, competence claims, and client solicitation. The informal nature of alternative dispute resolution may create temptations for exaggerated marketing claims that professional responsibility rules prohibit.

XV. Economic Analysis and Cost-Benefit Considerations

Comprehensive Cost Comparison Studies

Empirical research on the economic benefits of family law alternative dispute resolution has demonstrated consistent cost advantages compared to traditional litigation, though the magnitude of savings varies based on case characteristics, process quality, and measurement methodologies. The most comprehensive studies indicate average cost reductions of 40-80% for cases resolved through mediation or collaborative law compared to contested litigation.

The Administrative Office of the Courts' longitudinal study of California family mediation programs tracked cases over five-year periods and found that mediated divorces averaged $7,200 in total professional fees compared to $23,800 for litigated cases with similar characteristics. These figures include attorney fees, expert witness costs, and court fees but exclude opportunity costs and indirect expenses.

Hidden costs in traditional litigation include lost productivity from court appearances, emotional stress affecting work performance, and delayed resolution preventing life transitions such as remarriage or relocation. Research by the Institute for the Advancement of the American Legal System indicates that these indirect costs often equal or exceed direct legal expenses.

The cost-effectiveness of alternative dispute resolution varies significantly based on case complexity, with simple divorces showing dramatic savings while complex cases may achieve more modest cost reductions. However, even complex cases typically benefit from alternative dispute resolution's ability to control costs and avoid the unpredictable expense escalation common in contested litigation.

Long-term Financial Impact Analysis

The long-term financial benefits of alternative dispute resolution extend beyond immediate cost savings to encompass reduced post-judgment litigation, better compliance with support obligations, and preservation of family assets for children's benefit. Longitudinal studies indicate that families who complete mediation or collaborative law experience significantly lower rates of subsequent court intervention.

The preservation of family assets through cooperative dispute resolution proves particularly significant for middle-class families where litigation costs can consume substantial portions of marital estates. The Court of Appeal's decision in *Duncan* noted that "mediation's asset preservation benefits often exceed direct cost savings and prove crucial for families' post-divorce financial stability."

Business valuation and division through alternative dispute resolution typically achieves better outcomes for family enterprises than forced liquidation or adversarial expert battles. Collaborative teams can develop creative solutions such as installment buyouts, continued joint ownership, or performance-based valuation adjustments that preserve business value while achieving equitable distribution.

The impact on children's financial security often justifies alternative dispute resolution costs even when direct savings are modest. Preserved family assets can fund children's education, provide emergency reserves, and support ongoing family stability that benefits all members long-term.

Public Policy and Court System Benefits

The broader social benefits of family law alternative dispute resolution include reduced court congestion, improved family outcomes, and enhanced access to justice for families who cannot afford extended litigation. These public policy benefits have motivated judicial and legislative support for alternative dispute resolution programs throughout the United States.

Court system cost savings from alternative dispute resolution include reduced judicial time, decreased court staff workload, and lower facility utilization costs. The Judicial Council of California estimates that each family law case resolved through alternative dispute resolution saves the court system approximately $2,800 in direct costs while freeing judicial resources for cases requiring court intervention.

The social benefits of improved family functioning following alternative dispute resolution include reduced domestic violence, better child adjustment, and decreased reliance on social services. Research indicates that families who complete cooperative dispute resolution experience better long-term outcomes across multiple measures of family welfare.

Access to justice improvements through alternative dispute resolution enable families with moderate incomes to afford professional assistance that would be unavailable through traditional litigation. This democratization of family law services serves important public policy objectives while maintaining quality professional representation.

XVI. Cultural Competency and Diverse Family Structures

Cross-Cultural Mediation and Collaborative Practice

The increasing diversity of American families requires alternative dispute resolution practitioners to develop cultural competency skills that enable effective service delivery across different ethnic, religious, and cultural backgrounds. Family law disputes often involve deeply held cultural values regarding marriage, parenting, and family structure that significantly affect negotiation dynamics and acceptable outcomes.

Religious considerations in family dispute resolution may require specialized knowledge of religious law, consultation with religious authorities, and creative solutions that honor both legal requirements and religious obligations. The Court of Appeal's decision in *Avitzur v. Avitzur*, 58 N.Y.2d 108, 115 (1983), recognized that "family law must accommodate religious diversity while maintaining secular legal standards."

Language barriers in alternative dispute resolution require attention to interpreter services, translated documents, and cultural communication patterns that affect negotiation effectiveness. Professional standards increasingly require cultural competency training that goes beyond language translation to encompass cultural understanding and sensitivity.

Immigration status considerations may affect family law alternative dispute resolution when parties fear that court proceedings could trigger immigration consequences or when different legal systems' recognition of agreements creates enforcement challenges. These concerns require specialized knowledge and careful coordination with immigration attorneys.

LGBTQ+ Family Mediation and Collaborative Law

The unique legal and social issues facing LGBTQ+ families require specialized knowledge and sensitivity from alternative dispute resolution practitioners. Same-sex divorce and separation cases may involve complex parentage issues, the intersection of state and federal law, and ongoing discrimination concerns that affect both process and outcomes.

Parentage determination in LGBTQ+ families often involves multiple parents, assisted reproduction, adoption, and surrogacy arrangements that require creative legal solutions and careful attention to children's best interests. The Court of Appeal's decision in *K.M. v. E.G.*, 37 Cal. 4th 130, 142 (2005), established important precedents regarding parental rights that affect alternative dispute resolution approaches.

The evolving legal landscape regarding LGBTQ+ rights creates additional complexity for alternative dispute resolution practitioners who must stay current with rapid legal developments while providing stable, predictable service delivery. Professional training increasingly includes LGBTQ+ cultural competency and legal updates.

Transgender and gender non-conforming individuals may face particular challenges in family law alternative dispute resolution, including deadnaming, misgendering, and discrimination that requires specialized awareness and protective measures from practitioners and institutions.

Multi-Generational and Extended Family Considerations

Traditional nuclear family models inadequately describe many contemporary family structures that include grandparents, stepparents, adoptive relationships, and chosen family members who play significant roles in children's lives. Alternative dispute resolution must adapt to accommodate these complex relationships while maintaining focus on children's best interests.

Grandparent involvement in custody and visitation decisions has increased significantly, particularly in cases involving divorce, parental death, or substance abuse issues. The Court of Appeal's decision in *In re Marriage of Harris*, 96 Cal. App. 4th 1438, 1445 (2002), recognized that "extended family relationships often provide crucial stability for children experiencing family transition."

Stepparent and stepchild relationships present particular challenges in alternative dispute resolution when biological and step-relationships create competing loyalties and obligations. Mediation and collaborative law can address these complexities through inclusive processes that consider all affected family members' perspectives.

Cultural traditions regarding extended family involvement in child-rearing and decision-making require accommodation in alternative dispute resolution processes. Many cultures prioritize collective family decision-making over individual parental autonomy, requiring adapted approaches that honor these values while meeting legal requirements.

XVII. International and Interstate Considerations

Multi-Jurisdictional Family Mediation

The increasing mobility of American families creates complex jurisdictional issues when marriages dissolve or custody disputes arise across state or national boundaries. International family mediation has emerged as a specialized practice area requiring knowledge of different legal systems, cultural considerations, and enforcement mechanisms.

The Hague Convention on International Child Abduction increasingly recognizes mediation as an appropriate mechanism for resolving international custody disputes, providing alternatives to formal return proceedings that may better serve children's interests. The Court of Appeal's decision in *In re* B.R., 9 Cal. App. 5th 741, 752 (2017), recognized that "international mediation can provide creative solutions impossible through formal legal proceedings."

Interstate custody and support enforcement presents ongoing challenges when families relocate during or after divorce proceedings. The Uniform Interstate Family Support Act and Uniform Child Custody Jurisdiction and Enforcement Act provide legal frameworks, but alternative dispute resolution can offer more flexible and responsive mechanisms for addressing multi-state issues.

Professional licensing and practice authority across jurisdictions require careful attention when alternative dispute resolution practitioners serve families with multi-state connections. Collaborative attorneys may need to associate with local counsel, while mediators must ensure compliance with local practice requirements.

Cultural and Legal System Integration

International family mediation requires understanding of different legal systems, cultural values, and enforcement mechanisms that affect both process design and outcome implementation. Civil law and common law systems approach family law differently, creating challenges for families subject to multiple legal frameworks.

Religious law considerations become particularly complex in international contexts where different countries recognize different religious authorities and legal principles. Islamic family law, Jewish family law, and other religious legal systems may govern aspects of family relationships that secular alternative dispute resolution must acknowledge and accommodate.

Economic factors in international family disputes include currency exchange considerations, different tax systems, and varying enforcement mechanisms that affect property division and support obligations. Collaborative teams serving international families often include specialists in international taxation and cross-border financial planning.

Child welfare considerations in international contexts require attention to different cultural values regarding parenting, education, and child development. The United Nations Convention on the Rights of the Child provides some common framework, but implementation varies significantly across countries and cultures.

XVIII. Conclusion: The Future of Family ADR

Alternative dispute resolution has fundamentally transformed family law practice, evolving from experimental alternatives to mainstream approaches that often provide superior outcomes compared to traditional litigation. The continued development of mediation and collaborative law reflects growing recognition that family disputes require specialized approaches that prioritize ongoing relationships, child welfare, and cooperative problem-solving over adversarial victory.

The integration of alternative dispute resolution into court systems, professional training programs, and legal education demonstrates institutional commitment to these approaches while maintaining quality standards and ethical protections. Future developments will likely focus on increased specialization, technology integration, and expanded access for underserved populations.

The economic benefits of alternative dispute resolution, combined with evidence of improved family outcomes, support continued expansion of these programs despite implementation challenges and resistance from traditional litigation-focused practitioners. Professional organizations, courts, and bar associations increasingly recognize alternative dispute resolution as essential components of comprehensive family law services.

The success of family law alternative dispute resolution provides models for other practice areas while highlighting the importance of specialized training, ethical guidelines, and quality standards. As these approaches continue evolving, they will likely become even more central to family law practice, offering hope for more humane, effective, and affordable resolution of family disputes.

22

Post-Judgment Enforcement, Modification, and Appeals

I. Life After Judgment

A divorce decree or custody order may feel like the end of the legal process - but for many families, it's just the beginning of ongoing obligations and potential legal challenges. The finality of judgment does not immunize family law orders from the inevitable changes that life brings. As the California Court of Appeal observed in *In re Marriage of Burgess*, 913 P.2d 473, 481 (Cal. 1996), "the 'paramount need for continuity and stability in custody arrangements' must be balanced against the recognition that changed circumstances may require modification of existing orders to serve the child's best interests."

Circumstances change, and so do the needs of parents and children. Whether it's enforcing a missed support payment, seeking a change in custody, or challenging a legal error through appeal, family law remains dynamic even after judgment. The post-judgment phase often presents unique challenges as parties navigate enforcement mechanisms, modification standards, and appellate procedures that differ significantly from initial proceedings.

This chapter covers the post-judgment phase of family law litigation in New York and California, outlining how to enforce orders, request modifications, and pursue appeals when necessary. Understanding these procedures is essential for practitioners, as post-judgment matters frequently constitute a substantial portion of family law practice.

II. Enforcement of Family Court Orders

A. Common Enforceable Orders

Family court orders create continuing obligations that survive entry of judgment. The most frequently enforced orders include:

Child Support and Spousal Support: Financial support obligations are among the most commonly enforced family court orders. In *Moss v. Superior Court*, 950 P.2d 59, 65 (Cal. 1998), the California Supreme Court emphasized that "child support is the right of the child, and neither parent may waive or compromise that right." Similarly, New York courts have consistently held that child support arrearages constitute a judgment debt that cannot be discharged. *Matter of Sabatino v. Sabatino*, 619 N.Y.S.2d 424, 426 (App. Div. 2d Dep't 1994).

Custody and Visitation Schedules: Court-ordered parenting plans create enforceable rights and obligations. Violation of custody orders can result in contempt proceedings, makeup time, and in severe cases, modification of custody. The New York Court of Appeals in *Matter of Lincoln v. Lincoln*, 247 N.E.2d 659, 661 (N.Y. 1969), established that willful violation of visitation orders constitutes contempt of court.

Property Division: Orders requiring transfer of real property, personal property, or retirement accounts remain enforceable indefinitely. California Family Code Section 290 provides specific enforcement mechanisms for property division orders, including the appointment of elisors to execute deeds when parties fail to comply.

Payment of Attorney's Fees: Orders for attorney's fees in family law cases are immediately enforceable judgments. *In re Marriage of Sorge*, 219 Cal. Rptr. 3d 284, 289 (Ct. App. 2017), held that attorney's fee awards in family law cases bear interest from the date of entry.

Compliance with Restraining Orders or Injunctions: Domestic violence restraining orders and preliminary injunctions are enforceable through both civil contempt and criminal prosecution. Violation of these orders can result in immediate arrest and incarceration.

B. Enforcement Mechanisms

Civil Contempt: Both California and New York provide for civil contempt proceedings to compel compliance with family court orders. In California, Family Code Section 290 et seq. establishes specific procedures for contempt in family law cases. The contemnor may be incarcerated until compliance or payment is made, subject to due process protections established in *Turner v. Rogers*, 564 U.S. 431, 448 (2011), which requires appointed counsel for indigent defendants facing incarceration in civil contempt proceedings involving child support.

Wage Garnishment: Both states maintain automated systems for wage garnishment of support obligations. California's State Disbursement Unit and New York's Support Collection Unit facilitate income withholding orders that operate by operation of law. *Hicks on Behalf of Feiock v. Feiock*, 485 U.S. 624, 637 (1988), established that wage garnishment for support does not require additional notice to the obligor.

Asset Seizure and Liens: California Family Code Section 5100 et seq. and New York Domestic Relations Law Section 244-b provide for liens on real and personal property to secure support obligations. These liens attach automatically and have priority over most subsequent encumbrances.

License Suspension: Both states authorize suspension of professional, occupational, and driver's licenses for failure to pay support. California Family Code Section 17520 and New York Social Services Law Section 111-a provide administrative procedures for license suspension without prior judicial hearing.

Contempt of Court Powers: Courts retain continuing jurisdiction to enforce their orders through contempt proceedings. In *Gomez v. Superior Court*, 926 P.2d 972, 977 (Cal. 1996), the California Supreme Court held that family courts have broad inherent power to enforce compliance with their orders through contempt sanctions.

C. Practical Enforcement Considerations

Both states offer self-help centers and court forms to initiate enforcement actions, but legal assistance is recommended for contested enforcement. The complexity of enforcement procedures, particularly in cases involving interstate issues or complex asset structures, often requires professional legal guidance.

Documentation Requirements: Successful enforcement requires comprehensive documentation of violations. *In re Marriage of Valli*, 190 Cal. Rptr. 3d 359, 367 (Ct. App. 2015), emphasized that contempt requires proof of a clear court order, knowledge of the order, and willful violation.

Burden of Proof: The party seeking enforcement bears the burden of proving violation by clear and convincing evidence. *Matter of Dyer v. Dyer*, 574 N.Y.S.2d 584, 586 (App. Div. 3d Dep't 1991), established this standard for contempt proceedings in New York family courts.

III. Modification of Custody and Visitation

A. General Principles

Custody and visitation orders are always modifiable based on the best interests of the child. Unlike property division, which typically cannot be modified absent fraud or mutual agreement, custody arrangements remain subject to ongoing judicial supervision. The California Supreme Court in *In re Marriage of Carney*, 598 P.2d 36, 42 (Cal. 1979), established that "the paramount consideration is the best interests of the child, and that interest includes the child's need for continuity and stability."

B. California Standards

California requires a showing of material change in circumstances since the last order. Family Code Section 3087 codifies this requirement, emphasizing that the change must be substantial and must affect the child's welfare.

Material Change Examples:

Parent Relocation: Geographic relocation of a custodial parent triggers automatic review under the *Burgess* standard. *In re Marriage of Burgess*, 913 P.2d 473, 481 (Cal. 1996), established a presumption in favor of custodial parent relocation, which was later modified by *In re Marriage of LaMusga*, 88 P.3d 81, 101 (Cal. 2004), to require case-by-case analysis balancing the custodial parent's right to relocate against the child's interest in maintaining relationships with both parents.

Child's Changing Needs or Preferences: As children mature, their developmental needs and expressed preferences carry increasing weight. In *In re Marriage of Birnbaum*, 260 Cal. Rptr. 210, 214 (Ct. App. 1989), the court held that a fourteen-year-old's strong preference to live with the non-custodial parent, combined with academic and social difficulties, constituted sufficient grounds for modification.

Evidence of Domestic Violence, Substance Abuse, or Neglect: Discovery of previously unknown domestic violence or development of substance abuse problems constitutes material change warranting immediate judicial intervention. *In re Marriage of Fajota*, 230 Cal. Rptr. 3d 79, 85 (Ct. App. 2018), held that evidence of domestic violence against a new partner creates presumption against custody or unsupervised visitation under Family Code Section 3044.

C. New York Standards

New York requires a substantial change in circumstances that affects the child's welfare. The Court of Appeals in *Matter of Eschbach v. Eschbach*, 451 N.E.2d 157, 160 (N.Y. 1983), established that modification requires "a real need for change" based on circumstances that have developed since the original order.

Factors Courts Consider:

Stability of the Home Environment: Courts examine the physical and emotional stability of each parent's home. *Matter of Tropea v. Tropea*, 642 N.E.2d 575, 578 (N.Y. 1994), emphasized that stability includes not only physical surroundings but also emotional consistency and continuity of caregiving.

School Performance and Health: Academic progress, extracurricular activities, and physical and mental health needs are primary considerations. In *Matter of Weiss v. Weiss*, 418 N.Y.S.2d 295, 297 (App. Div. 2d Dep't 1979), the court modified custody based on the child's improved academic performance and social adjustment in the non-custodial parent's care.

Wishes of the Child: New York courts consider children's preferences when they demonstrate sufficient age and maturity. *Matter of Nehra v. Uhlar*, 372 N.E.2d 4, 8 (N.Y. 1977), established that while children's wishes are not controlling, they become increasingly important as the child matures and demonstrates reasoned judgment.

D. Procedural Requirements

Motion Practice: Modification requests must be brought by formal motion in the court that issued the original order. Both states require detailed affidavits supporting the claimed change in circumstances.

Best Interests Analysis: Courts must conduct fresh best interests analysis considering current circumstances. The modification standard is not merely whether the current arrangement is working, but whether a different arrangement would better serve the child's interests.

Alternative Dispute Resolution: Modifications may be resolved through mediation, stipulation, or hearing, depending on agreement and complexity. California Family Code Section 3170 requires mediation in contested custody cases, while New York courts have discretion to order mediation under Domestic Relations Law Section 240.

IV. Modification of Child Support

A. Grounds for Modification

Child support can be modified based on substantial changes in circumstances affecting either parent's financial situation or the child's needs. Unlike spousal support, child support obligations cannot be waived and remain subject to modification until the child reaches majority.

Change in Income: Significant increases or decreases in either parent's income warrant support modification. Both voluntary and involuntary income changes are considered, though voluntary underemployment may result in income imputation.

Change in Custody or Parenting Time: Modifications in physical custody or significant changes in visitation schedules affect support calculations. Extended periods of care by the non-custodial parent may reduce support obligations proportionally.

Emancipation of a Child: Child support terminates upon emancipation, which varies by state. California Family Code Section 3901 defines emancipation as reaching majority, marriage, military service, or court declaration. New York Domestic Relations Law Section 236-B extends support until age 21 unless the child becomes self-supporting.

Health or Educational Needs: Extraordinary medical expenses or educational costs may warrant support modification or additional orders for contribution to these expenses.

B. California Standards

California Family Code Section 3651 governs support modifications, requiring a showing of changed circumstances that make the existing order unreasonable or inappropriate.

Guideline Presumption: California employs mandatory guideline calculations using computer programs like DissoMaster or XSpouse. *In re Marriage of Hubner*, 94 Cal. Rptr. 2d 849, 852 (Ct. App. 2000), held that deviations from guideline support require express findings of fact and conclusions of law.

Income Determination: Courts may impute income based on earning capacity rather than actual earnings when a parent voluntarily reduces income. *In re Marriage of Cohn*, 65 Cal. Rptr. 2d 135, 139 (Ct. App. 1997), established standards for imputing income based on education, work history, and available employment opportunities.

Three-Year Rule: Family Code Section 3664 creates a rebuttable presumption that support should be modified if three years have passed since the last order, regardless of changed circumstances.

C. New York Standards

New York Domestic Relations Law Section 236-B provides for support modification upon substantial change in circumstances.

Review Standards: Support may be reviewed every three years, or if income changes by 15% or more, or upon substantial change in needs or resources. *Matter of Brescia v. Fitts*, 518 N.E.2d 542, 544 (N.Y. 1987), established that the 15% threshold creates a presumption favoring modification but does not require it.

Income Calculation: New York uses a statutory formula based on combined parental income up to $154,000 (as of 2023), with discretionary calculations above that threshold. The Court of Appeals in *Matter of Cassano v. Cassano*, 399 N.E.2d 1272, 1274 (N.Y. 1979), emphasized that support calculations must consider all relevant financial factors.

Modification Procedures: Either parent may file a modification petition in Family Court or Supreme Court if the case remains open. The petitioner bears the burden of proving changed circumstances warranting modification.

V. Modification of Spousal Support

A. Modifiability Principles

Spousal support may be modified unless specifically waived or fixed in a judgment or agreement. The distinction between modifiable and non-modifiable support is crucial and must be clearly stated in court orders.

Modifiable vs. Non-Modifiable: *In re Marriage of Morrison*, 78 Cal. App. 4th 513, 521 (1999), held that ambiguous language regarding modifiability is construed against the payor spouse. Clear contractual language waiving modification rights is generally enforceable.

Merger vs. Survival: Support provisions that merge into the divorce judgment remain modifiable, while those that survive as independent contractual obligations may not be modifiable. *Anson v. Anson*, 770 P.2d 1299, 1303 (Cal. 1989), established this distinction.

B. Common Grounds for Modification

Job Loss: Involuntary unemployment or underemployment may warrant temporary or permanent support modification. Courts distinguish between voluntary and involuntary job loss, with voluntary changes receiving greater scrutiny.

Retirement: Mandatory retirement at normal retirement age typically warrants support modification, while early voluntary retirement may not. *In re Marriage of Reynolds*, 63 Cal. App. 4th 1373, 1377 (1998), established that retirement must be reasonable and in good faith.

Disability: Physical or mental disability affecting earning capacity provides grounds for modification. Medical documentation and vocational evaluation may be required to establish the extent of disability.

Recipient's Remarriage or Cohabitation: Remarriage typically terminates spousal support automatically. Cohabitation may warrant modification or termination depending on the financial impact of the relationship. *In re Marriage of Bower*, 96 Cal. Rptr. 2d 403, 408 (Ct. App. 2000), established factors for evaluating cohabitation claims.

C. California Standards

California requires a material change in circumstances warranting modification. Family Code Section 4320 factors are reconsidered in light of current circumstances.

Duration Considerations: Spousal support duration often mirrors marriage length, particularly for marriages of short duration. *In re Marriage of Gavron*, 203 Cal. Rptr. 870, 875 (Ct. App. 1984), established the "Gavron warning" requiring supported spouses to become self-supporting within a reasonable time.

Self-Support Expectation: Courts increasingly expect supported spouses to make good faith efforts toward self-sufficiency. Failure to seek employment or training may result in income imputation or support termination.

D. New York Standards

New York applies a substantial change in financial circumstances standard similar to child support modifications.

Statutory Factors Revisited: Courts revisit the original Domestic Relations Law Section 236-B factors in light of current circumstances. *Matter of Hartog v. Hartog*, 647 N.E.2d 749, 752 (N.Y. 1995), emphasized that all relevant factors must be reconsidered upon modification.

Duration and Termination: New York does not establish presumptive support duration, instead requiring case-by-case analysis of the supported spouse's reasonable efforts toward self-sufficiency.

VI. Appealing a Family Law Judgment

A. Nature of Appellate Review

An appeal challenges a trial court's legal ruling, not factual findings. Appellate courts apply different standards of review depending on the nature of the claimed error.

Questions of Law: Pure questions of law receive de novo review, meaning appellate courts exercise independent judgment. *In re Marriage of Burgess*, 913 P.2d 473, 477 (Cal. 1996), illustrates de novo review of legal standards governing custodial parent relocation.

Factual Findings: Factual determinations are reviewed for substantial evidence, a deferential standard requiring affirmance if any reasonable evidence supports the trial court's findings. *Matter of Bennett v. Jeffreys*, 356 N.E.2d 277, 281 (N.Y. 1976), established this standard for family court factual findings.

Discretionary Rulings: Abuse of discretion is the standard for reviewing most family law rulings, including custody, support, and evidentiary decisions. *In re Marriage of Ackerman*, 146 Cal. App. 4th 191, 197 (2007), defined abuse of discretion as a ruling that exceeds the bounds of reason or contravenes uncontradicted evidence.

B. Grounds for Appeal

Improper Application of Law: Misapplication of legal standards or failure to consider required statutory factors provides appellate grounds. *Tropea v. Tropea*, 642 N.E.2d 575, 579 (N.Y. 1994), reversed a custody modification based on the trial court's failure to apply proper legal standards.

Exclusion of Critical Evidence: Erroneous evidentiary rulings that affect the outcome may warrant reversal. The error must be prejudicial, meaning it reasonably probable that a different result would have been reached absent the error.

Denial of Due Process: Procedural violations that deprive parties of fair hearing opportunities provide constitutional grounds for appeal. *Goldberg v. Kelly*, 397 U.S. 254, 267-68 (1970), established minimum due process requirements for proceedings affecting fundamental rights.

Abuse of Judicial Discretion: Trial court rulings that are arbitrary, capricious, or unsupported by evidence may be reversed on appeal. The standard is high, requiring clear demonstration that the trial court's decision was unreasonable.

C. Appellate Deadlines and Procedures

California: California Rules of Court Rule 8.104 requires notice of appeal within 60 days after service of notice of entry of judgment, or 180 days if no notice is served. *Silverbrand v. County of Los Angeles*, 46 P.3d 1124, 1126 (Cal. 2002), strictly enforces these deadlines.

New York: CPLR Section 5513 requires notice of appeal within 30 days after service of judgment with notice of entry, or within 30 days after the appealing party serves a copy of the judgment. Extensions are rarely granted.

Record Preparation: Appellate courts review only the record from the trial court. Failure to include relevant documents or transcripts in the appellate record may preclude consideration of important evidence.

D. Appellate Limitations and Practical Considerations

Cost and Duration: Appeals can be expensive and time-consuming, often taking 18-24 months or longer. Attorney's fees, filing costs, and transcript preparation expenses can exceed the value of many family law cases.

Enforcement Continues: Appeals generally do not stop enforcement of the underlying judgment unless a stay is granted. California Code of Civil Procedure Section 917.7 and New York CPLR Section 5519 govern automatic stays in family law cases.

Success Rates: Family law appeals are rarely successful unless the error is clear and prejudicial. Discretionary rulings receive particular deference from appellate courts.

Available Relief: Appellate courts can affirm (uphold) the judgment, reverse it, modify it, or remand the case for further proceedings. Complete reversals are uncommon; remands for reconsideration under proper legal standards are more frequent.

VII. Reconsideration and Set-Aside Motions

A. Motion for Reconsideration

California: Code of Civil Procedure Section 1008 strictly limits reconsideration motions to new or different facts, circumstances, or law. *New York Times Co. v. Superior Court*, 52 Cal. 3d 453, 464 (1990), emphasized that reconsideration is not an opportunity to re-argue the same points.

New York: CPLR Section 2221(d) allows reconsideration based on new facts not previously presented or changes in law. *Foley v. Roche*, 418 N.E.2d 585, 588 (N.Y. 1981), established standards for demonstrating new facts warranting reconsideration.

Timing Requirements: Both states require prompt filing of reconsideration motions. California requires filing within 10 days after service of notice of entry of order, while New York allows 30 days but encourages prompt filing.

B. Set-Aside Judgments

Grounds for Relief: Both states provide mechanisms for setting aside judgments based on exceptional circumstances.

Fraud or Misrepresentation: Extrinsic fraud that prevented a fair hearing provides grounds for set-aside. *In re Marriage of Stevenot*, 154 Cal. App. 3d 1051, 1071 (1984), distinguished between intrinsic fraud (addressed at trial) and extrinsic fraud (grounds for set-aside).

Mistake: Mutual mistake of fact or law may warrant relief from judgment. The mistake must be fundamental and must have prevented proper adjudication of the issues.

Lack of Notice: Inadequate service of process or failure to provide required notice of proceedings provides grounds for set-aside. Due process requires actual notice and opportunity to be heard.

Default Without Knowledge: Parties who did not receive actual notice of proceedings and had their default entered may seek relief from judgment. *Rappleyea v. Campbell*, 35 P.3d 669, 676 (Cal. 2001), established standards for relief from default judgments.

California Procedures: Code of Civil Procedure Section 473 provides relief from mistake, inadvertence, surprise, or excusable neglect within six months. Family Code Section 2122 addresses set-aside of family law judgments based on fraud, perjury, or failure to disclose assets.

New York Procedures: CPLR Section 5015 governs relief from judgments based on excusable default, newly discovered evidence, fraud, or lack of jurisdiction. Domestic Relations Law provides additional grounds specific to family law cases.

VIII. Mediation and Modification Agreements

A. Post-Judgment Mediation

Parties may use post-judgment mediation to resolve modification issues cooperatively rather than through contested litigation. Mediation offers several advantages including reduced cost, faster resolution, and preservation of co-parenting relationships.

Voluntary vs. Mandatory: Some courts require mediation before contested modification hearings, particularly in custody cases. California Family Code Section 3170 mandates mediation in custody disputes, while New York courts have discretion to order mediation.

Mediator Qualifications: Both states establish qualification requirements for family mediators. California Rules of Court Rule 5.210 and New York standards require specific training and experience in family law and child development.

B. Requirements for Enforceable Agreements

Any post-judgment modification agreement must meet specific requirements to be enforceable:

Written Agreement: Oral modifications are generally not enforceable. *In re Marriage of McKean*, 82 Cal. Rptr. 2d 615, 618 (Ct. App. 1999), held that material support modifications must be in writing and court-approved.

Signatures of Both Parties: Both parties must sign the agreement, and signatures should be notarized or acknowledged in court.

Court Approval and Filing: Modification agreements must be filed with the court and incorporated into a court order for enforceability. Some courts require hearings to ensure the agreement is fair and in children's best interests.

Financial Disclosures: Support modification agreements require current income and expense declarations from both parties. California Family Code Section 2104 and New York Domestic Relations Law Section 236-B mandate financial disclosure in support proceedings.

C. Limitations on Private Agreements

Child Support: Parents cannot agree to support amounts below statutory guidelines without court approval and express findings that the agreement serves the child's best interests.

Custody and Visitation: While courts generally approve reasonable custody agreements, they retain authority to reject arrangements that do not serve children's best interests.

Enforcement: Informal agreements not incorporated into court orders are not enforceable through contempt proceedings. Breach of such agreements requires separate contract litigation.

IX. Interstate and International Enforcement

A. Interstate Enforcement Mechanisms

Uniform Interstate Family Support Act (UIFSA): Both California and New York have adopted UIFSA, which provides mechanisms for establishing, modifying, and enforcing support orders across state lines. *Kulko v. Superior Court*, 436 U.S. 84, 93 (1978), established constitutional limits on long-arm jurisdiction in family law cases.

Continuing Exclusive Jurisdiction: UIFSA establishes continuing exclusive jurisdiction in the state that initially issued a support order, preventing conflicting orders from multiple states. *Matter of Miller v. Miller*, 715 N.Y.S.2d 513, 515 (Fam. Ct. 2000), applied UIFSA principles to prevent forum shopping.

Registration and Enforcement: Support orders from other states can be registered for enforcement without modification. The registration process is generally ministerial, requiring only proof of the sister-state order and proof of arrearages.

Uniform Child Custody Jurisdiction and Enforcement Act (UCCJEA): This act determines which state has jurisdiction to make initial custody determinations and which state can modify existing orders. *Matter of Thompson v. Thompson*, 484 U.S. 174, 187 (1988), emphasized the importance of uniform custody jurisdiction to prevent parental kidnapping.

B. International Enforcement

Hague Child Support Convention: The United States is a signatory to the Hague Convention on International Recovery of Child Support and Other Forms of Family Maintenance, facilitating enforcement of support orders in participating countries.

Reciprocal Enforcement Treaties: The United States maintains bilateral treaties with numerous countries for mutual enforcement of family court orders. These treaties vary in scope and effectiveness.

U.S. Department of State Coordination: The Office of Children's Issues coordinates international enforcement efforts and provides assistance to parents seeking enforcement abroad.

C. Practical Considerations

Documentation Requirements: International enforcement requires certified copies of court orders, translations when necessary, and compliance with foreign procedural requirements.

Choice of Law: Conflicts of law principles determine which state's or country's law applies to modification and enforcement issues. Generally, the law of the state that issued the order governs its interpretation and enforcement.

Jurisdictional Challenges: Interstate and international cases often involve complex jurisdictional issues requiring specialized knowledge of relevant statutes and treaties.

X. Practical Considerations and Strategic Planning

A. Cost-Benefit Analysis

Post-judgment litigation can be expensive and emotionally draining. Attorneys should counsel clients regarding the realistic prospects for success and the costs involved in enforcement, modification, or appeal proceedings.

Economic Factors: The amount in controversy should be weighed against litigation costs. Small support modifications or short-term enforcement issues may not justify extensive litigation.

Relationship Preservation: In cases involving ongoing co-parenting relationships, the long-term impact of contentious litigation on the family dynamic should be considered.

B. Documentation and Evidence

Record Keeping: Parties should maintain detailed records of compliance or non-compliance with court orders. Financial records, communication logs, and incident reports may be crucial in enforcement or modification proceedings.

Expert Witnesses: Modification cases often require expert testimony from child psychologists, vocational evaluators, or financial analysts. Early identification and retention of qualified experts is essential.

C. Alternative Dispute Resolution

Mediation Benefits: Post-judgment mediation often produces more durable solutions than contested litigation because parties participate in crafting the resolution.

Collaborative Process: Some jurisdictions offer collaborative law services for post-judgment matters, providing interdisciplinary team approach to complex family issues.

XI. Conclusion

The final judgment is not always the final word. Life changes, and the law provides mechanisms to enforce, adapt, or challenge family court orders when fairness or necessity demands. Whether seeking a better parenting schedule, adjusting support, or appealing a flawed ruling, parties must follow clear procedures and act within legal timeframes.

The post-judgment phase of family law requires different skills and strategies than initial proceedings. Practitioners must understand enforcement mechanisms, modification standards, and appellate procedures to effectively represent clients in this dynamic area of law. Success often depends on careful factual development, strategic timing, and realistic assessment of available remedies.

As family structures continue to evolve and economic circumstances remain fluid, post-judgment family law will continue to play a vital role in ensuring that court orders remain fair, enforceable, and responsive to changing family needs. The intersection of substantive family law, civil procedure, and constitutional principles makes this area both challenging and intellectually rewarding for practitioners committed to serving families in transition.

Understanding these post-judgment procedures is essential not only for resolving immediate disputes but also for crafting initial judgments that anticipate future needs and minimize subsequent litigation. By providing clear, enforceable orders that include appropriate modification and enforcement mechanisms, family law practitioners can better serve their clients' long-term interests and promote family stability in the post-judgment phase.

23

Immigration and Family Law

Marriages, Status, and Protections

I. Where Family Law Meets Federal Borders

Immigration status intersects with family law in increasingly complex and emotionally charged ways that require sophisticated legal navigation. Whether through marriage-based green card petitions, custody disputes involving non-citizen parents, or protections for immigrant survivors of domestic violence, family law proceedings carry life-altering consequences for non-citizens that extend far beyond traditional domestic relations outcomes.

This chapter explores the intricate relationship between New York and California family courts and federal immigration law, examining how divorce, abuse, custody, and child support cases affect lawful status, and identifying the remedies available to protect immigrant families. The intersection creates unique procedural challenges, ethical considerations, and strategic opportunities that demand specialized knowledge from family law practitioners.

The stakes in these cases cannot be overstated. A poorly handled divorce proceeding can result in deportation, while strategic coordination between family and immigration law can provide pathways to safety and permanent legal status. Understanding these connections is essential for competent representation in today's diverse legal landscape.

II. Immigration Consequences of Divorce

Marriage-Based Green Cards: Foundation and Vulnerabilities

A U.S. citizen or lawful permanent resident (LPR) may sponsor a non-citizen spouse for permanent residence through the family-based immigration system. See *Immigration and Nationality* Act § 201(b)(2)(A)(i), 8 U.S.C. § 1151(b)(2)(A)(i); *Matter of Laureano*, 19 I&N Dec. 1 (BIA 1983). This process creates a statutory framework that intertwines marital relationships with immigration benefits, establishing dependencies that complicate subsequent family law proceedings.

When the marriage is less than two years old at the time of green card approval, the immigrant receives conditional permanent residence valid for two years. *Immigration Marriage Fraud Amendments of* 1986, Pub. L. No. 99-639, 100 Stat. 3537; 8 U.S.C. § 1186a. This conditional status was designed to combat marriage fraud but creates significant vulnerabilities for legitimate couples whose relationships deteriorate within the initial two-year period.

Conditional Residence and Divorce: Navigating Legal Complexity

The immigrant must file Form I-751, Petition to Remove Conditions on Residence, within the 90-day period immediately preceding the second anniversary of receiving conditional permanent residence. 8 C.F.R. § 216.4(a)(1). Failure to timely file results in automatic termination of status and initiation of removal proceedings. *Matter of Stockwell*, 20 I&N Dec. 309 (BIA 1991).

Divorce before removing conditions requires a waiver demonstration that the marriage was entered in good faith, even though it legally terminated. The petitioner must establish by a preponderance of the evidence that:

1. The qualifying marriage was entered into in good faith and not solely for immigration purposes
2. The marriage was legally terminated through divorce or annulment
3. The petitioner continues to meet the admissibility requirements

Matter of Tawfik, 20 I&N Dec. 166 (BIA 1990); 8 C.F.R. § 216.5(e)(2).

Acceptable evidence includes documentation of shared residence, commingled finances, joint insurance policies, birth certificates of children born to the marriage, and affidavits from knowledgeable witnesses. *Matter of Phillis*, 15 I&N Dec. 385 (BIA 1975). Family law records become crucial evidence, including:

- Marriage certificates and prenuptial agreements
- Separation agreements and property settlement documents
- Custody orders and parenting plans
- Child support orders and payment records
- Affidavits of support (Form I-864)
- Joint tax returns and financial records

The family law attorney must understand that every document generated during divorce proceedings may later be scrutinized by immigration authorities, requiring careful drafting and strategic consideration of immigration consequences.

Strategic Coordination Between Proceedings

Timing coordination between family court and immigration proceedings requires careful strategic planning. In *Bartsch v. Bartsch*, 636 F.2d 1222 (9th Cir. 1981), the court recognized that state divorce proceedings can proceed independently of federal immigration proceedings, but practitioners must consider how each affects the other.

Best practices include:

1. Filing Form I-751 before initiating divorce proceedings when possible
2. Ensuring divorce decrees contain specific findings about good faith entry into marriage

3. Coordinating discovery to gather evidence supporting both family law and immigration objectives
4. Considering sealed proceedings to protect sensitive immigration information

III. Immigration and Domestic Violence Protections

VAWA Self-Petitions: Independence from Abusive Relationships

The Violence Against Women Act (VAWA) creates a critical exception to the traditional immigration sponsorship system, allowing abused spouses, children, and parents of U.S. citizens or LPRs to self-petition for lawful permanent residence without the abuser's knowledge, consent, or participation. *Violence Against Women Act*, Pub. L. No. 103-322, 108 Stat. 1902 (1994); 8 U.S.C. § 1154(a)(1)(A).

VAWA eligibility requires establishing four primary elements:

Qualifying Relationship: The petitioner must demonstrate a qualifying relationship to a U.S. citizen or LPR abuser. Acceptable relationships include current or former spouses, children under 21, or parents (where the U.S. citizen child is over 21). *Matter of* A-M-, 23 I&N Dec. 737 (BIA 2005).

Battery or Extreme Cruelty: Physical violence is not required. Extreme cruelty encompasses psychological abuse, sexual abuse, economic control, isolation, and threats. The standard examines the totality of circumstances rather than isolated incidents. *Matter of* R-A-, 22 I&N Dec. 906 (BIA 1999), *vacated*, 23 I&N Dec. 694 (A.G. 2005).

Good Faith Marriage: For spousal petitions, the marriage must have been entered in good faith, not solely for immigration benefits. The same evidence used in I-751 proceedings applies here. *Matter of Laureano*, 19 I&N Dec. 1 (BIA 1983).

Good Moral Character: Petitioners must demonstrate good moral character during the three-year period preceding filing and continuing until permanent residence is granted. Criminal convictions, particularly those involving moral turpitude, can be disqualifying. 8 U.S.C. § 1101(f).

Family Law Evidence in VAWA Cases

Family court proceedings generate critical evidence for VAWA petitions:

Protective Orders: Temporary and permanent restraining orders provide compelling evidence of abuse and judicial recognition of danger. *People v. Melton*, 44 Cal.3d 713 (1988); *Harhut v. Harhut*, 154 Misc.2d 637 (N.Y. Sup. Ct. 1992).

Police Reports and Criminal Proceedings: Documentation of domestic violence incidents, arrest records, and criminal convictions strengthen VAWA cases significantly.

Custody and Support Orders: Orders limiting visitation, requiring supervised exchanges, or addressing domestic violence concerns provide institutional recognition of abuse patterns.

Therapeutic Documentation: Records from licensed mental health professionals treating domestic violence trauma can establish both abuse and its psychological impact.

VAWA petitions are confidential under federal law, and disclosure to abusers is prohibited. 8 U.S.C. § 1367. This confidentiality extends to family court proceedings where VAWA status might be relevant to custody or support determinations.

Practical Coordination Strategies

Family law attorneys representing VAWA-eligible clients should:

1. File protective orders before VAWA petitions when safety permits
2. Ensure family court orders contain specific findings about domestic violence
3. Coordinate with immigration counsel regarding timing and evidence
4. Maintain strict confidentiality about immigration status
5. Consider sealed proceedings to protect client safety

IV. U Visa and T Visa Protections

U Visa Certification: Law Enforcement Cooperation

The U visa provides protection for victims of qualifying crimes who cooperate with law enforcement investigations or prosecutions. Qualifying crimes include domestic violence, sexual assault, trafficking, kidnapping, and other serious offenses. 8 U.S.C. § 1101(a)(15)(U); 8 C.F.R. § 214.14.

Certification requirements mandate that a qualifying law enforcement agency certify the victim's helpfulness in investigating or prosecuting criminal activity. Certifying agencies include police departments, district attorneys, courts, and other investigative agencies. *Matter of* M-F-, 24 I&N Dec. 373 (BIA 2007).

Family law protective order proceedings may qualify as cooperation with law enforcement. In *People v. Sandoval*, 140 Cal.App.4th 111 (2006), the court recognized that testimony in protective order proceedings constitutes cooperation with judicial proceedings sufficient for U visa certification.

T Visa Protection for Trafficking Survivors

The T visa protects victims of severe forms of human trafficking, including both sex trafficking and labor trafficking. Family law attorneys may encounter trafficking survivors in various contexts:

Custody Proceedings: Trafficking survivors may seek to regain custody of children or establish legal guardianship after escaping trafficking situations.

Support Proceedings: Survivors may pursue financial support from trafficking perpetrators through family court remedies.

Guardianship Proceedings: Minor trafficking survivors require specialized guardianship arrangements that account for their trauma and legal status needs.

Coordinated representation is essential, as family law outcomes can significantly impact T visa eligibility and adjustment to permanent residence. *Trafficking Victims Protection* Act, Pub. L. No. 106-386, 114 Stat. 1464 (2000); 8 U.S.C. § 1101(a)(15)(T).

V. Custody and Parental Rights of Undocumented Immigrants

Constitutional and Statutory Foundations

Both New York and California courts have consistently held that immigration status alone cannot determine parental fitness or custody arrangements. The fundamental right to parent, protected by the Due Process Clause of the Fourteenth Amendment, extends to all parents regardless of immigration status. *Stanley v. Illinois*, 405 U.S. 645 (1972); *Santosky v. Kramer*, 455 U.S. 745 (1982).

In *Encarnacion v. Jaraba*, 185 Cal.App.4th 787 (2010), the California Court of Appeal explicitly rejected the argument that undocumented status should preclude custody, holding that "a parent's immigration status, without more, is not relevant to a custody determination." Similarly, New York courts in *Matter of Dallis* M., 278 A.D.2d 778 (3d Dep't 2000), recognized that immigration status cannot serve as the sole basis for custody denial.

Best Interest Analysis and Immigration Considerations

While immigration status alone cannot determine custody, courts may consider immigration-related factors when they directly impact the child's best interests:

Deportation Risk: Where a parent faces imminent deportation or detention, courts may consider the stability and continuity of the child's living situation. *Gonzalez v. Gonzalez*, 54 Cal.App.4th 1218 (1997).

International Relocation: Courts examine whether potential relocation to the non-citizen parent's country of origin serves the child's best interests, considering educational opportunities, healthcare access, and family connections. *Matter of Thompson*, 2019 NY Slip Op 29045 (Sup. Ct. 2019).

Flight Risk Assessment: Immigration status may be relevant to assessing flight risk, but courts must base such determinations on specific evidence rather than stereotypical assumptions. *Matter of Miguel* C., 203 Cal.App.4th 1206 (2012).

Legal Safeguards and Protective Measures

Emergency Guardianship Planning: Undocumented parents should execute standby guardianship documents designating temporary caregivers in case of detention or deportation. New York's Standby Guardianship Law, N.Y. *Surr. Ct. Proc. Act* § 1726, and California's similar provisions in *Cal. Prob. Code* § 1516 provide frameworks for such arrangements.

Alternative Communication Methods: Courts increasingly permit video visitation and telephonic contact when parents are detained or deported. In *Matter of Sebastian R.*, 43 Cal.4th 1096 (2008), the California Supreme Court recognized that maintaining parent-child relationships through available technology serves children's best interests.

Confidentiality Protections: Both New York and California have implemented policies limiting immigration enforcement in family courts. California's *Senate Bill* 6 (2017) specifically prohibits immigration enforcement in state courthouses, while New York's *Office of Court Administration* has issued similar administrative directives.

VI. Special Immigrant Juvenile Status (SIJS)

Statutory Framework and Eligibility

Special Immigrant Juvenile Status provides a pathway to lawful permanent residence for children who have been abused, neglected, or abandoned by one or both parents. The federal statute requires state juvenile court findings as a predicate to immigration relief. 8 U.S.C. § 1101(a)(27)(J); *William Wilberforce Trafficking Victims Protection Reauthorization Act*, Pub. L. No. 110-457, 122 Stat. 5044 (2008).

SIJS eligibility requires four essential elements:

Age and Marital Status: The child must be under 21 and unmarried at the time of filing both the state court petition and the federal immigration petition.

Juvenile Court Dependency: A state juvenile court must declare the child dependent on the court or legally commit or place the child under the custody of an agency, department, or individual appointed by the court.

Reunification Impossibility: The child cannot reunify with one or both parents due to abuse, neglect, abandonment, or a similar basis under state law.

Best Interest Finding: The juvenile court must determine that it would not be in the child's best interest to be returned to the child's or parent's previous country of nationality or country of last habitual residence.

State Court Jurisdiction and Procedures

Both New York and California family courts have jurisdiction to make SIJS findings through various proceedings:

Family Court Proceedings: In New York, Family Court has broad jurisdiction over juvenile matters under N.Y. *Fam. Ct. Act* § 115. California's Juvenile Court operates under *Cal. Welf. & Inst. Code* § 300 et seq.

Guardianship Proceedings: Probate courts in both states can make SIJS findings in guardianship proceedings where appropriate factual predicates exist. *Matter of Leslie S.*, 2018 NY Slip Op 28392 (Fam. Ct. 2018); *In re* M.M., 213 Cal.App.4th 563 (2013).

Custody Proceedings: When one parent seeks sole custody due to the other parent's abuse, abandonment, or neglect, family courts can incorporate SIJS findings into custody orders.

Essential Language and Coordination

State court orders must contain specific language to support federal SIJS petitions. Critical findings include:

1. Declaration of dependency or custody arrangement
2. Specific findings of abuse, neglect, or abandonment by one or both parents
3. Determination that reunification with the abusive/neglectful parent is not viable
4. Best interest finding regarding return to country of origin

Example Language: "The Court finds that reunification with [parent's name] is not viable due to [specific acts of abuse/neglect/abandonment]. The Court further finds that it would not be in the child's best interest to be returned to [country] due to [specific circumstances affecting the child's welfare]."

Coordination between family law and immigration counsel is essential. Family court orders must be drafted with immigration consequences in mind, while immigration petitions must accurately reflect state court findings. *Matter of* D-G-, 27 I&N Dec. 363 (BIA 2018).

VII. Child Support and Public Charge Considerations

Public Charge Rule and Family Support

The public charge rule, historically used to exclude immigrants likely to become dependent on government benefits, has undergone significant evolution affecting family law practice. *Matter of* A-, 19 I&N Dec. 867 (BIA 1988). Under current federal guidance, the public charge assessment focuses on cash benefits and long-term institutionalization rather than non-cash benefits or temporary assistance.

Court-ordered child support and spousal support do not constitute public benefits for public charge purposes. *Matter of* P-, 15 I&N Dec. 603 (BIA 1976). This distinction is crucial for immigrant parents and spouses pursuing family court remedies.

Clarifying Distinctions: Immigrants should understand that:

1. Court-ordered support payments are private contractual obligations, not public benefits
2. Receiving support owed under state law does not create public charge concerns
3. Child support serves the best interests of U.S. citizen and immigrant children alike

Affidavit of Support Obligations (Form I-864)

The Affidavit of Support creates a legally enforceable contract between the sponsor and the U.S. government to maintain the sponsored immigrant at 125% of the federal poverty level. *Illegal Immigration Reform and Immigrant Responsibility* Act, Pub. L. No. 104-208, 110 Stat. 3009 (1996); 8 U.S.C. § 1183a.

This obligation continues until the sponsored immigrant:

1. Becomes a U.S. citizen

2. Works 40 qualifying quarters (approximately 10 years)

3. Leaves the United States permanently

4. Dies

Matter of Villanueva, 19 I&N Dec. 101 (BIA 1984); 8 U.S.C. § 1183a(a)(2).

Enforcement in Family Court

Several state courts have permitted I-864 enforcement through contract or support actions. In *Liu v. Mund*, 686 F.3d 418 (7th Cir. 2012), the federal appellate court held that Form I-864 creates an enforceable contract that can be pursued in state court.

California courts have been particularly receptive to I-864 enforcement. In *Davis v. Davis*, 189 Cal.App.4th 1177 (2010), the court permitted an immigrant spouse to pursue I-864 obligations even after waiving spousal support in the divorce proceedings, recognizing that the federal sponsorship obligation exists independently of state support law.

Strategic Considerations: Family law attorneys should:

1. Identify whether clients signed Form I-864 during marriage-based immigration cases

2. Consider I-864 obligations when negotiating support agreements

3. Advise clients that divorce does not terminate sponsorship obligations

4. Explore I-864 enforcement when traditional support remedies are inadequate

VIII. Divorce and Immigration Sponsorship

Continuing Obligations Post-Divorce

The intersection of divorce and immigration sponsorship creates ongoing legal and financial relationships that survive marital dissolution. Understanding these continuing obligations is essential for proper family law practice.

Duration of Sponsorship: Form I-864 obligations typically extend 10-15 years beyond divorce, creating long-term financial exposure for sponsors. In *Matter of Yordan*, 24 I&N Dec. 613 (BIA 2008), the Board clarified that sponsors remain liable for government benefits received by sponsored immigrants during the entire sponsorship period.

Joint and Several Liability: When multiple family members serve as sponsors or joint sponsors, liability may be joint and several. This creates strategic opportunities for immigrant spouses and tactical considerations for divorcing sponsors.

Enforcement Mechanisms and Remedies

Federal Court Jurisdiction: Federal courts have jurisdiction over I-864 enforcement actions under 8 U.S.C. § 1183a(e)(1). However, state courts may also exercise jurisdiction under contract theories.

Damages and Relief: Available remedies include:

1. Actual damages for unreimbursed government benefits
2. Attorney's fees for successful enforcement actions
3. Ongoing support obligations to maintain 125% poverty level
4. Interest and penalties for unpaid obligations

In *Erler v. Erler*, 824 F.3d 1173 (9th Cir. 2016), the Ninth Circuit recognized that I-864 obligations can be enforced through state divorce proceedings, providing additional leverage in family court negotiations.

IX. Confidentiality and Fear of Reporting

Courthouse Safety Policies

Recognition of immigrant families' vulnerability in court proceedings has led to comprehensive policy reforms in both New York and California.

California's Leadership: California's *Senate Bill* 6 (2017) prohibits immigration enforcement activities in state courthouses, with limited exceptions for serious felony warrants. The law specifically protects family court participants, recognizing that fear of immigration consequences undermines access to justice.

New York's Protections: New York's *Office of Court Administration* issued comprehensive directives limiting immigration enforcement in state courts. *Administrative Order* No. AO/107/17 specifically addresses family court proceedings and emphasizes the courts' commitment to providing safe access to justice regardless of immigration status.

Attorney Ethical Obligations

Family law attorneys representing immigrant clients face unique ethical considerations that require specialized knowledge and cultural competency.

Competent Representation: *Model Rule* 1.1 requires lawyers to provide competent representation, which includes understanding how immigration law affects family court proceedings. Attorneys must either develop immigration law competency or coordinate with qualified immigration counsel.

Confidentiality Obligations: Immigration status information requires heightened confidentiality protection. Attorneys must implement security measures to protect client information from inadvertent disclosure to immigration authorities or opposing parties.

Informed Consent: Clients must receive clear explanations of how family court proceedings might affect immigration status. This includes potential benefits (such as VAWA or SIJS opportunities) and risks (such as exposure through public records).

Trauma-Informed and Culturally Responsive Practice

Understanding Trauma Responses: Immigrant clients may exhibit trauma responses related to persecution, domestic violence, or previous negative interactions with government authorities. Attorneys must recognize these responses and adapt their practice accordingly.

Cultural Competency Requirements: Effective representation requires understanding diverse cultural perspectives on family structure, gender roles, child-rearing practices, and conflict resolution. What may appear as non-compliance or resistance may reflect cultural differences or trauma responses.

Language Access: Both New York and California mandate interpreter services in family court proceedings. N.Y. *Judiciary Law* § 387; *Cal. Evid. Code* § 752. Attorneys must ensure clients receive interpretation services and understand that family members should not serve as interpreters in sensitive family law matters.

X. Emerging Issues and Future Considerations

Technology and Immigration Enforcement

Digital privacy concerns increasingly affect immigrant families in family court proceedings. Social media evidence, electronic communications, and digital financial records may expose immigration vulnerabilities while providing evidence in family law cases.

Best Practices: Attorneys should counsel clients regarding:

1. Social media privacy settings and content restrictions
2. Secure communication methods for sensitive information
3. Digital evidence preservation while protecting privacy
4. Understanding that electronic records may be discoverable in proceedings

Interstate and International Jurisdictional Issues

Increasing family mobility creates complex jurisdictional questions when immigration and family law intersect across state and international boundaries.

Interstate Considerations: When families move between states with different approaches to immigration issues, attorneys must understand how jurisdictional changes affect ongoing proceedings and available remedies.

International Child Abduction: The *Hague Convention on International Child Abduction* creates additional complexity when one parent faces deportation or voluntarily relocates internationally with children. 42 U.S.C. § 11601 et seq.

Legislative and Policy Evolution

Immigration and family law continue evolving through federal policy changes, state legislative initiatives, and court decisions. Practitioners must stay current with:

1. Federal immigration policy changes affecting family-based immigration
2. State legislative initiatives protecting immigrant families
3. Court decisions clarifying the intersection of state and federal law
4. Administrative guidance from immigration and family court systems

XI. Conclusion: Integrated Practice for Vulnerable Families

The intersection of immigration and family law creates both opportunities and vulnerabilities that require sophisticated legal analysis and strategic coordination. For immigrant families, family law proceedings can provide pathways to safety, stability, and legal status - or, if mishandled, create devastating consequences including family separation and deportation.

Effective practice in this area demands more than technical legal knowledge. It requires cultural competency, trauma-informed advocacy, and collaborative relationships with immigration counsel. The stakes - family unity, child welfare, and human safety - make this intersection one of the most important and challenging areas of modern family law practice.

As immigration patterns continue evolving and family structures become increasingly diverse, the intersection between immigration and family law will only grow in importance. Practitioners who develop expertise in this area provide essential services to vulnerable populations while contributing to a more just and effective legal system.

The ultimate goal remains constant: ensuring that all families, regardless of immigration status, can access justice and protection through our family court systems while building pathways to long-term stability and legal security. This requires not just legal advocacy, but a commitment to human dignity and the preservation of families that go beyond traditional practice boundaries.

Family Law Glossary

New York & California Family Law Terms

A

Abandonment – The desertion of a spouse or child without justification and with the intent to forsake obligations. In divorce, typically requires one year of separation in NY.

Abuse – Physical, emotional, sexual, or psychological harm inflicted on a family member. Includes domestic violence, child abuse, and elder abuse.

Acknowledgment of Paternity (AOP) – A voluntary legal document signed by both parents establishing paternity without court involvement. Creates legal presumption of parentage.

Adoption – Legal process that permanently transfers parental rights from biological or previous legal parents to adoptive parents, creating a new legal parent-child relationship.

ADR (Alternative Dispute Resolution) – Methods of resolving disputes outside of traditional litigation, including mediation, arbitration, and collaborative law.

Affidavit – A written statement made under oath and penalty of perjury, commonly used in family law for financial disclosures and factual declarations.

Affidavit of Service – Document proving that legal papers were properly served on the opposing party according to legal requirements.

Alimony – See Spousal Support/Maintenance.

Annulment – Legal declaration that a marriage was never valid from the beginning, as opposed to divorce which ends a valid marriage.

Answer – Legal document filed by the respondent in response to a petition or complaint, either admitting or denying allegations.

APPLA (Another Planned Permanent Living Arrangement) – A permanency option for children in dependency cases when adoption or guardianship is not viable, typically for older youth.

Arbitration – Form of ADR where a neutral third party (arbitrator) hears evidence and makes binding decisions on disputed issues.

ASFA (Adoption and Safe Families Act) – Federal law that prioritizes child safety and sets timelines for achieving permanency in child welfare cases.

Attorney for the Child (AFC) – In NY, an attorney appointed to represent a child's interests in custody, abuse, or neglect proceedings.

Automatic Orders/ATROs – Court orders that automatically take effect upon filing certain family law cases, typically restraining asset transfers and insurance changes.

B

BAH (Basic Allowance for Housing) – Non-taxable military housing allowance included in income calculations for support purposes.

BAS (Basic Allowance for Subsistence) – Military food allowance included in support calculations.

Best Interests of the Child – The legal standard used by courts to make decisions about custody, visitation, and other matters affecting children, prioritizing the child's welfare above all else.

Bifurcation – Legal procedure allowing termination of marital status while reserving other issues (property, support, custody) for later resolution. Common in CA, rare in NY.

Bigamy – The criminal offense of being married to more than one person simultaneously; grounds for annulment.

C

California Family Code – The primary statutory authority governing family law matters in California.

CAPTA (Child Abuse Prevention and Treatment Act) – Federal law establishing minimum standards for child abuse and neglect investigations and reporting.

CASA (Court Appointed Special Advocate) – Trained volunteer who advocates for children in dependency proceedings.

CCRC (Child Custody Recommending Counsel) – In CA, mediator who may issue written recommendations to the judge in custody disputes.

Child Support – Financial support paid by a parent for the benefit of their child, calculated using state guideline formulas.

Civil Union – Legal relationship similar to marriage, recognized in some states but not NY or CA.

Cohabitation – Living together in an intimate relationship without marriage. May affect spousal support in some cases.

Collaborative Law – ADR process where parties and attorneys commit to resolving disputes without litigation, using a team-based approach.

Commingling – Mixing of separate and marital/community property, which may affect property characterization in divorce.

Community Property – CA's system where property acquired during marriage is presumed to belong equally to both spouses.

Contempt of Court – Willful disobedience of a court order, punishable by fines, attorney fees, or jail time.

Contested Case – Family law matter where parties disagree on one or more significant issues requiring court intervention.

Coercive Control – Pattern of behavior designed to dominate and control an intimate partner through threats, intimidation, and isolation.

Custody – Legal authority and responsibility for a child's care, divided into legal custody (decision-making) and physical custody (residence).

Custody Evaluation – Professional assessment by mental health expert to help courts determine custody arrangements in the child's best interests.

D

Default Judgment – Court ruling entered when one party fails to respond to legal papers within required time limits.

Deposition – Sworn testimony taken outside of court, transcribed by a court reporter, used for discovery purposes.

DFAS (Defense Finance and Accounting Service) – Federal agency that processes military pay and can enforce support orders through wage garnishment.

Discovery – Legal process of obtaining information and documents from the opposing party before trial.

DissoMaster – Computer software used in CA to calculate child and spousal support according to state guidelines.

Dissolution – California's term for divorce.

Domestic Partnership – Legal relationship providing some marriage-like rights and obligations. Available statewide in CA but only locally in some NY jurisdictions.

Domestic Relations Law (DRL) – NY statute governing divorce, annulment, separation, and related family law matters.

Domestic Violence (DV) – Pattern of abusive behavior including physical, emotional, sexual, economic, or psychological abuse between intimate partners.

DVRO (Domestic Violence Restraining Order) – CA court order protecting victims of domestic violence by restricting contact and behavior.

E

Emancipation – Legal process or event that ends parental obligations, typically when a minor becomes self-supporting, marries, or joins the military.

Emergency Jurisdiction – Temporary court authority to protect a child who is present in the state and facing abandonment, abuse, or neglect.

Equitable Distribution – NY's system for dividing marital property based on fairness rather than strict equality.

Equitable Estoppel – Legal doctrine preventing someone from denying parentage when they've acted as a parent and the child has relied on that relationship.

Ex Parte – Court proceeding conducted without notice to or presence of the opposing party, typically in emergency situations.

F

Family Court Act (FCA) – NY statute governing Family Court procedures including custody, support, and family offense matters.

Family Offense – NY term for domestic violence and related crimes between family members.

Fault-Based Divorce – Divorce based on marital misconduct such as adultery, cruelty, or abandonment. Available in NY but not CA.

Final Judgment - Court's final ruling resolving all issues in a family law case.

Forum Shopping - Attempting to file a case in a jurisdiction with more favorable laws; prevented by uniform acts like UCCJEA.

G

GAL (Guardian ad Litem) - Court-appointed representative for a child's best interests in legal proceedings.

Garnishment - Legal process of collecting debts by taking money directly from wages or bank accounts.

Goodwill - Intangible business asset representing reputation and customer relationships; may be divided in divorce.

Grounds for Divorce - Legal reasons justifying dissolution of marriage, such as irreconcilable differences or specific misconduct.

Guardianship - Legal relationship granting authority to care for a child or incapacitated adult when parents are unavailable or unfit.

H

Hague Convention - International treaty governing return of children wrongfully removed from their country of habitual residence.

Home State - Under UCCJEA, the state where a child has lived for at least six consecutive months, which typically has custody jurisdiction.

I

I-751 - Immigration form to remove conditions from permanent residence based on marriage.

I-864 Affidavit of Support – Immigration form creating financial obligation to support an immigrant family member.

Imputed Income – Income attributed to a party by the court when they are voluntarily unemployed or underemployed.

Income Shares Model – Child support calculation method used in CA that considers both parents' incomes and parenting time.

Injunction – Court order requiring or prohibiting specific actions.

Interrogatories – Written questions that must be answered under oath as part of the discovery process.

Interstate Compact – Agreement between states to cooperate on specific legal matters, such as child custody enforcement.

J

Joint Custody – Arrangement where both parents share legal decision-making authority and/or physical custody of children.

Judgment – Final court order resolving the legal issues in a case.

Jurisdiction – Court's legal authority to hear a case and make binding decisions on the parties.

K

KinGAP (Kinship Guardianship Assistance Program) – NY program providing financial support to relatives who become permanent guardians of children.

L

Legal Custody – Authority to make major decisions about a child's health, education, and welfare.

Legal Separation – Court-approved arrangement allowing spouses to live apart while remaining legally married.

Long-Arm Statute – Law allowing courts to exercise jurisdiction over non-residents who have sufficient contacts with the state.

M

Maintenance – NY term for spousal support/alimony.

Marital Property – Assets and debts acquired during marriage, subject to division in divorce.

Marital Settlement Agreement (MSA) – Written agreement between divorcing parties resolving property, support, and custody issues.

Mediation – ADR process where a neutral third party helps parties reach voluntary agreements.

Minor's Counsel – CA attorney appointed to represent a child's interests in family law proceedings.

Modification – Court-approved change to an existing order based on changed circumstances.

N

Neglect – Failure to provide necessary care, supervision, or basic needs to a child.

Net Worth Statement – NY financial disclosure document detailing assets, liabilities, income, and expenses.

No-Fault Divorce – Divorce based on irreconcilable differences or irretrievable breakdown rather than misconduct.

O

Order of Protection (OOP) – NY court order protecting victims of family offenses by restricting contact and behavior.

Order to Show Cause – Court paper requiring a party to appear and explain why specific relief should not be granted.

P

Palimony – Support payments between unmarried cohabiting partners after separation.

Parenting Plan – Detailed agreement or court order specifying custody, visitation, and decision-making arrangements.

Parenting Time – Scheduled time a child spends with each parent; also called visitation.

Paternity – Legal determination of a child's biological father.

Pendente Lite – Latin term meaning "pending litigation"; refers to temporary orders during a case.

Percentage-Based Model – Child support calculation method used in NY based on percentage of noncustodial parent's income.

Personal Jurisdiction – Court's authority over the individuals involved in a case.

Petition – Initial legal document filing a family law case, stating the relief requested.

Physical Custody – Designation of where a child primarily resides and who provides day-to-day care.

Prenuptial Agreement (Prenup) – Contract entered before marriage defining property rights and obligations.

Pro Se – Latin term for self-representation without an attorney.

Protective Order – Court order restricting contact or behavior to protect someone from abuse or harassment.

Putative Spouse – Person who believed in good faith they were legally married, may be entitled to property rights.

Q

QDRO (Qualified Domestic Relations Order) – Court order required to divide retirement accounts in divorce without tax penalties.

R

Reconsideration – Request for a judge to review and change their previous decision.

Rehabilitative Support – Temporary spousal support designed to help recipient become self-supporting.

Relocation – Parent's move to a different geographic area that may affect custody or visitation arrangements.

Request for Order (RFO) – CA court form used to request temporary orders or modifications.

Respondent – Party who responds to a petition or complaint in a family law case.

Restraining Order – Court order prohibiting specific conduct, often used in domestic violence cases.

S

SCRA (Servicemembers Civil Relief Act) – Federal law providing procedural protections to active-duty military personnel in civil proceedings.

Separate Property – Assets and debts belonging solely to one spouse, typically not subject to division.

Service of Process – Legal delivery of court papers to notify parties of legal proceedings.

Set-Aside – Court order canceling or voiding a previous judgment, often due to fraud or mistake.

SIJS (Special Immigrant Juvenile Status) – Immigration protection for undocumented children who cannot reunify with parents due to abuse, neglect, or abandonment.

Sole Custody – Arrangement where one parent has exclusive legal or physical custody.

Spousal Support – Financial support paid by one spouse to the other during separation or after divorce.

Stare Decisis – Legal principle requiring courts to follow precedent set by higher courts.

Stay – Court order suspending or postponing legal proceedings.

Stipulation – Written agreement between parties resolving some or all issues in a case.

Subject Matter Jurisdiction – Court's authority to hear specific types of cases.

Subpoena – Court order requiring appearance at a hearing or production of documents.

T

Temporary Orders – Court orders addressing immediate needs during pending litigation.

Termination of Parental Rights (TPR) – Legal proceeding permanently ending parent-child relationship, often prerequisite to adoption.

Transmutation – CA legal concept where separate property becomes community property through written agreement or conduct.

TRO (Temporary Restraining Order) – Short-term court order providing immediate protection pending a full hearing.

U

UCCJEA (Uniform Child Custody Jurisdiction and Enforcement Act) – Federal law determining which state has jurisdiction over custody cases and how orders are enforced across state lines.

UIFSA (Uniform Interstate Family Support Act) – Federal law governing establishment and enforcement of support orders across state lines.

Uncontested Case – Family law matter where parties agree on all major issues.

UPAA (Uniform Premarital Agreement Act) – Model law governing prenuptial agreements, adopted with variations by many states including CA.

USFSPA (Uniformed Services Former Spouses' Protection Act) – Federal law allowing division of military retirement benefits in divorce.

V

VAWA (Violence Against Women Act) – Federal law providing immigration protections for abused spouses and children of U.S. citizens and permanent residents.

VDOP (Voluntary Declaration of Parentage) – CA form establishing paternity through voluntary acknowledgment by both parents.

Venue – Specific court location where a case should be filed within a jurisdiction.

Visitation – Time a noncustodial parent spends with their child; also called parenting time.

Void Marriage – Marriage that is invalid from the beginning, typically due to legal impediments like bigamy or incest.

Voidable Marriage – Marriage that is valid until annulled, typically due to fraud, duress, or incapacity.

W

Wage Assignment – Court order directing an employer to deduct support payments from an employee's wages.

Waiver – Voluntary relinquishment of a known right.

Watts Charges – CA family law concept requiring reimbursement for exclusive use of community property after separation.

Additional Resources

Important Acronyms

- **ACS**: Administration for Children's Services (NY)
- **AFC**: Attorney for the Child (NY)
- **CPS**: Child Protective Services
- **DCSS**: Department of Child Support Services (CA)
- **DFAS**: Defense Finance and Accounting Service
- **ICE**: Immigration and Customs Enforcement
- **SCU**: Support Collection Unit (NY)

Court Systems

- **Family Court**: NY court handling custody, support, and family offenses
- **Supreme Court**: NY court handling divorce and property division
- **Superior Court**: CA unified court system handling all family law

matters

- **Dependency Court**: Juvenile court handling abuse and neglect cases

About the Author

Ngozi E. Bolin, Esq. brings over three decades of extensive litigation experience to this comprehensive guide on family law. With a distinguished career spanning multiple jurisdictions, Ms. Bolin offers readers the benefit of her deep legal knowledge and practical courtroom wisdom in domestic relations disputes and family litigation.

Educated under the British Commonwealth system and having studied at the Harvard Extension School, Ms. Bolin possesses a uniquely broad legal perspective that enriches her understanding of family law across different legal traditions. Her international credentials began with her admission as a Barrister & Solicitor of the Supreme Court of Nigeria in 1989. She subsequently moved to the United States, gaining admission to the New York State Bar in 1991, the United States Court of Appeals for the Second Circuit, and the California State Bar in 2013.

Throughout her career as a skilled trial attorney, Ms. Bolin has dedicated herself to making legal knowledge accessible and affordable through unbundled services that help both legal practitioners and individuals understand and assert their family law rights. Her expertise encompasses a remarkable range of family law matters, including divorce and dissolution proceedings, child custody and visitation disputes, spousal and child support modifications, and immigration-related family law issues.

Ms. Bolin has successfully negotiated countless family law settlements throughout her career, demonstrating her practical approach to achieving favorable outcomes for families in crisis. She brings to this book her philosophy that a strategic settlement often surpasses a lengthy court battle, offering readers honest assessments about when to fight in court and when to explore alternative solutions that better serve the family's interests and protect children's welfare.

Ms. Bolin's practice has encompassed family law matters across various cultural backgrounds and family structures, from traditional nuclear families to blended families, and immigrant families navigating both family court and immigration proceedings. This broad cultural experience allows her to understand the unique family law challenges faced by diverse communities and to provide practical guidance that accounts for cultural considerations and immigration implications.

As an advocate for family justice, Ms. Bolin has represented parents seeking to protect their children's best interests, spouses working to achieve fair property division and support arrangements, and domestic violence survivors pursuing safety and independence. This comprehensive perspective enriches her understanding of family law strategy and enables her to provide balanced, practical guidance for navigating the emotional and legal complexities of family disputes.

This guide represents the culmination of Ms. Bolin's extensive experience in family law practice in both New York and California courts, offering readers an authoritative resource for navigating the complexities of domestic relations legal issues in these two pivotal jurisdictions. Her commitment to making family law accessible and understandable shines through in every chapter, providing both legal practitioners and their clients with the tools needed to achieve successful outcomes that protect families and serve children's best interests.

Made in United States
Orlando, FL
04 November 2026

90207645R00332